AF579414

THE ART OF

JOHN HARRIS

BEYOND THE HORIZON

THE ART OF JOHN HARRIS – BEYOND THE HORIZON

ISBN: 9781781168424
Limited Edition ISBN: 9781783293155

Published by
Titan Books
A division of Titan Publishing Group Ltd.
144 Southwark St.
London
SE1 0UP

First edition: May 2014
10 9

EU RP (for authorities only)
eucomply OÜ Pärnu mnt 139b-14 11317
Talinn, Estonia
hello@eucompliancepartner.com
+3375690241

Front cover illustration for the standard edition commissioned by Irene Gallo of Tor Books for use on the cover of the book by John Scalzi, *The Human Division*.

A CIP catalogue record for this title is available from the British Library.

Printed and bound in China.

THE ART OF

JOHN HARRIS

BEYOND THE HORIZON

FOREWORD BY
JOHN SCALZI

COMMENTARY BY
THE ARTIST

TITAN BOOKS

FOREWORD

In my career as an author, I've found John Harris' work incredibly inspiring. And no, I don't mean that simply as a compliment. I mean it in the sense that a significant part of my written work started with me staring at a picture of his artwork and having ideas come from there.

The best example of this is my novel *The Ghost Brigades*, part of my 'Old Man's War' series. Tor, my publisher, decided to have John do the art for trade paperback of *Old Man's War* and at the same time commissioned the cover to *The Ghost Brigades*, which I was then writing – because sometimes in publishing you get a cover even before you have a manuscript. My editor showed both to me with a flourish. Both were quintessential John Harris space art: vibrantly colored, impressionist yet technical, implying a whole universe outside the borders of the cover.

As it happened, as Patrick was showing me these covers, I had written myself into a corner with *The Ghost Brigades*. I needed to move the story forward but I was a bit at a loss as to how to do it. John's cover for the book showed a space station hovering above the ring system of an otherwise Earth-like planet – and as I looked at John's art, I could almost physically feel the gears engage in my head. I knew what that planet was and why is was important and why a space station would be near its ring system ... and I went off to write, happily unjammed.

The cover to *The Ghost Brigades* describes the content of the novel, because it inspired it. And speaking as the author, I can say that the book is better because of John's cover. It was the first time I've used his work as a creative spur, but it's not been the last.

This isn't surprising to me, because I knew John's work as a reader long before I worked with him as a creator. John's artwork, like that of Richard Powers or Frank Kelly Freas, is iconic, and also Bookstore Iconic – which is to say you can see it from across a bookstore, and when you see it, you know what you're going to get in the pages of that book: A damn fine read that takes you places you can't go any other way. People forget that cover art isn't just good art, it's also, in a practical sense, a form of advertisement. It's also, in a very real way, a promise.

Perhaps it's unfair to put all that on the artist – to require the artist to promote the author, assure the reader and still make good art. But then one of the reasons John Harris is in such demand is that he does all of that. Authors and readers both want what's inside their books to match what's on the outside.

I've been lucky to have John as an inspiration. Perhaps his work will inspire you too. I hope it does.

JOHN SCALZI
NOVEMBER 2013

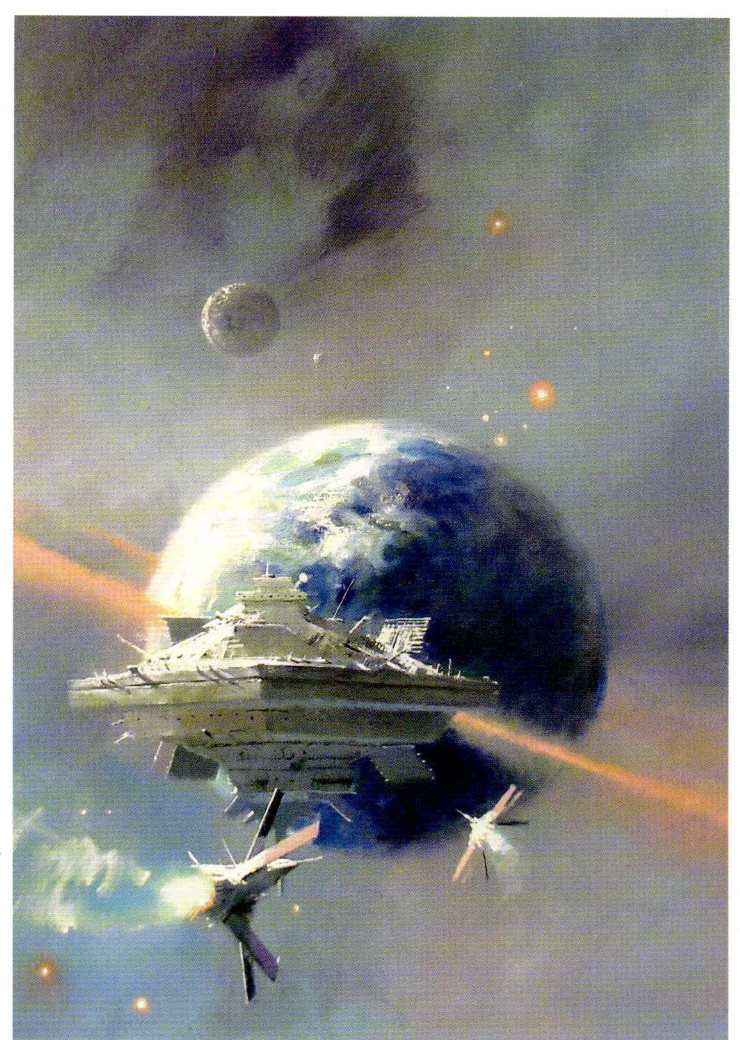

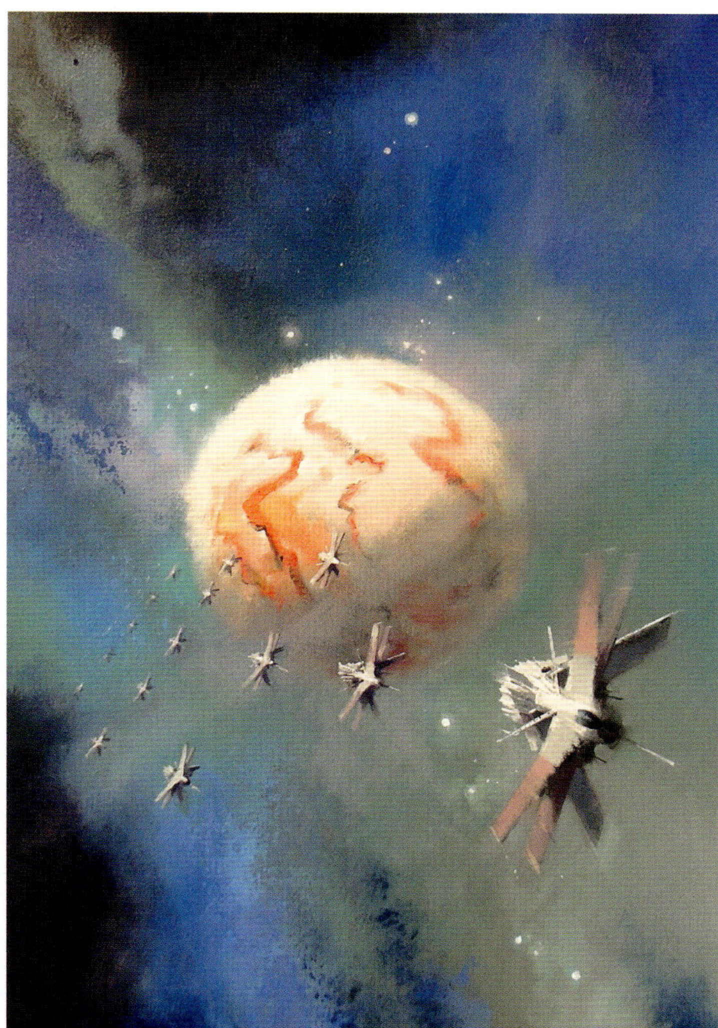

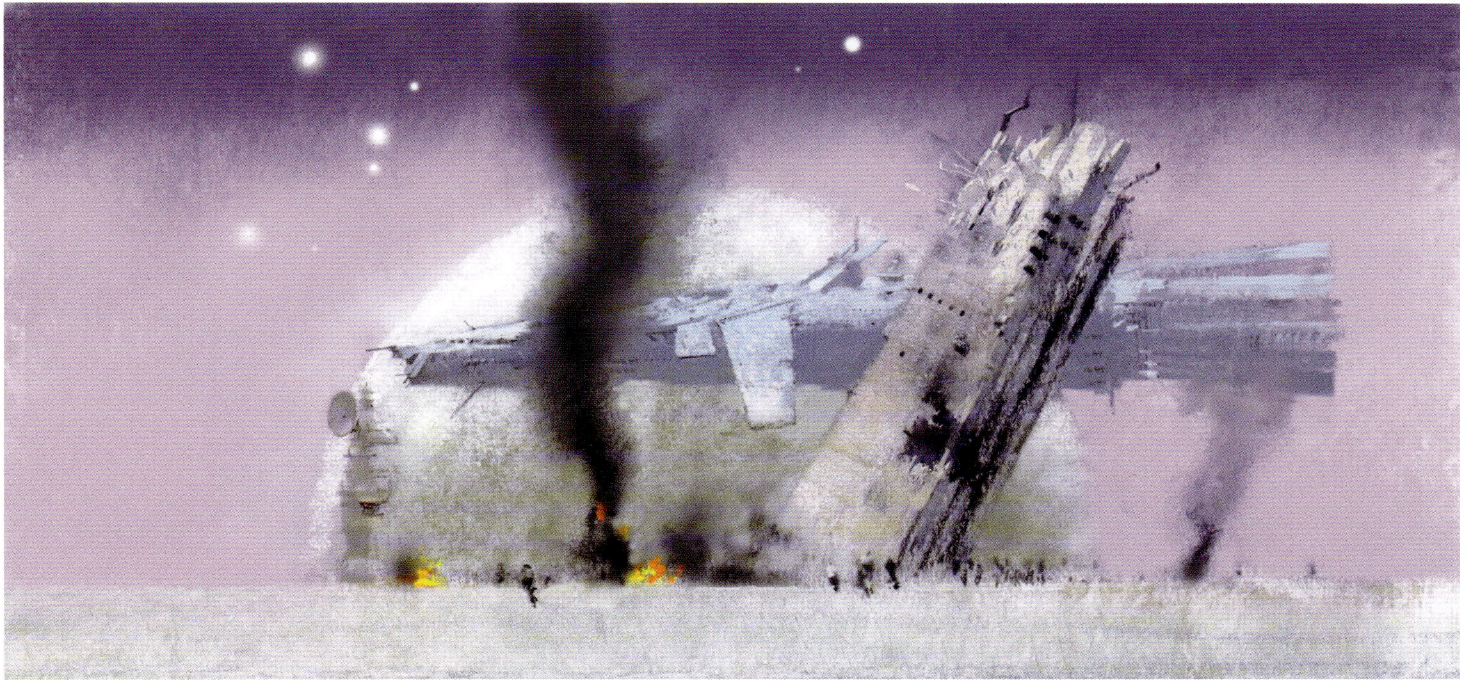

Top Left: *The Ghost Brigades*. 2005

Top Right: *Old Man's War*. 2005

Bottom: *After the Coup*, a sketch for the book by John Scalzi. 2008

INTRODUCTION

The world of science fiction is now so much a part of our culture, it is hard to imagine a time when it was not. The act of fantasising a future, complete with its social mores, its technology, architecture, fashion, even language, now seems such a natural and commonplace activity – and a defining characteristic of our age. Yet, before the nineteenth century, the concept of 'the future' was hardly ever considered. The rare occasions when it surfaced was in the domain of satirists and visionaries such as Jonathan Swift and William Blake. But the work of such figures was more about alternative views of reality than of the future.

When the Industrial Revolution got underway, all that changed. The concept of technology became the defining force that literally shaped our future and our awareness of it. The advent of writers like H.G. Wells and, later, Arthur C. Clarke and Isaac Asimov, brought into the forefront of our awareness the manner of how technology might create new worlds (both metaphoric and actual) to live in. By the 1960s, the generation of SF writers that included Clarke and Asimov had created a distinctive new field of thought – and the real world was only one step behind.

John Harris was one week short of 21 when *Apollo 19* reached the moon. By this time, he had already absorbed much of the world view of those writers, and they undoubtedly shaped him. This what he has to say about that:

"When I was first introduced to science fiction in the early sixties, there was a flavour to the genre, best expressed by people like the late Arthur C. Clarke, Alfred Bester, George R. Stewart and Isaac Asimov. I grew up with their books and their preoccupations became mine. Expansive perspectives, big spaces and bigger questions. The emotional colour that prevailed was, to my eyes, joyous, and to this day I am still inspired by the visions of those figures of the past."

Much of the work in this collection is undoubtedly 'hard-core' and represents a preoccupation with hardware. But the real meat of these images is the sense of scale, atmosphere and the space which this 'junk' occupies. And of these three elements, hard to separate, there is often a tussle in the artist's mind, as to which is most important. But the one which is most intangible – and yet most fulfilling, is the sense of atmosphere. Here in these pieces, often with accompanying sketches, the full display of these elements can be seen. Planetary bodies and vast megalithic structures hang weightless in a vaster space, as if waiting for the Last Trump. The air crackles with expectation and a sense of imminent thunder. This is the stage that is set, recalling, oddly, the Romantic tradition of 19th century artists. It is a collection of images spanning thirty-five years or more, and while it reveals an evolution of technique, it remains consistent in a vision that aims to inspire.

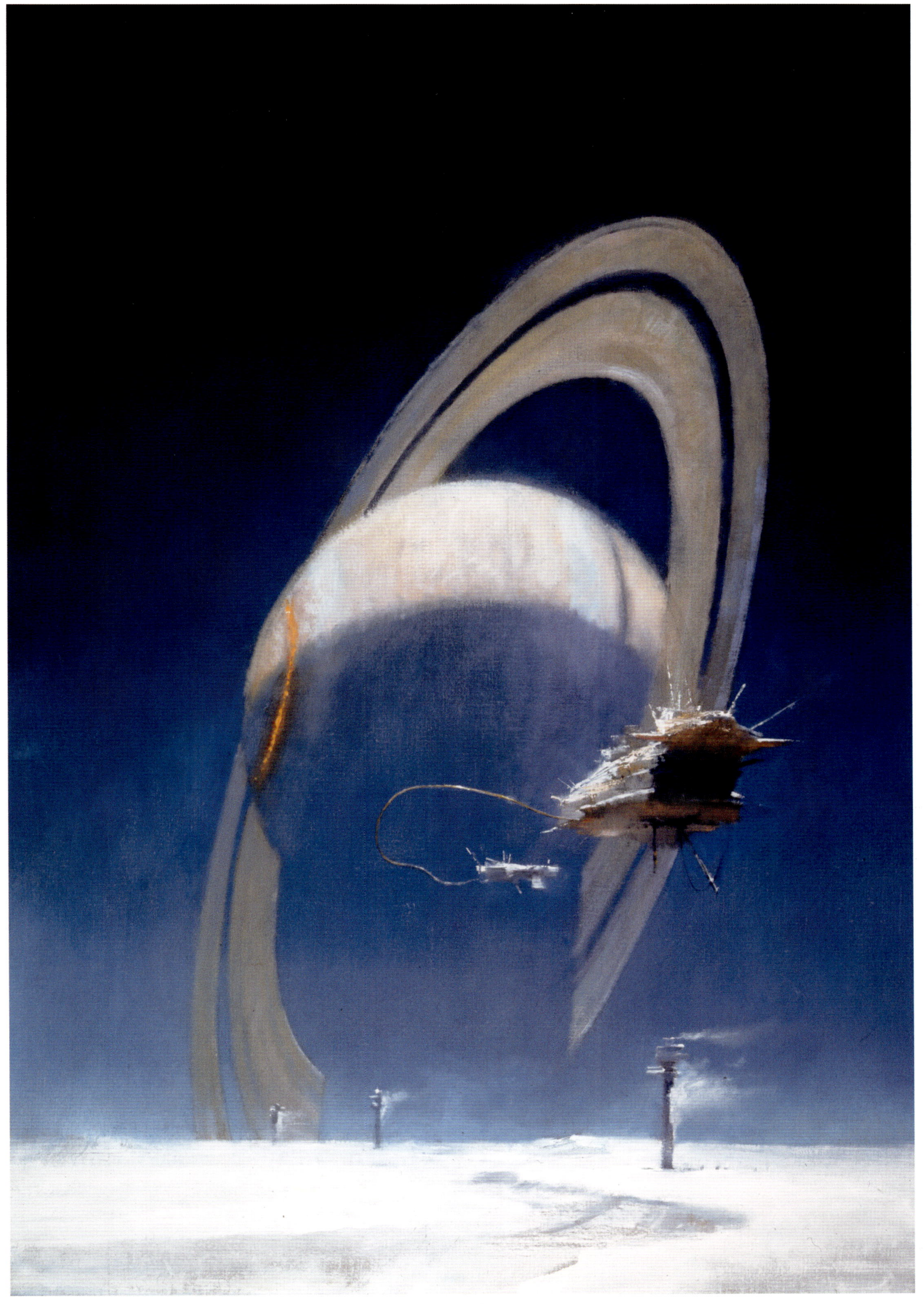

Above: *Saturn*, produced for the cover of the book of the same name by Ben Bova. 2002

It is impossible to talk in any meaningful way about the images in this book without referring to the origin of the various motifs that appear repeatedly in the work. Though the images are fundamentally the product of imagination, many of them have their basis in actual experiences viscerally felt by the artist. So, for example, the images of massive objects floating in space are not simply the result of knowing about the lack of gravity in space, but are the result of actual bodily experiences of weightlessness in transcendental meditation. Similarly, the images of cracking moons and their scale in relation to the horizon were provoked by things witnessed in lucid dreaming.

The connection to actual bodily sensations of such experiences has inevitably given rise to imagery that has its own logic, which may be contrary to known science. For instance, the piece entitled *The Building of FTL1* (on pages 14-15), while paying lip service to an entirely plausible reality of a huge spaceship being constructed in freefall (enclosed in an atmospheric shell), has lines and cables hanging off it as if under the influence of gravity, and that contradiction gives rise to precisely the feeling of something weighty that shouldn't be able to float.

This is all to emphasise that although science has a large part to play in the production of many of these paintings, it is not the guiding light of the imagery. It is simply the male half of the artist's brain acting as a ground on which the more female intuitive half can dance.

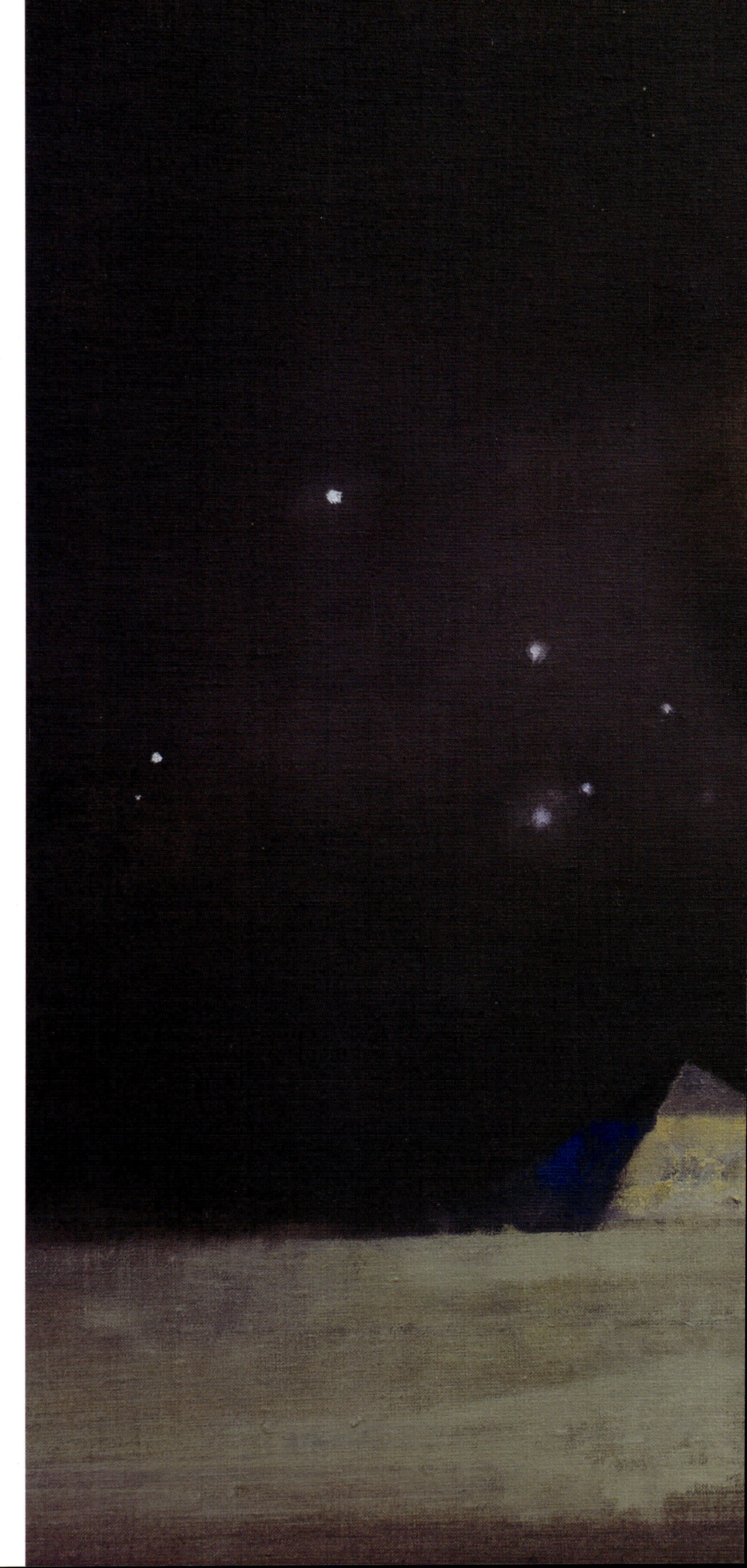

Right: *Migration*, 2011

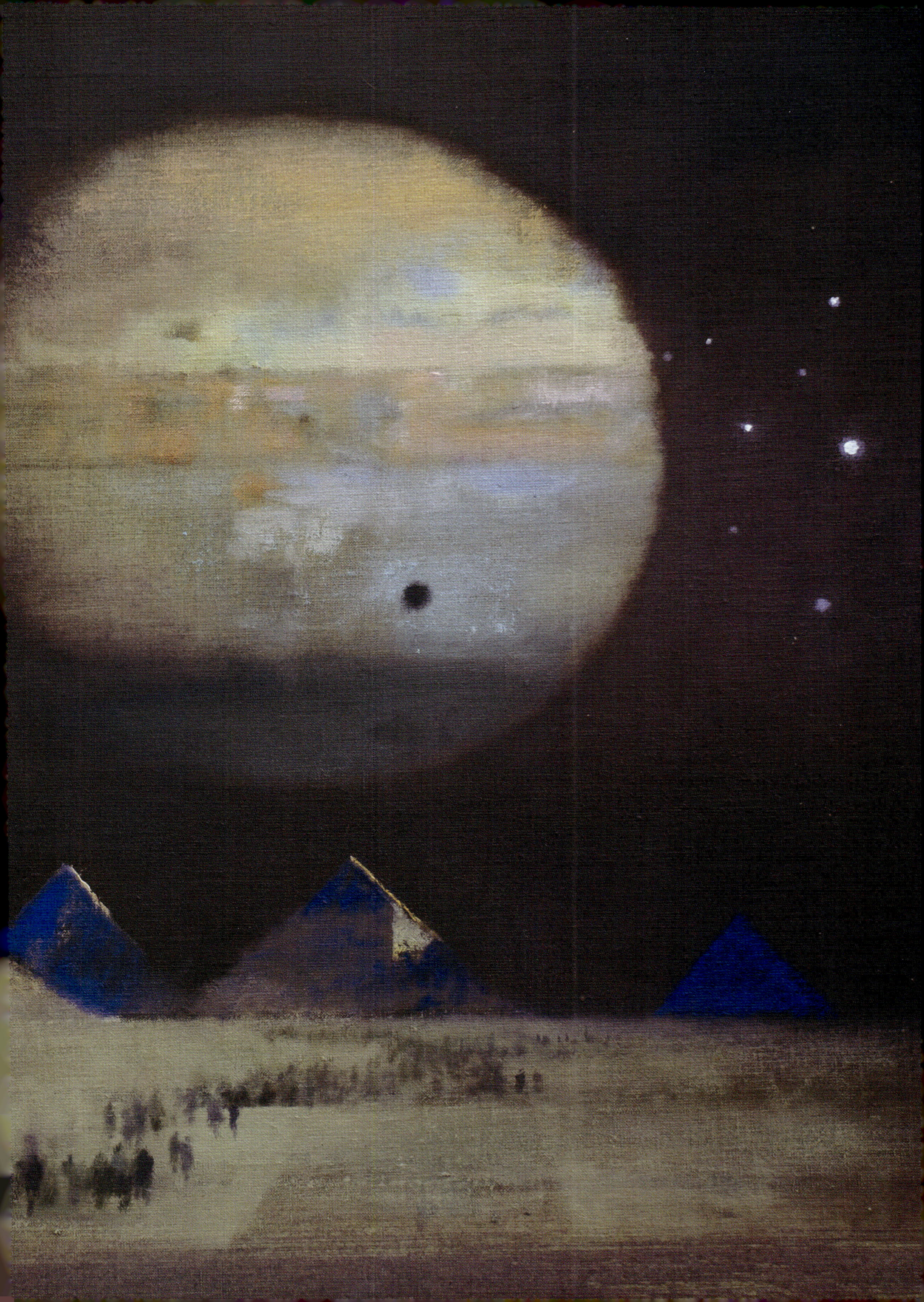

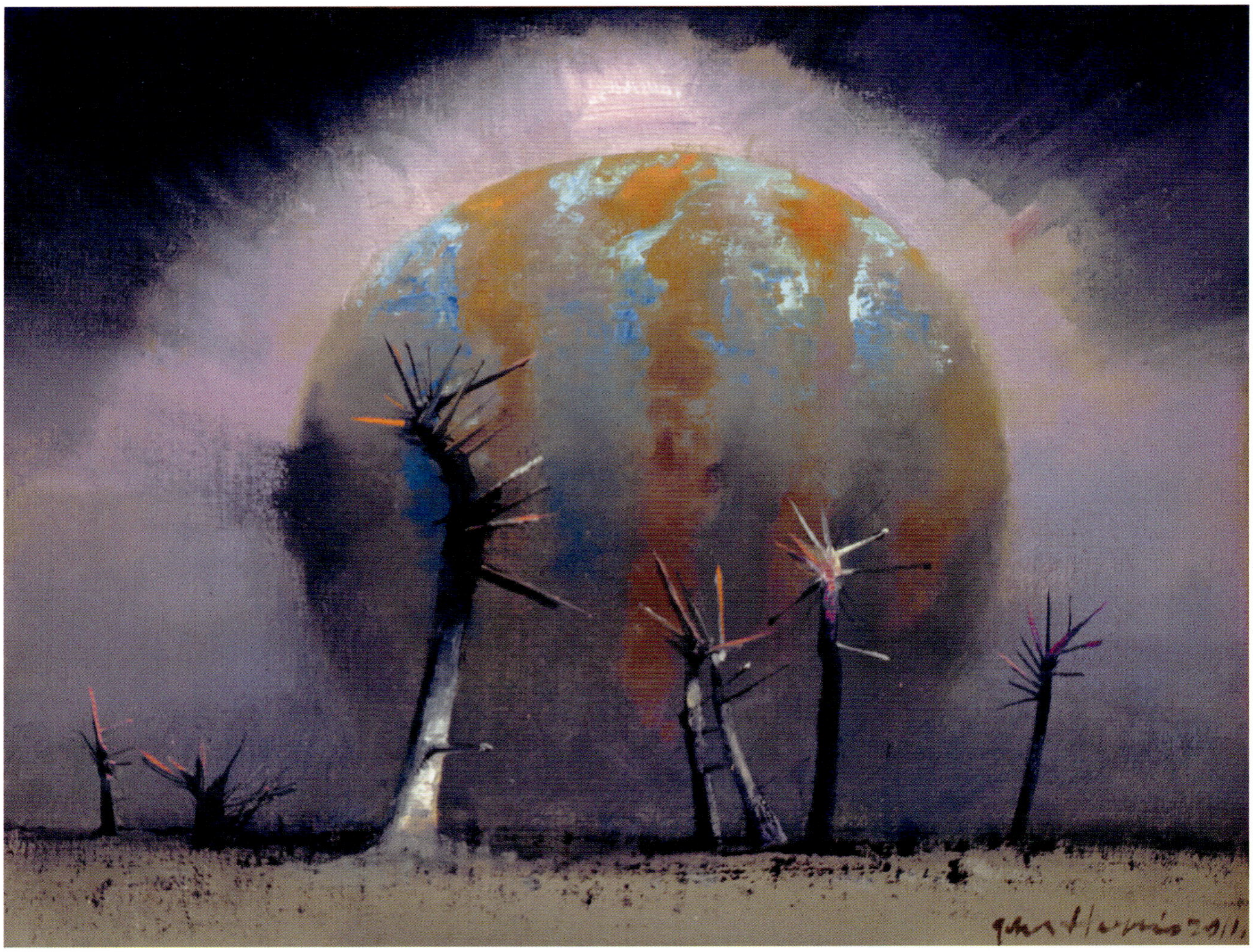

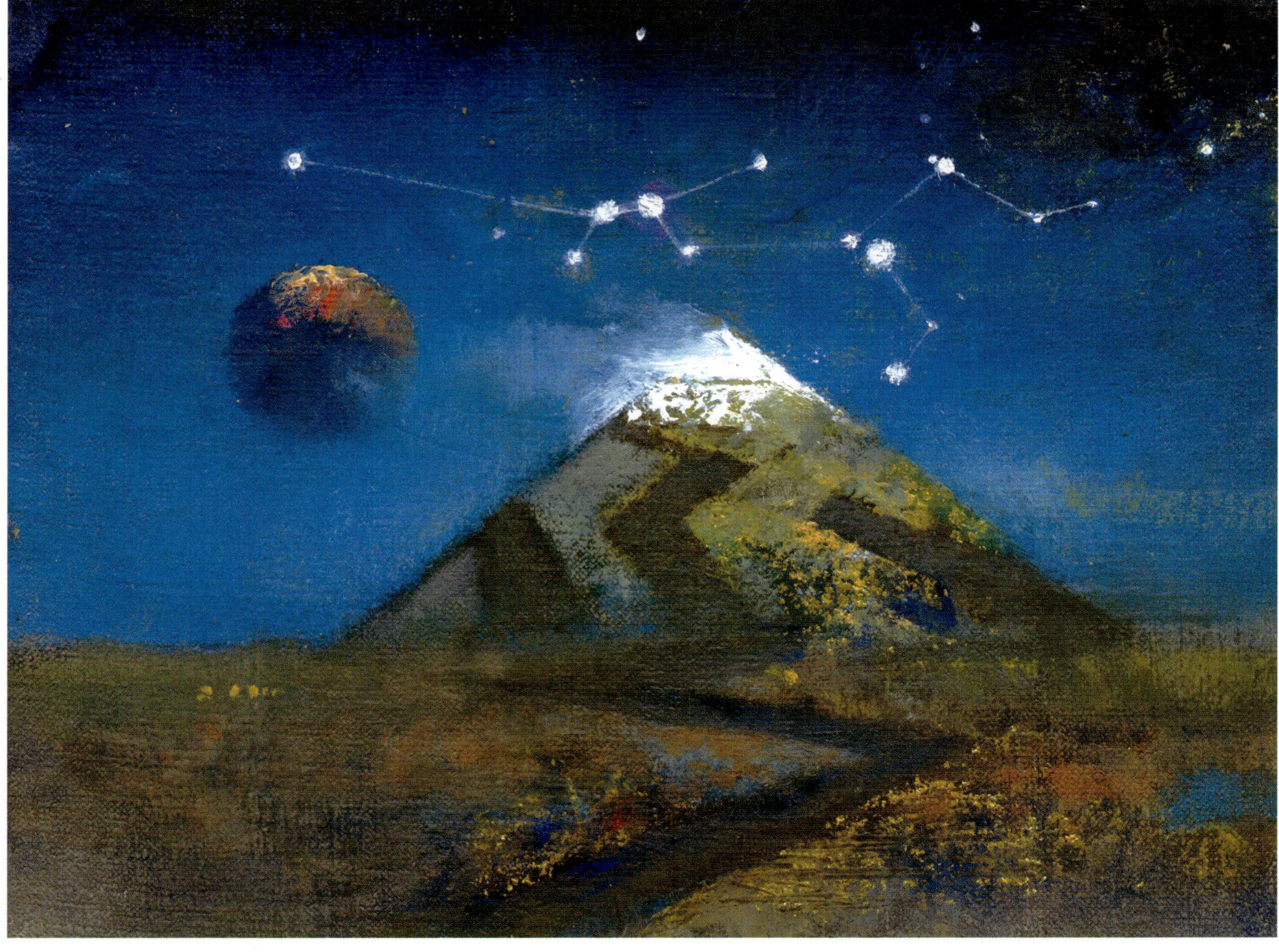

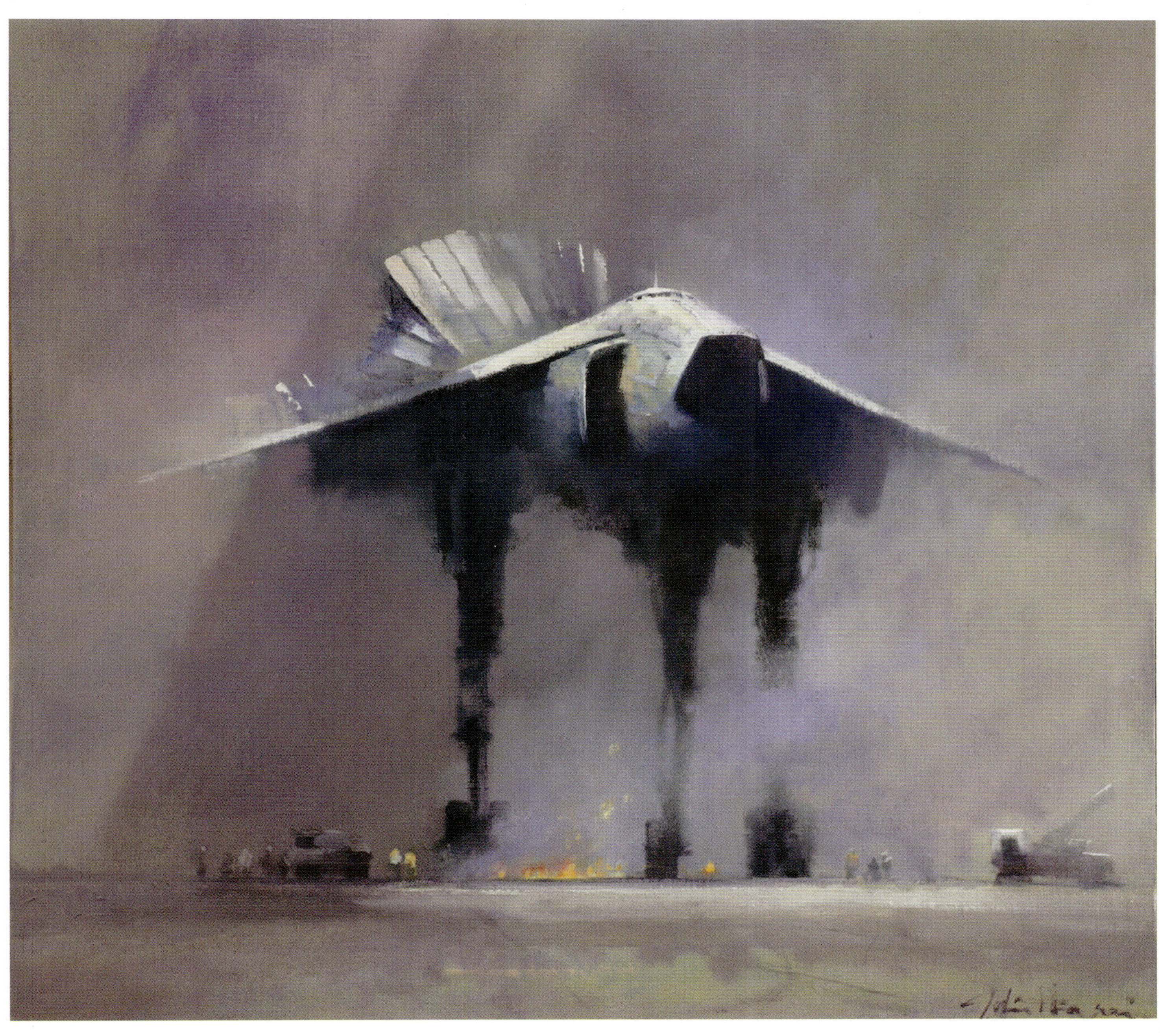

Above: *A Minor Incident*. 2011

Opposite Top: *Harvest*. 2011

Opposite Bottom: *The Pyramid of New Draco*, a sketch initially producec for a quilt design. 2012

Following Spread: *Quiet Night*, the first version. 1979

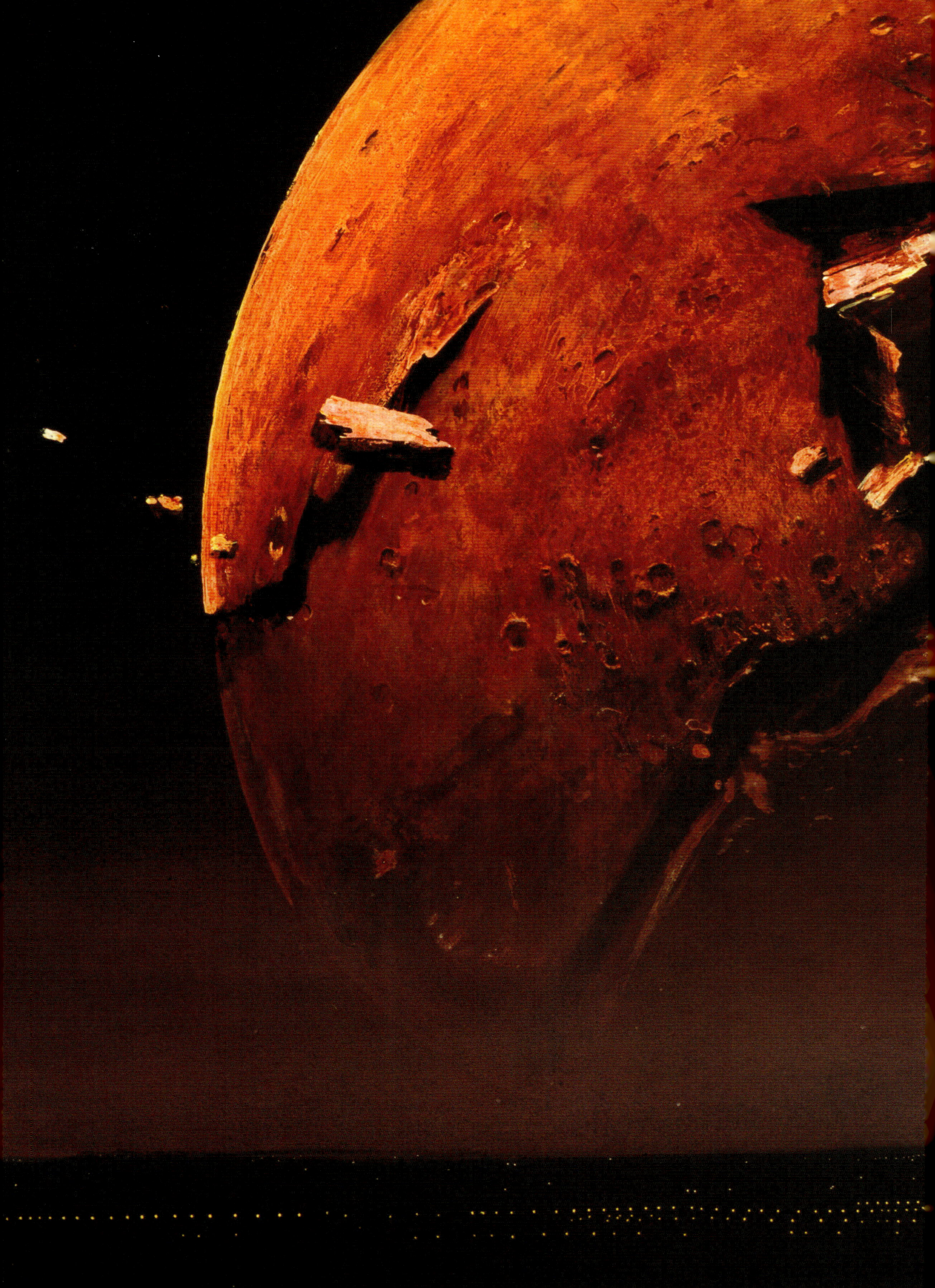

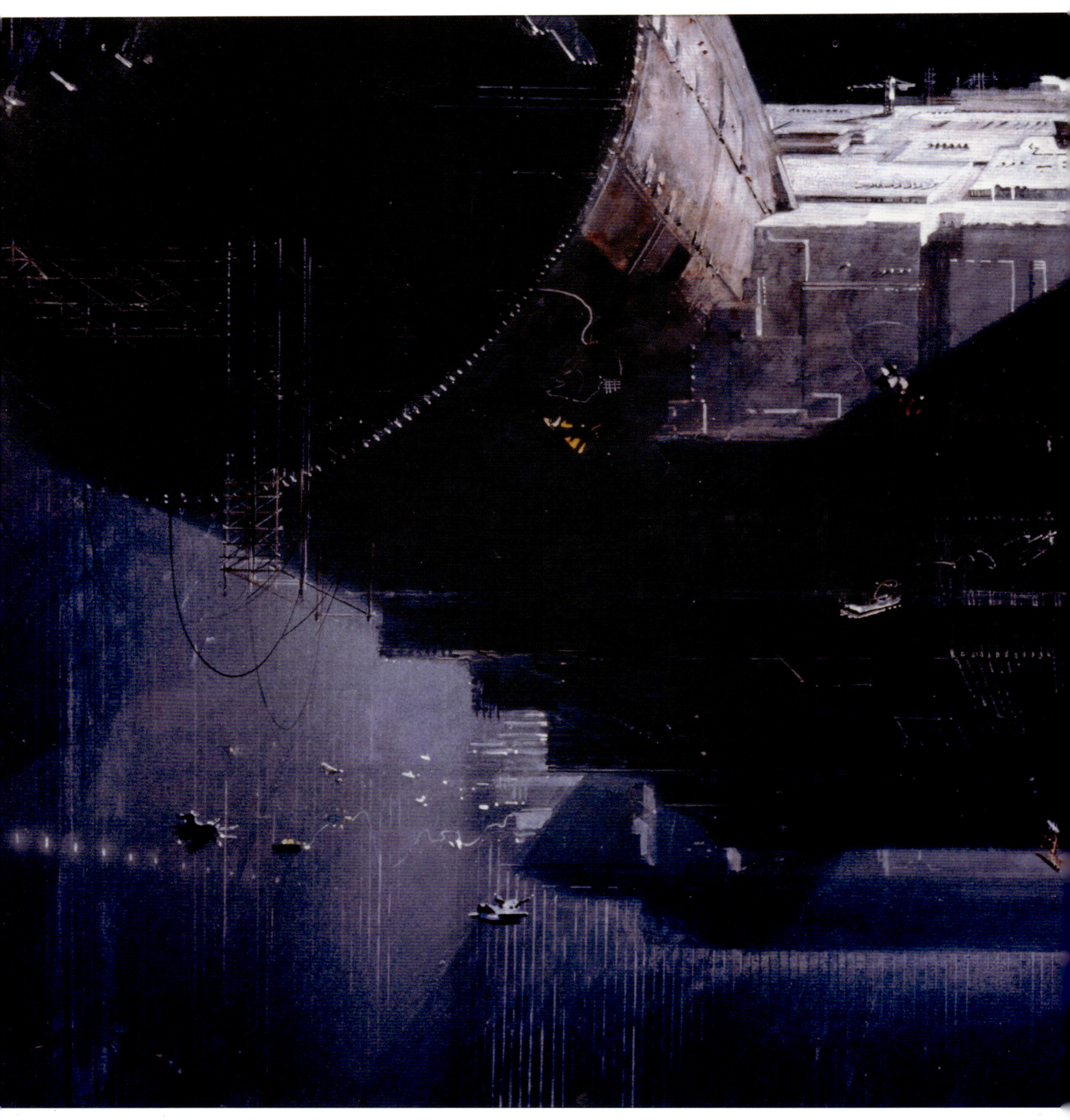

FLOATING MASS

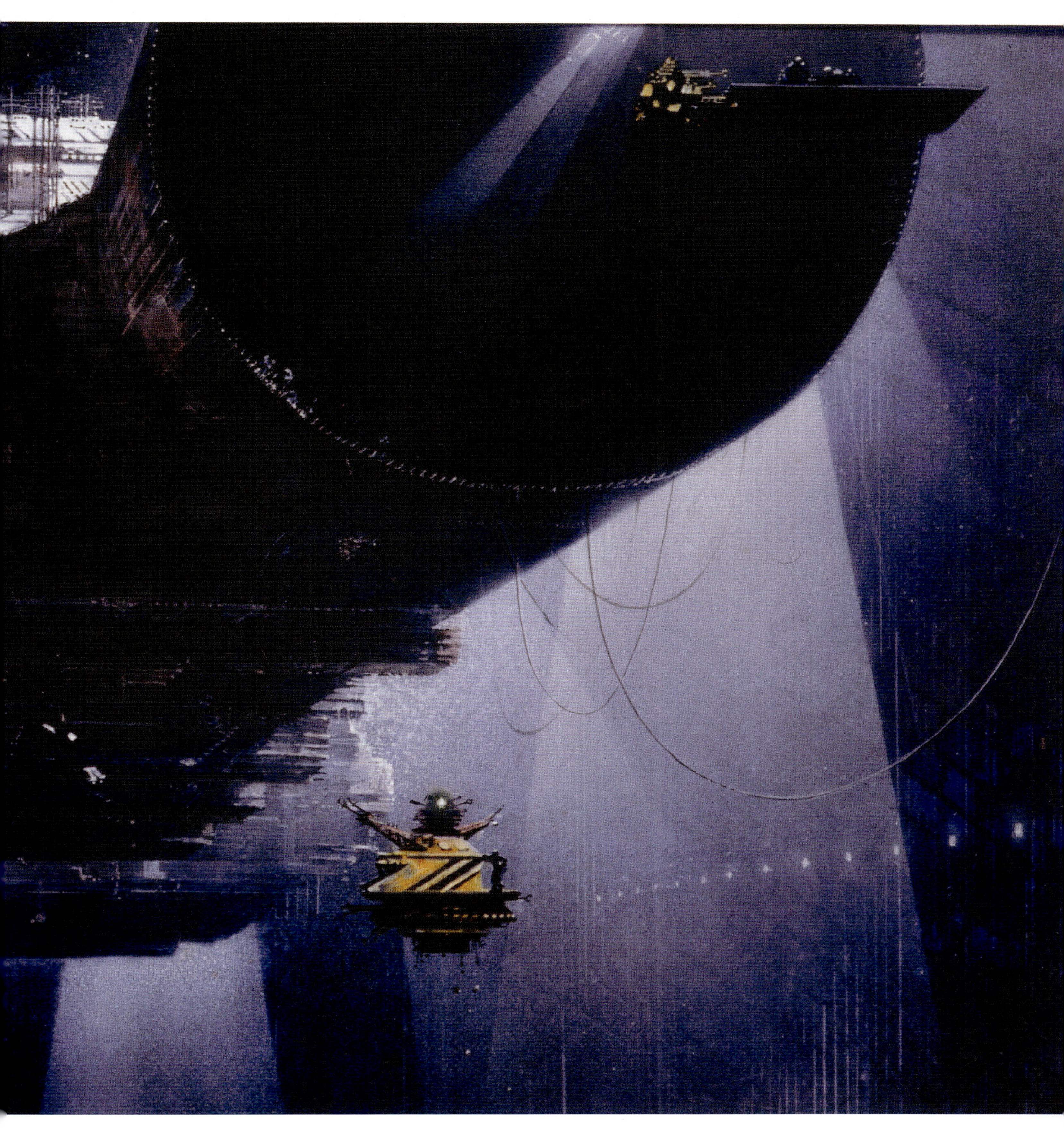

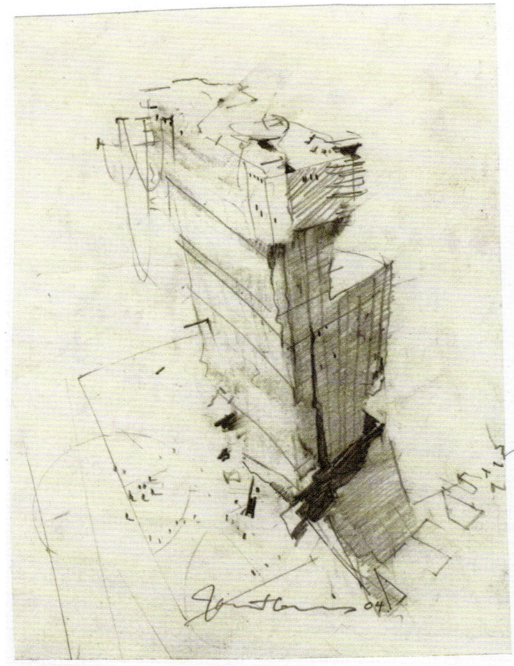

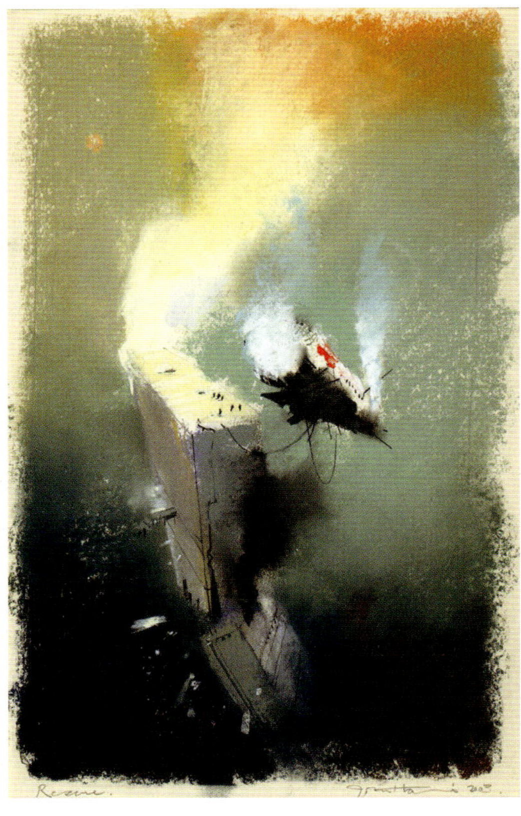

Previous Spread: *The Building of FTL1.* 1979

This Page: *Rescue*, sketches and painting for the cover of *General Practice*, by James White. 2002

Opposite: *Ports of Call*, for the book of short stories by Jack Vance. 2004

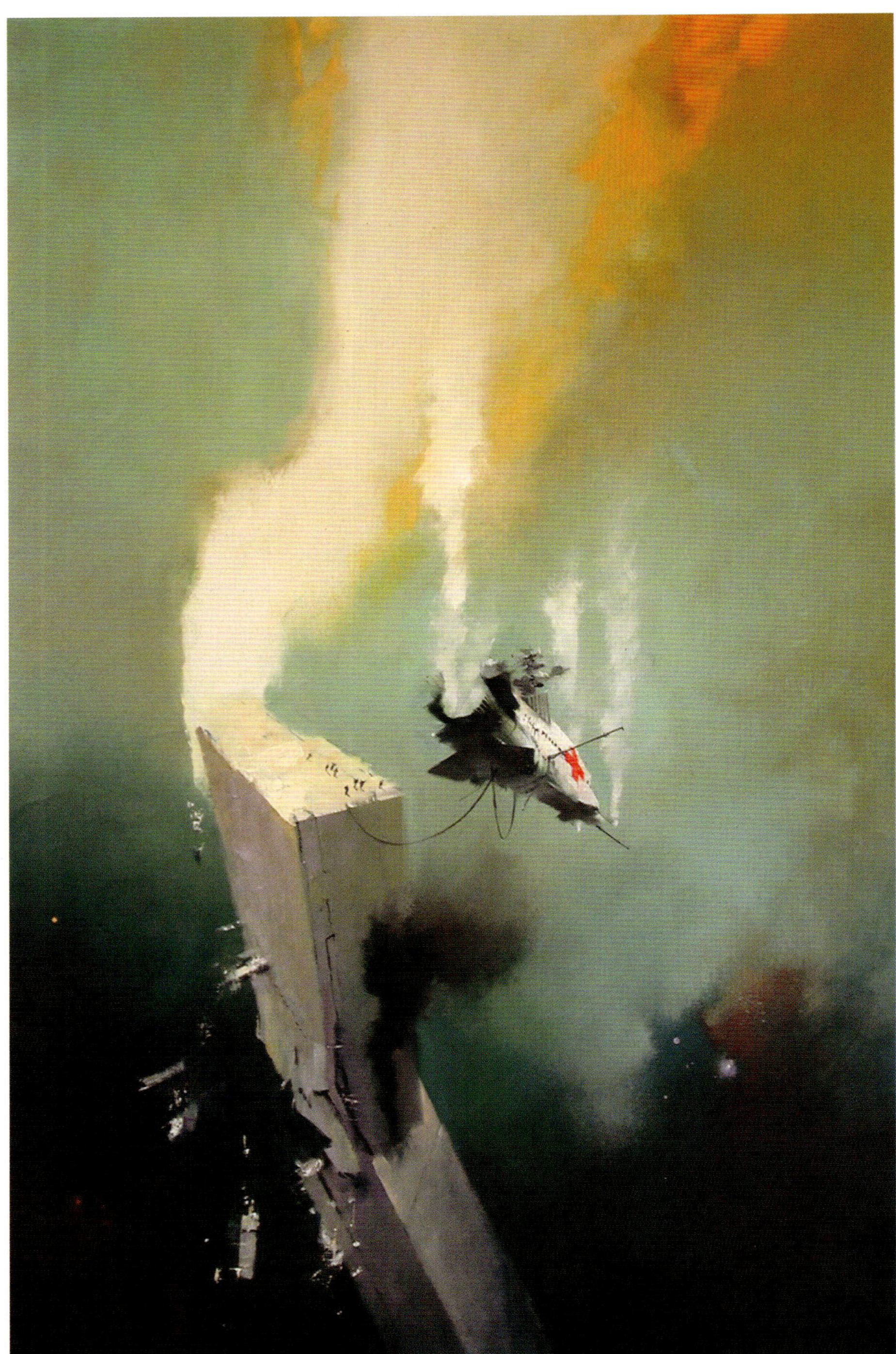

The view of an object travelling at speed through the air is one which we are all familiar with and, consequently, is easily forgotten. The image of a heavy object suspended motionless in a void is a different matter, implying a technology beyond our own. This simple contradiction lends such an image many overtones, both of narrative and emotional significance. I have played with this motif many times over the years, but probably the most effective versions were the earliest ones, when the sensation of floating yet having weight was a new and fresh experience for me. This connection, between a viscerally felt sensation and the creating of an image is a crucial part of my process. The following images are variations of that theme. In some of them, I added the contrary element of hanging lines drooping in loops (obviously under the influence of gravity). This served to add intensity to the sensation of 'otherness' that I try to invest in such pictures. On other occasions, I have introduced a sense of ascent (against gravity) by placing an object like a spaceship against a motif of aurora borealis, as in *Echo* or *Radio Freefall*, which gives the impression of the folds of a curtain hanging downwards under gravity. Paintings like *Sector General* and *Rescue* use an effect of 'falling', lending a paradoxical effect of weightlessness on the viewer. There are countless ways one might make the observer feel something in the pit of the stomach akin to the sensation of floating. These are just some of them.

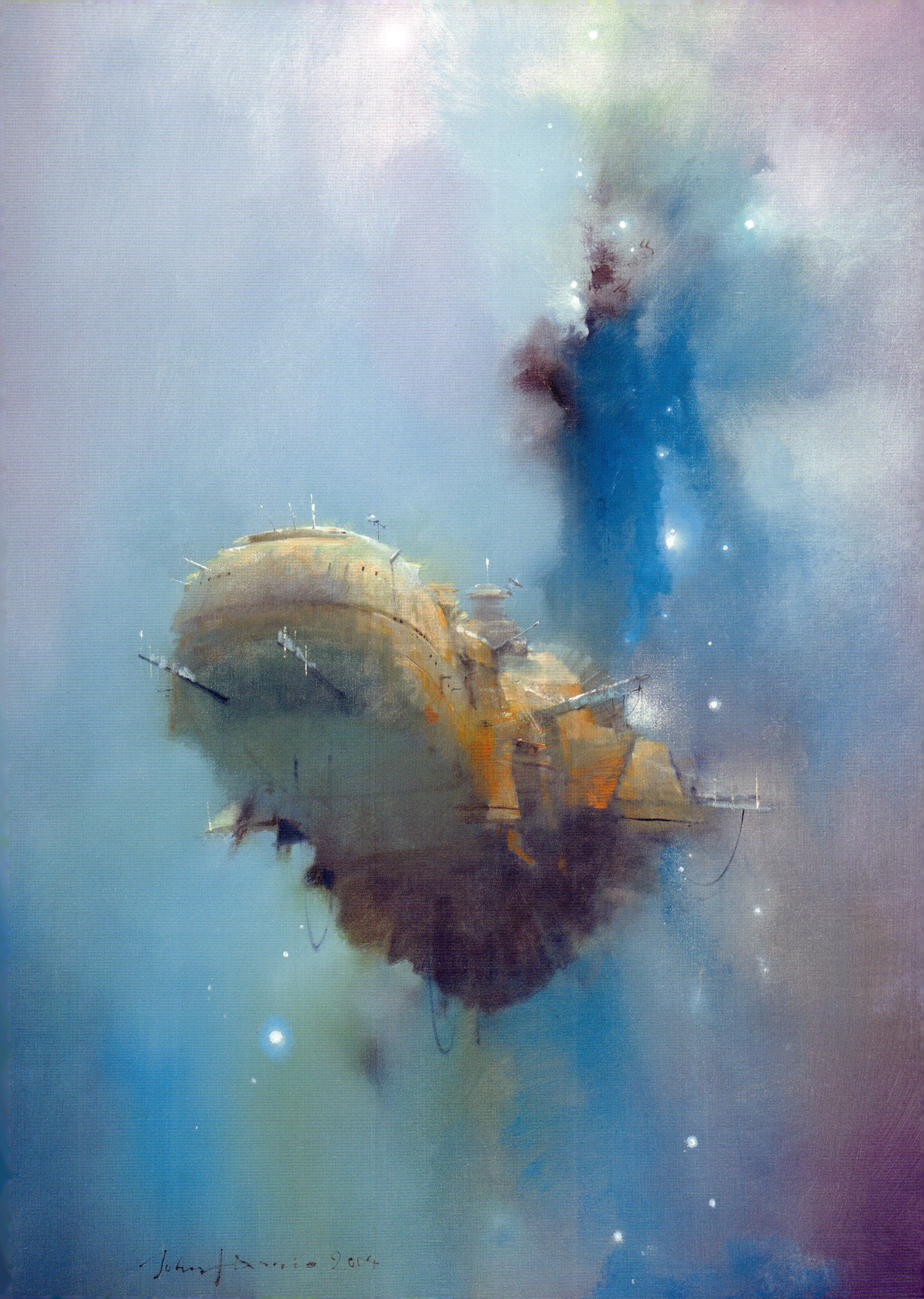

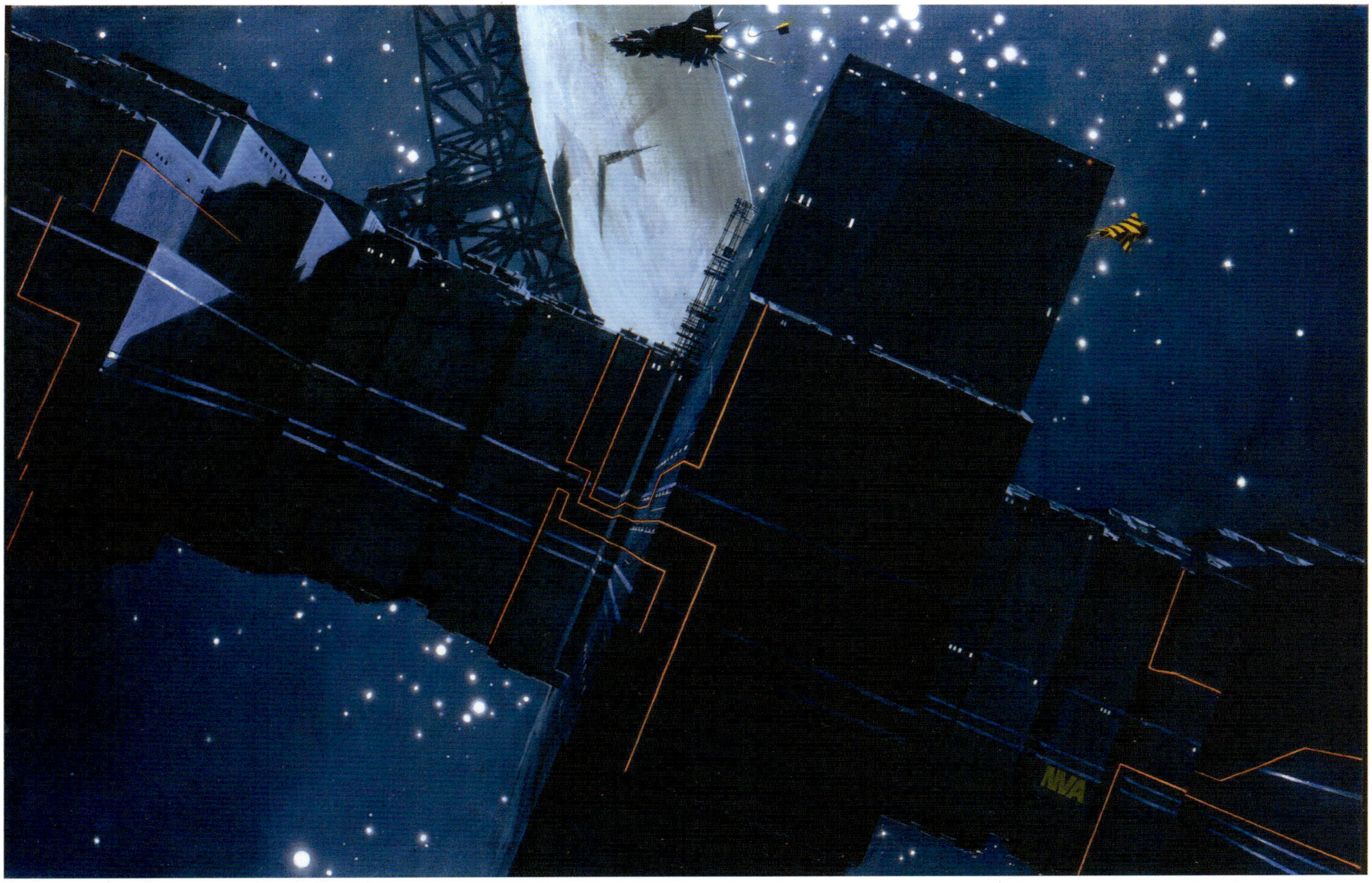

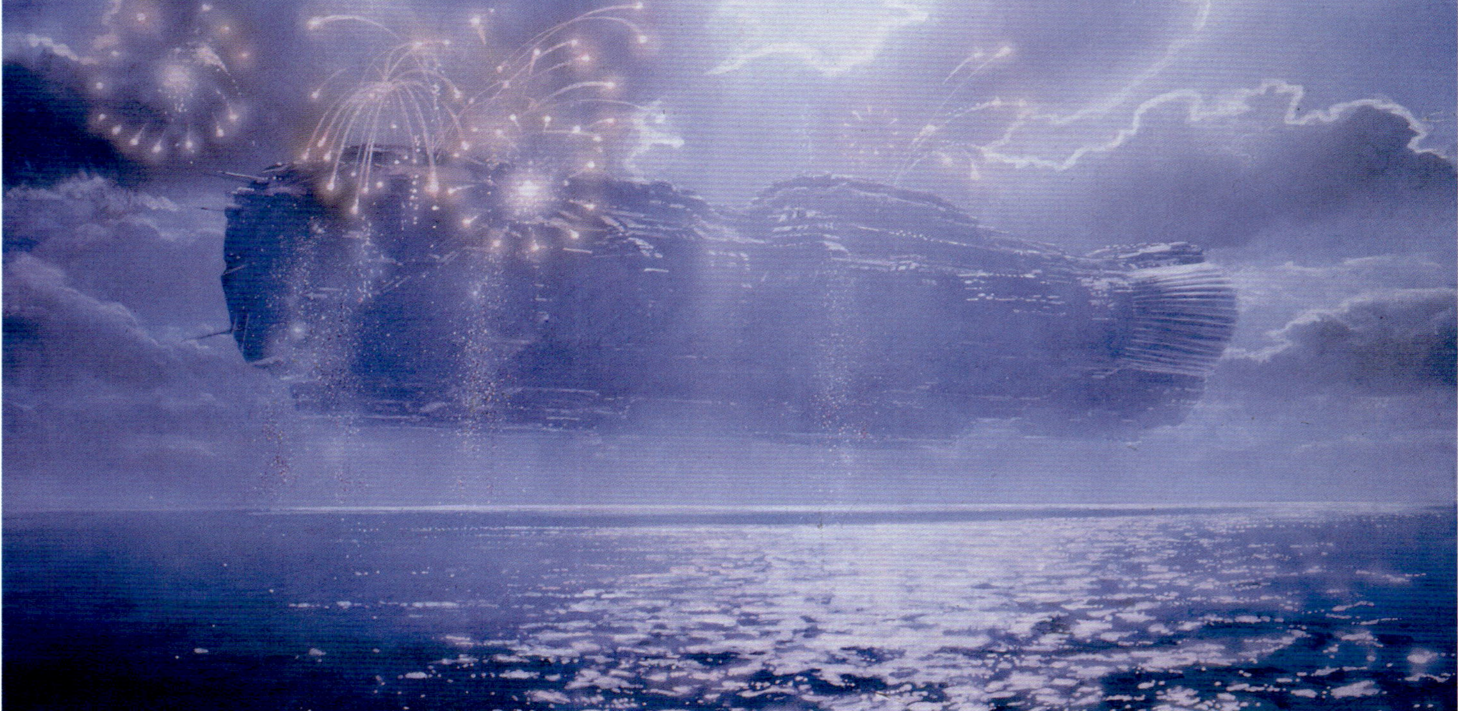

Top: *A Dream of Starlight*, a large painting commissioned by NVA Consultants. 1983

Bottom: *Mass: Planetfall*, one of the early shellac paintings. 1979

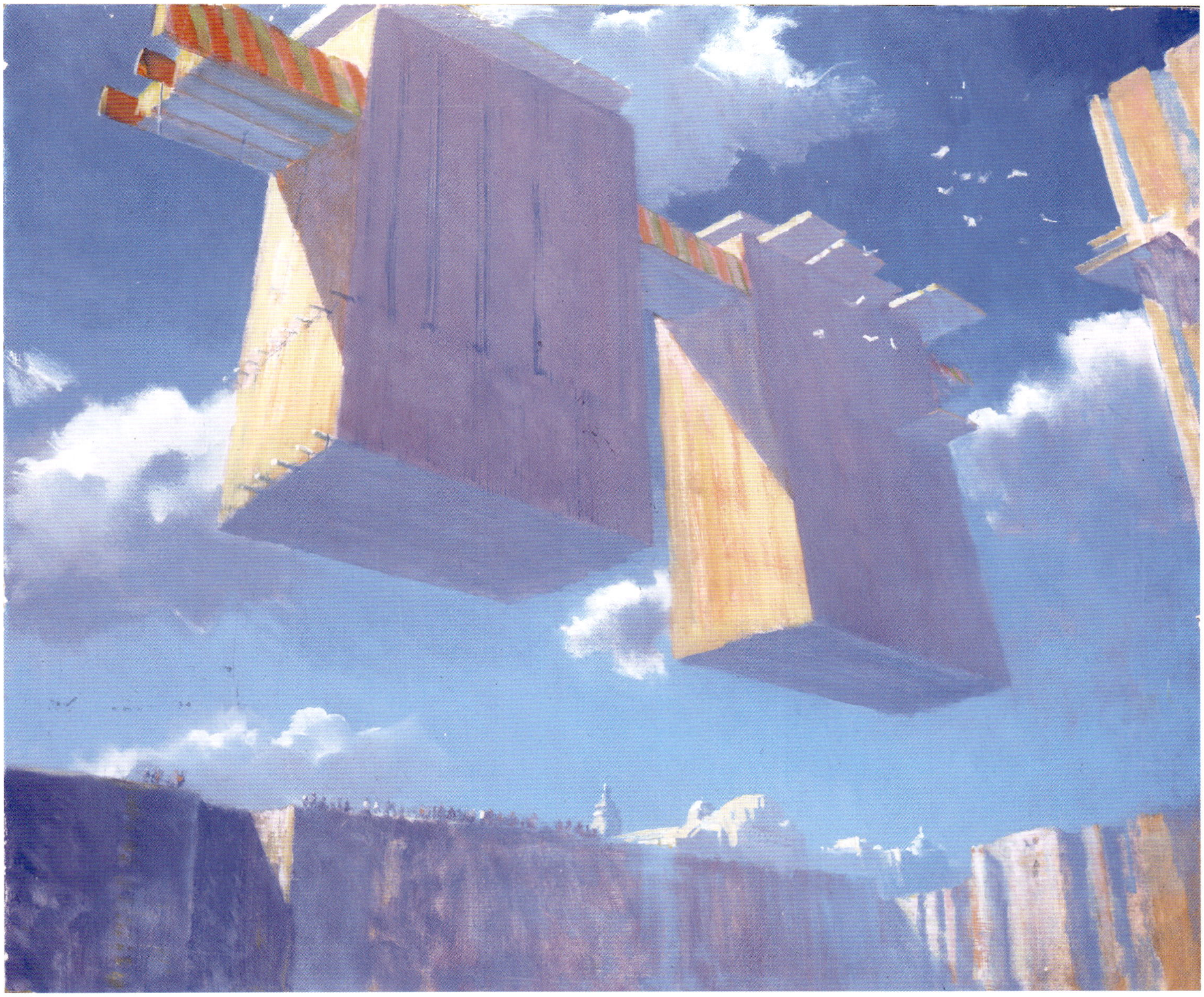

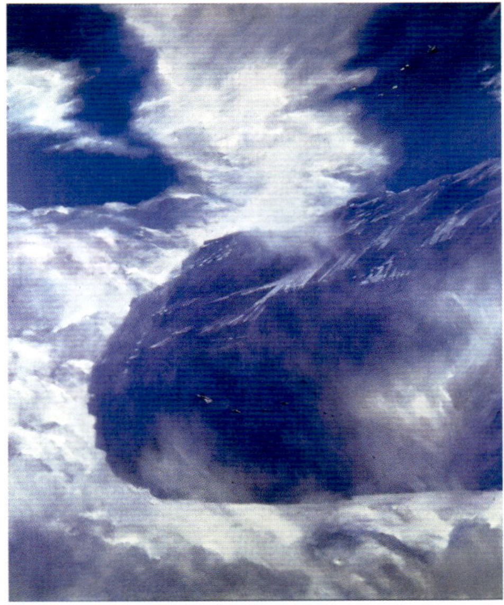

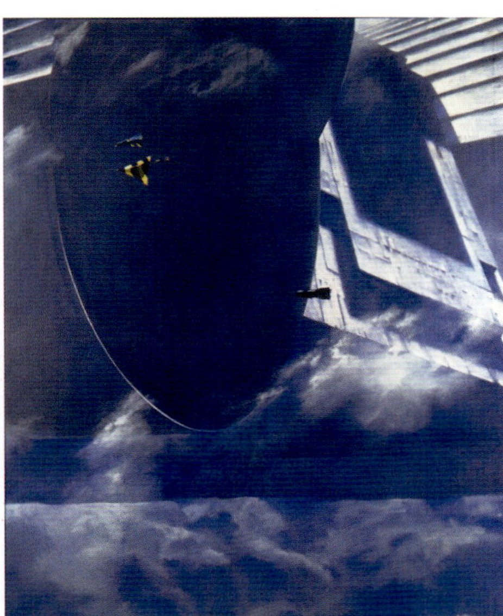

Top: *The Building of Atlantis.* 1997

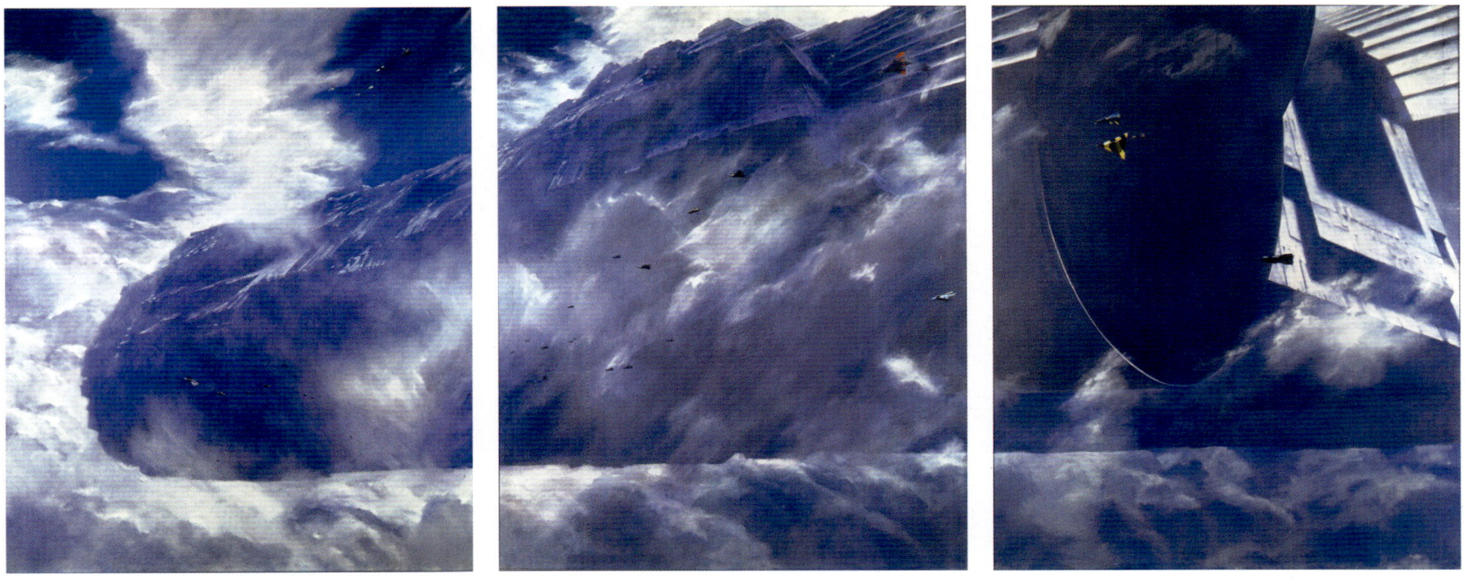

Bottom: *Mass: Leviathan,* a triptych of canvases measuring a total of 6 x 15 feet. 1979

This Page: *Horizons*, sketches and painting for the book by Mary Rosenblum. 2006

Opposite: *The Currents of Space (cropped)*, the cover for a book by Isaac Asimov. 1993

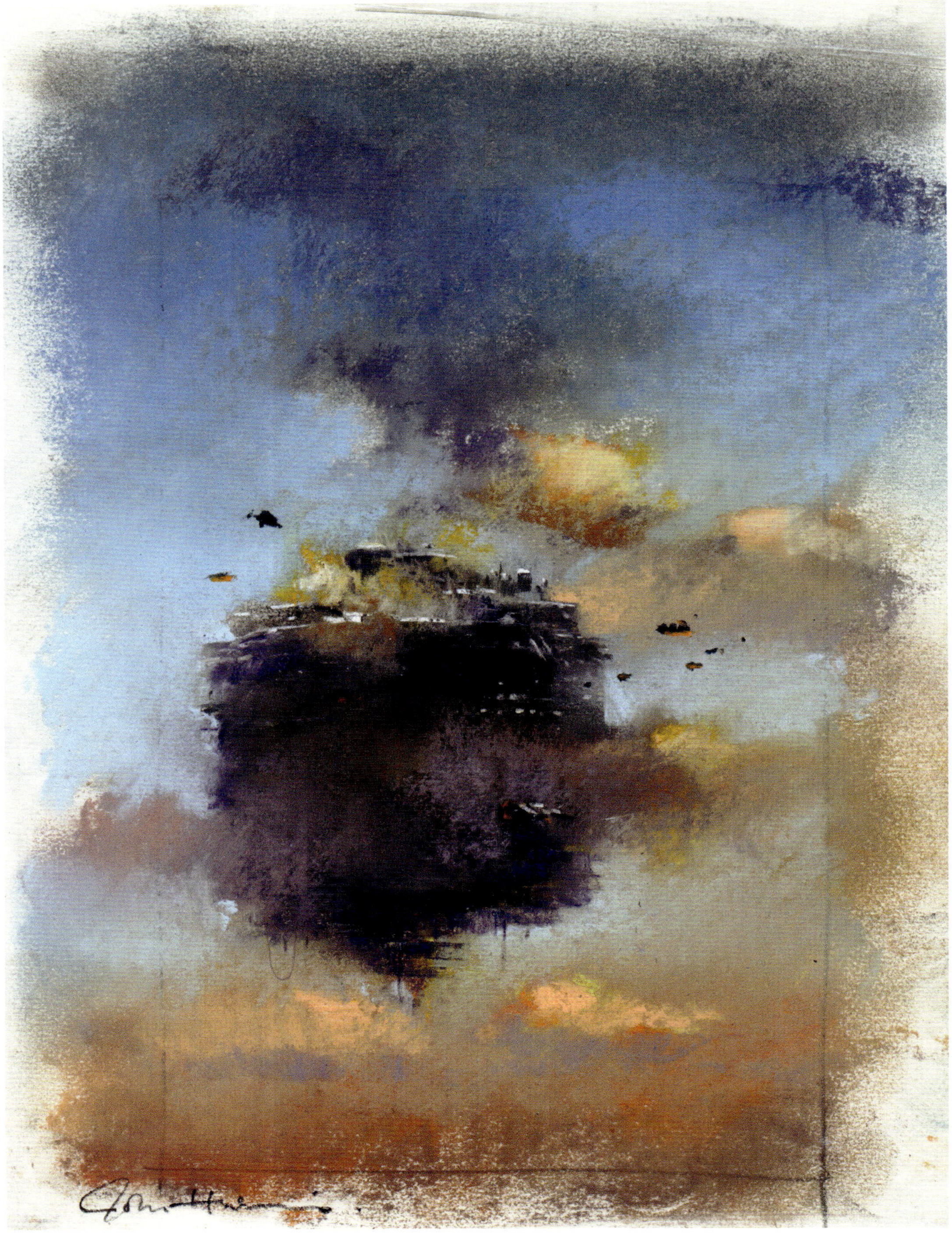

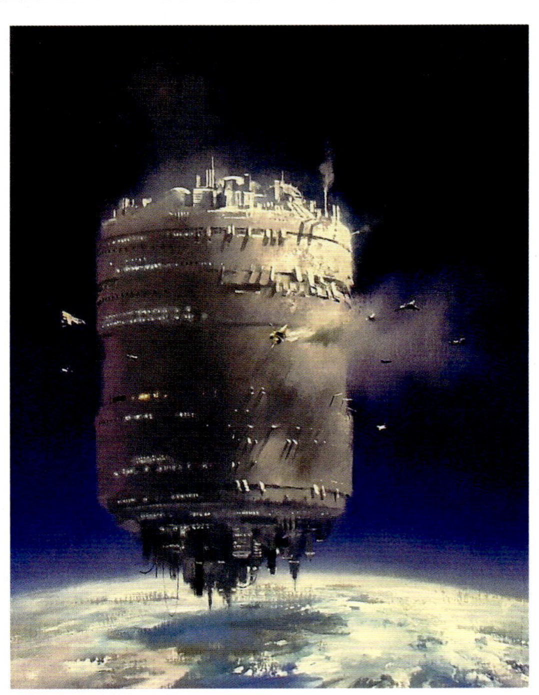

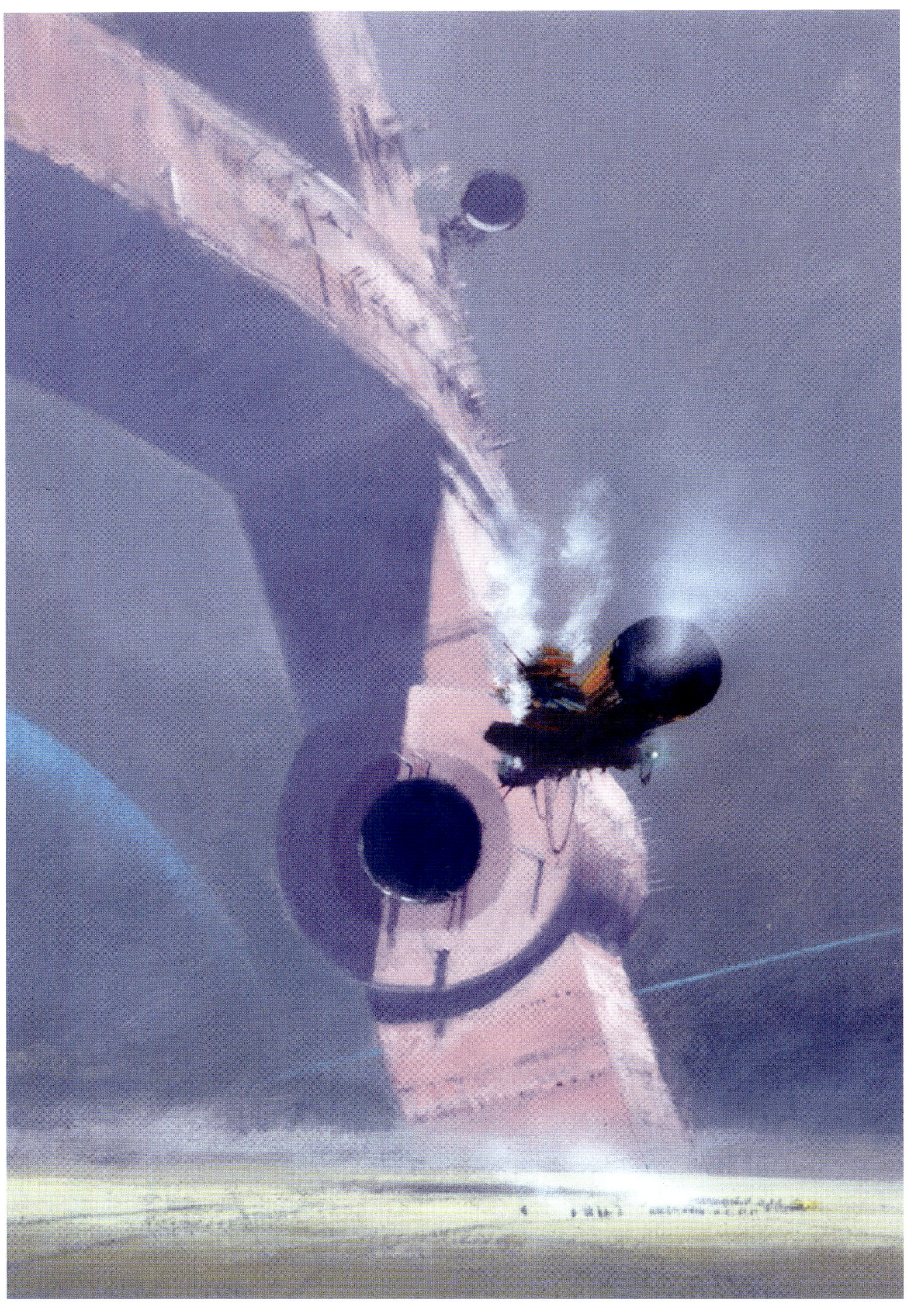

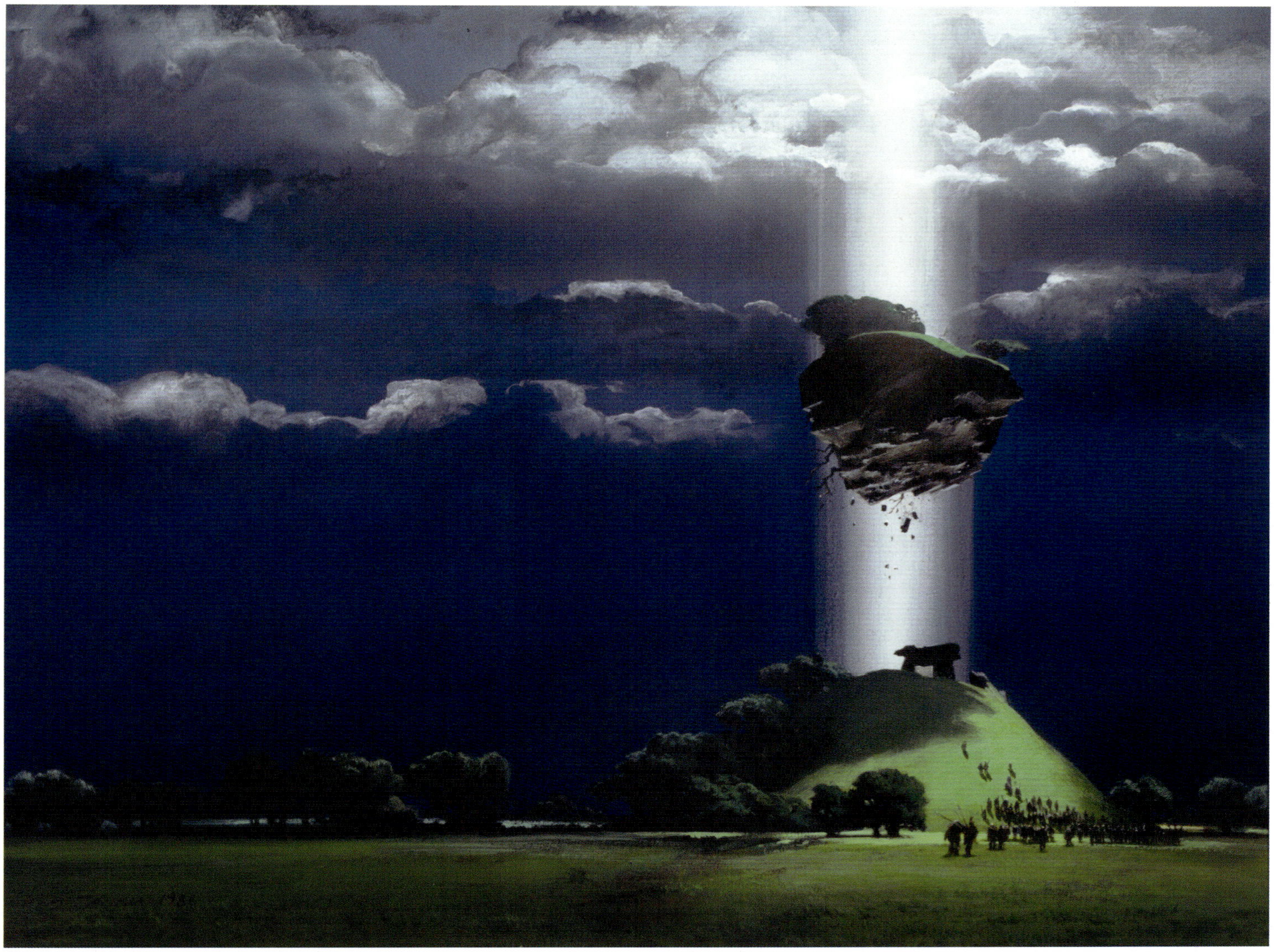

Above: *Corridors of Time*, for the cover of the book by Poul Anderson. 1985

Right: *Ancillary Justice*, preliminary pastel sketch. 2013

Opposite: *Radio Freefall*, the cover of the book by Matthew Jarpe. 2006

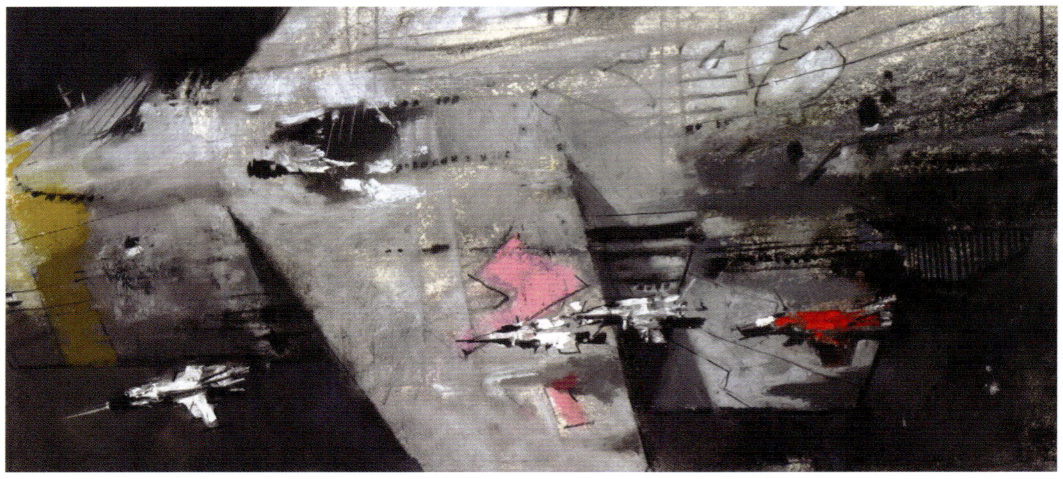

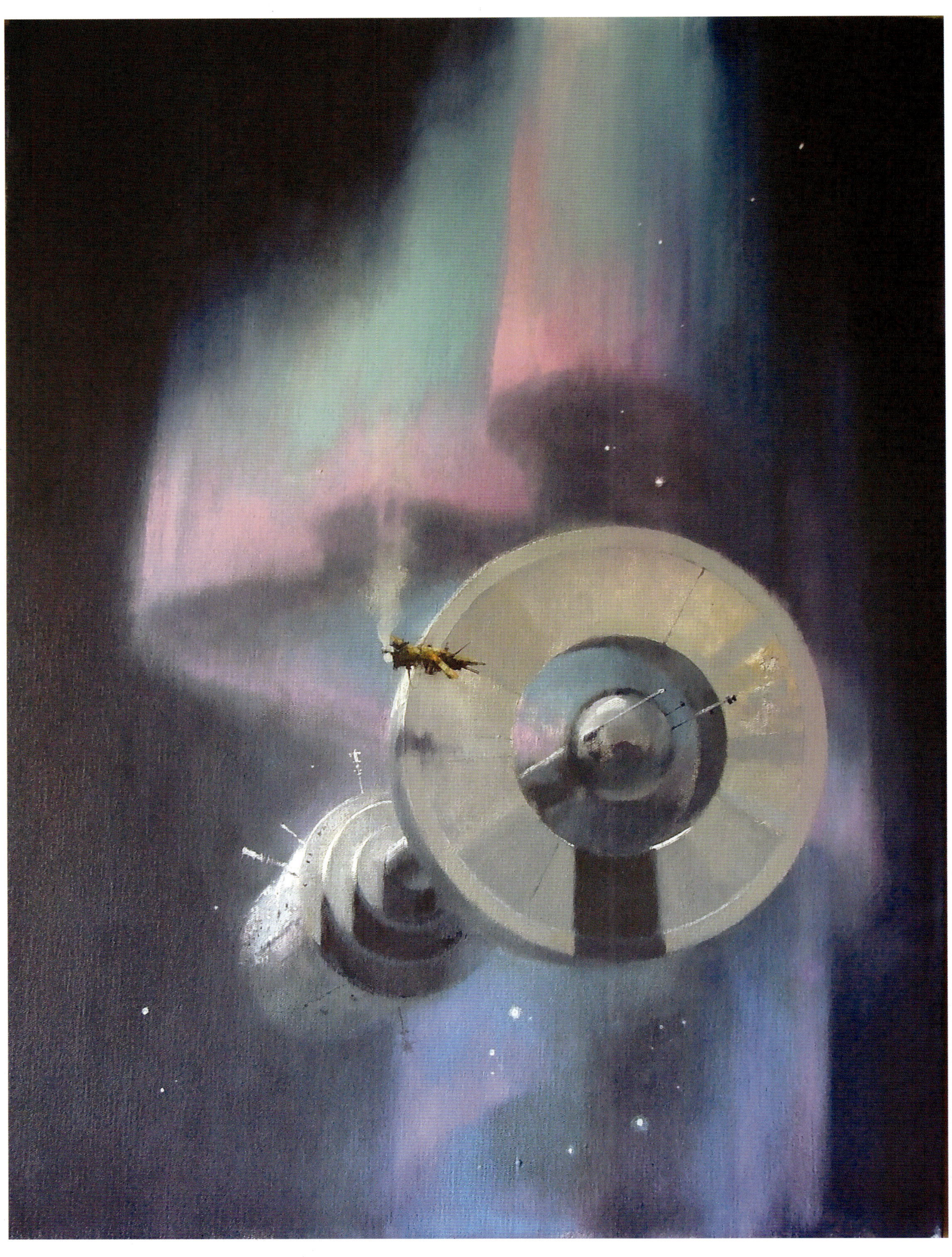

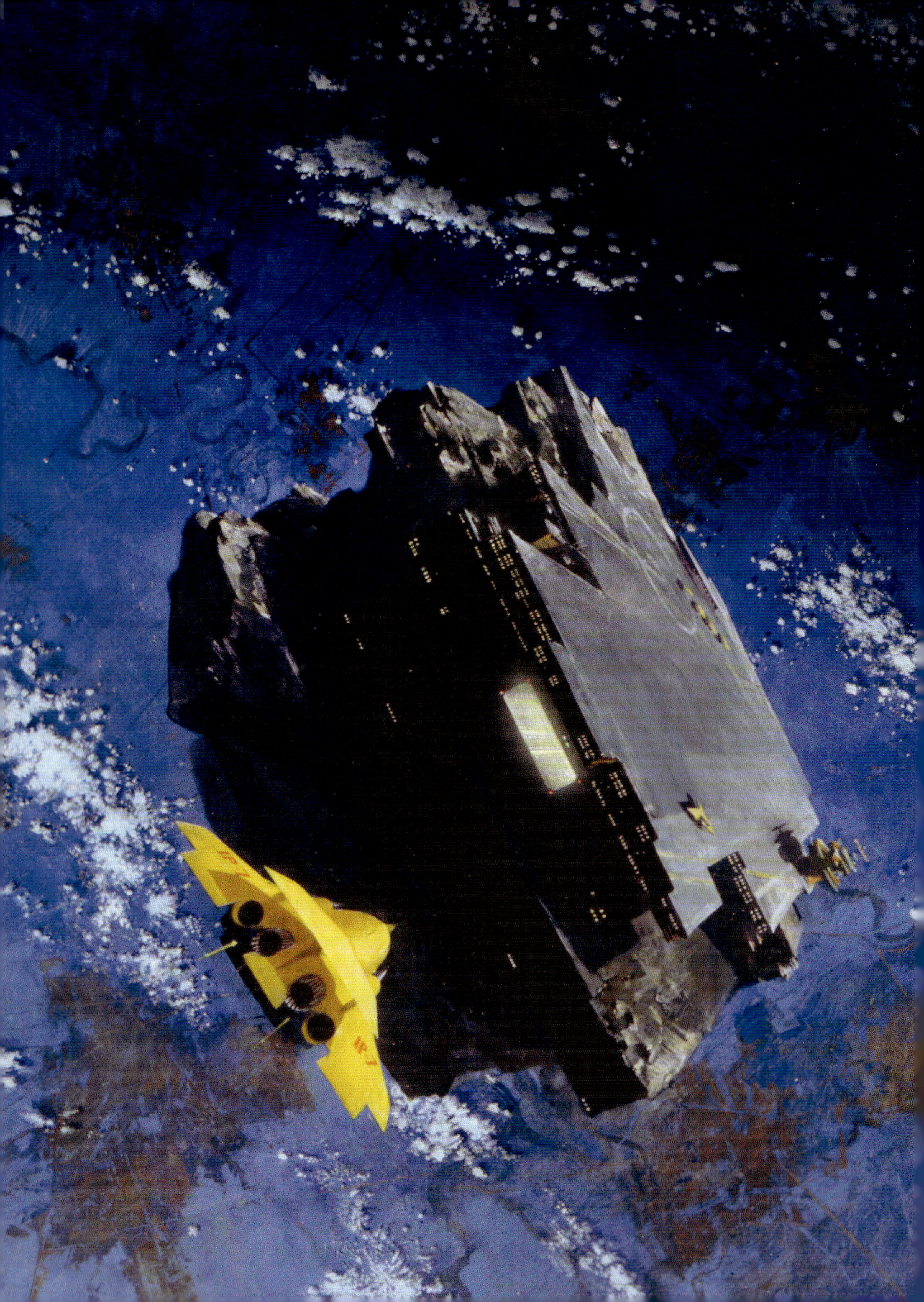

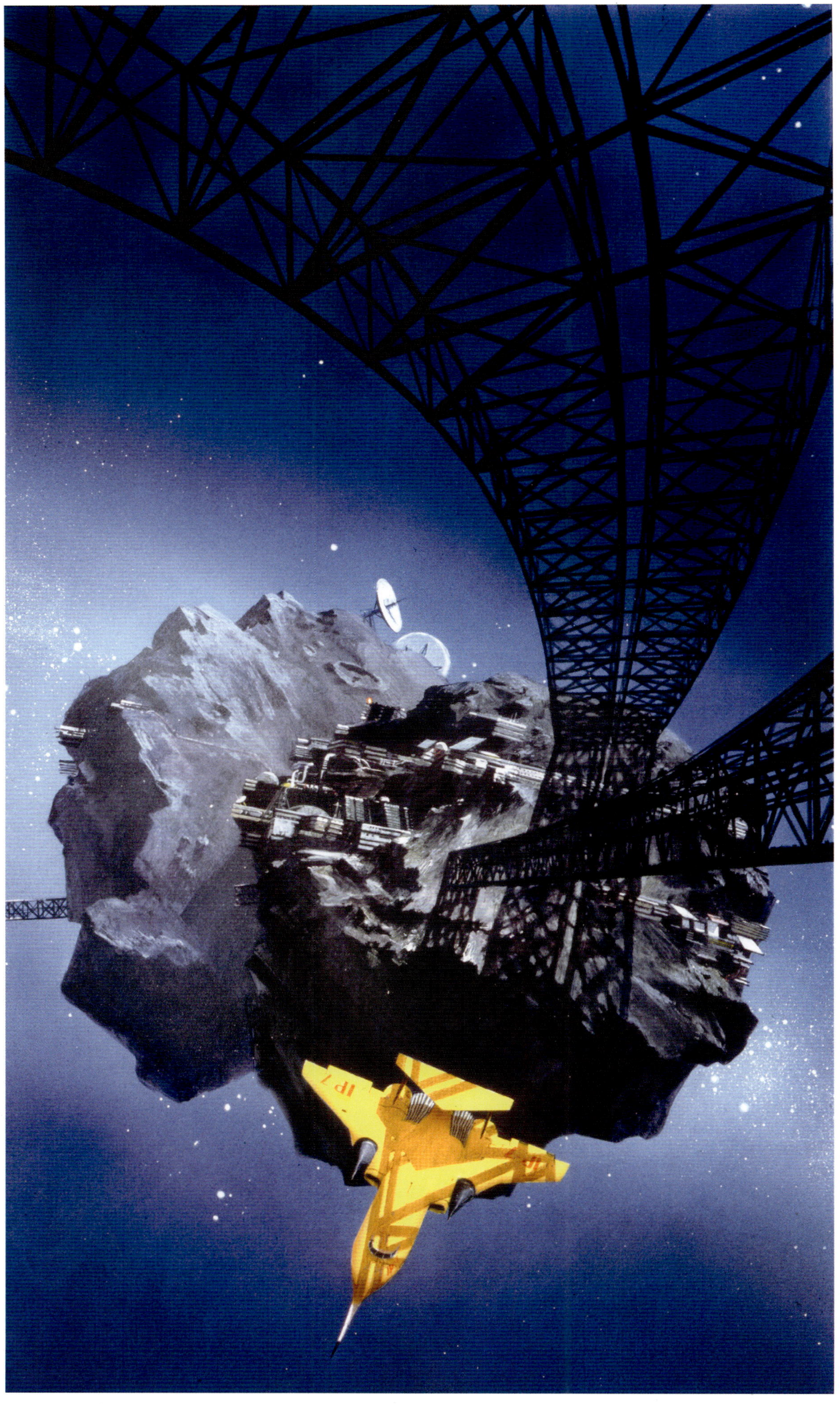

This Spread: *Worlds* and *Worlds Apart*, a brace of covers for the books by Joe Haldeman, 1994

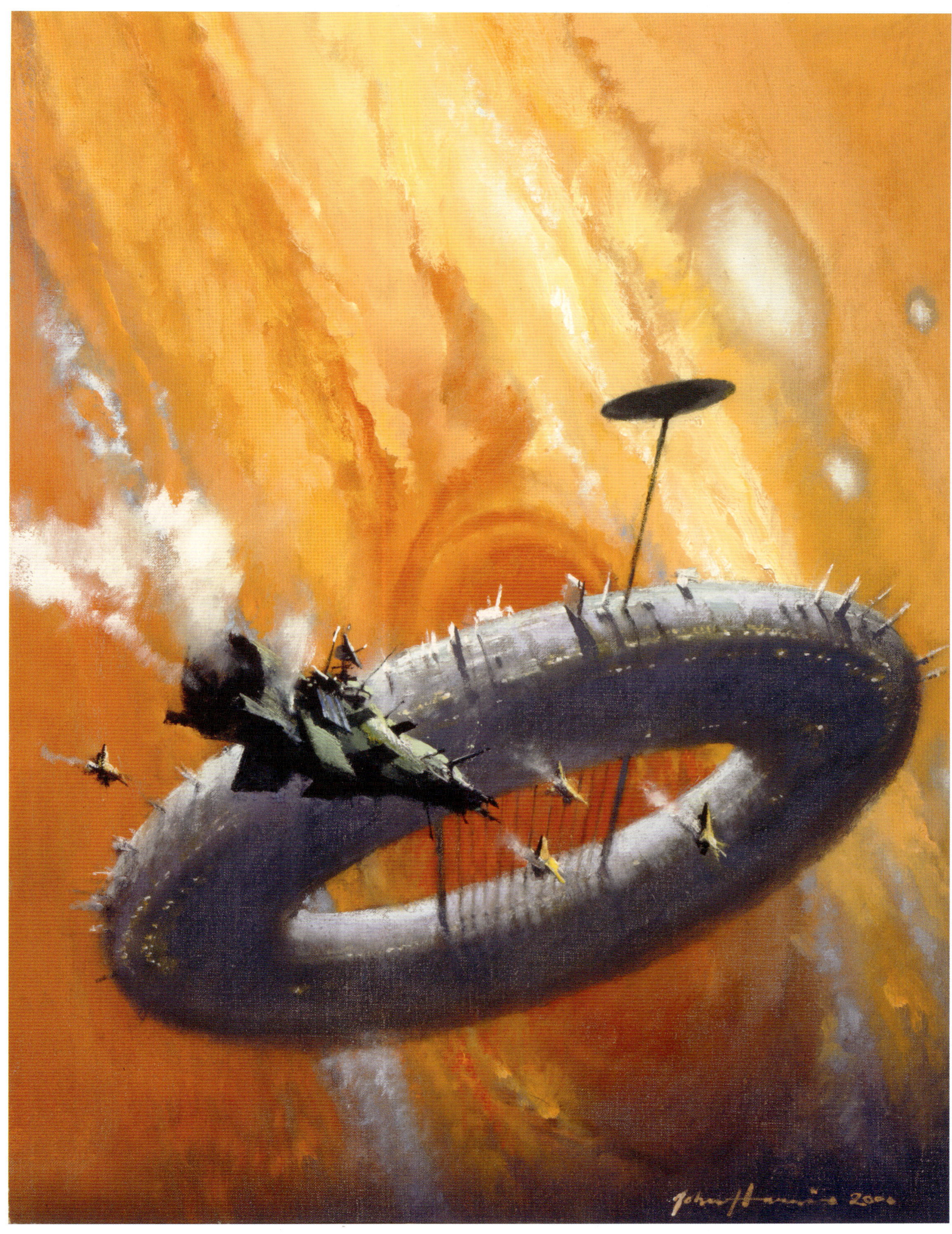

Above: *Jupiter*, for the cover of the book by Ben Bova. 2000

Opposite: *Earth Awakens*, for the cover of the book by Orson Scott Card and Aaron Johnston. 2013

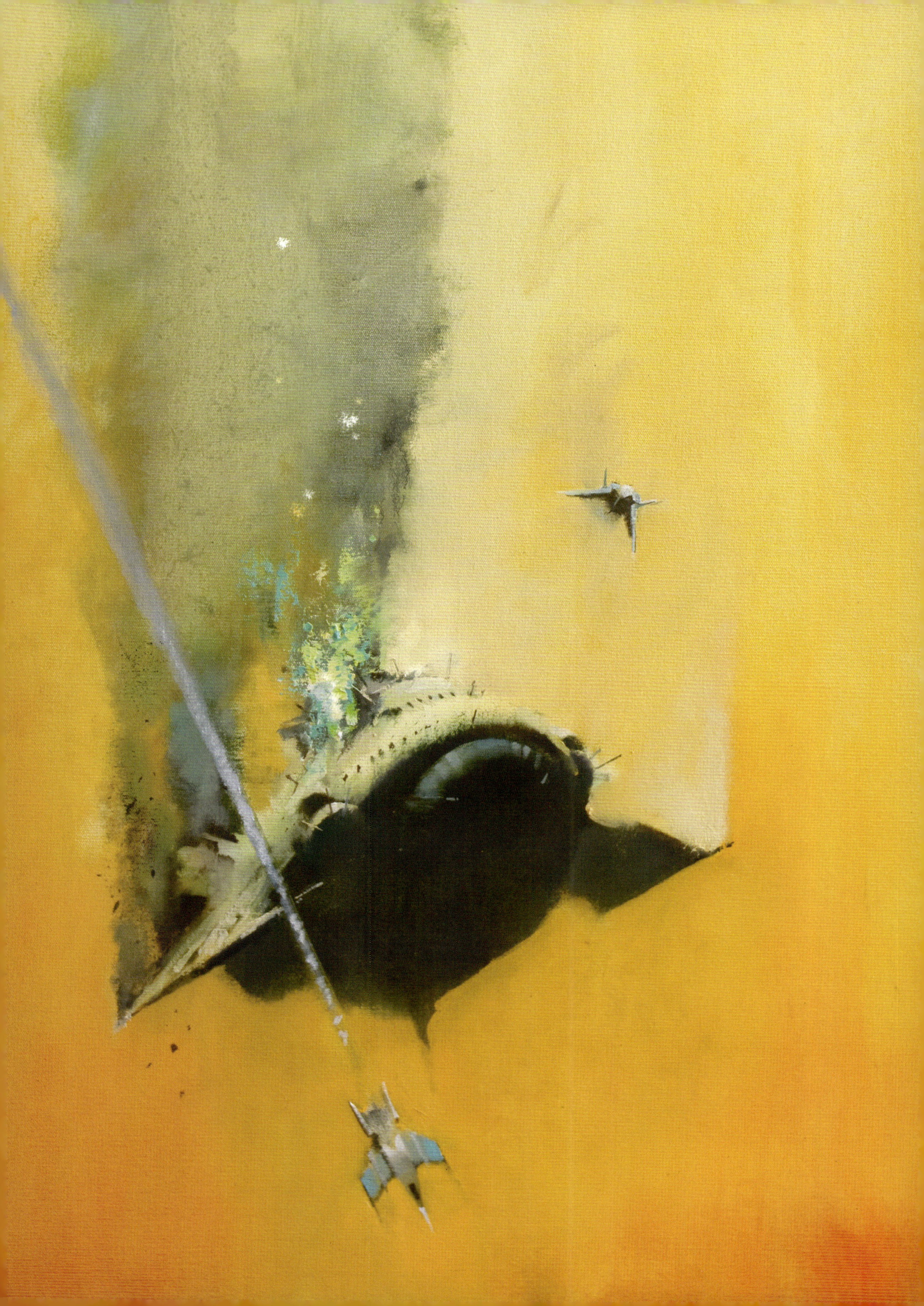

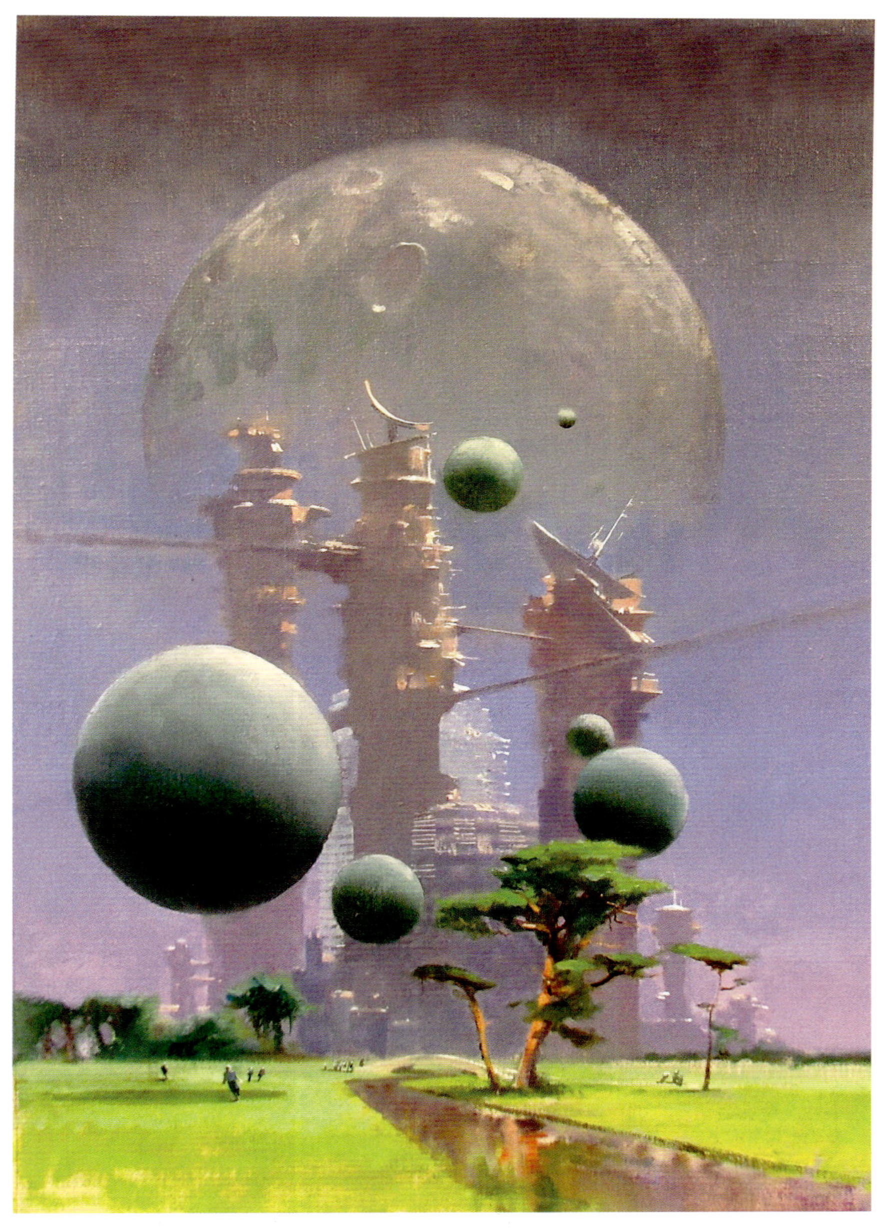

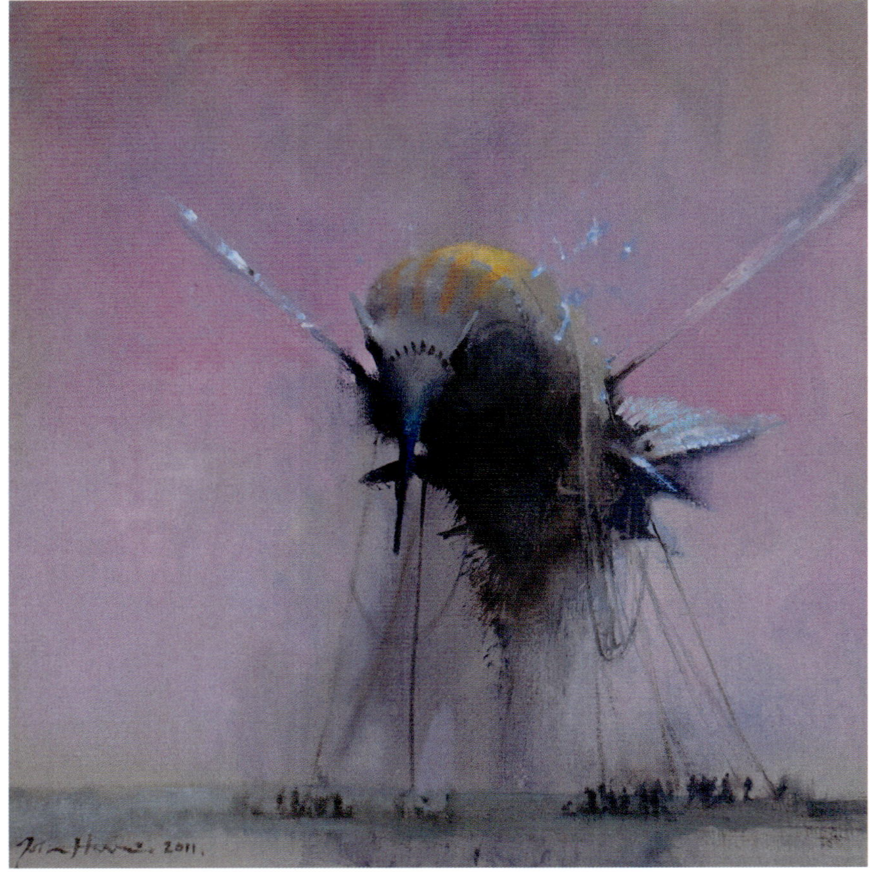

Top: *Armies of Memory*, for the cover of the book by John Barnes. 2006

Right: *Netting the Vespatron*. 2011

Opposite: *Ascent*. 2009

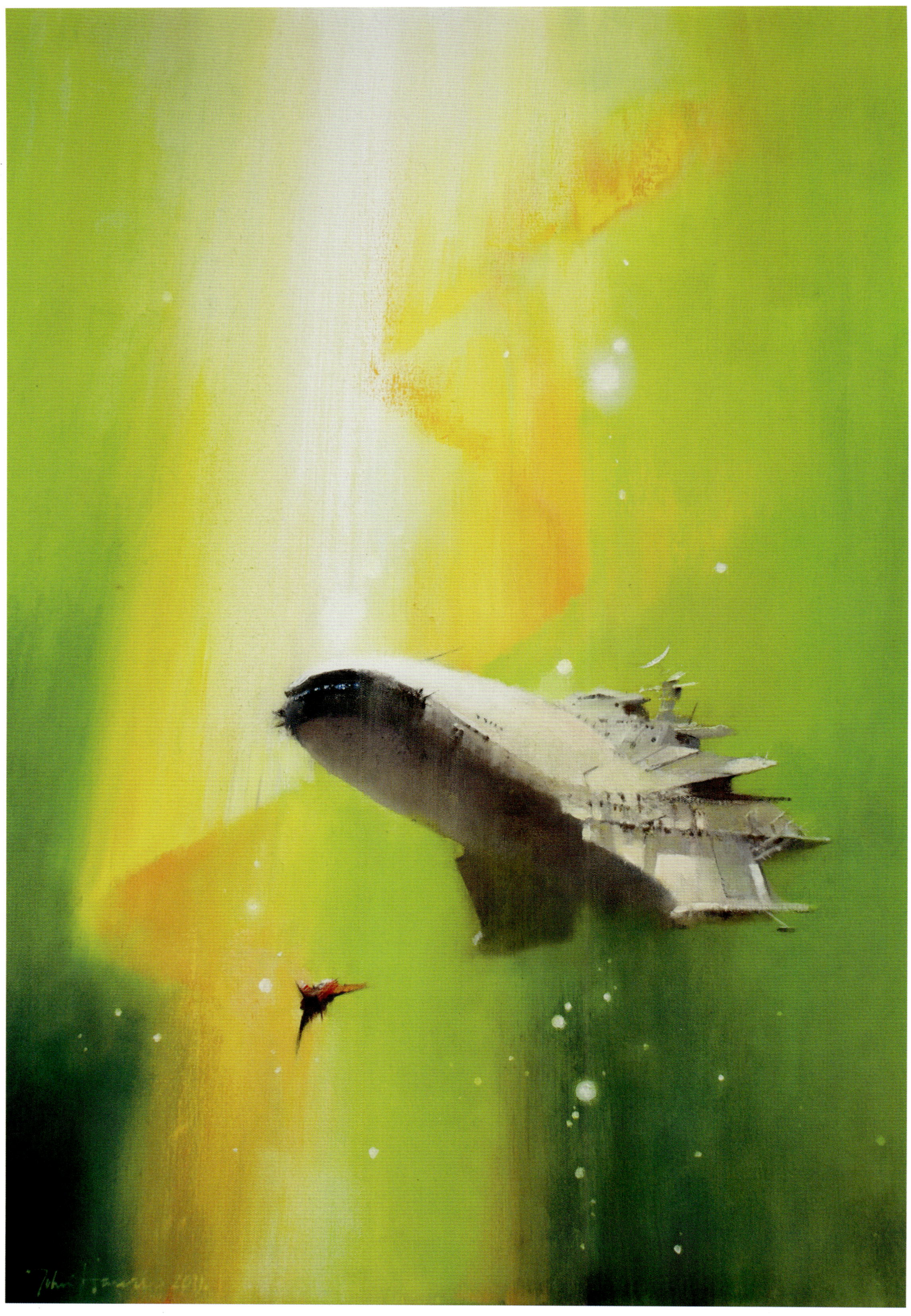

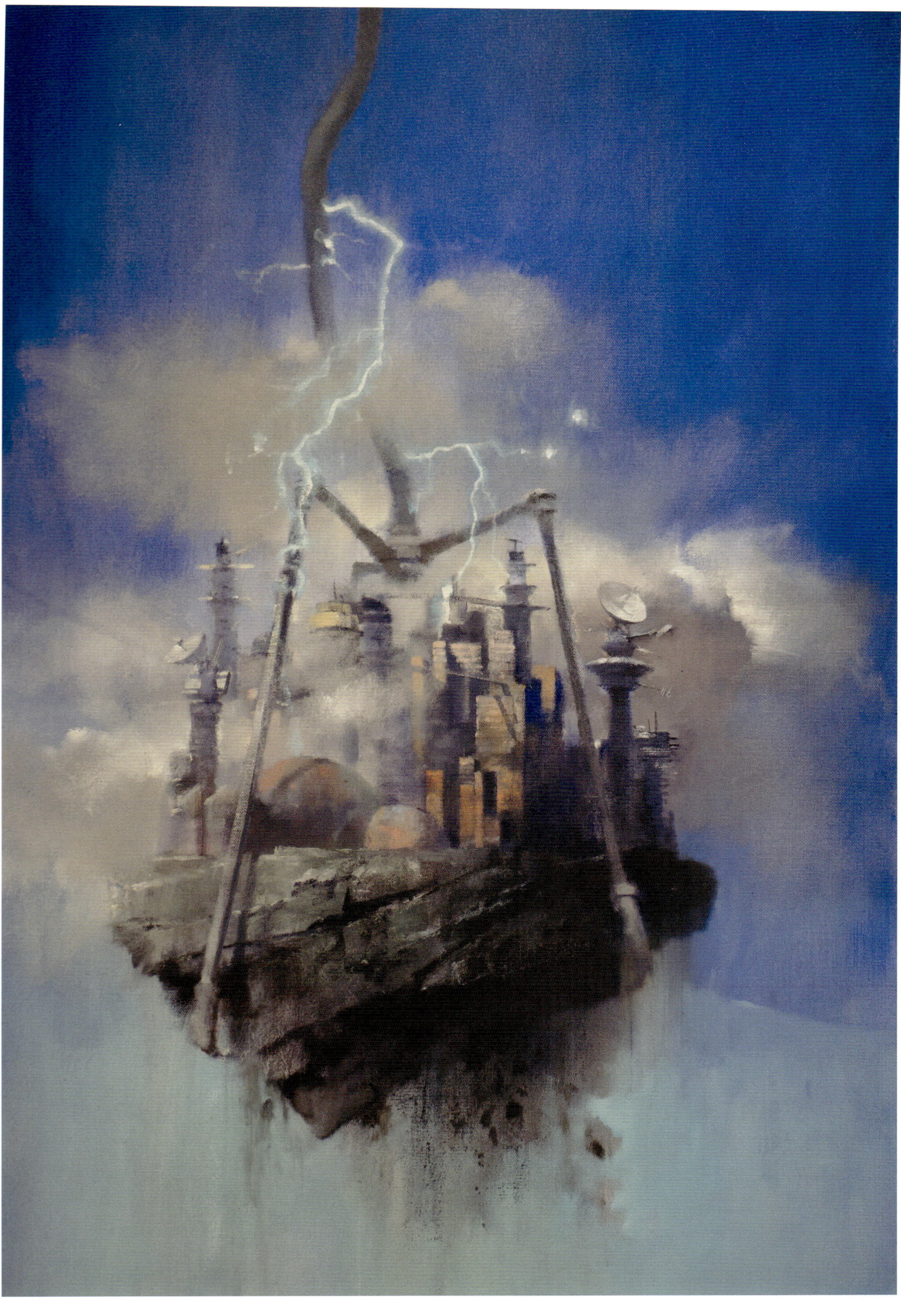

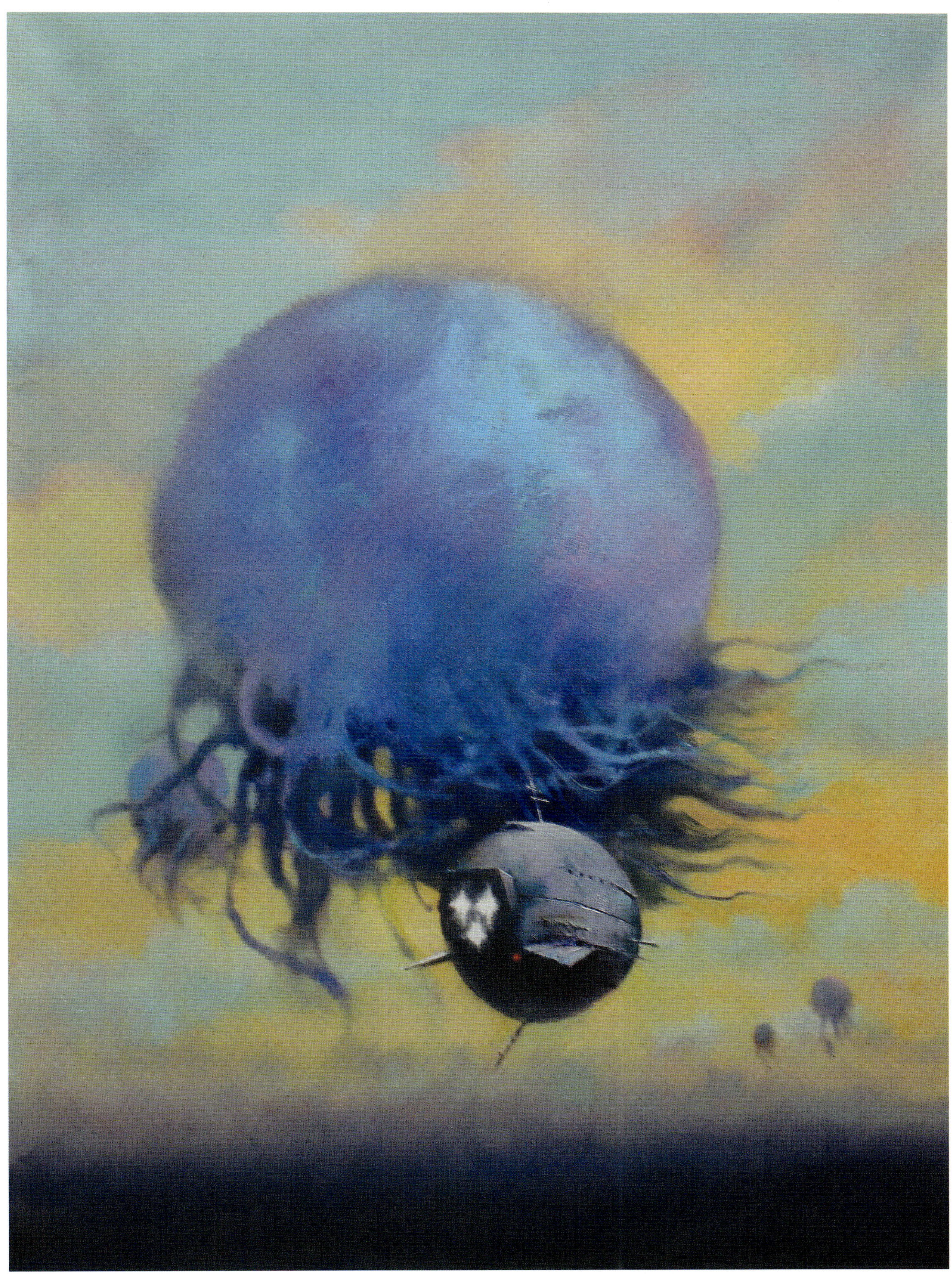

Above: *Leviathans of Jupiter*, for the cover of the book by Ben Bova. 2010

Opposite: *Judge of Ages*, for the cover of the book by John C Wright. 2012

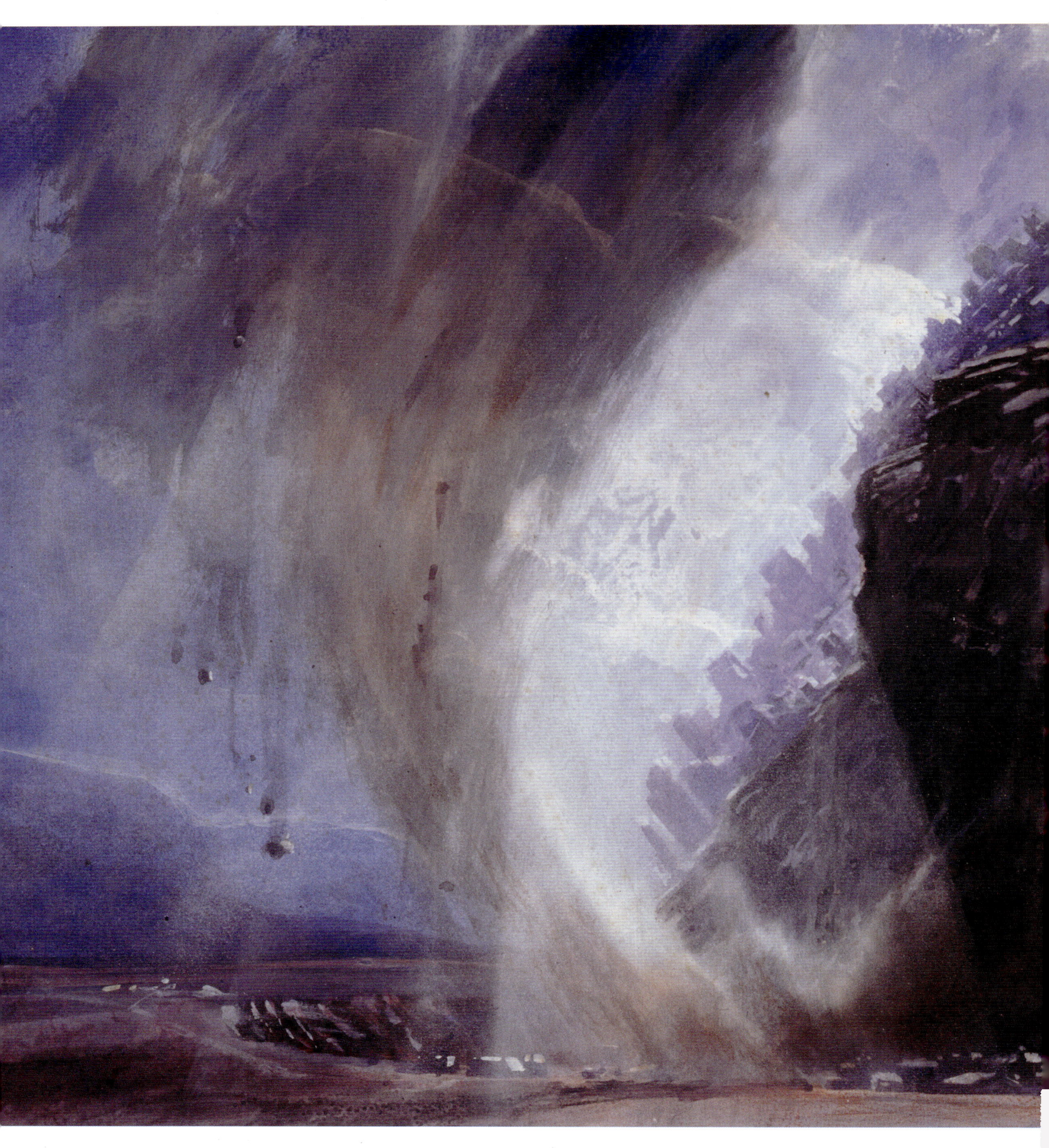

DUST TO DUST

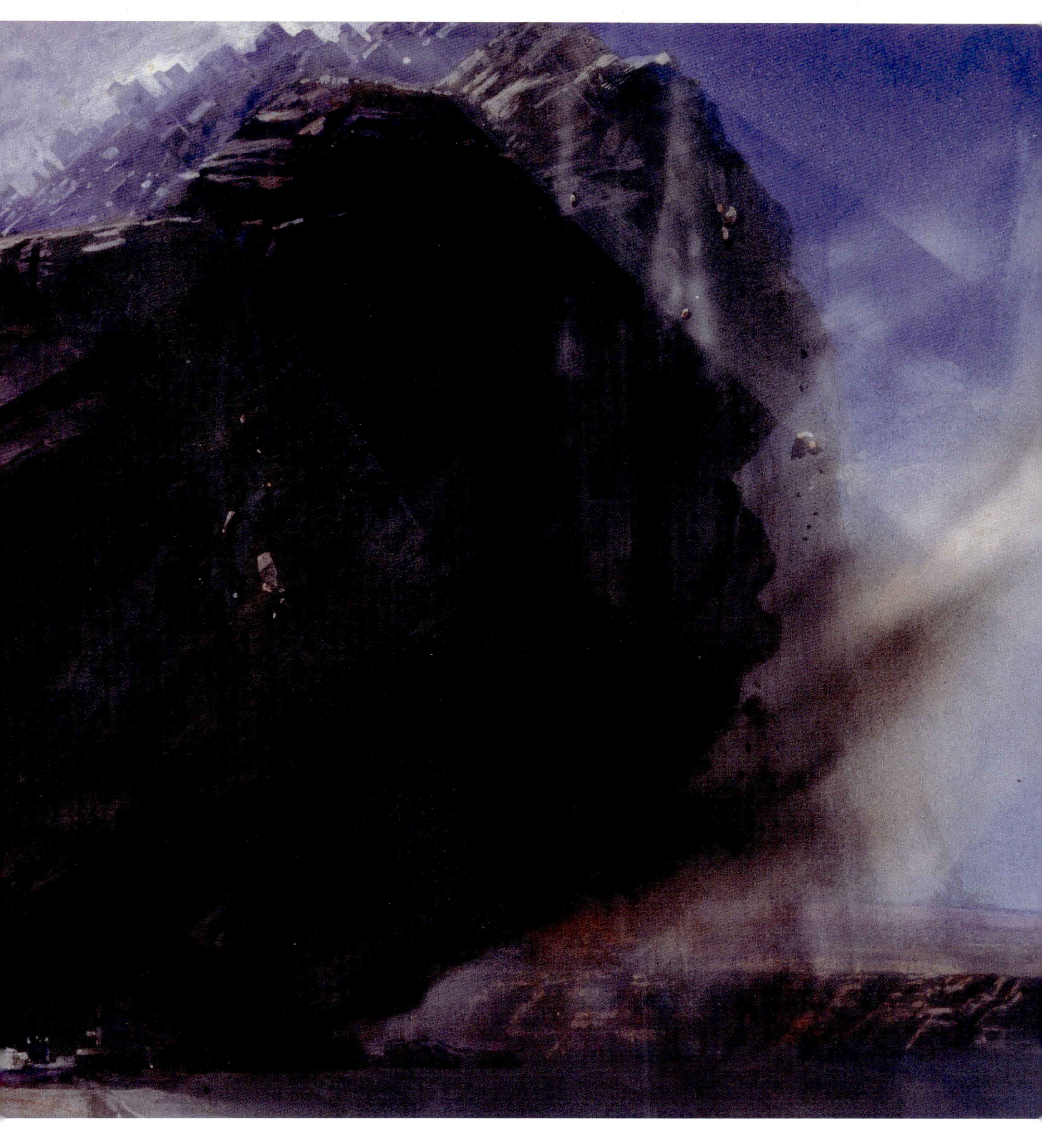

Like many children born just after the Second World War, I spent much of my early childhood exploring the ruins of abandoned bunkers and the jetsam of an industrialised society. Even where I lived, in the rural area to the south of London, there was the fading evidence of a recent heavily mechanised conflict, hidden in the scrubby woods. The broken air-raid shelters, amid brackish pools of water stained with oil. Bits of steel hawser curving out of broken blocks, mixed with briars mimicking the enemy in the war of reclamation. Fields of concrete – the remains of an aerodrome – were giving up the unequal fight against time and the thistles, and all of these things spoke a melancholic tale of past efforts, sidelined by a change of circumstance.

Growing up in this environment, it is, I suppose, inevitable that images of aspiration and fall have such a large part to play in my pictures. This preoccupation was given enormous impetus by the atmosphere of the times, which were dominated by the Cold War. Even as a thirteen year-old, I was, like many others of my generation in the early 1960s, acutely aware of the very precarious state of the world. This was the time of the Cuban Crisis and there was the very real possibility that our known world could suddenly become history. In short, the images of power and permanence that our society would like to claim as our reality was plainly nothing of the sort. What follows shows the two sides of the same coin.

Previous Spread: *Spindizzy,* to illustrate *Cities in Flight* by James Blish. 1977

Right: *The Far Shore of Time,* for the cover of the book by Frederick Pohl. 1998

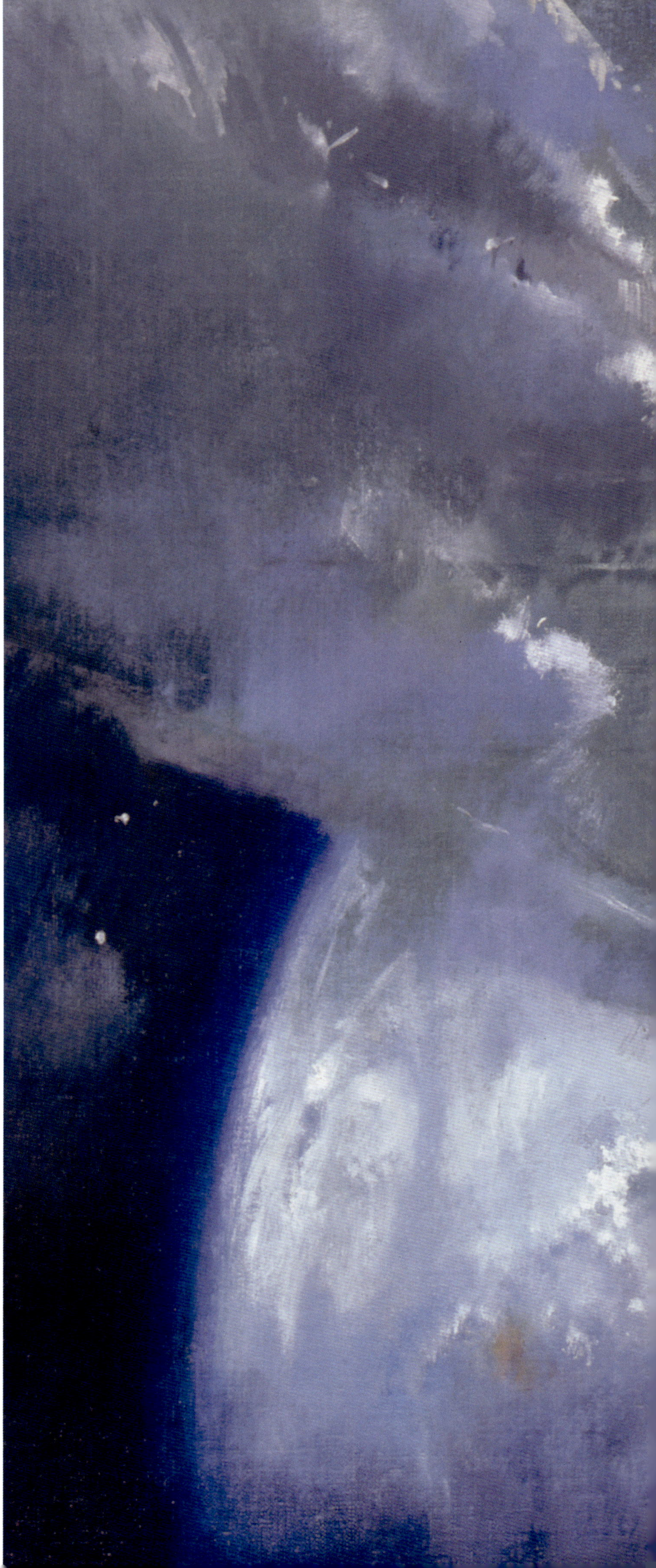

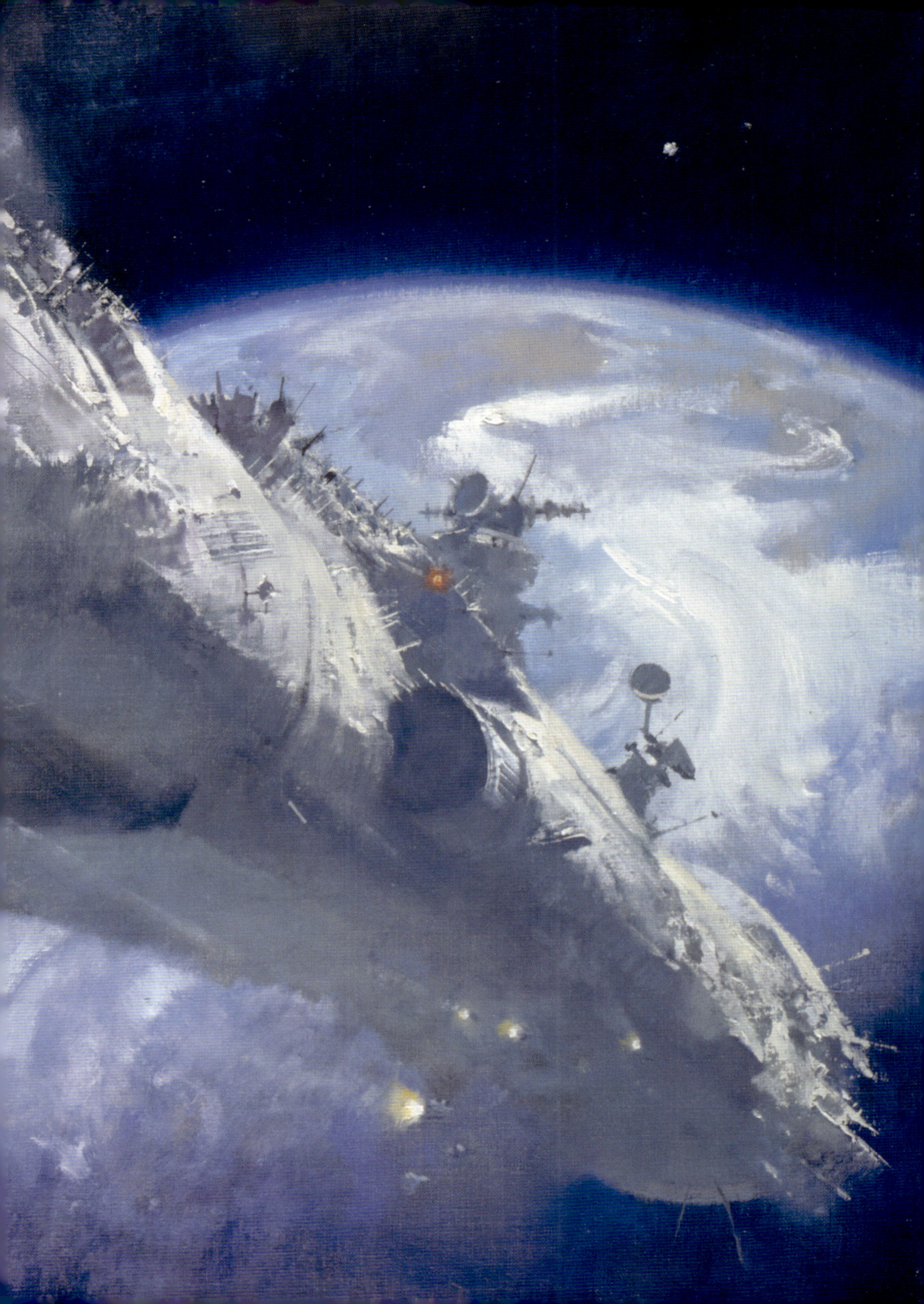

TOWERS IN STARLIGHT

In the first half of this collection are pictures which reflect the upcurving, more aspirational side of the coin, such as *The Welcome, Grand Tour,* et al. Each expresses the hubris of a race reaching for the stars, though some of these are inevitably tinged with melancholy, as if the heart already knows the emptiness that is yet to come.

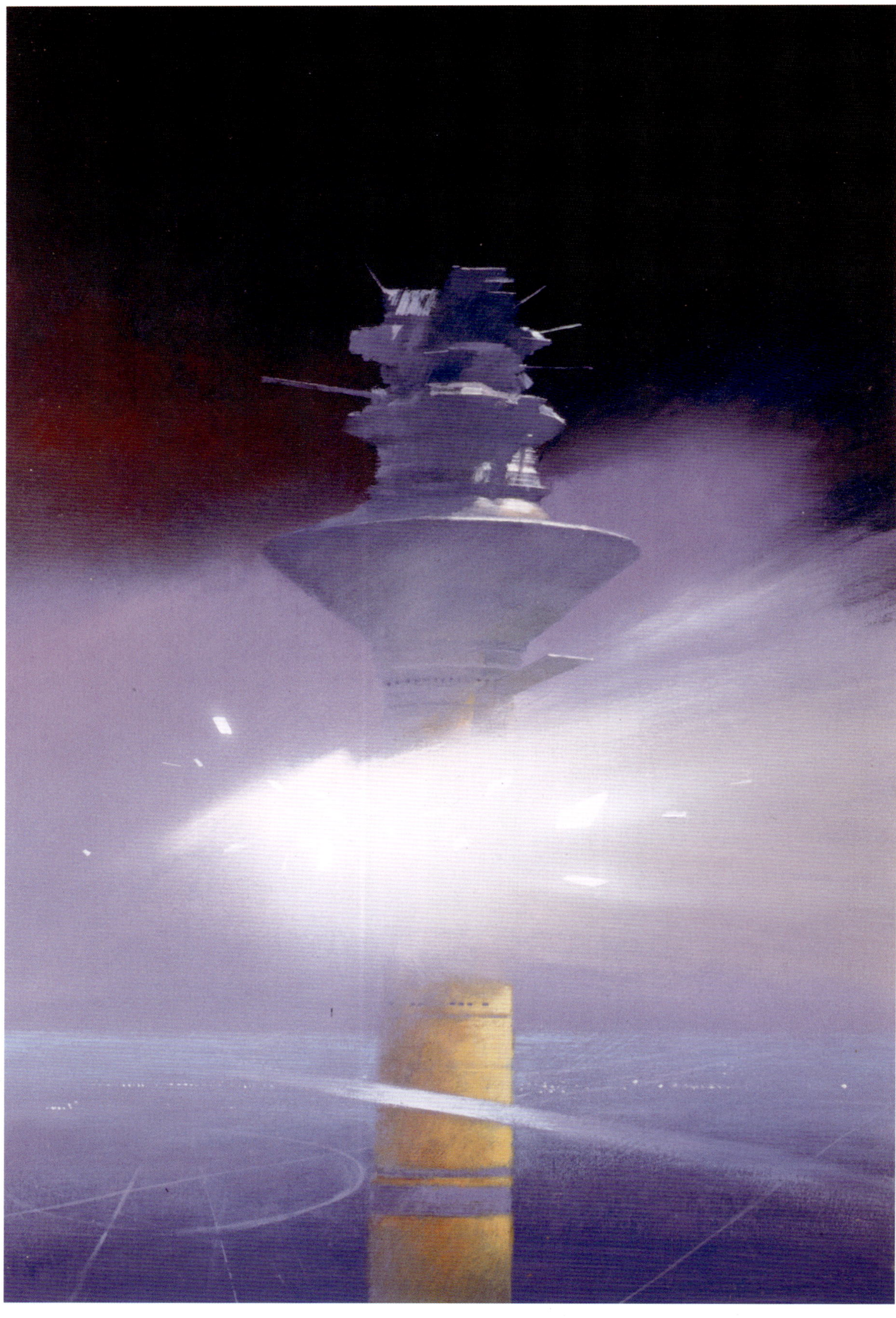

Above: *Driftglass*, for the cover of the book by Samuel R Delany. 1979

Right: *The Grand Tour*, for the cover of the book by Ben Bova. 2002

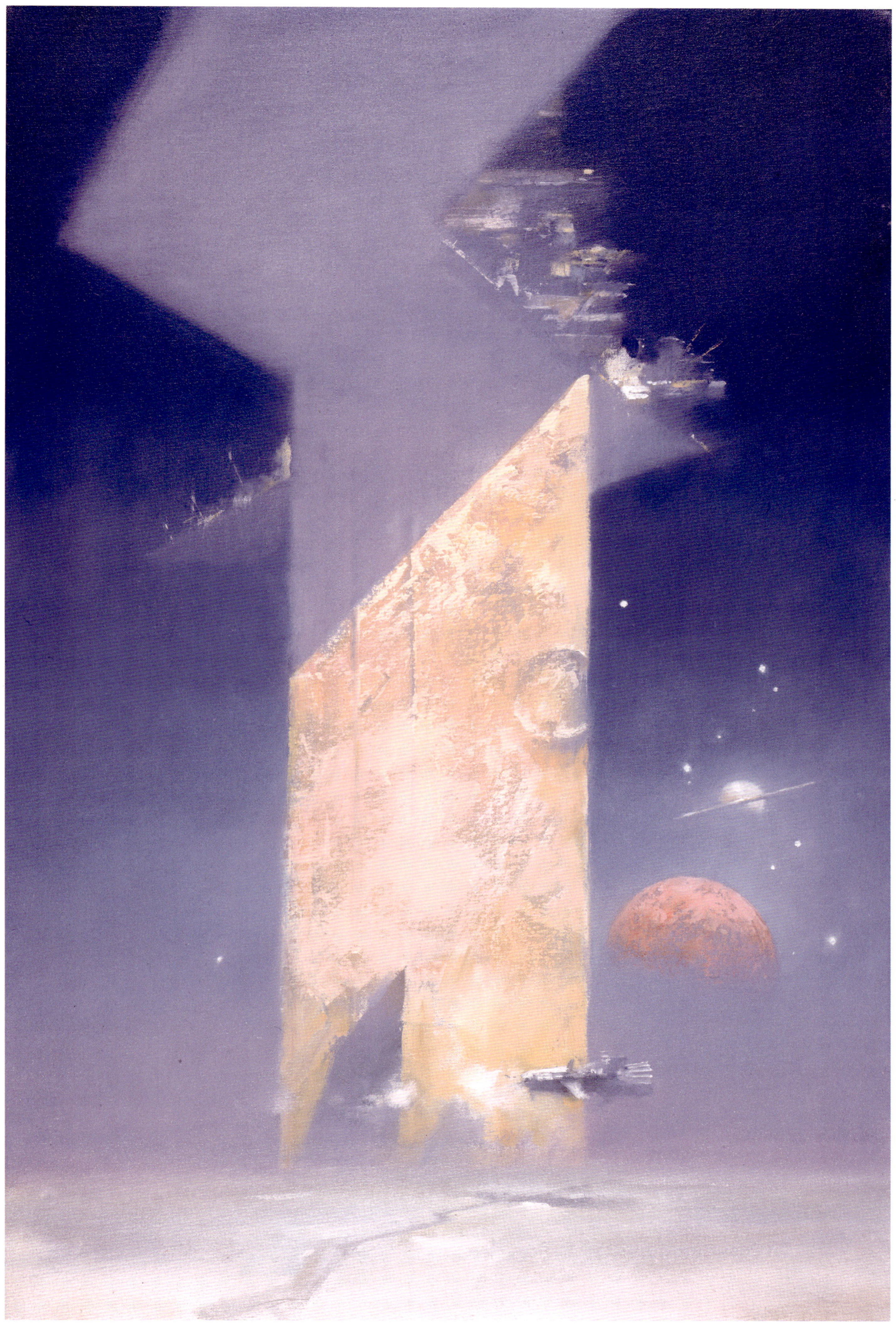

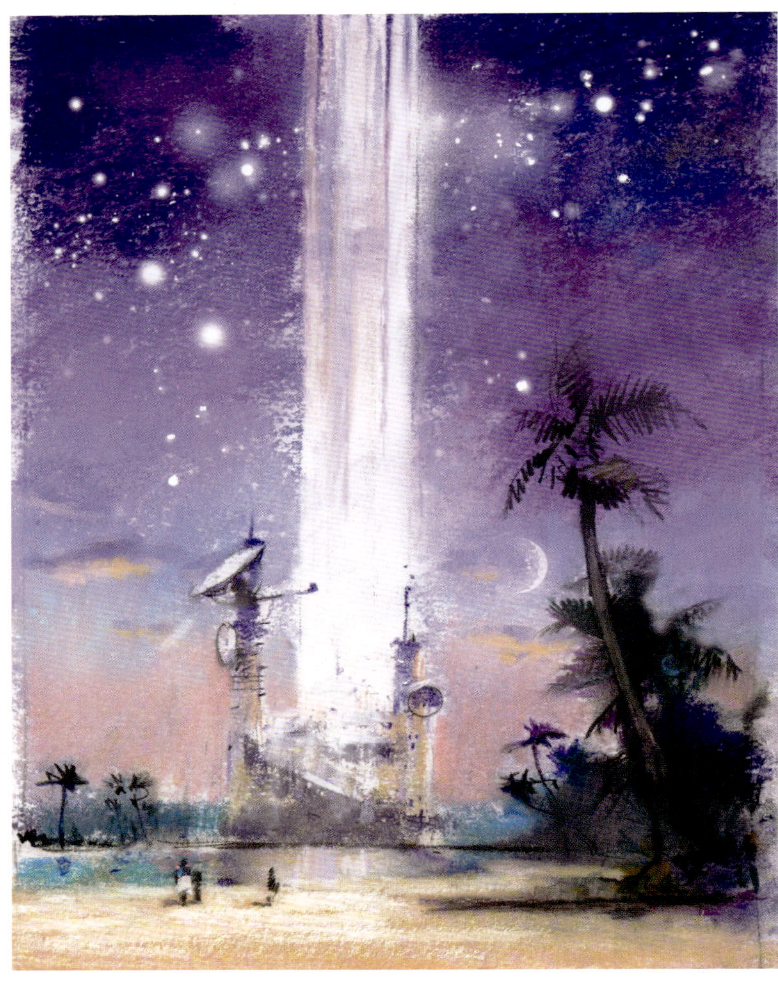

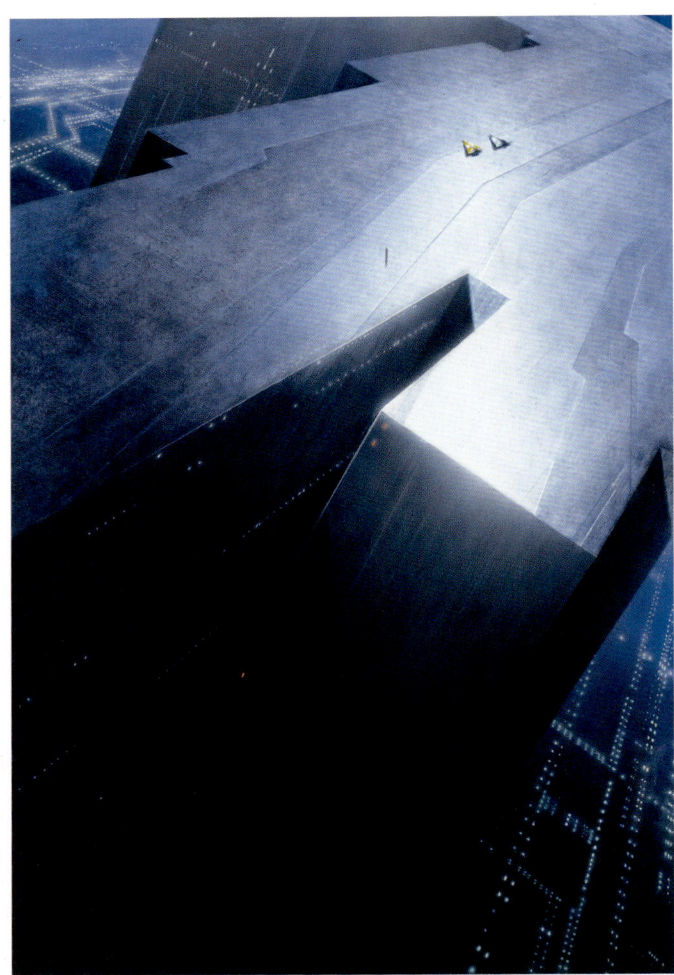

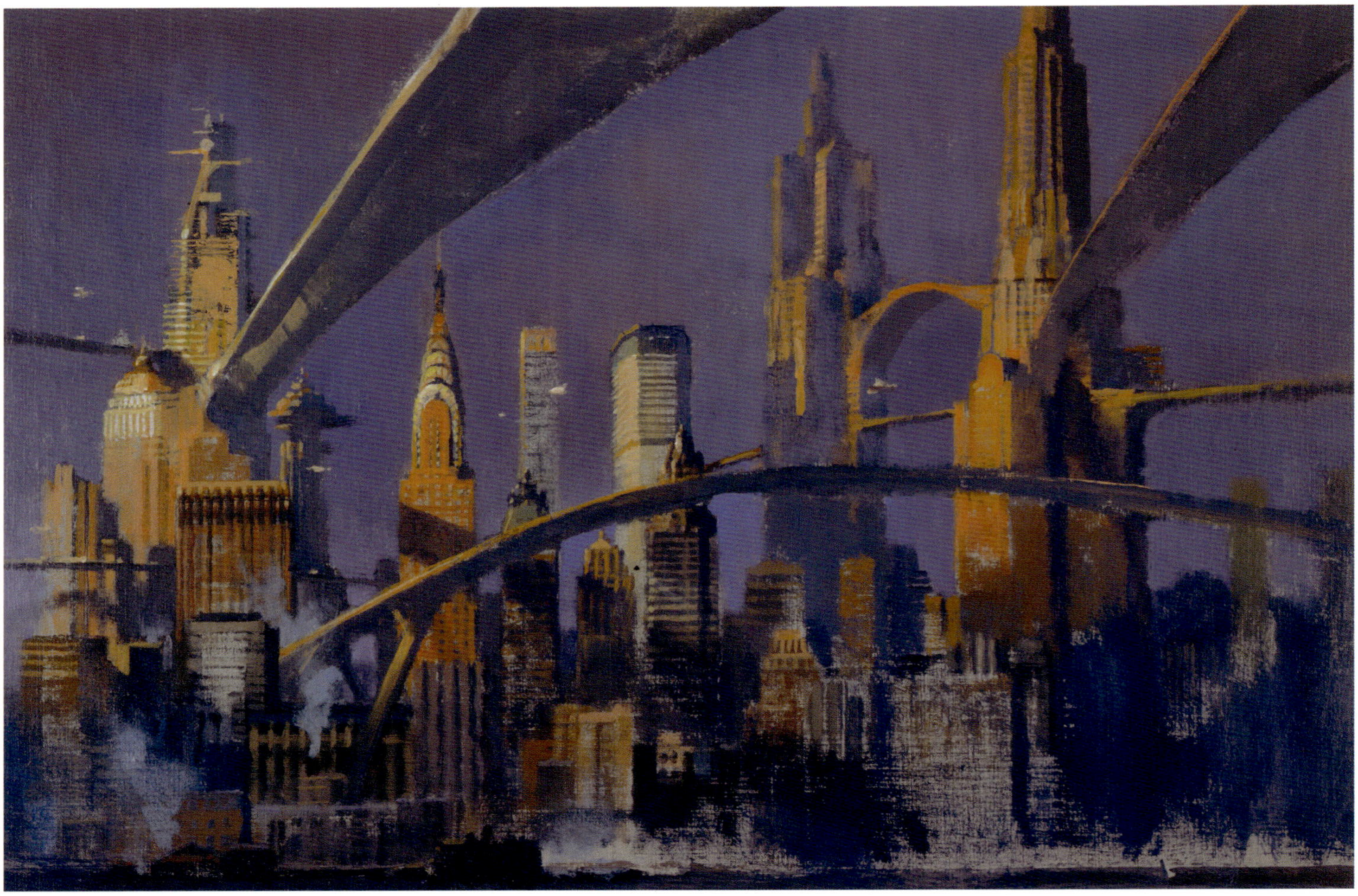

Above Left: *The Dream*, sketch for *The Last Theorem*, Arthur C Clarke's last book. 2008

Above Right: *ZX81*. 1981

Bottom: *The Siege of Eternity*, for the book by Frederick Pohl. 1998

Opposite: *The Welcome*, produced for the cover of *The Best of Trek 15*. 1989

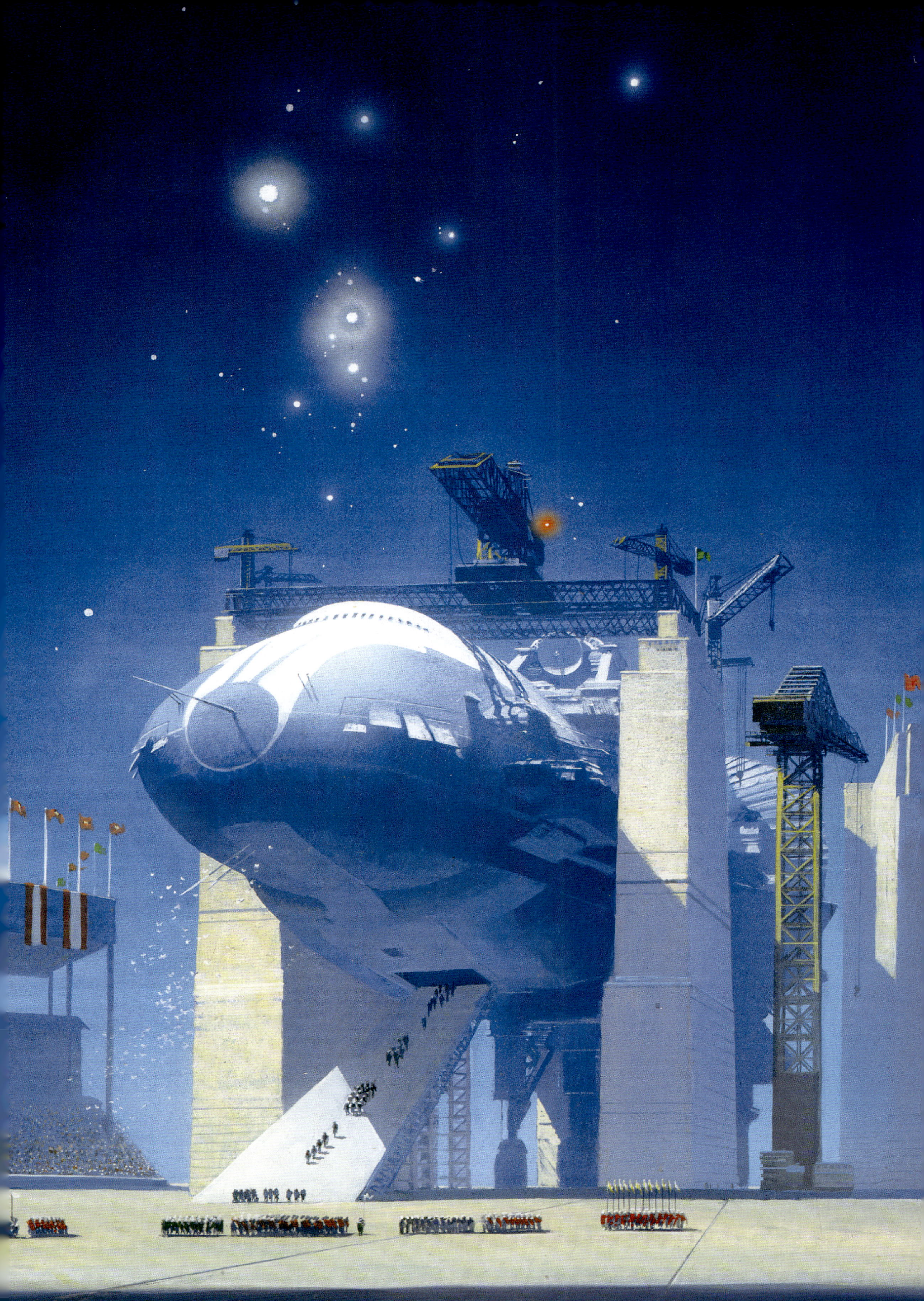

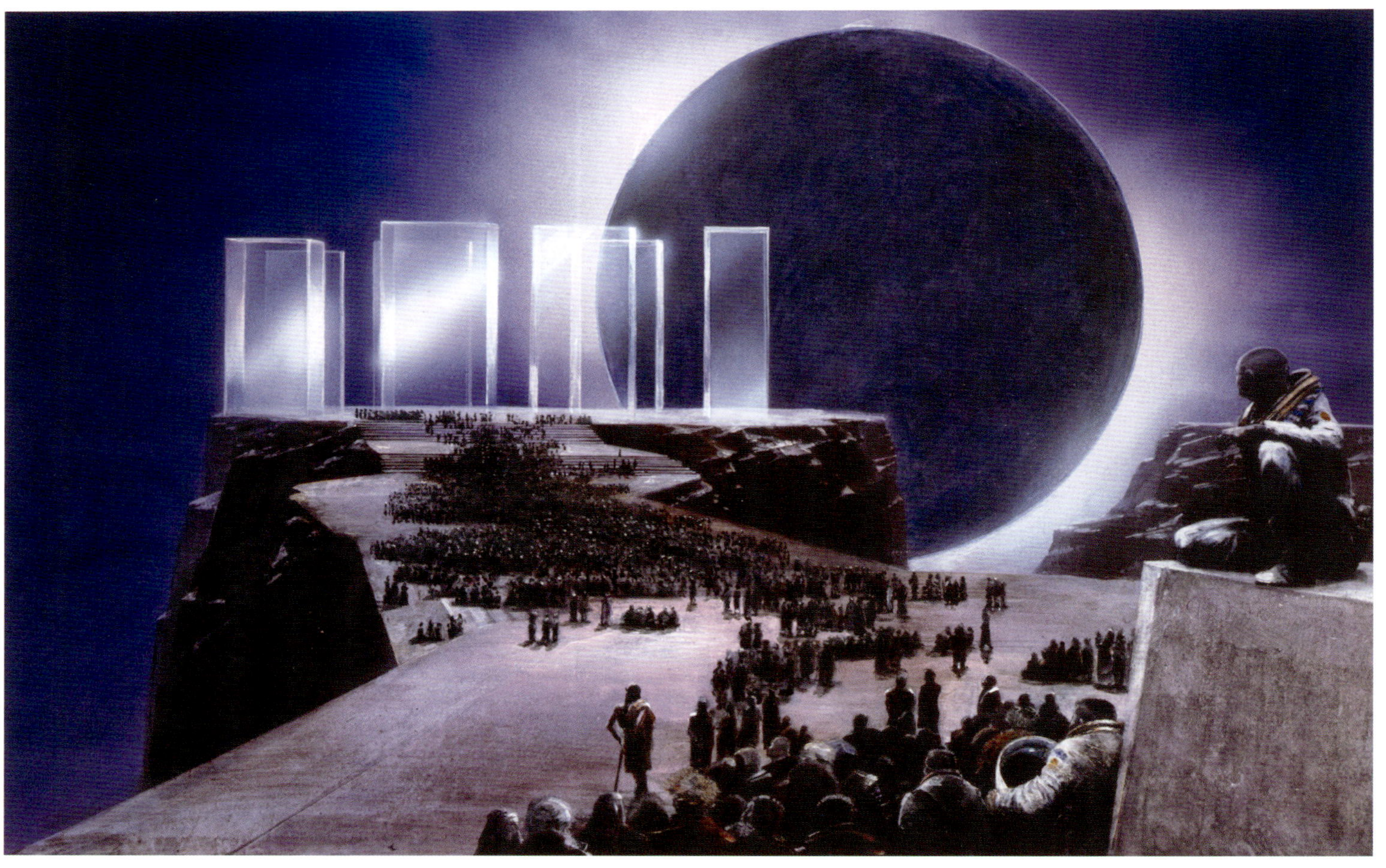

Above: *Mass: Crystal Henge*. 1979

Below: *The Twin Parliaments of Pyrrhus*, produced to illustrate an online segment of *The Human Division* by John Scalzi. 2012

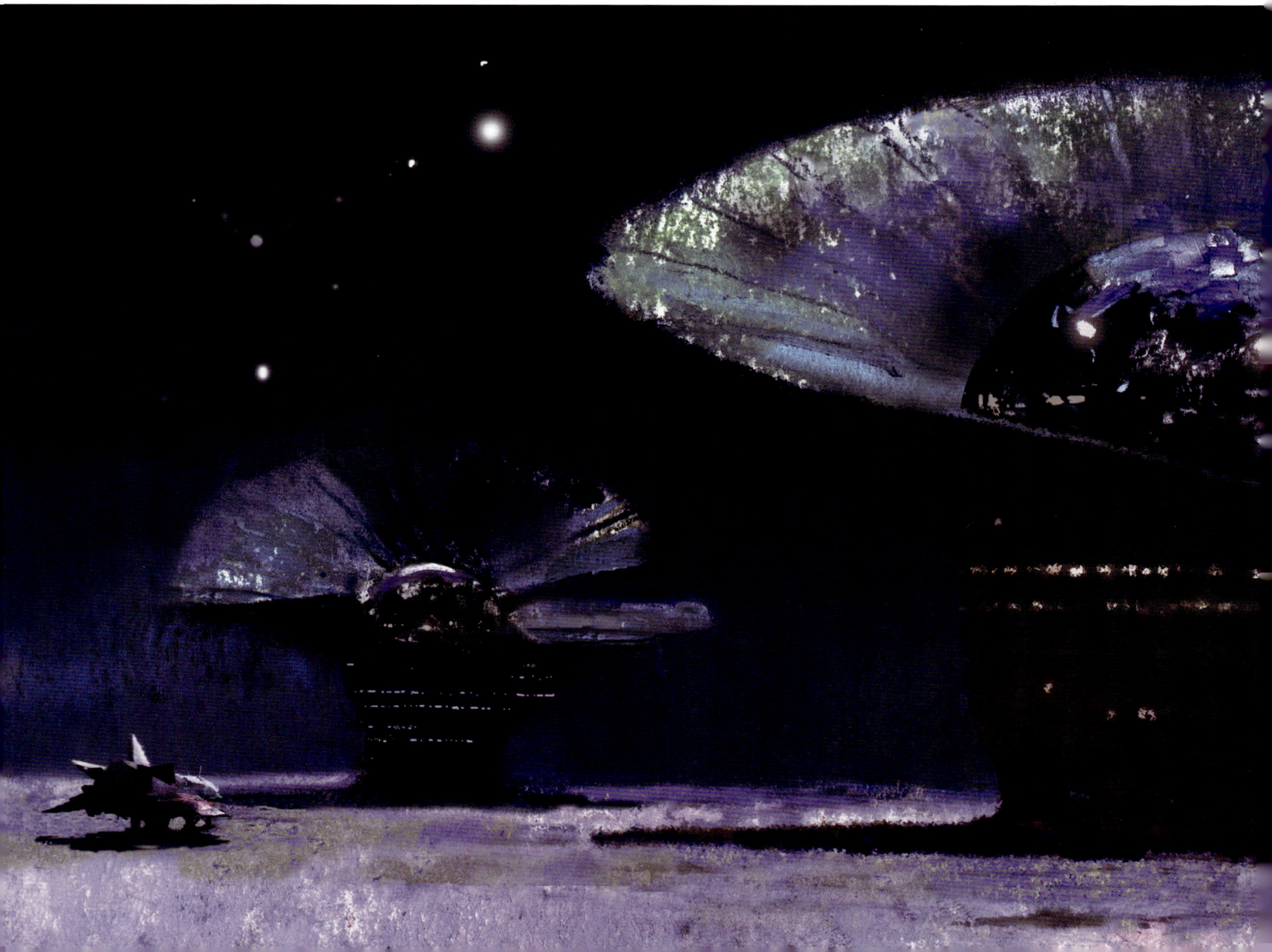

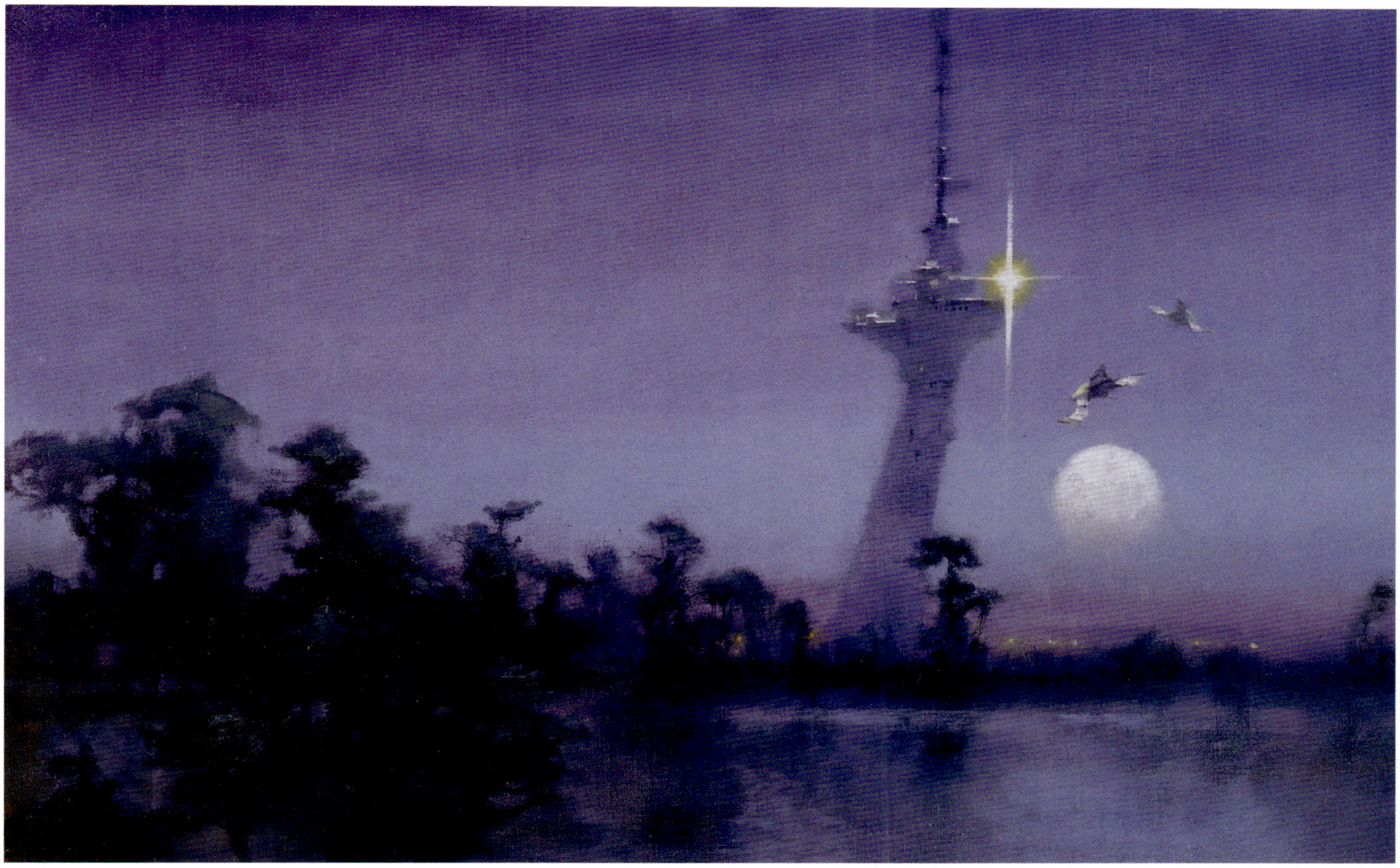

Above: *Eyes of the Calculor*, for the cover of the book by Sean McMullen. 2000

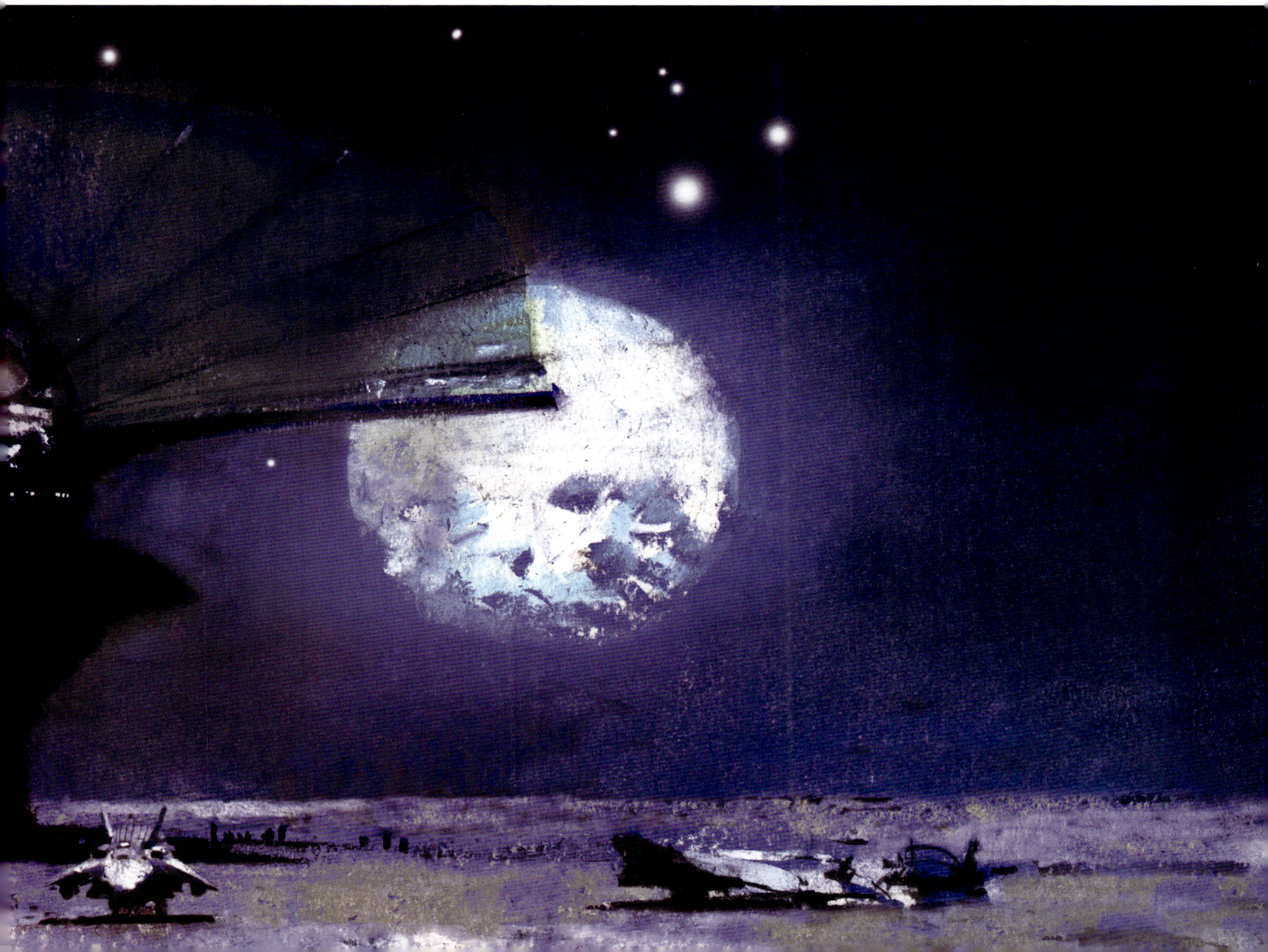

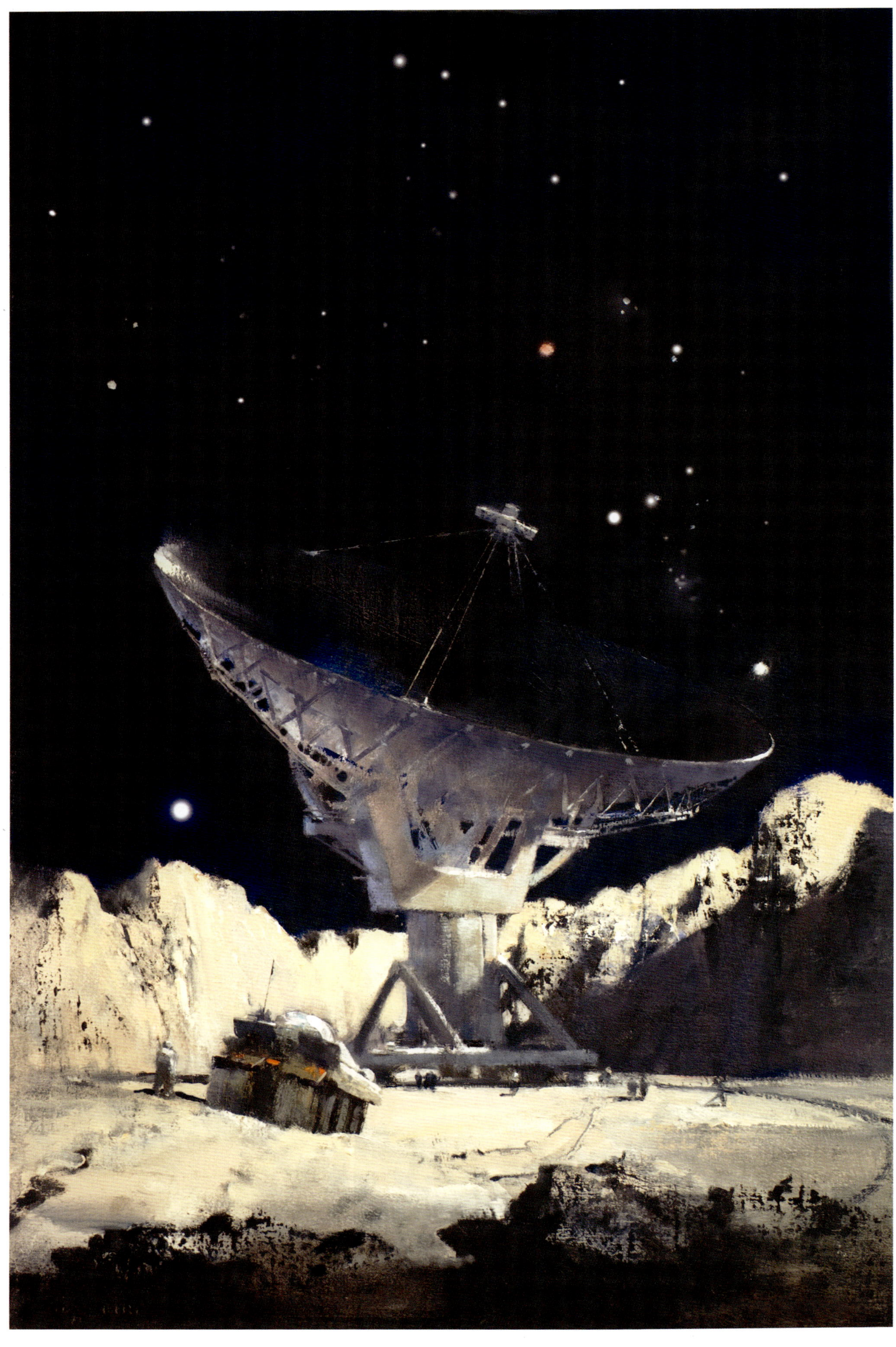

Above: *Farside*, for the cover of the book by Ben Bova. 2013

Opposite: *Phoenix*. 1990

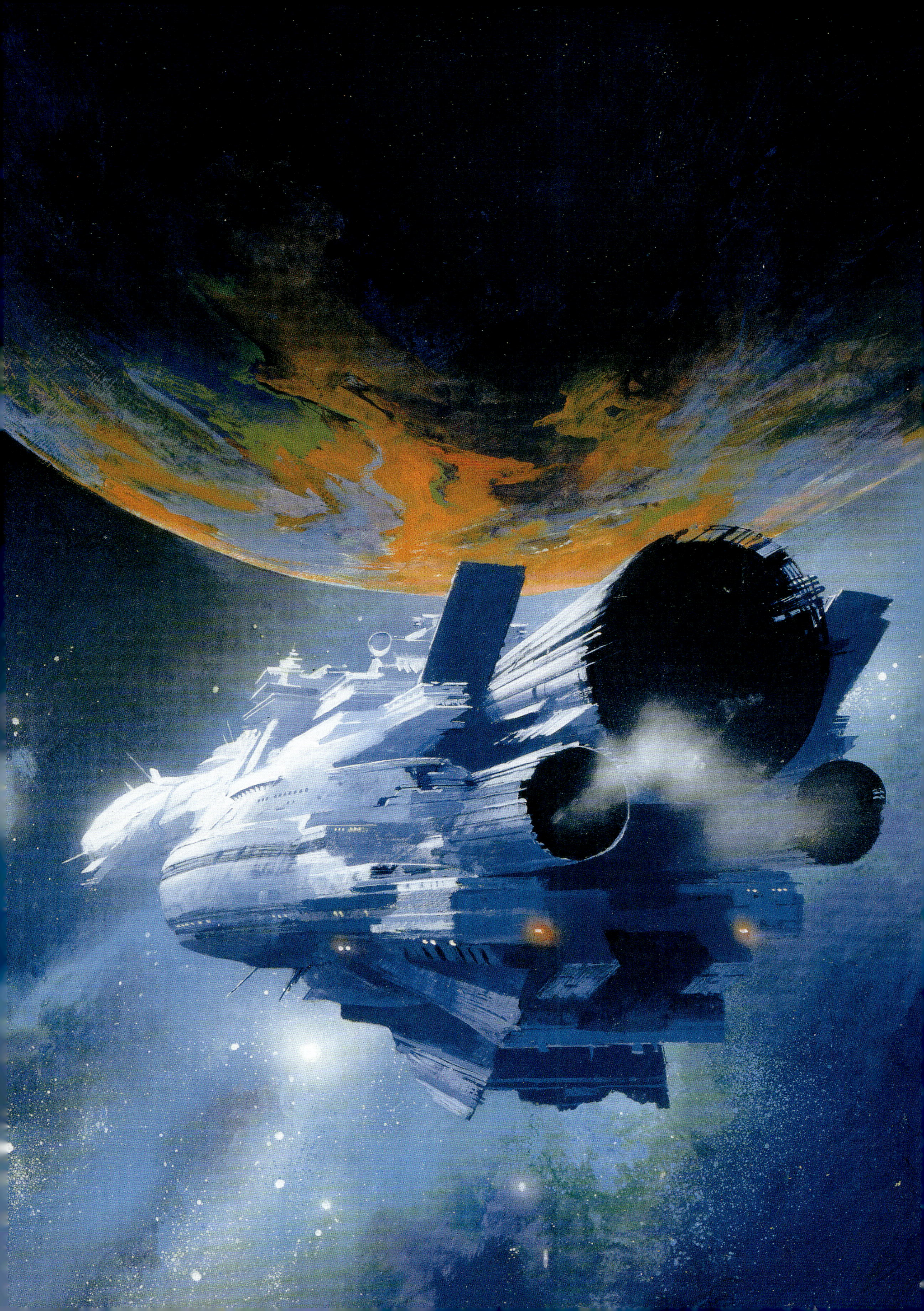

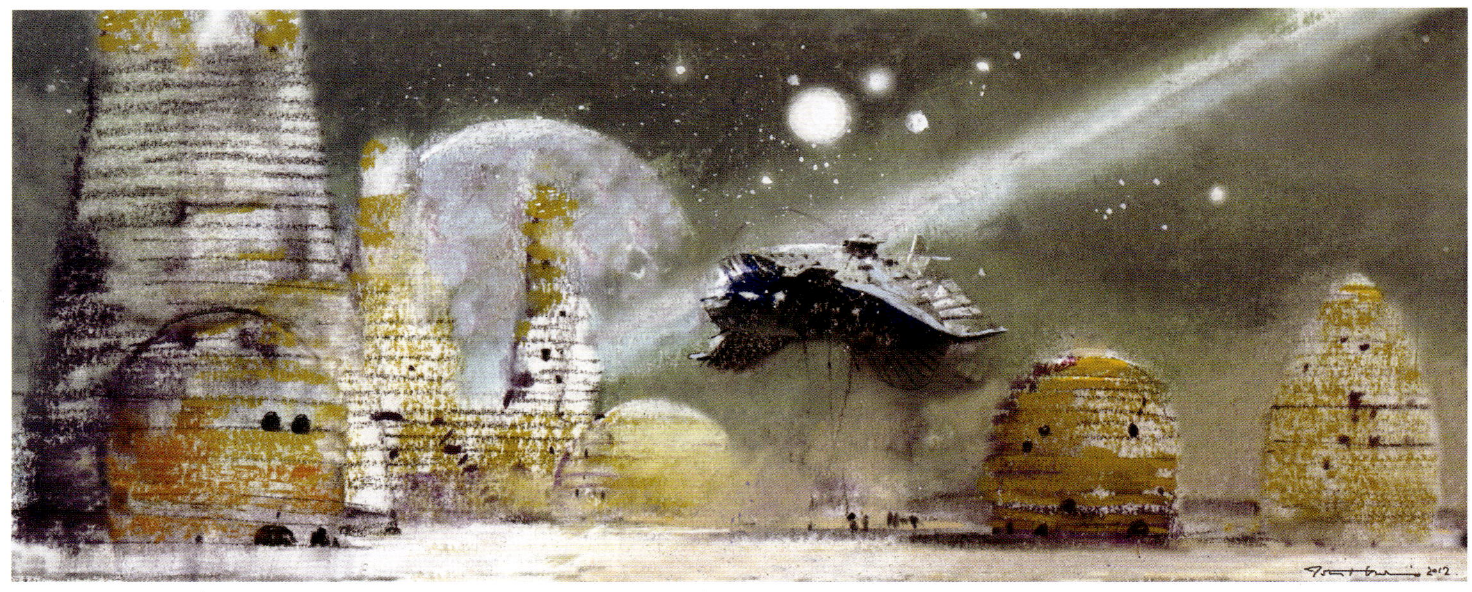

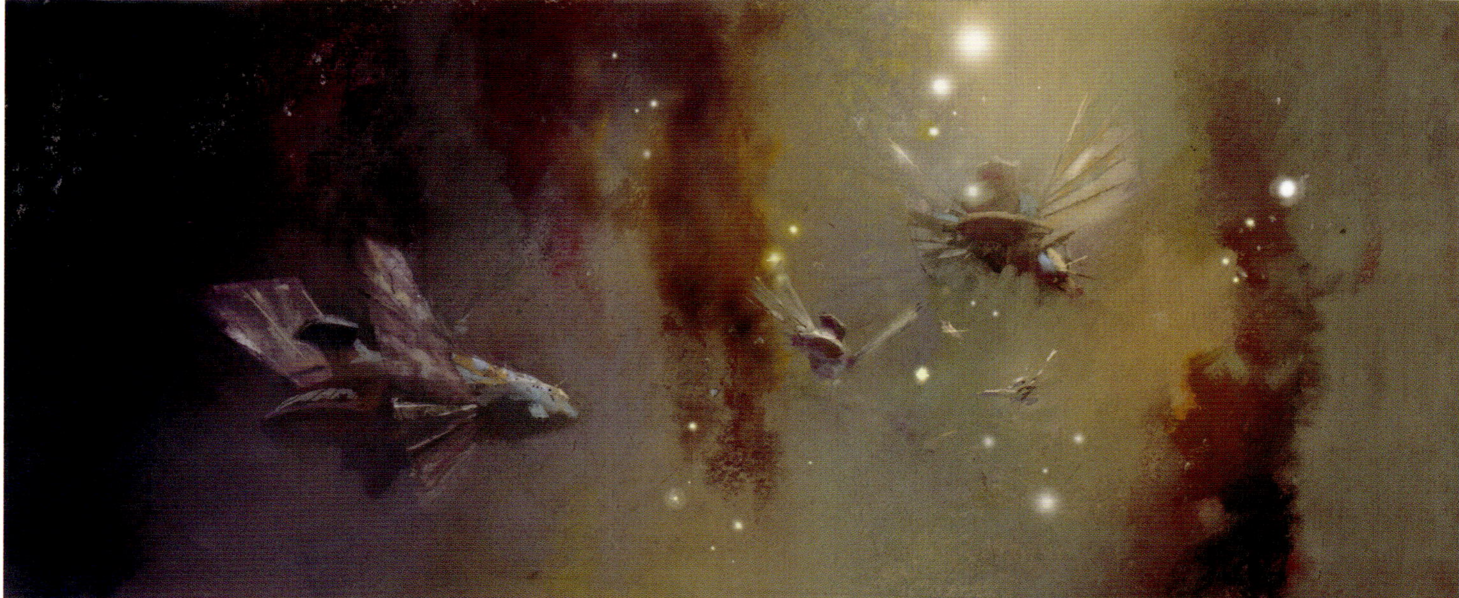

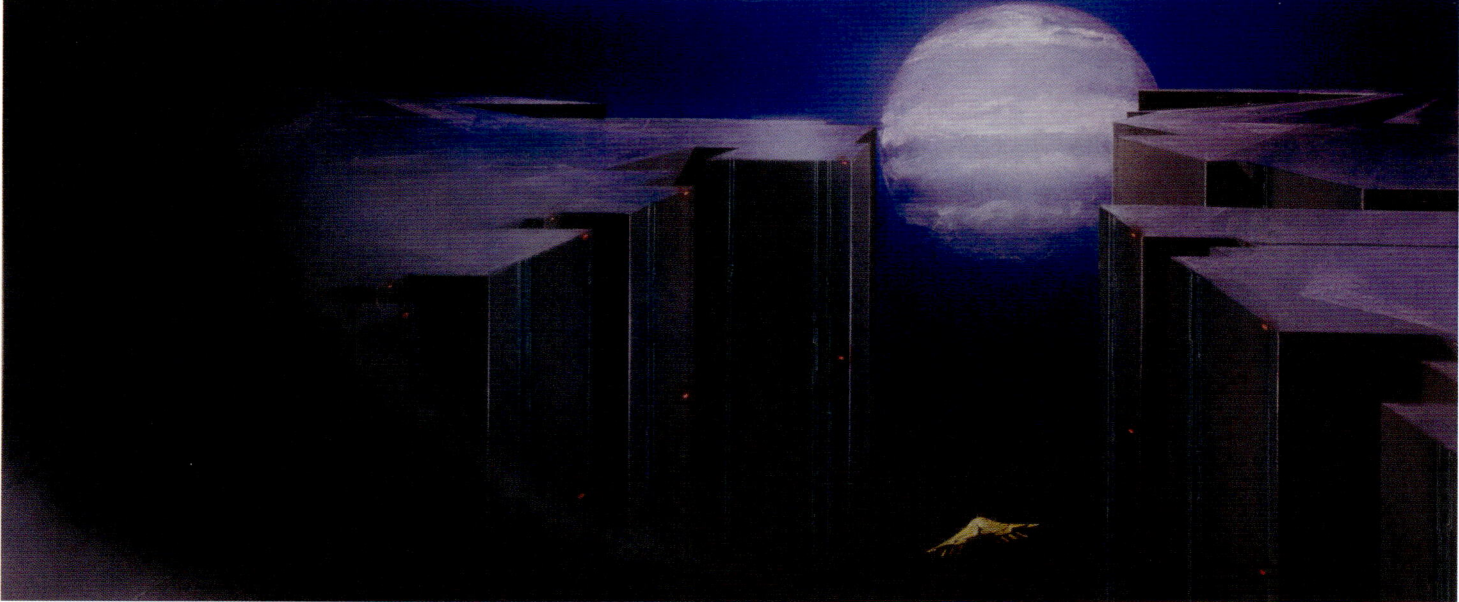

Top: *Deserted Village*, produced to illustrate an online segment of *The Human Division* by John Scalzi. 2012

Centre: *The Bright Diaspora*. 2011

Bottom: *Mass: Pegasus 1*. 1979

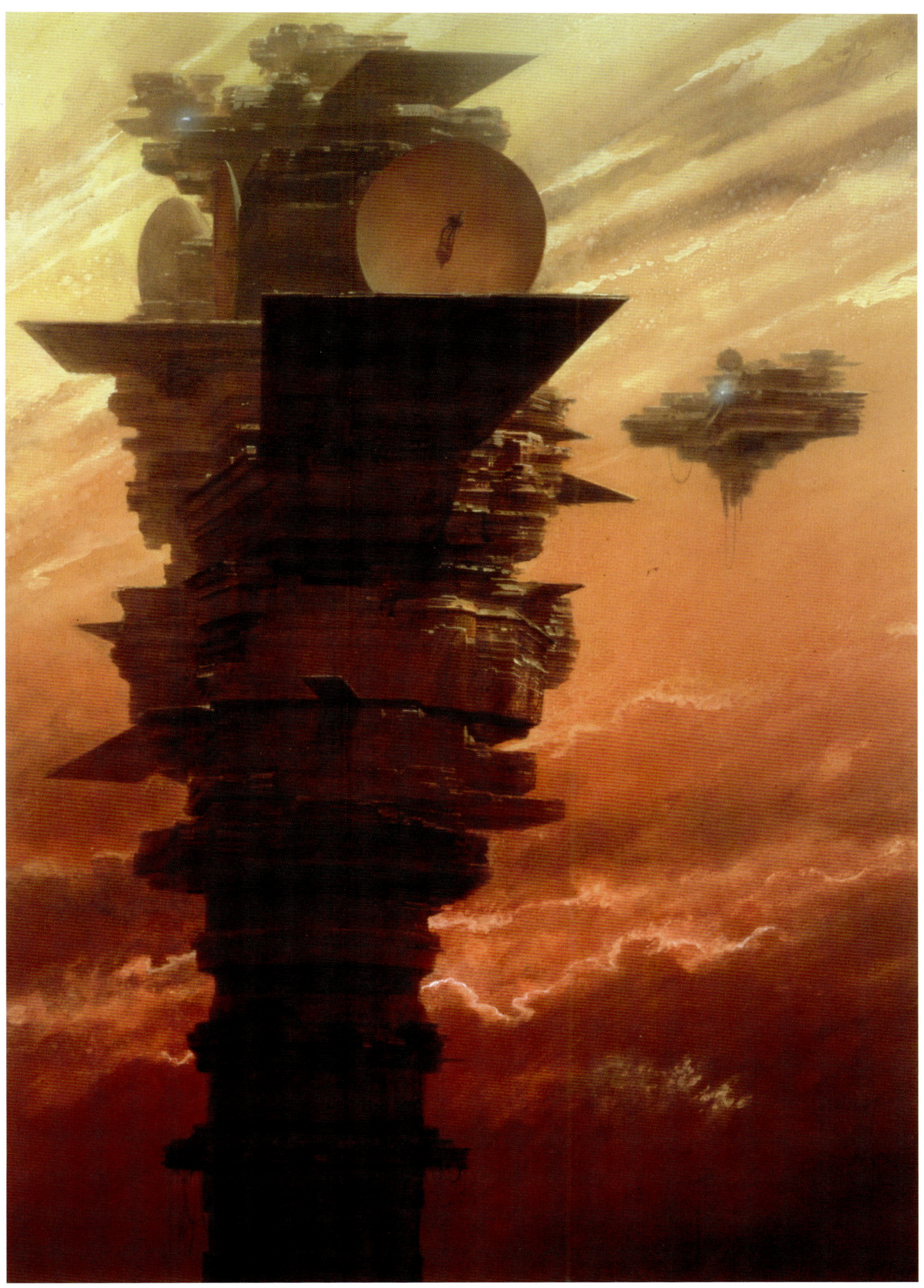

Above: *Microdrive*, the cover for the Spectrum computer manual. 1983

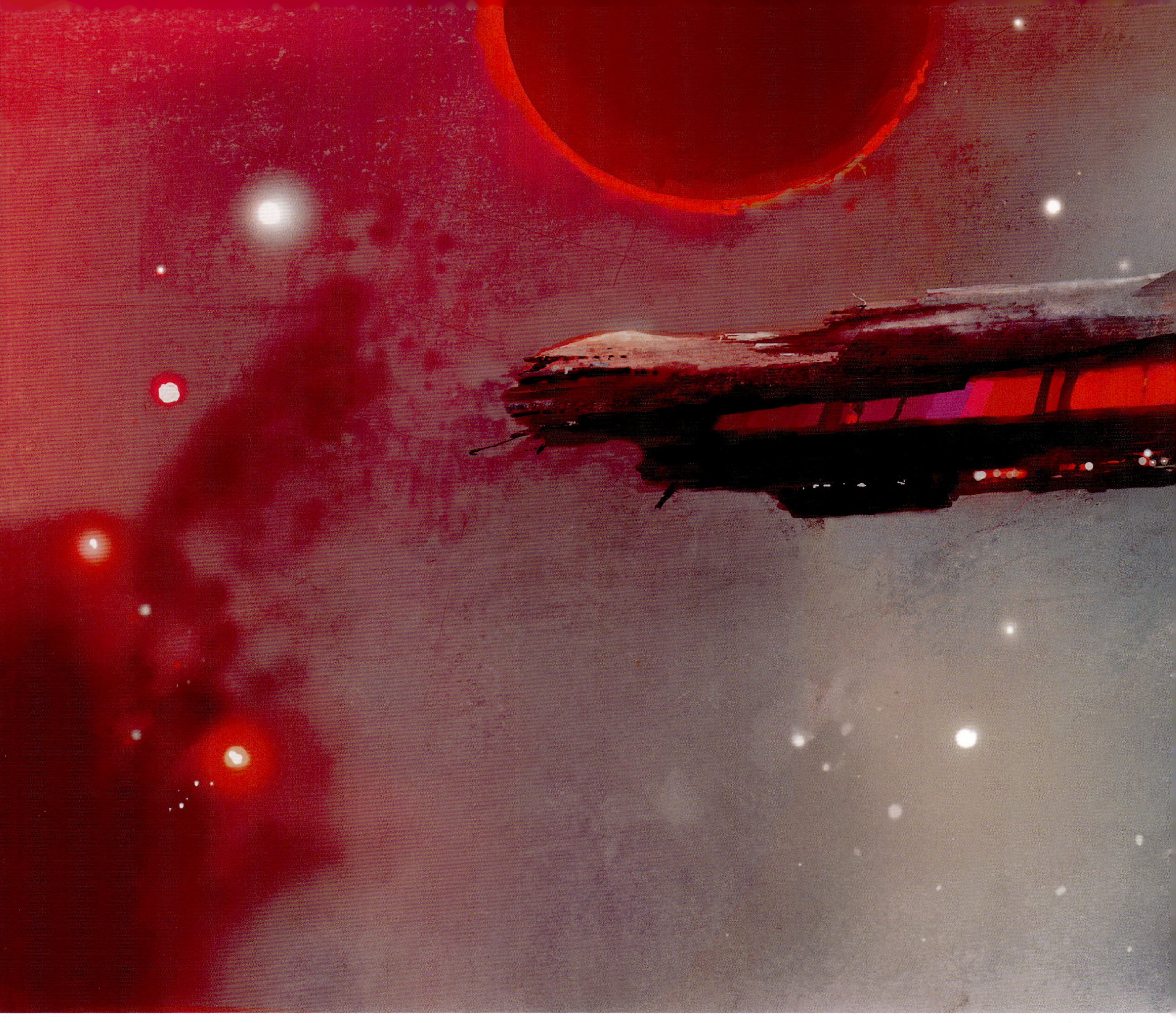

Above: *Spectral Lines.* 2011
Right: Pastel sketch

In 2011, Irene Gallo of Tor commissioned me to do a series of pieces specifically designed to be seen as title images for short stories to be seen online. The first one I was given to do in this way, was John Scalzi's *After the Coup* (see Foreword). This was followed by an extraordinary piece by the writer Yoon Ha Lee, called *A Vector Alphabet of Interstellar Travel.*

In this story , she posits the idea of the way different races might respond to the upward and outward urge to leave their home planets, like fledglings leaving their nests. Amongst them was a race who "conceive of the journey between stars as the sailing of bright ships...Some look upon their far-voyaging as a migratory imperative, and name their vessels after birds and butterflies..." It was this kind of beautiful writing that inspired *The Bright Diaspora* (see previous page) and the painting above, of a race so in love with their home sun that they scorched its spectral lines on the sides of their ships.

On a practical point, the speed which was required to complete these pieces, forced me to adopt a different process than the way I normally work. Having produced a pastel rough, I then tweaked it digitally to produce the final piece. I have never really liked to do this in the past, partly because I do not like the physical act of sitting in front of a computer screen, or the bloodless nature of the medium, and also because there's no piece of artwork you can lay your hands on at the end of it. But needs must and, ultimately, I was relatively happy with the result.

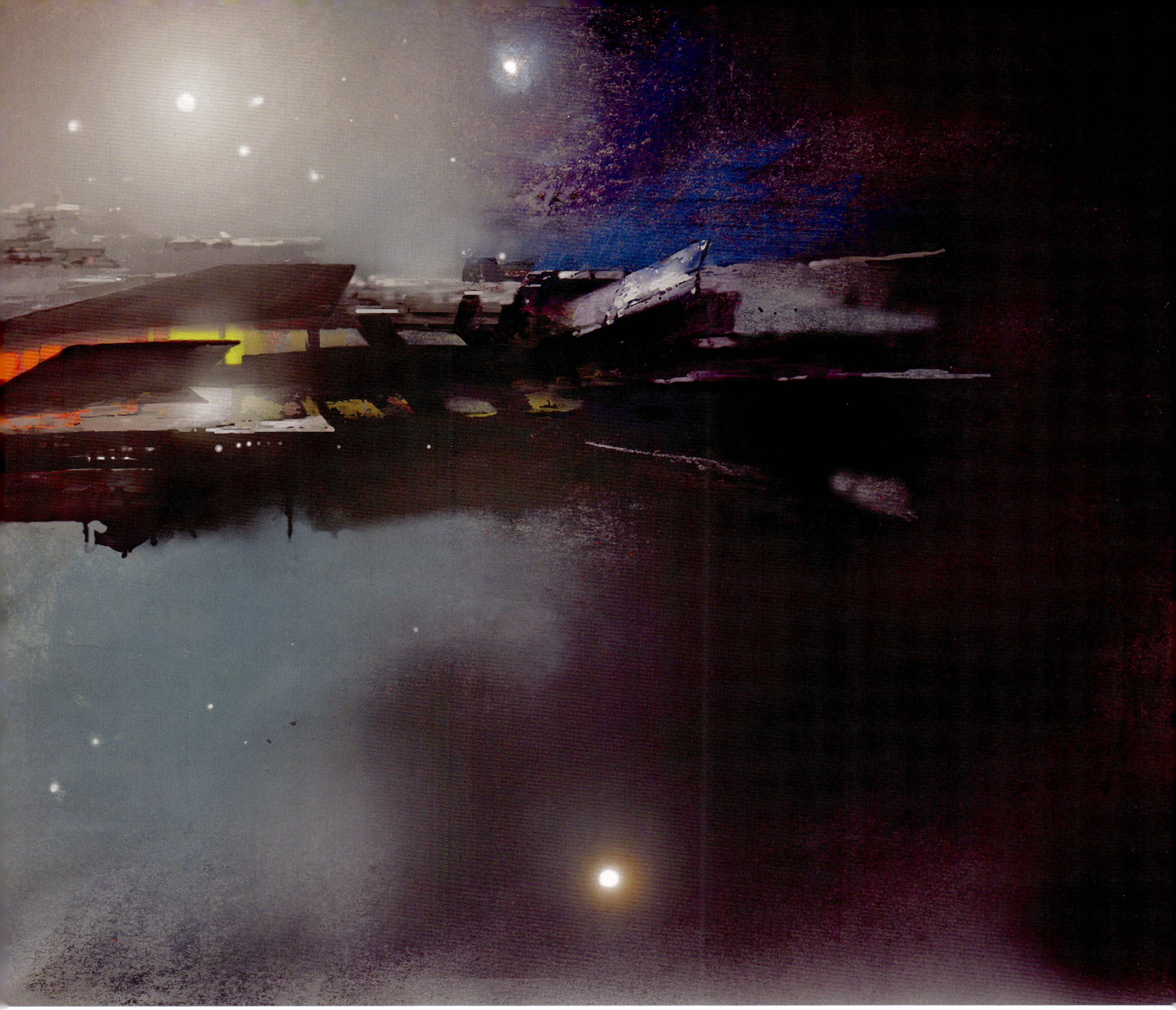

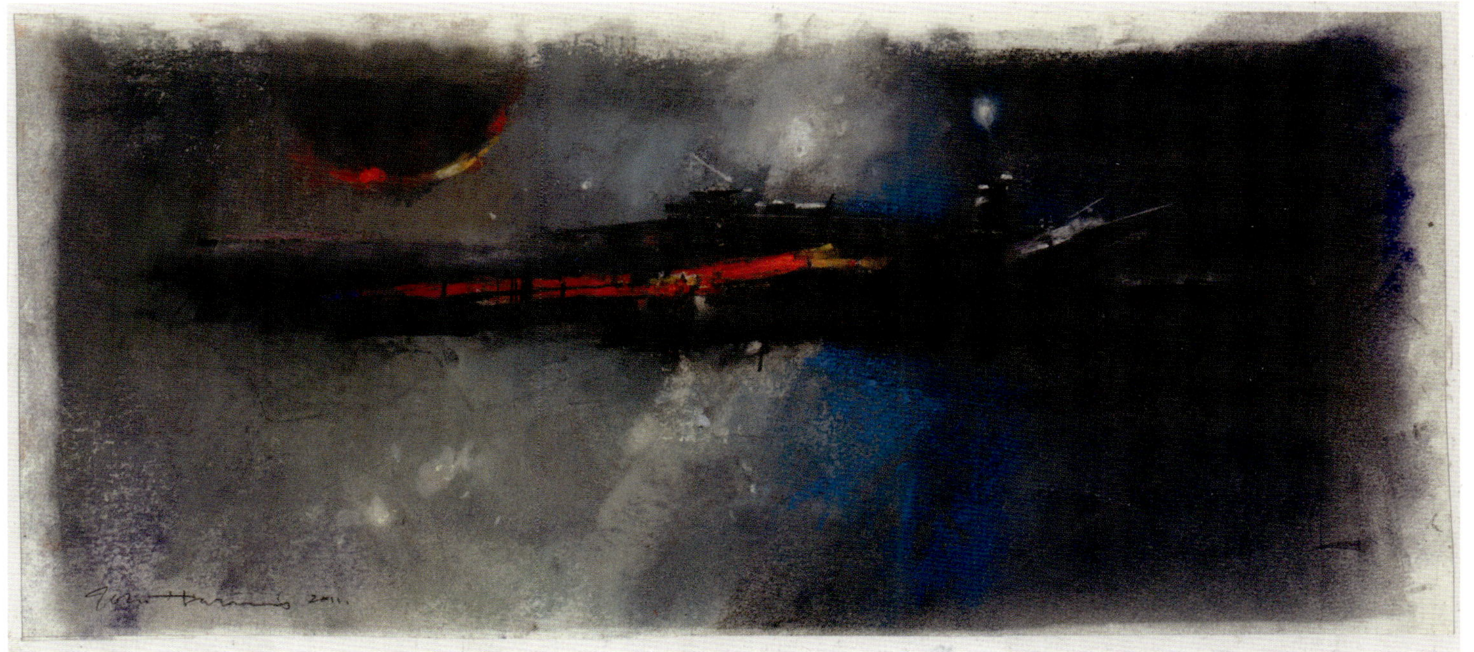

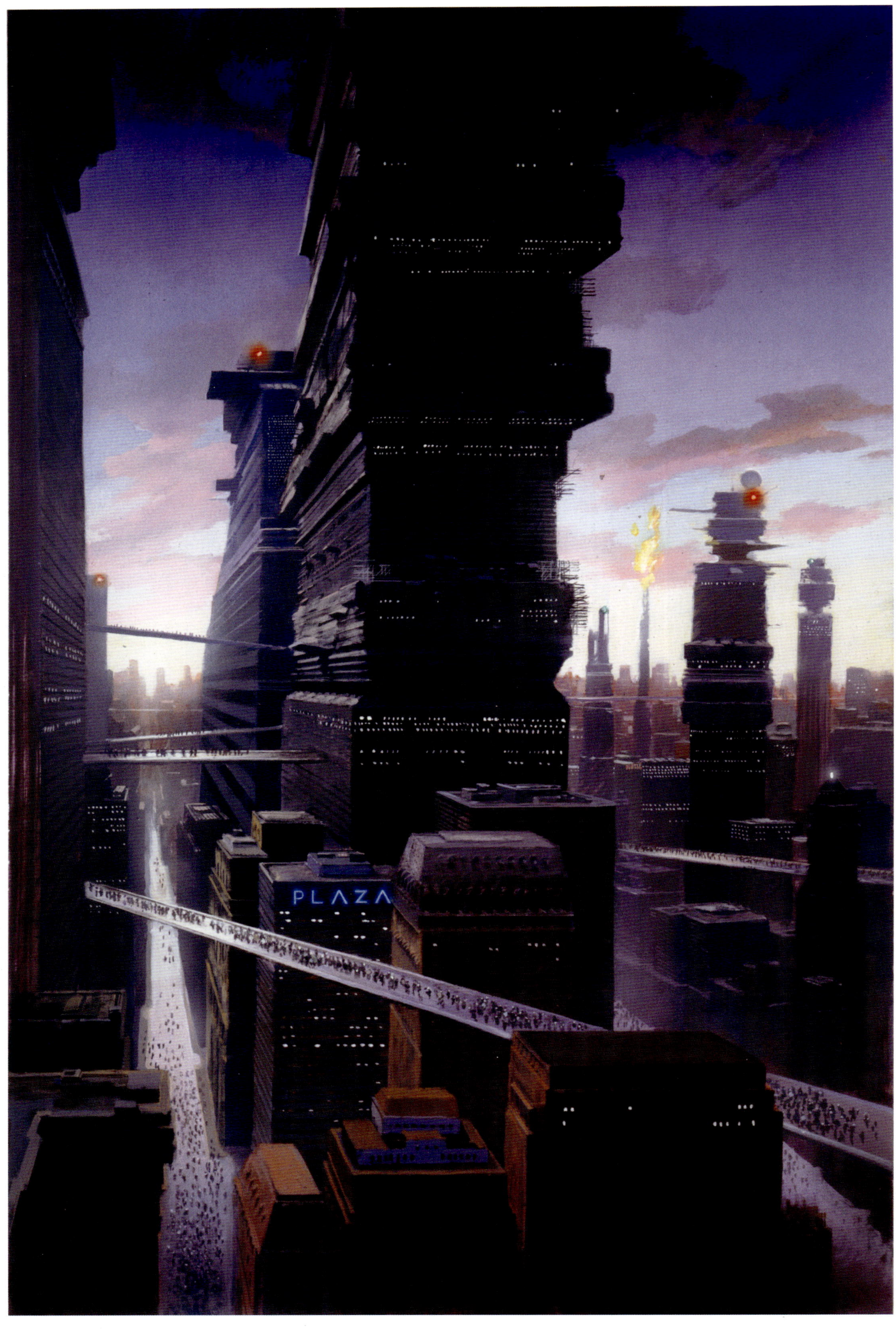
PLAZA

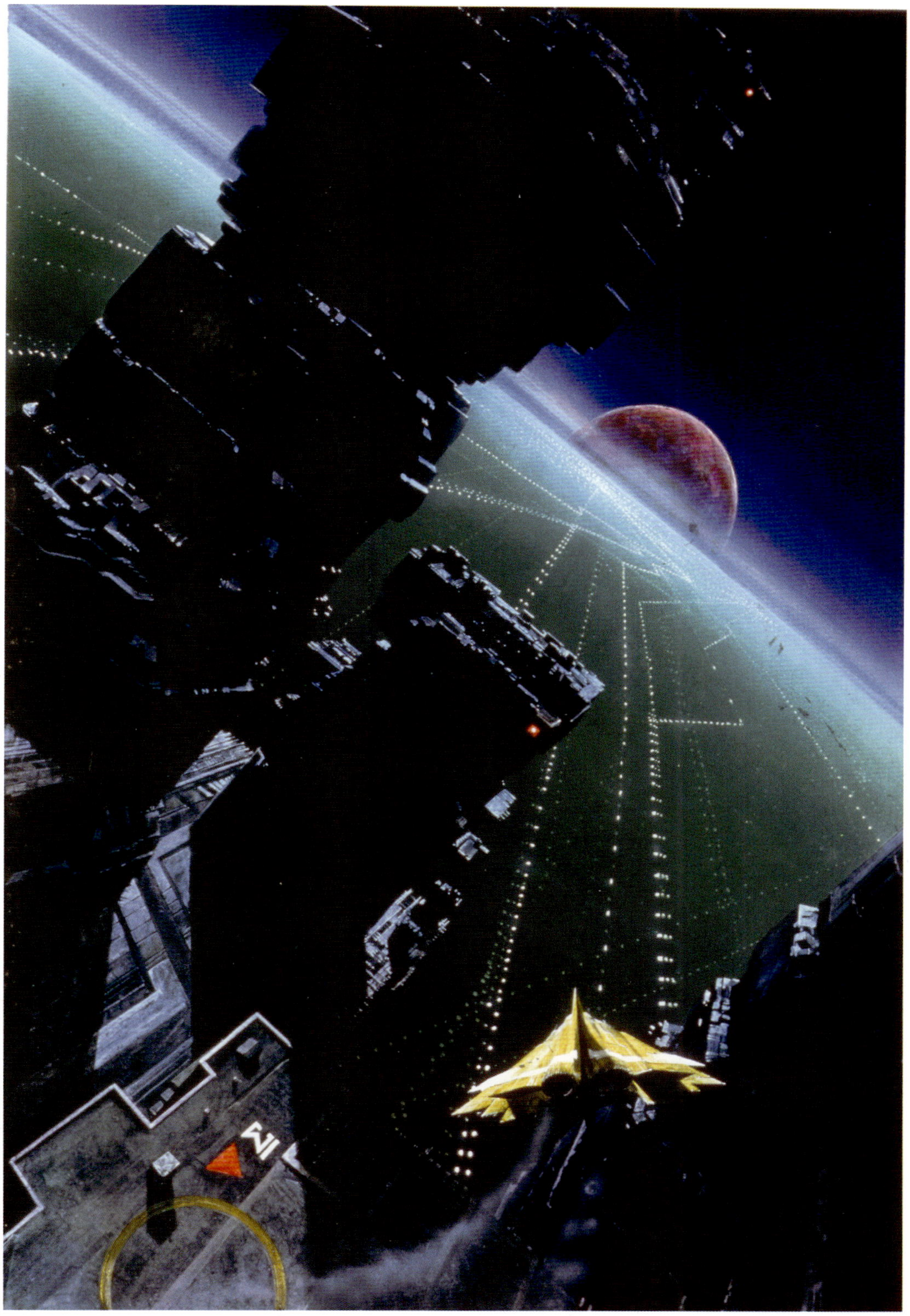

Left: *Drunkard's Walk*, subsequently used for the cover of *Ender's Game* by Orson Scott Card. 1979

Below: *Mass: Pegasus 3*. 1979

Opposite: *Body Mortgage*, for the cover of the book by Richard Engling. 1989

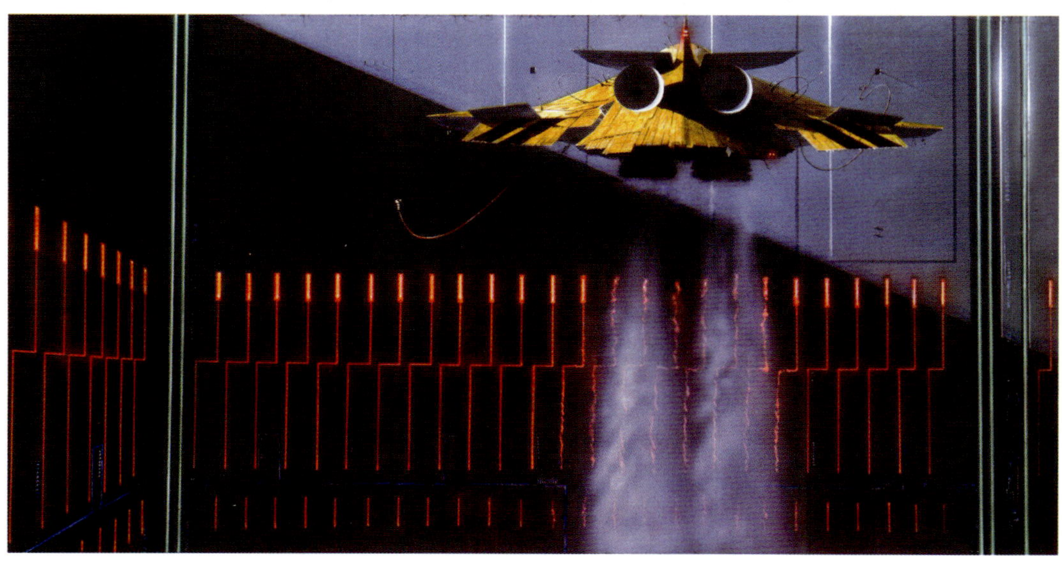

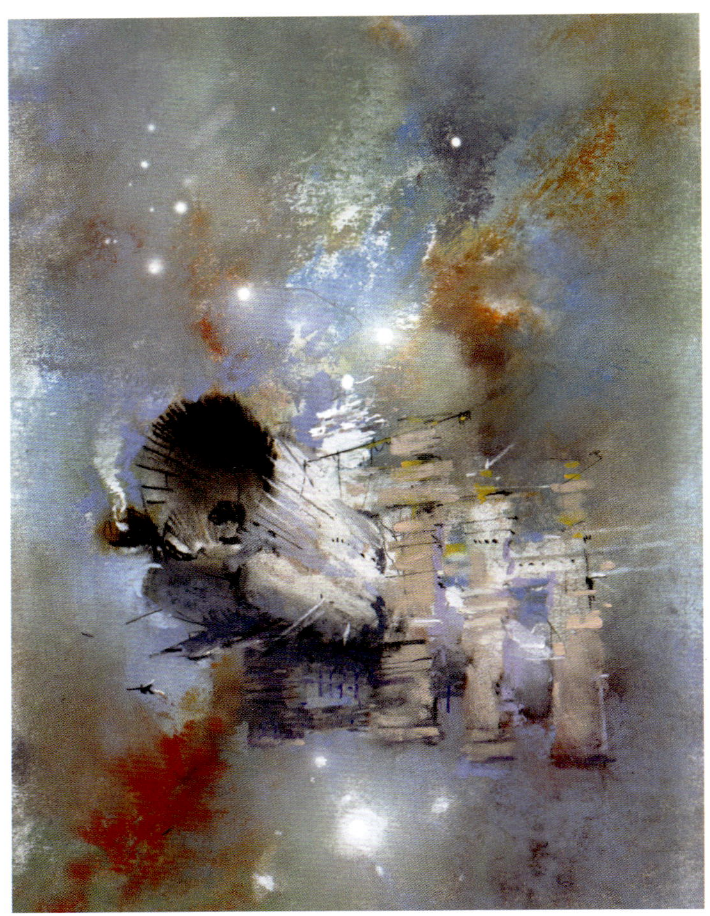

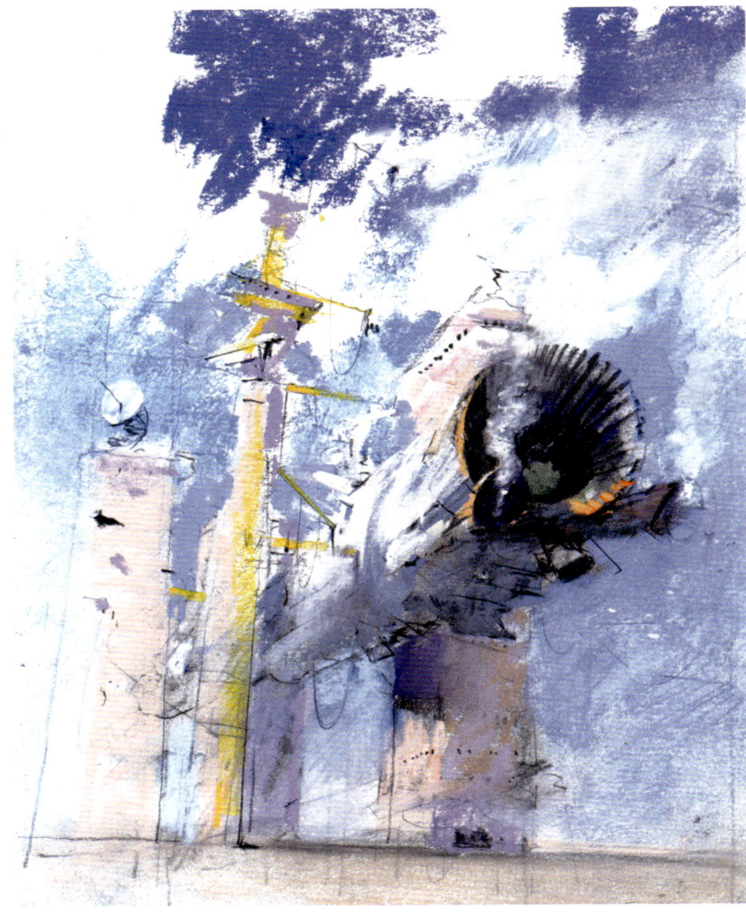

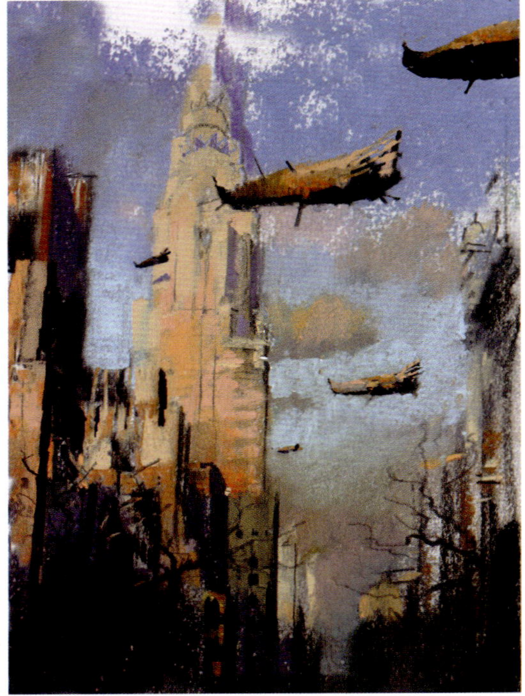

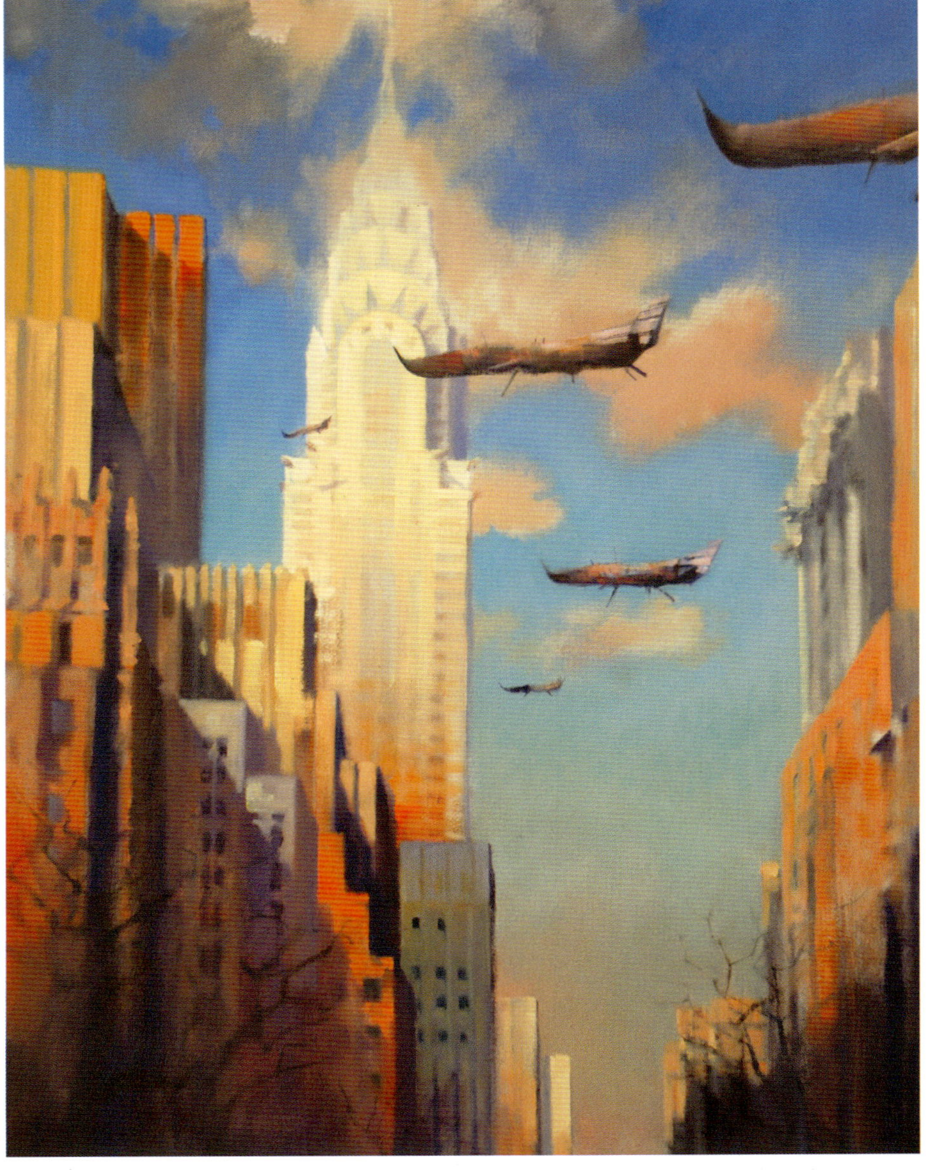

Top: *Spindrift* sketches, produced for the book by Allen Steele

Bottom: *Invasion of the Canoes*, sketch and painting for *The Last Theorem* by Arthur C Clarke. 2008

Opposite: *Ender in Exile*, for the cover of the book by Orson Scott Card. 2008

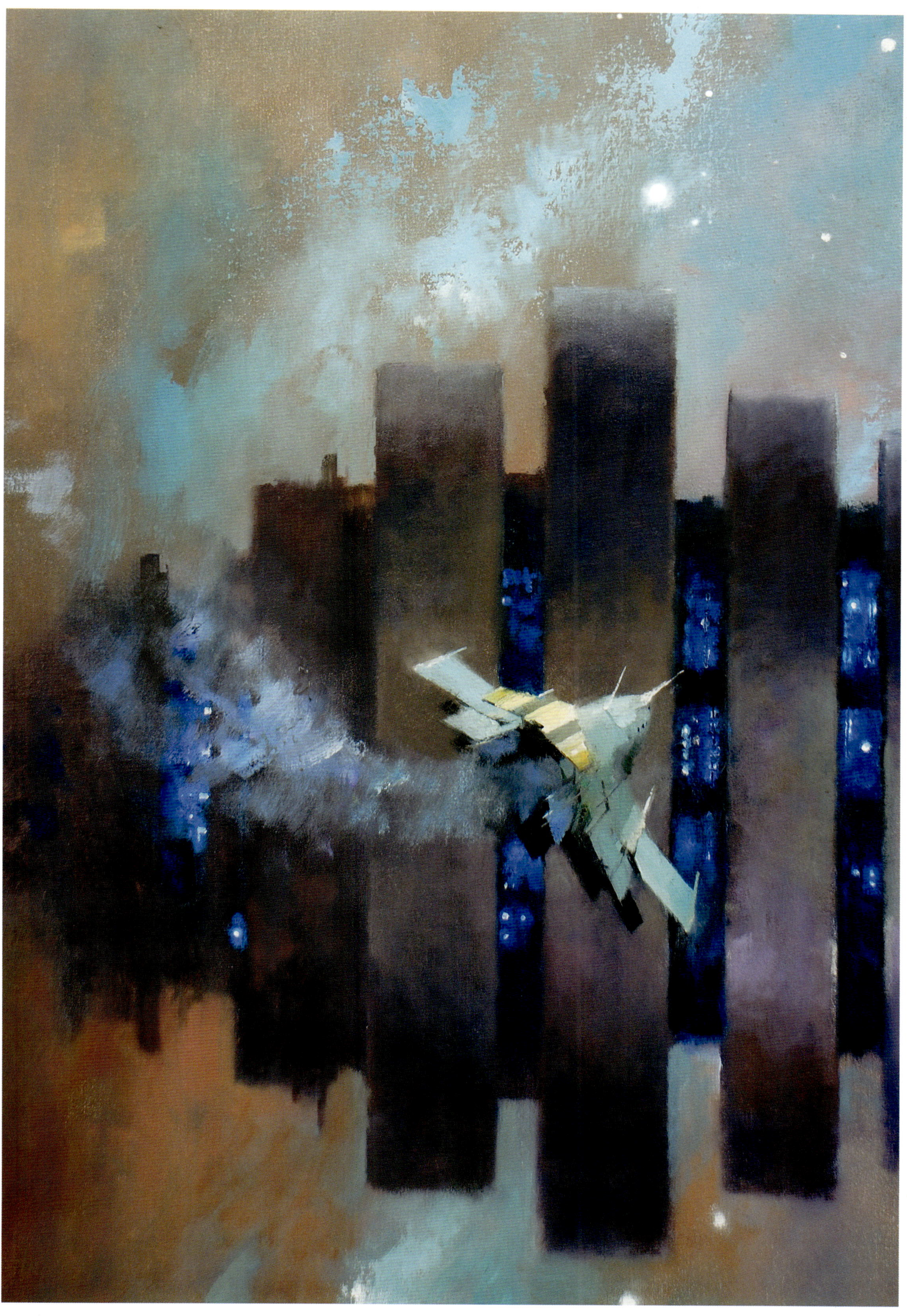

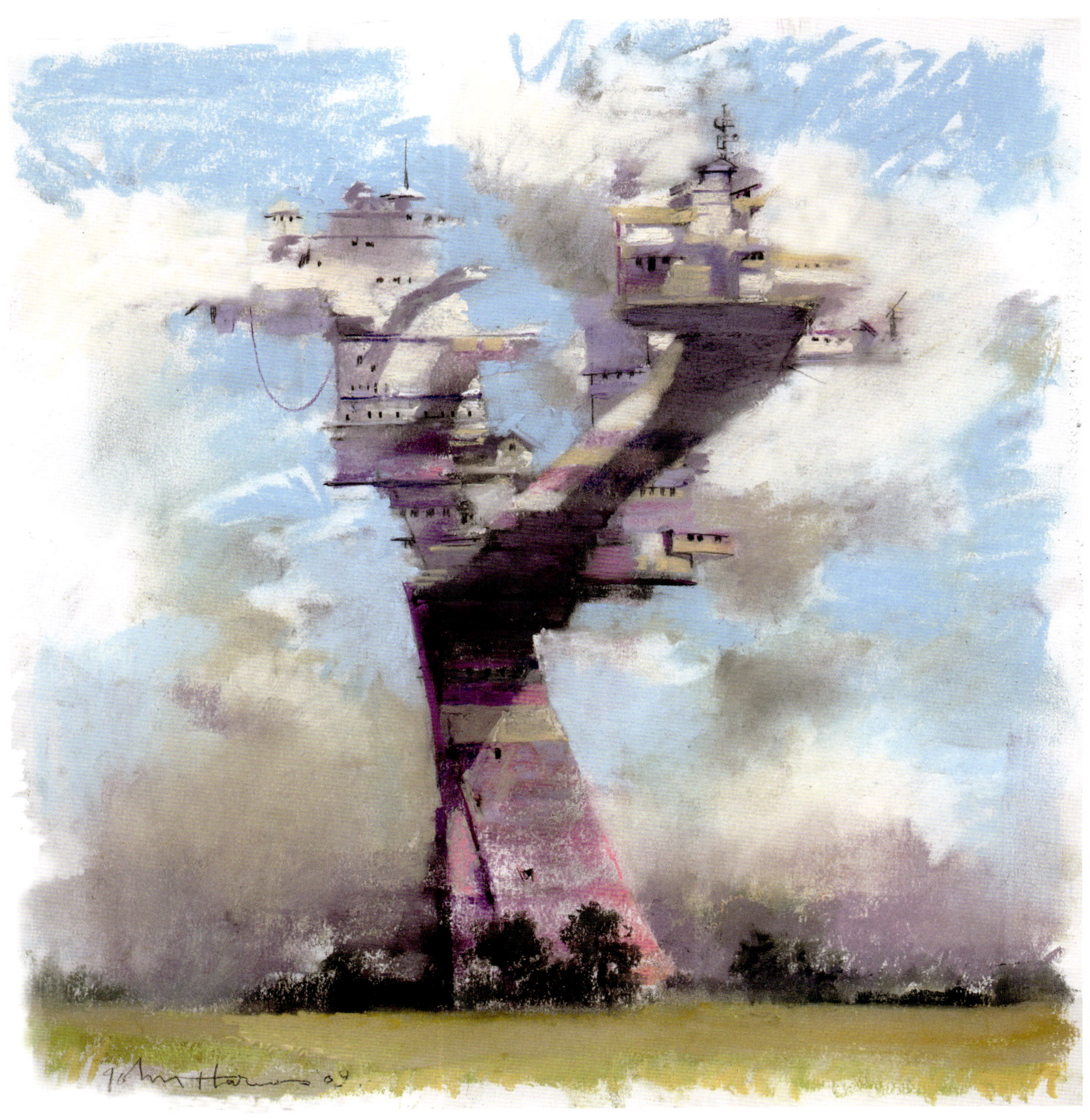

Above: *Treetown*. 2010

Opposite: *The Blue Rocket*. 2012

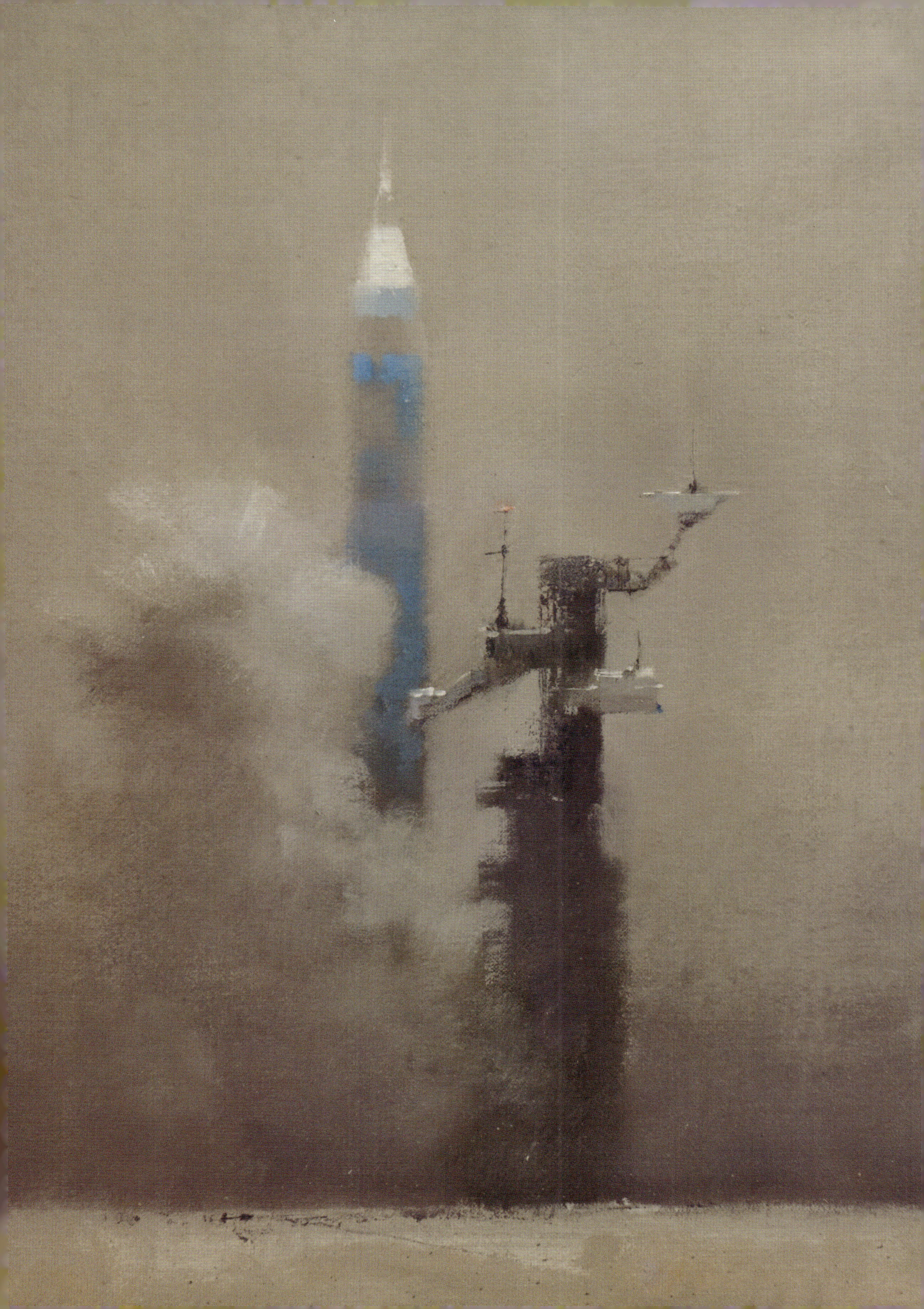

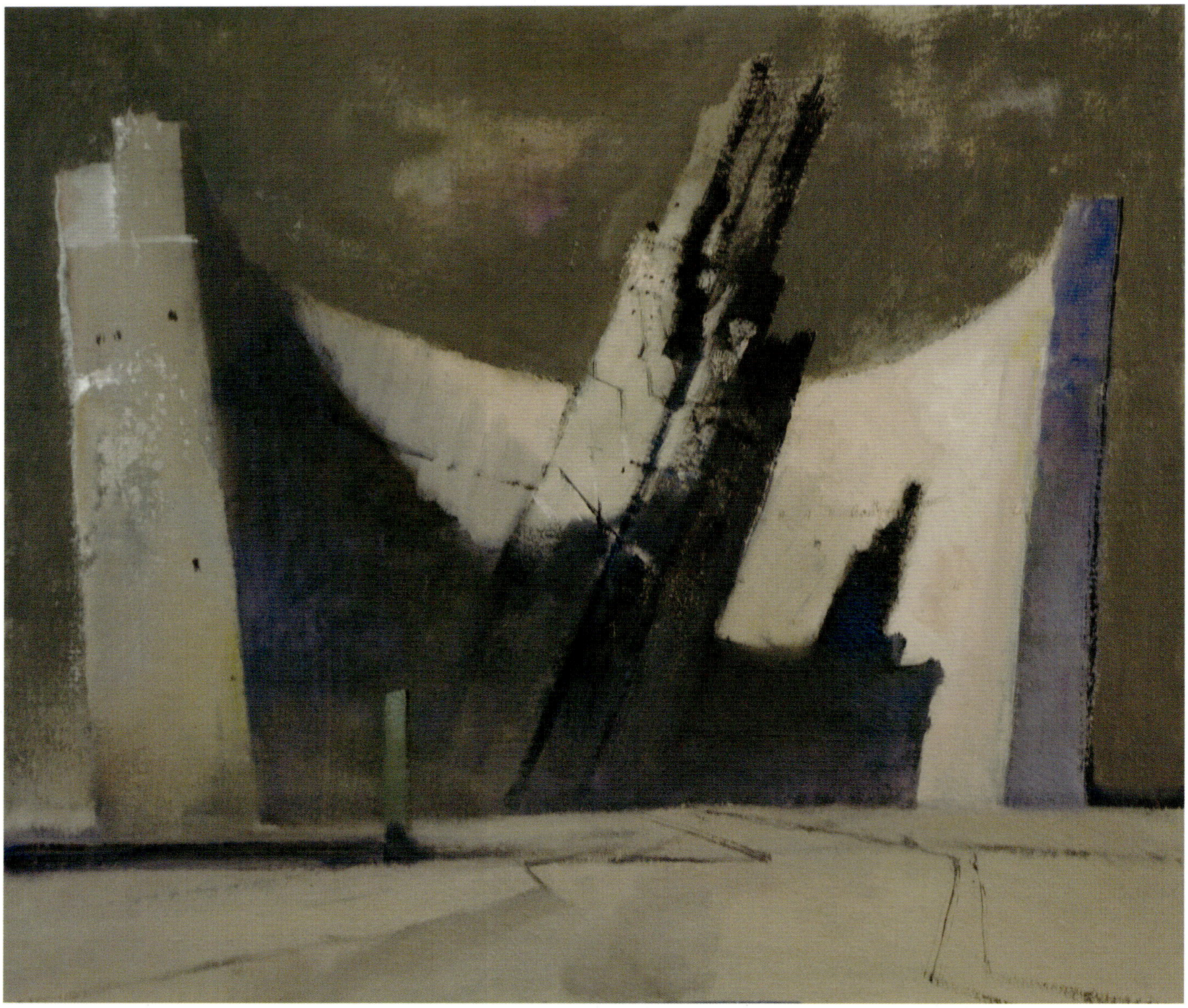

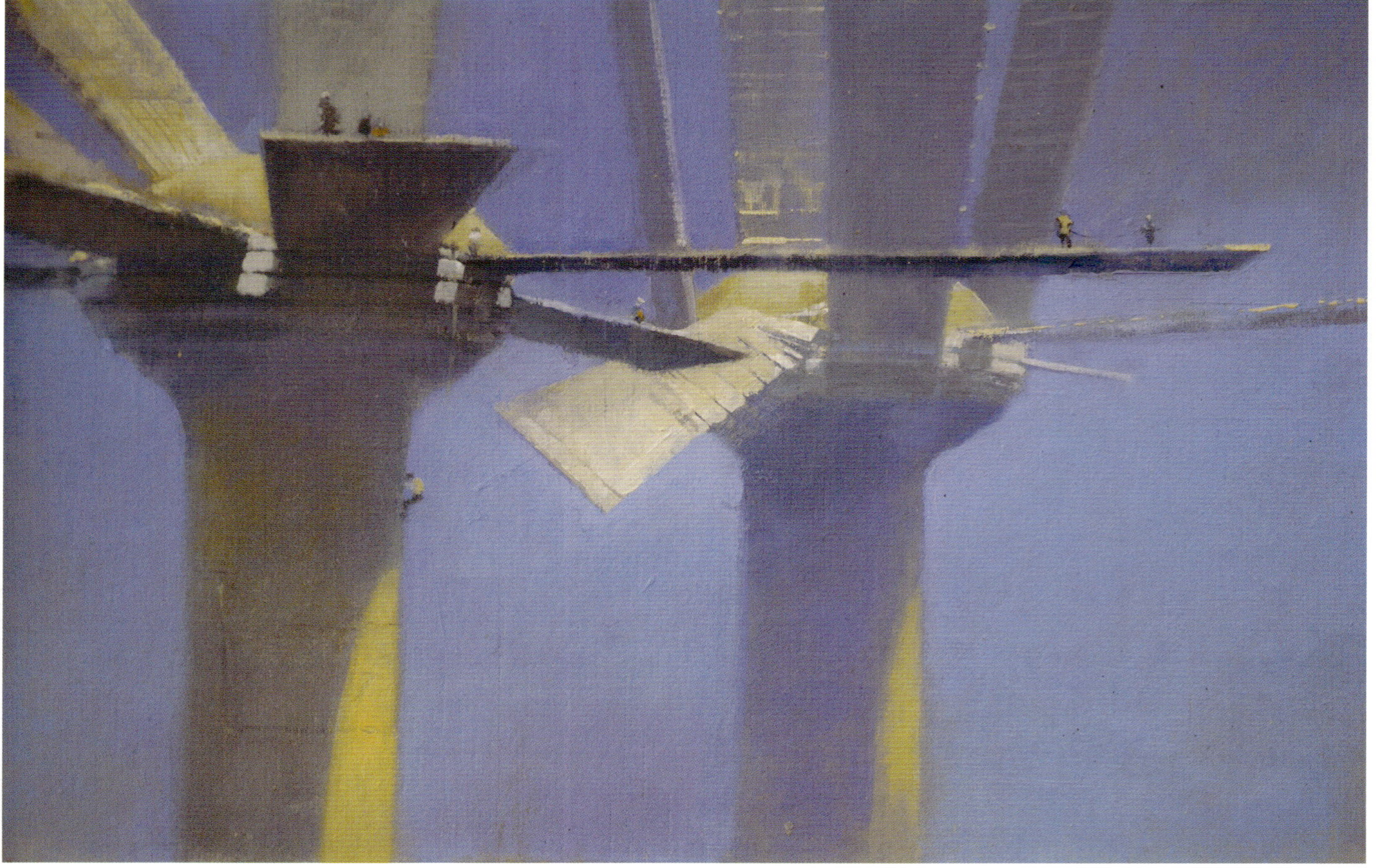

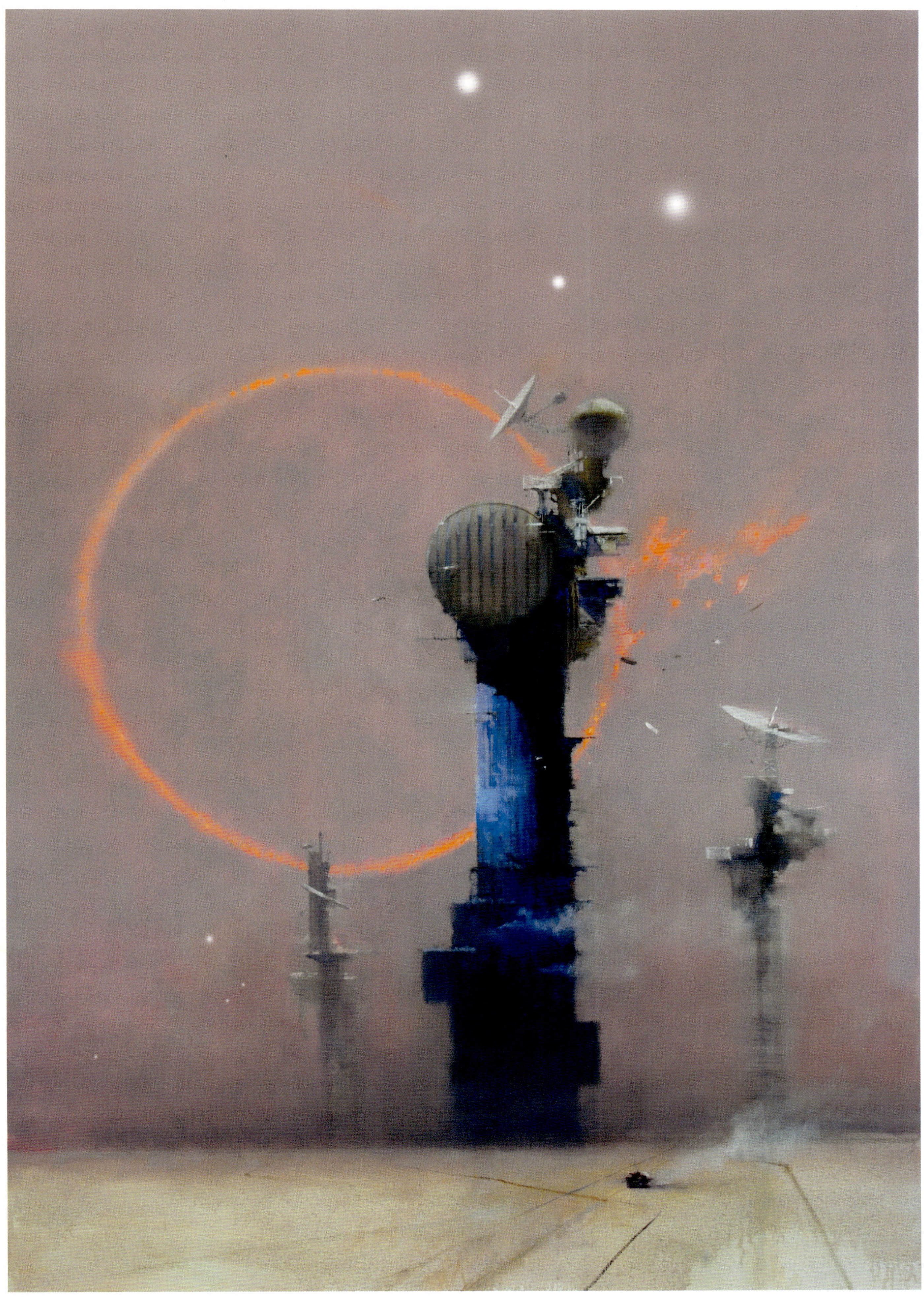

Above: *Way Station*, for the cover of *New Frontiers* by Ben Bova. 2013

Opposite Top: *The Pestel of Canopus*. 2012

Opposite Bottom: *Fire: The Sunflowers*

Following Spread: *Sunflowers in Starlight*. 2013

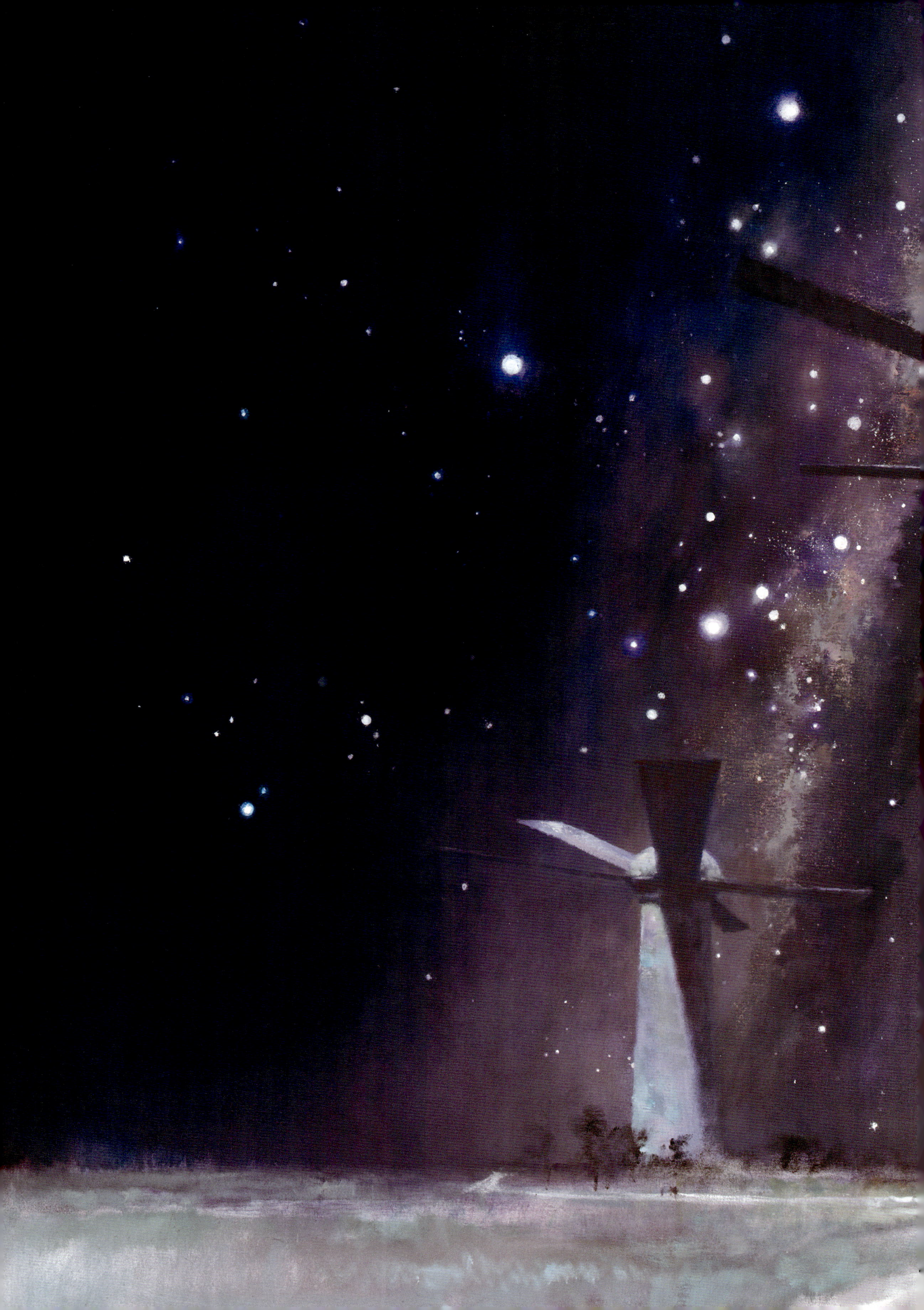

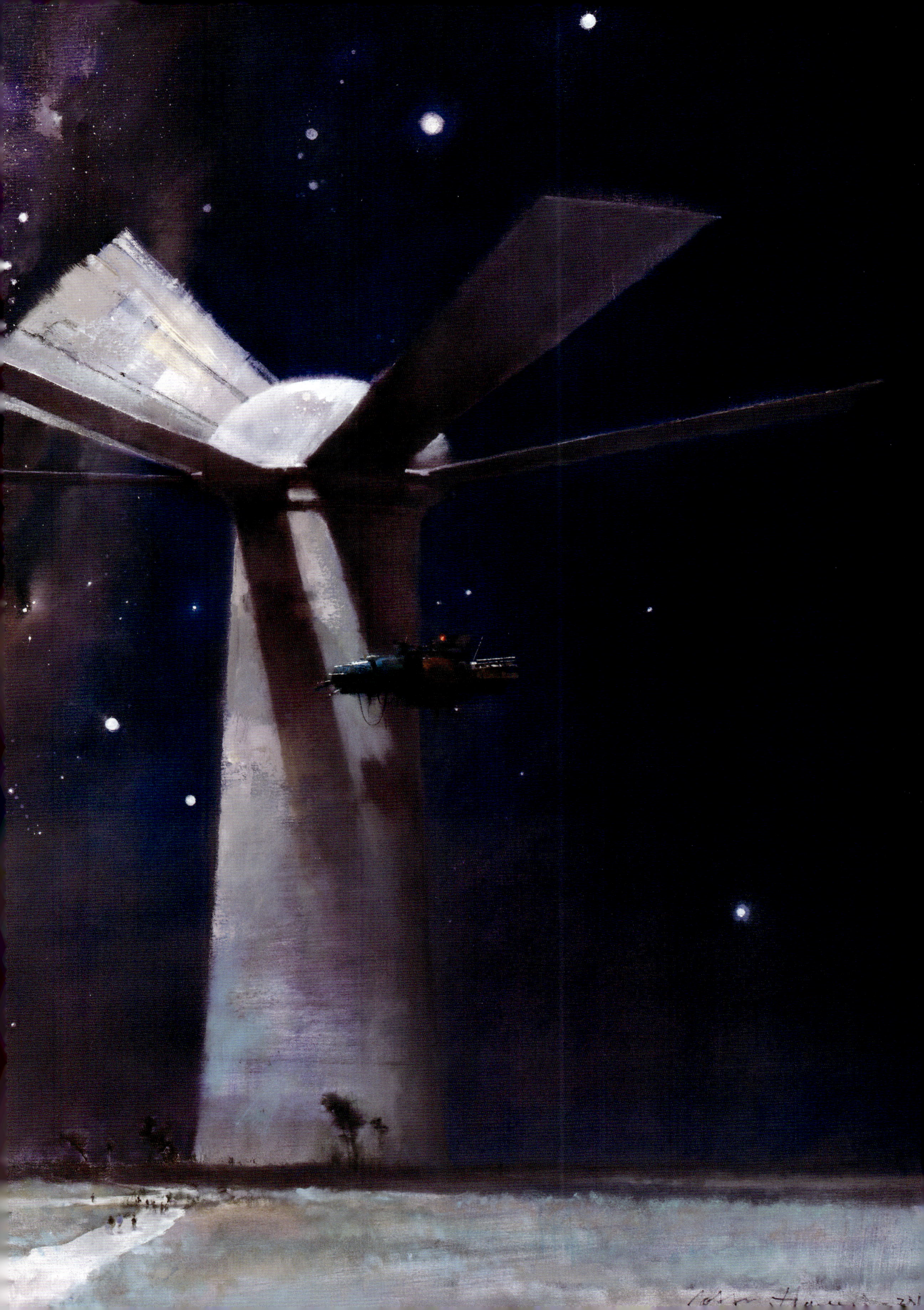

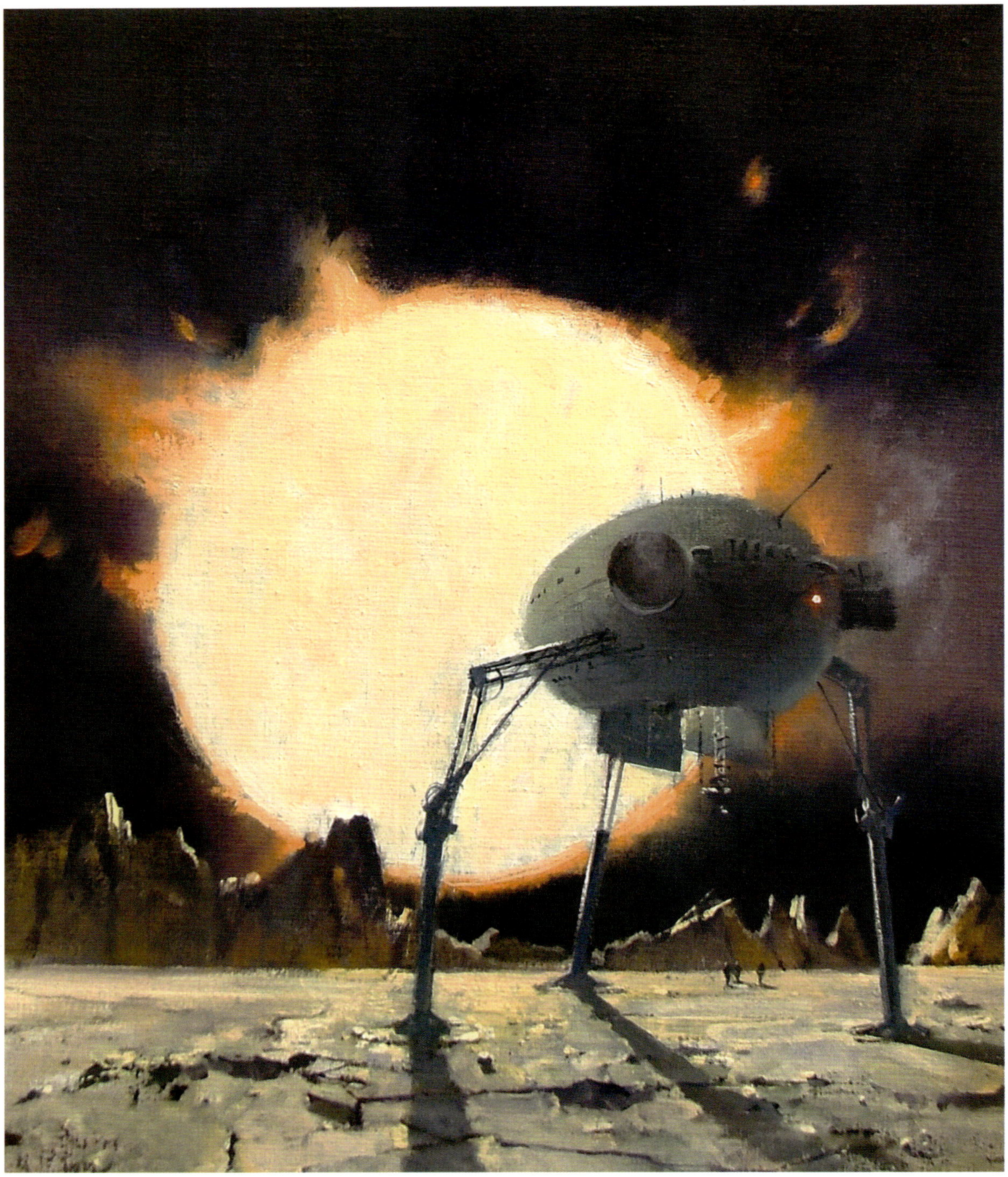

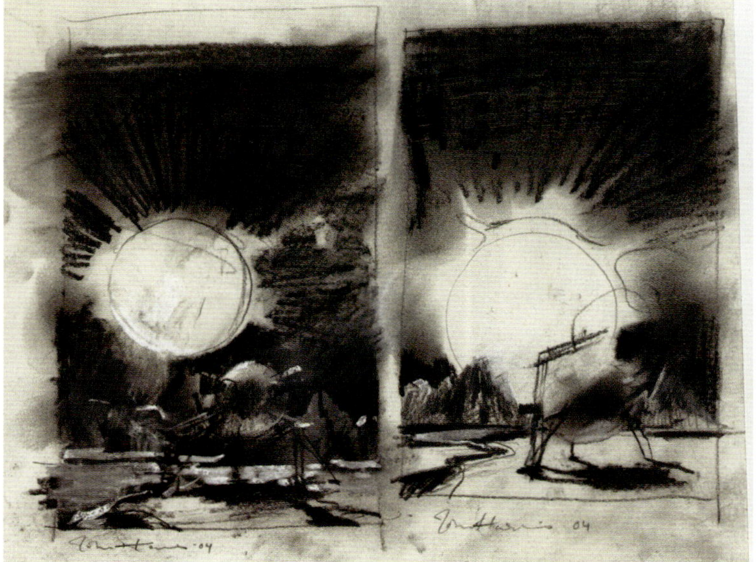

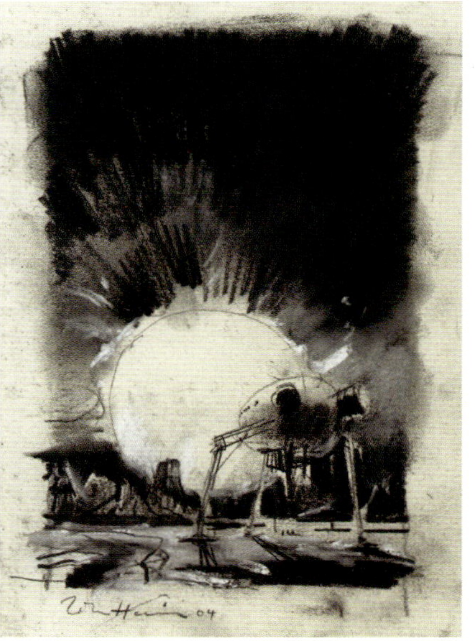

Above: *Mercury,* charcoal sketches and painting for the cover of the book by Ben Bova. 2004

Opposite: *Echo,* for the cover of the book by Jack McDevitt. 2009

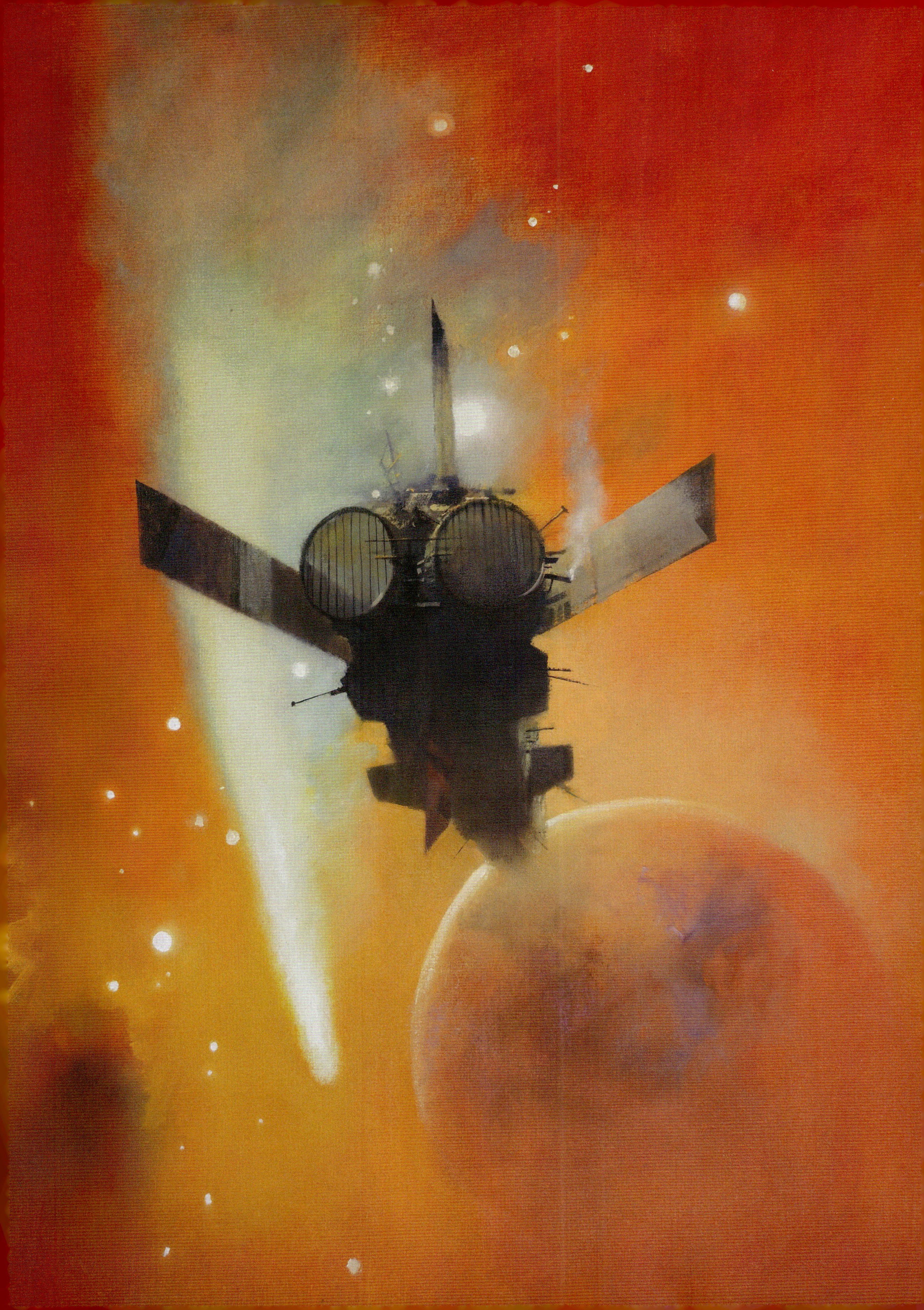

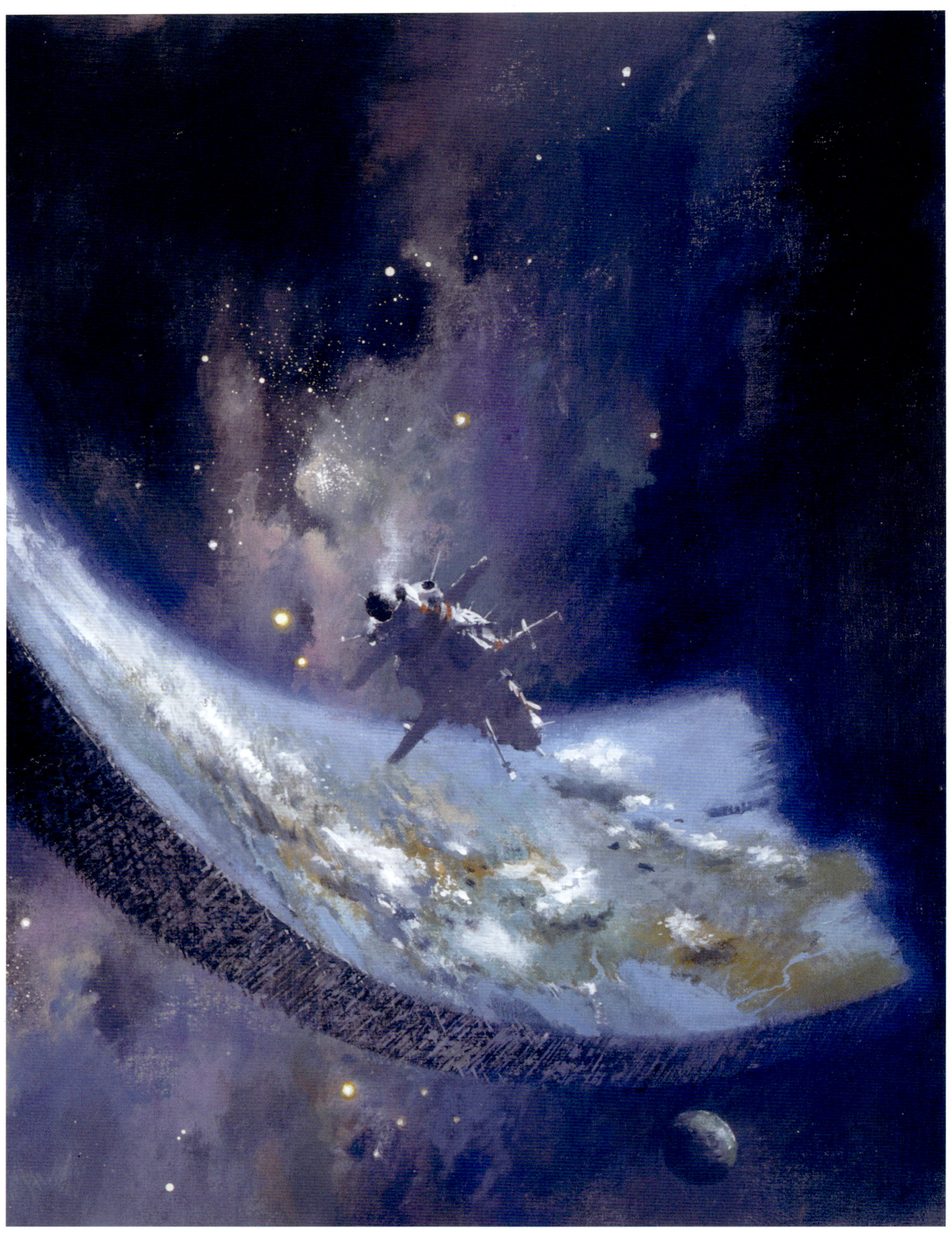

Above: *Ringworld Throne*, produced for the cover of the book by Larry Niven. 1996

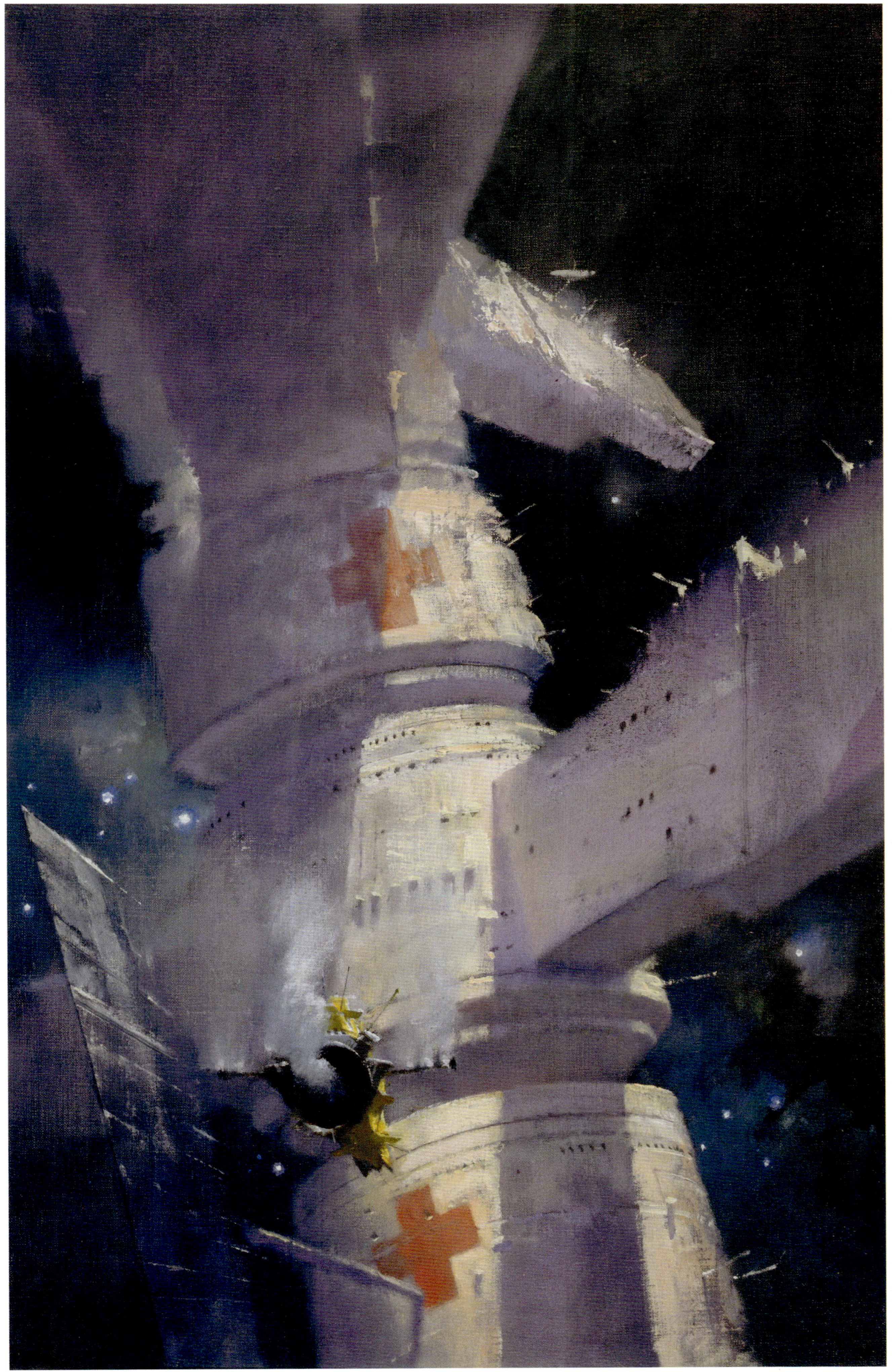

Above: *Double Contact*, for the cover of the book by James White. 2002

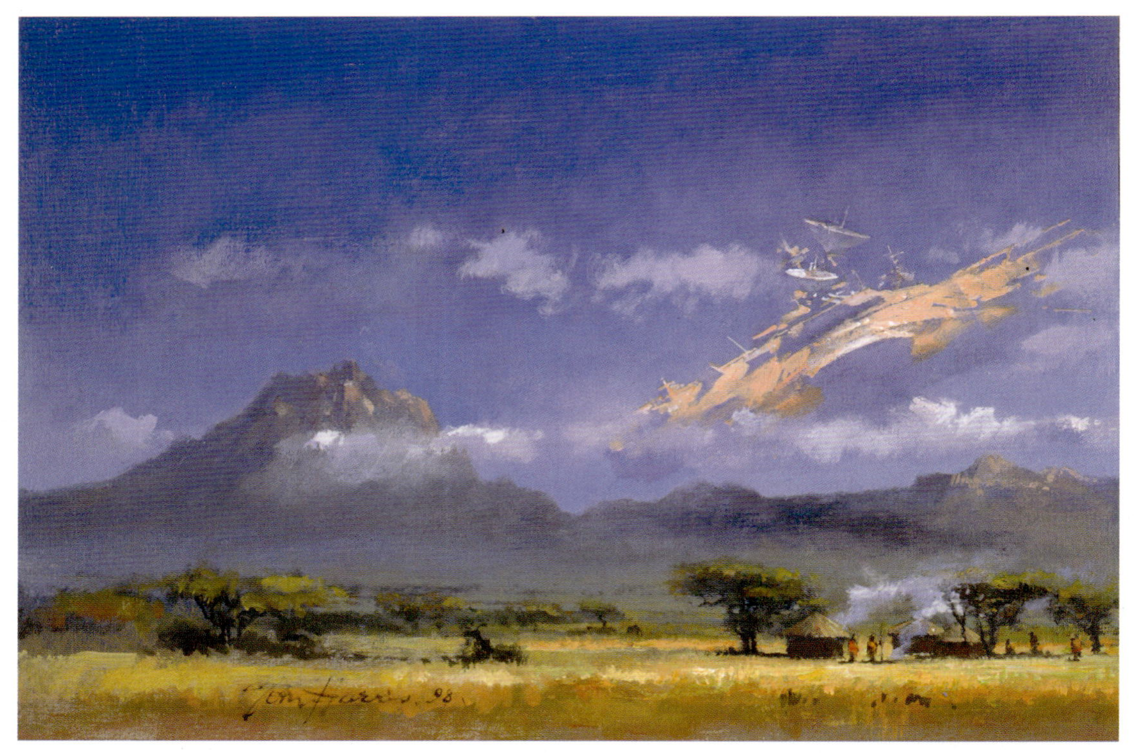

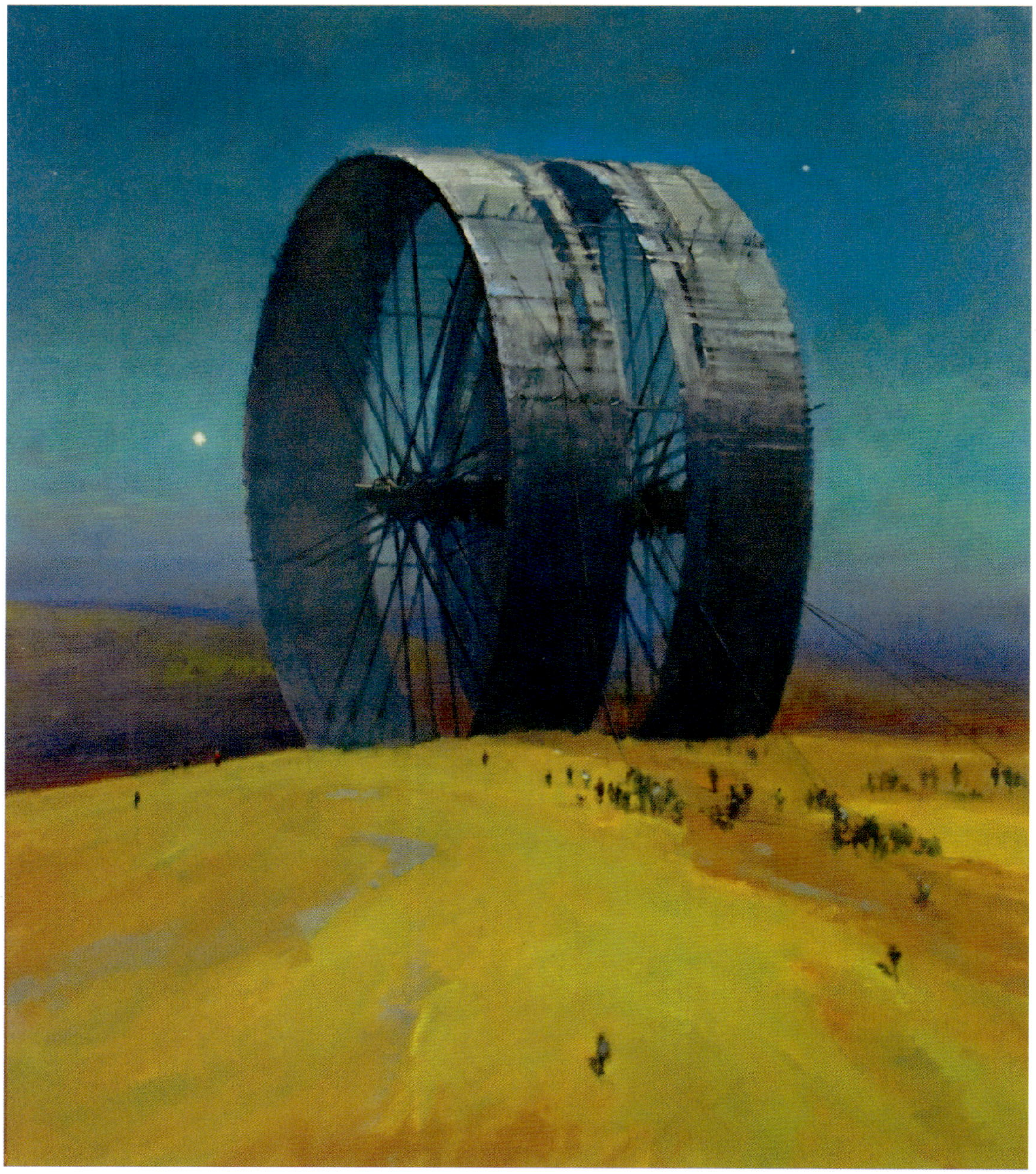

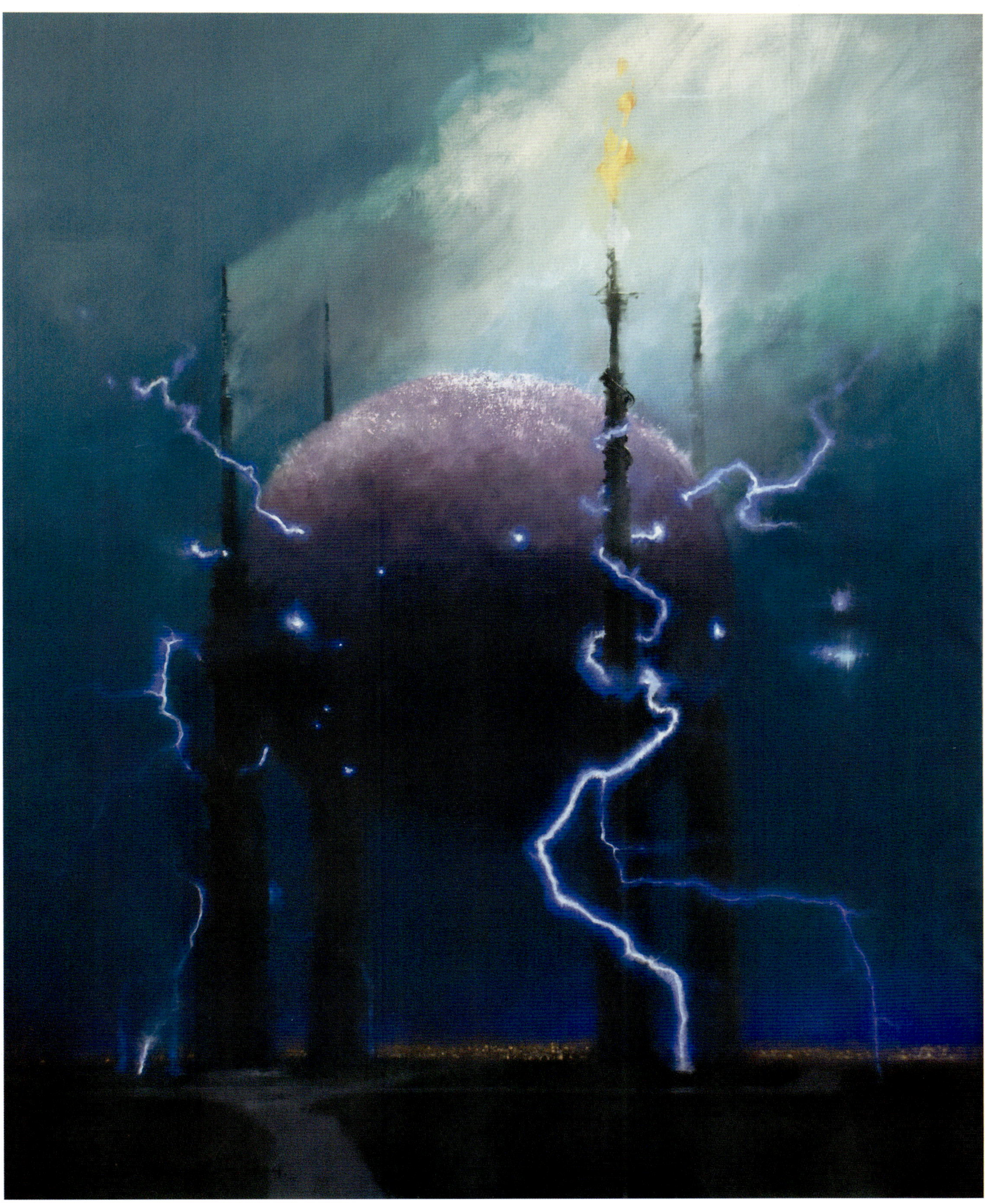

Above: *The Big Generator.* 2000

Opposite Top: *Kirinyaga*, for the cover of the book by Mike Resnick. 1997

Opposite Bottom: *The Long Way Home.* 1999

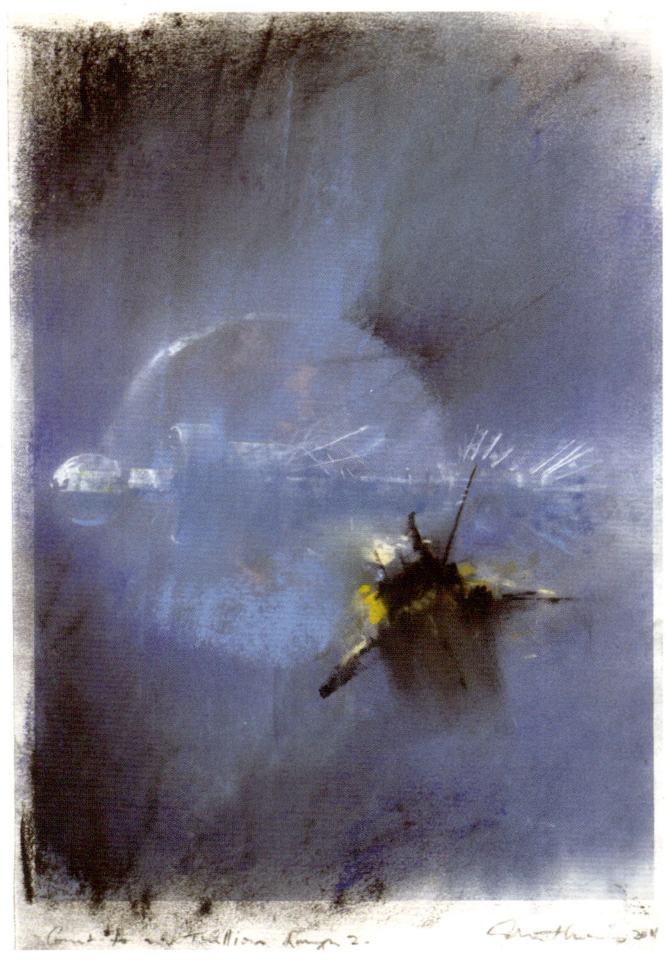

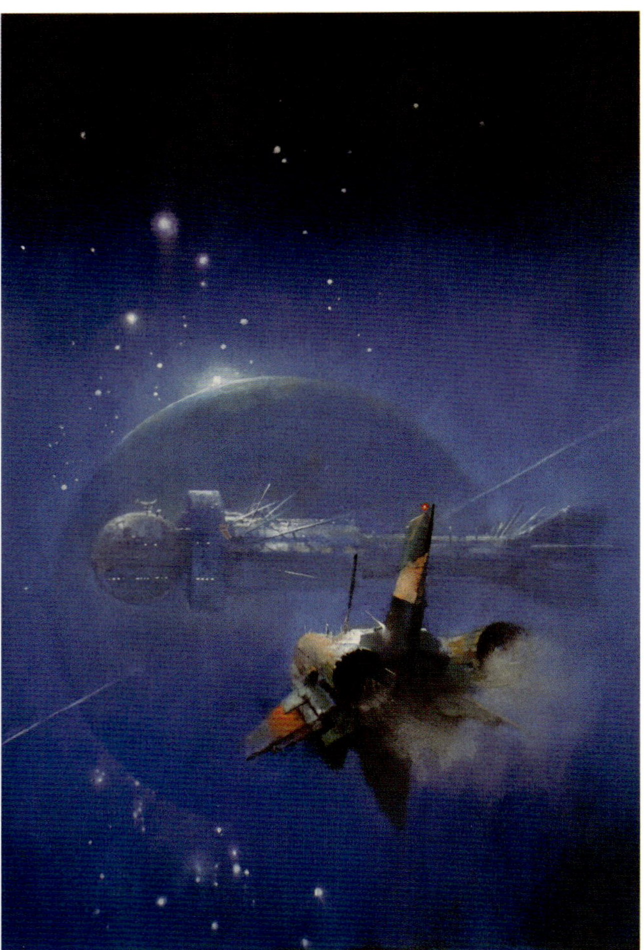

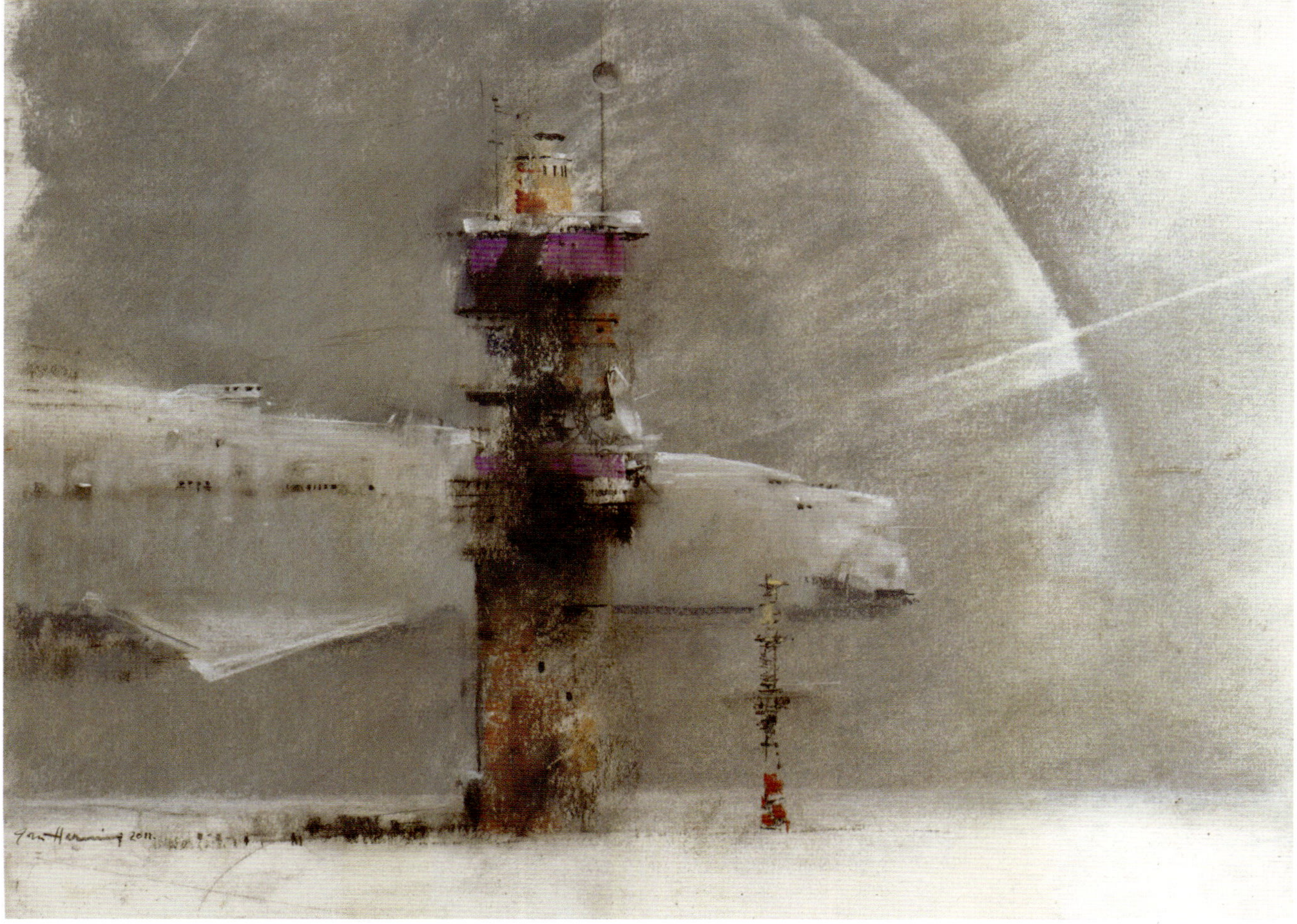

Top: *Count to a Trillion*, sketch and painting. 2010

Bottom: *Loading*. 2011

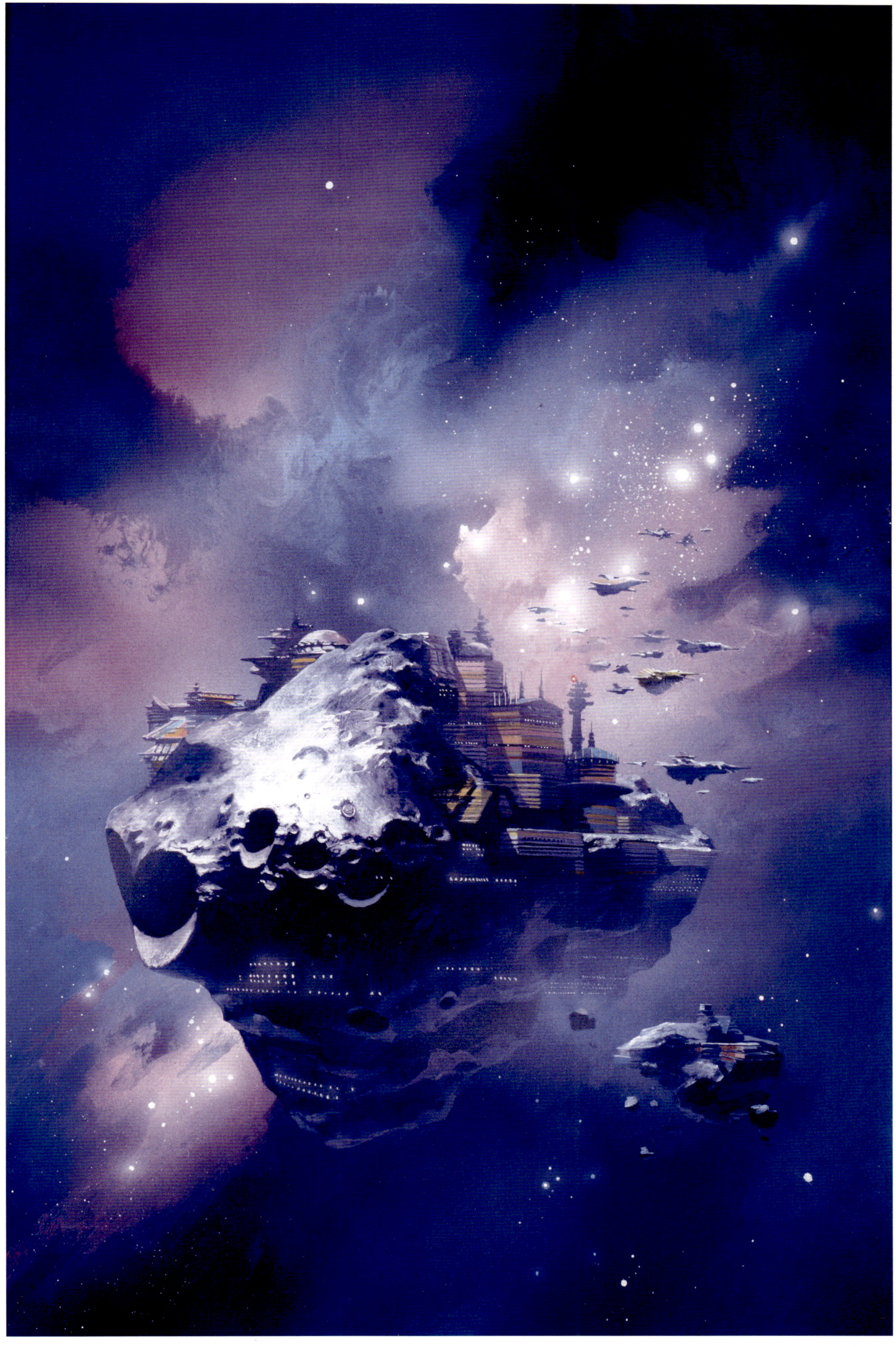

Above: *Astropolis*. 1987

THE RUINATION OF THINGS

There is nothing quite like a ruin to turn the attention inward. This introversion has been a habit of mine from as early as I can remember. The end of things has a timeless fascination and can come about in all sorts of ways, of course, but the final state is always a reduction, a simplification. In short: entropy. It seems that the bigger and more epic the objects created or the structures raised, the more violent their demise. In spite of the poet's prophecy that the world will not end with a bang but a whimper, there's much that might precede that finality, involving all sorts of cracking, thumping and good old fashioned explosions. Quite apart from anything else, they are fun to paint, but I have to admit to preferring the coda. The wistfulness of *A Visit to the Ruined World* or *The Search* (illustrating the search by mankind for other races, ultimately frustrated by the vastness of time and space, where races have risen and fallen long before man comes on the scene), come from a deeper part of my being and are consequently more fulfilling to produce. But: here are some variations on the way things come to pass.

Below & Right: *The Last Colony*, (previously *Off Armageddon Reef*), sketch and painting, for the book by John Scalzi, 2006

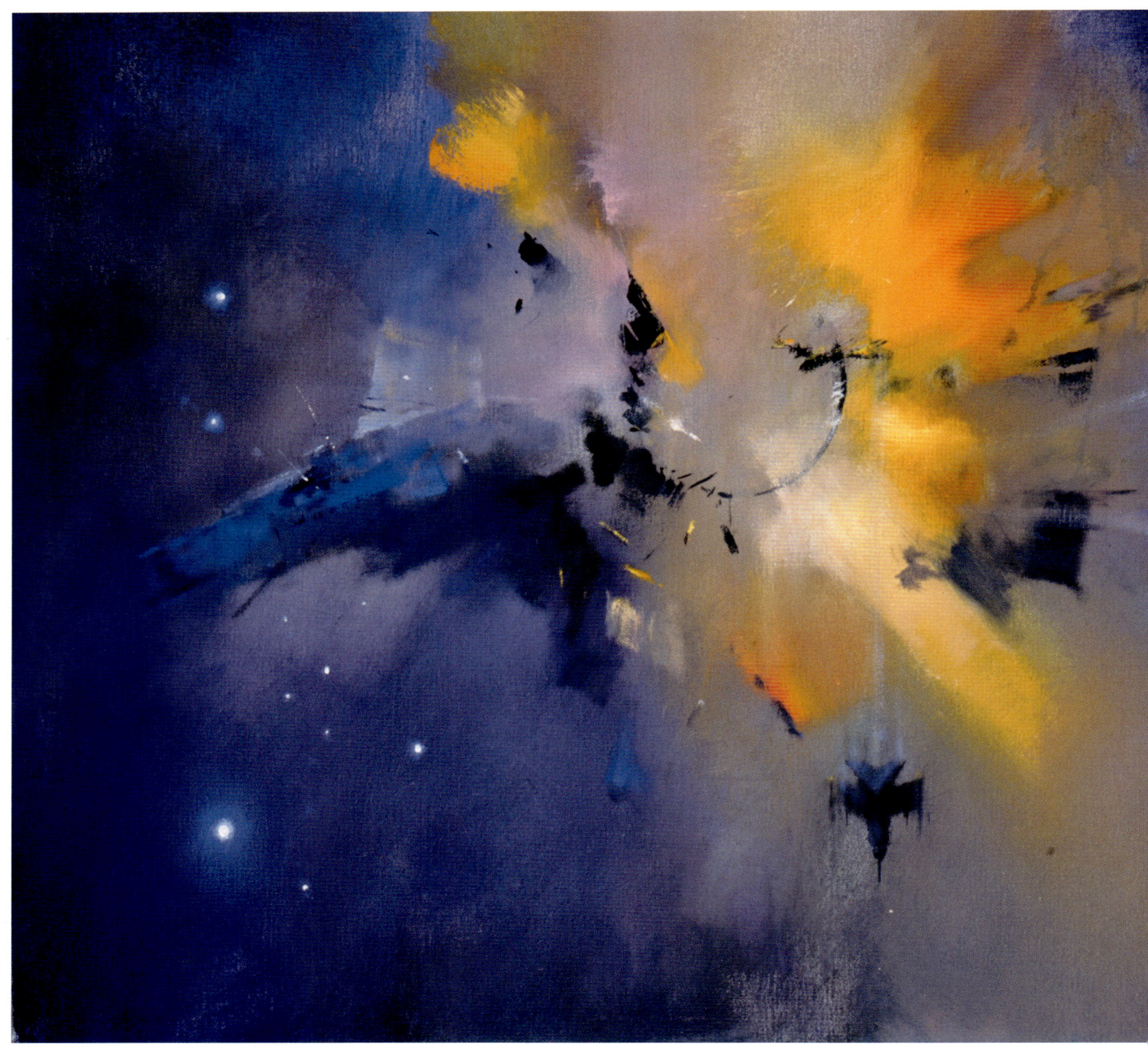

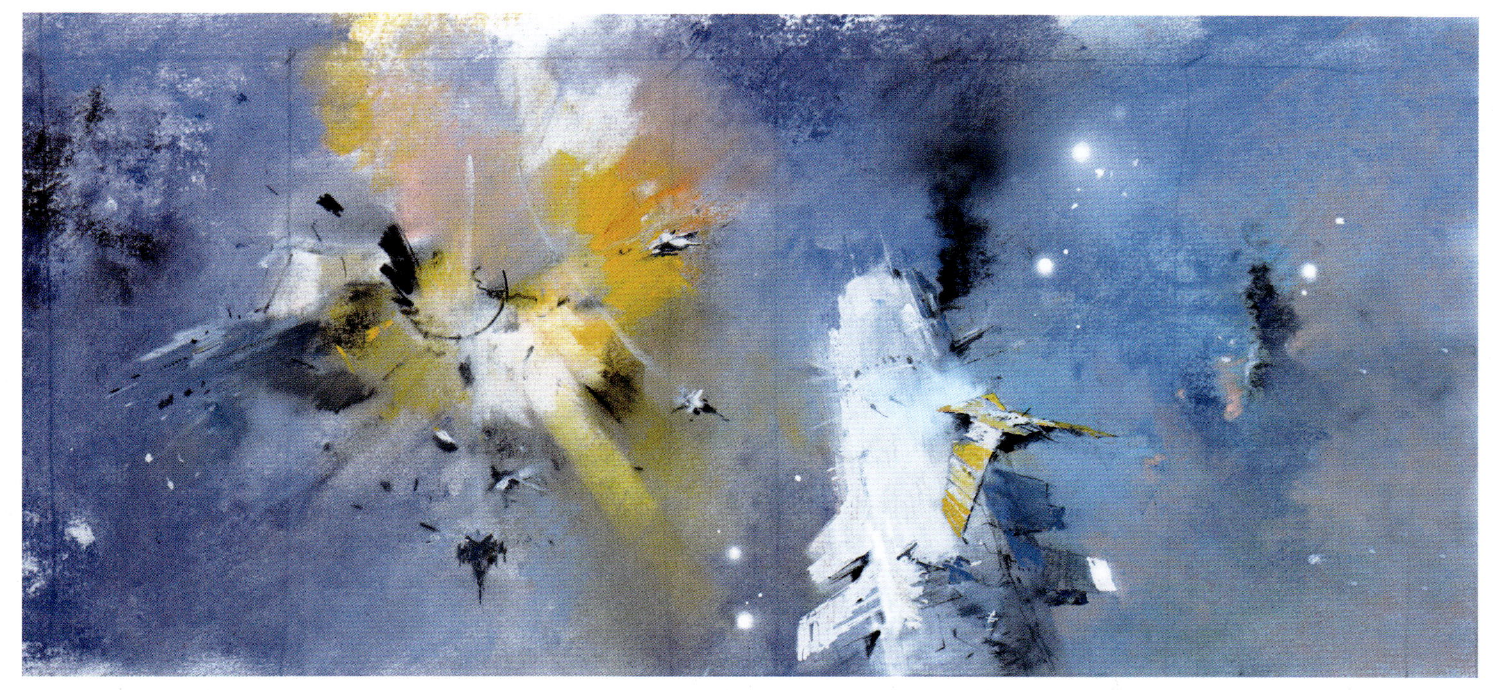

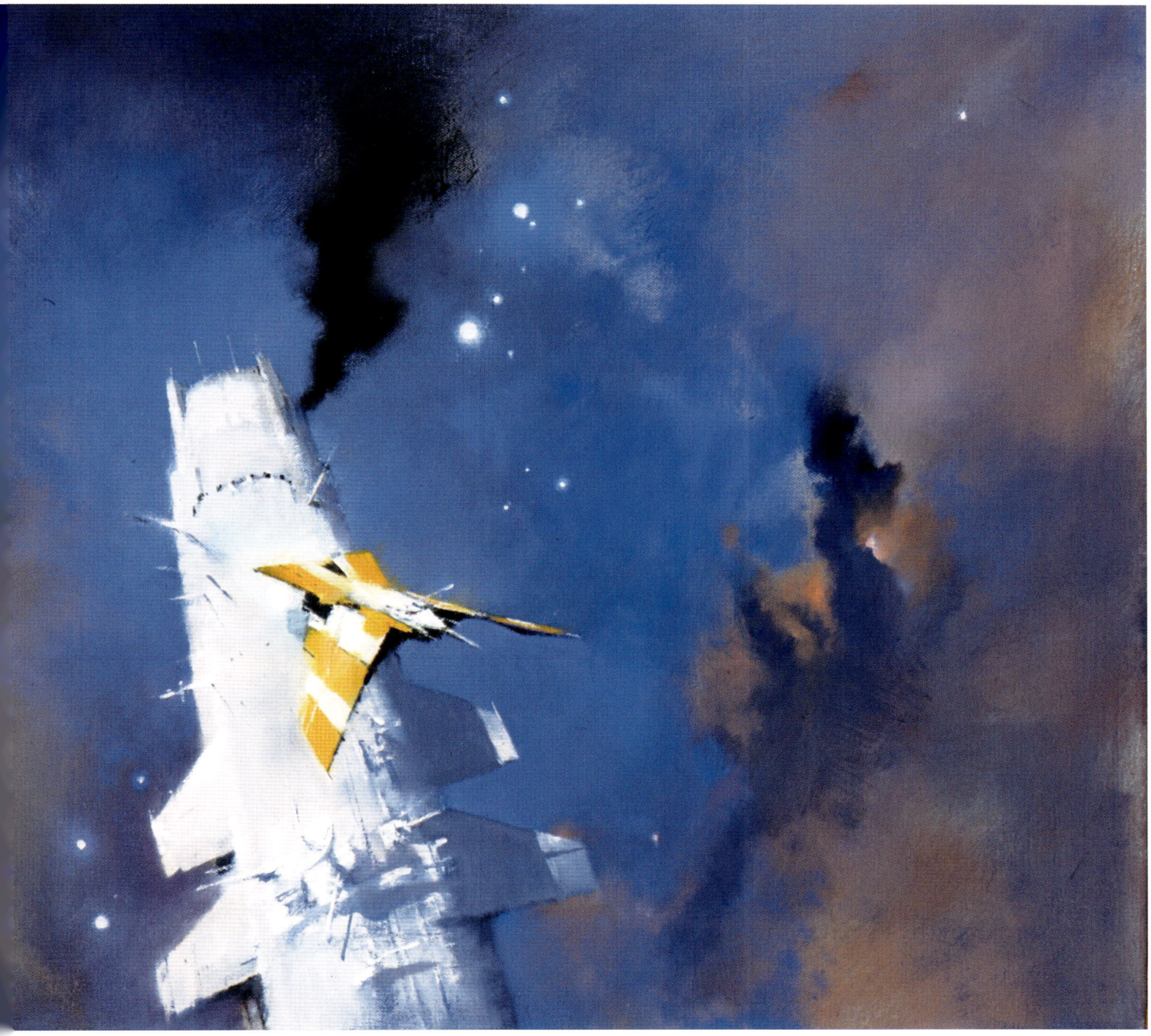

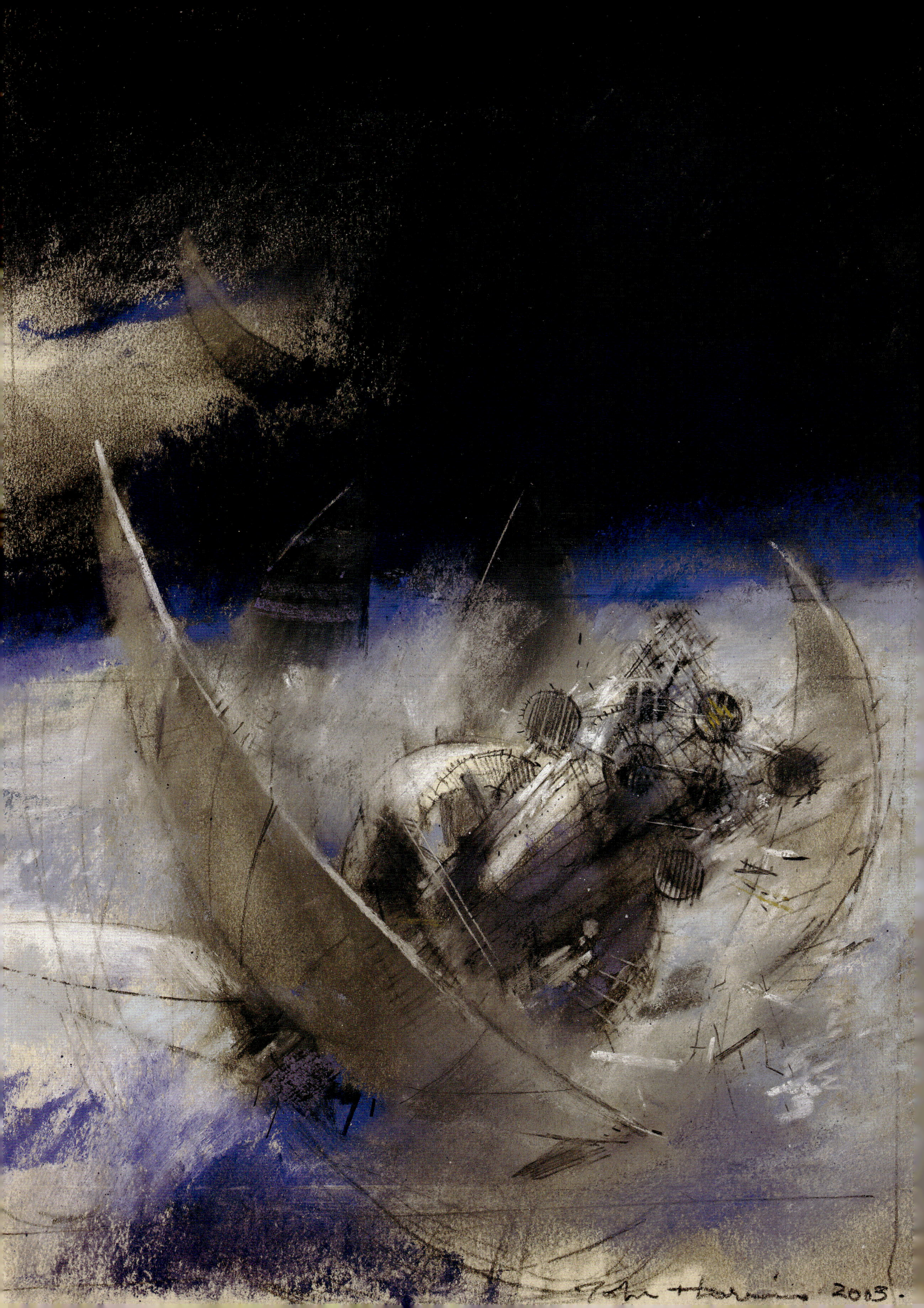

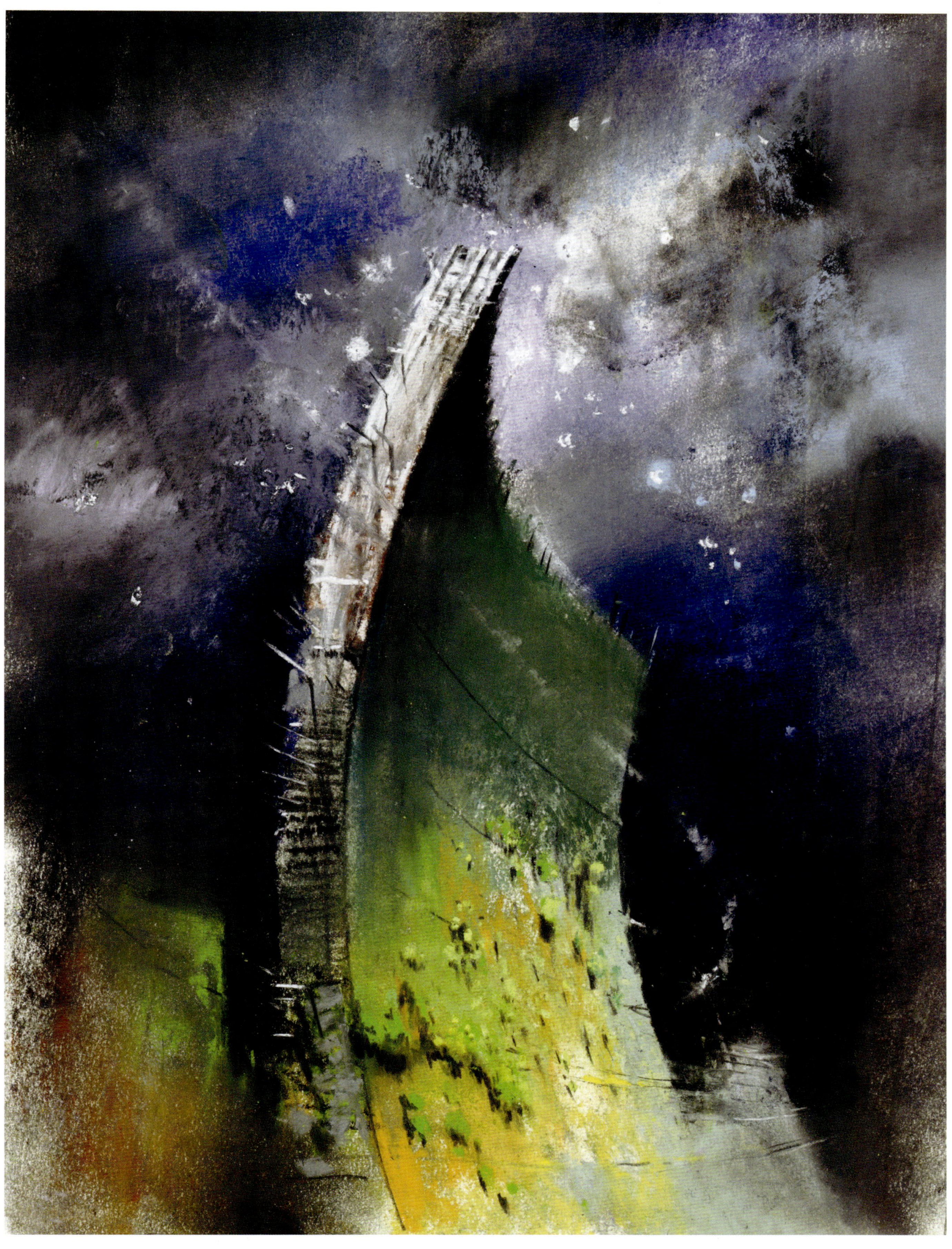

Above: *Learning of the World, sketch 3.* 2004

Opposite: *Pandora's Star, sketch.* 2003

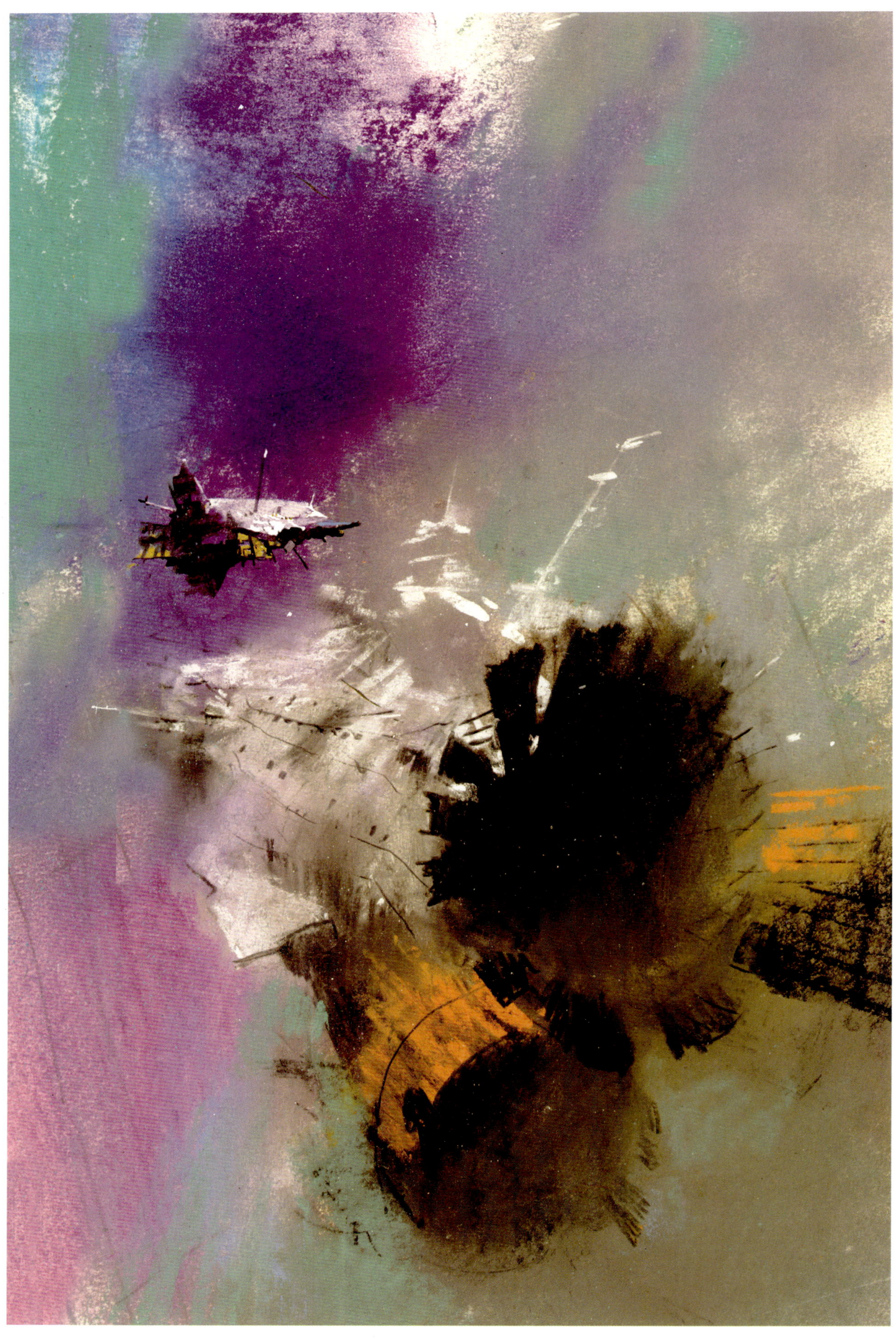

Above: *Seeker,* sketch for the cover of the book by Jack McDevitt. 2004

Opposite: *Alien Emergencies,* for the cover of the book by James White. 2001

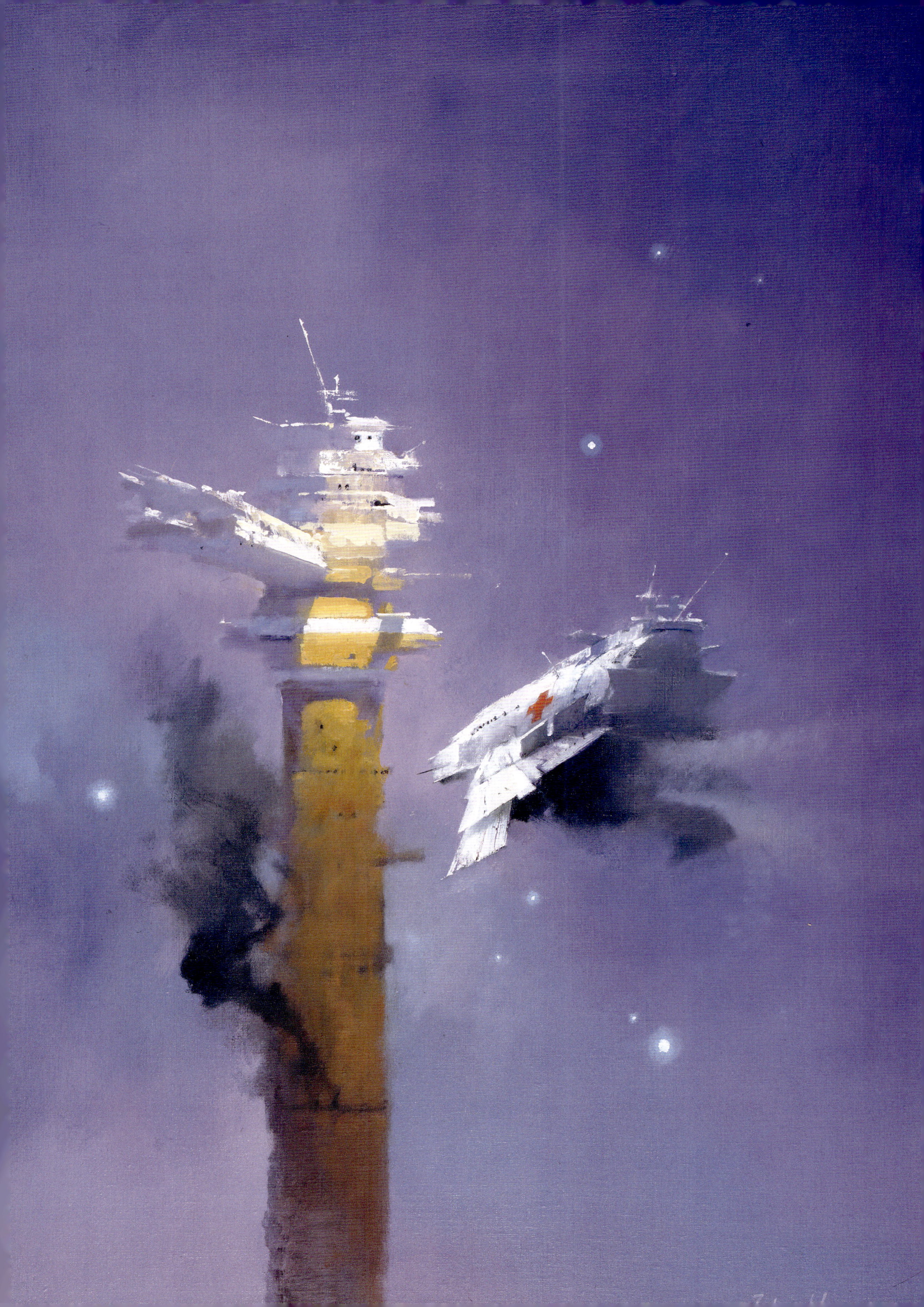

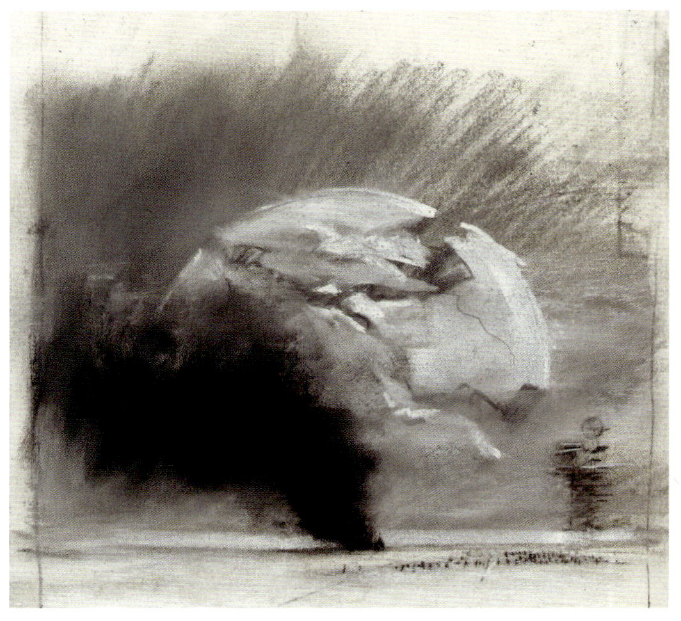

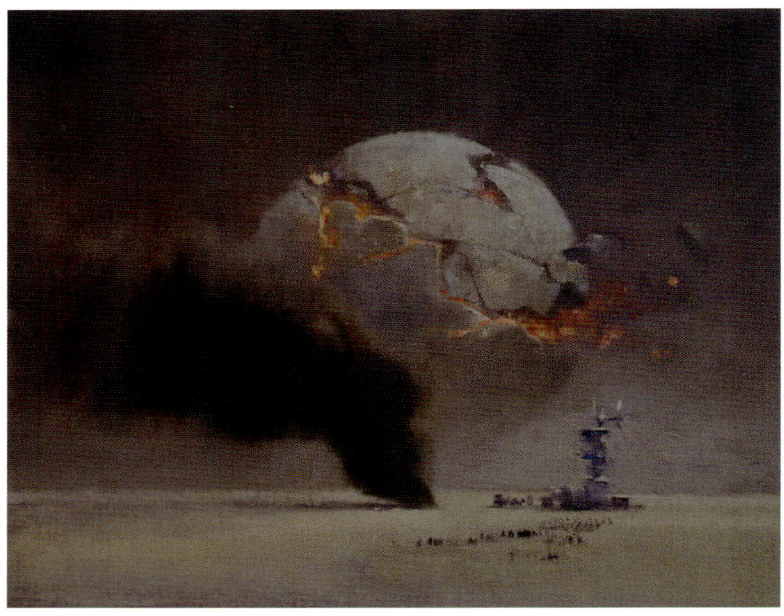

Above: *The First System War*, sketch and painting. 2010

Below: *Downfall*, produced to illustrate an online segment of *The Human Division* by John Scalzi. 2012

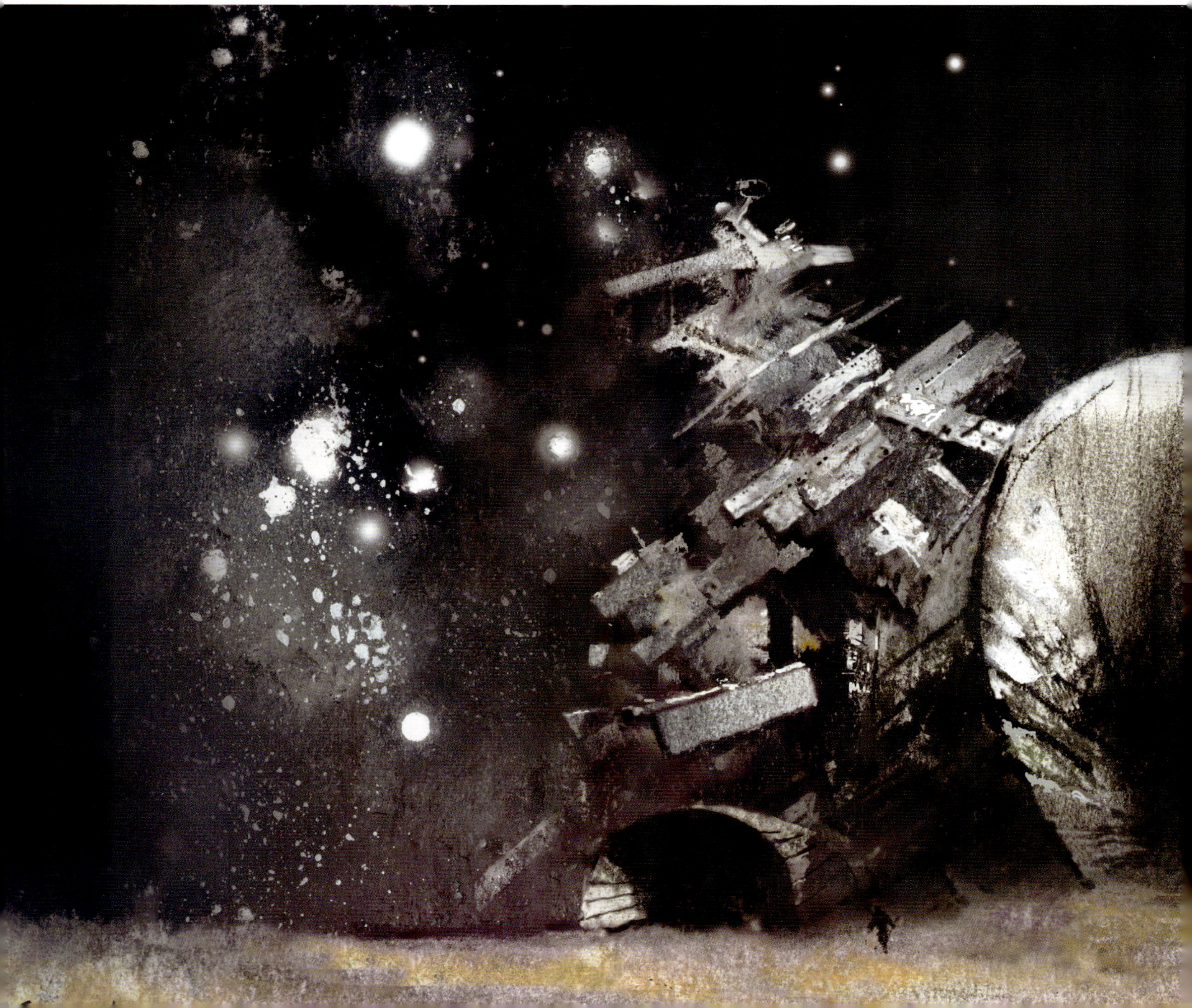

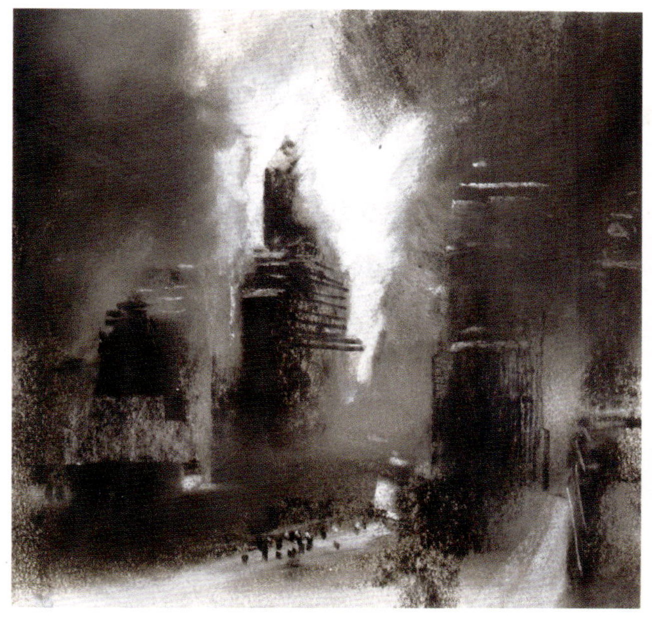

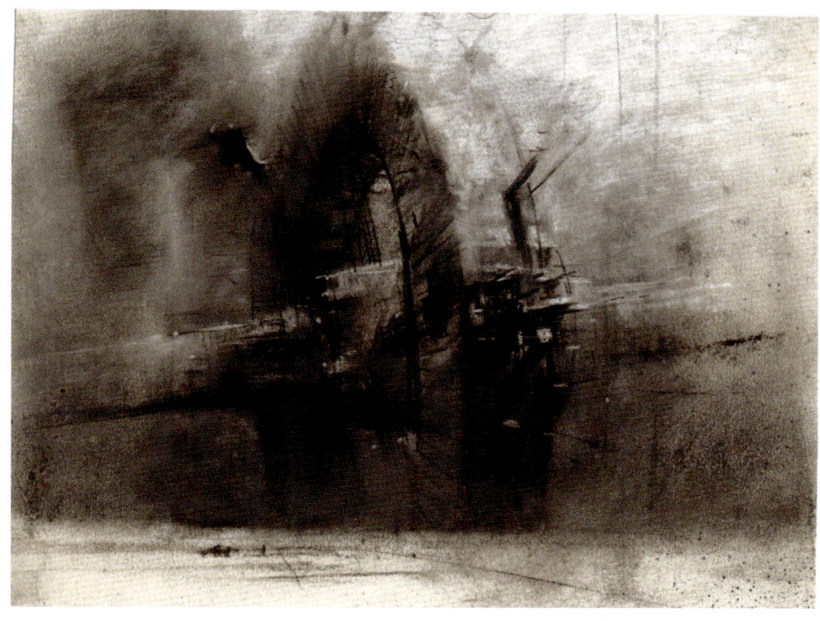

Above Left: *The Last Days of London.* 1991
Above Right: *The Materialist's Dream.* 2009

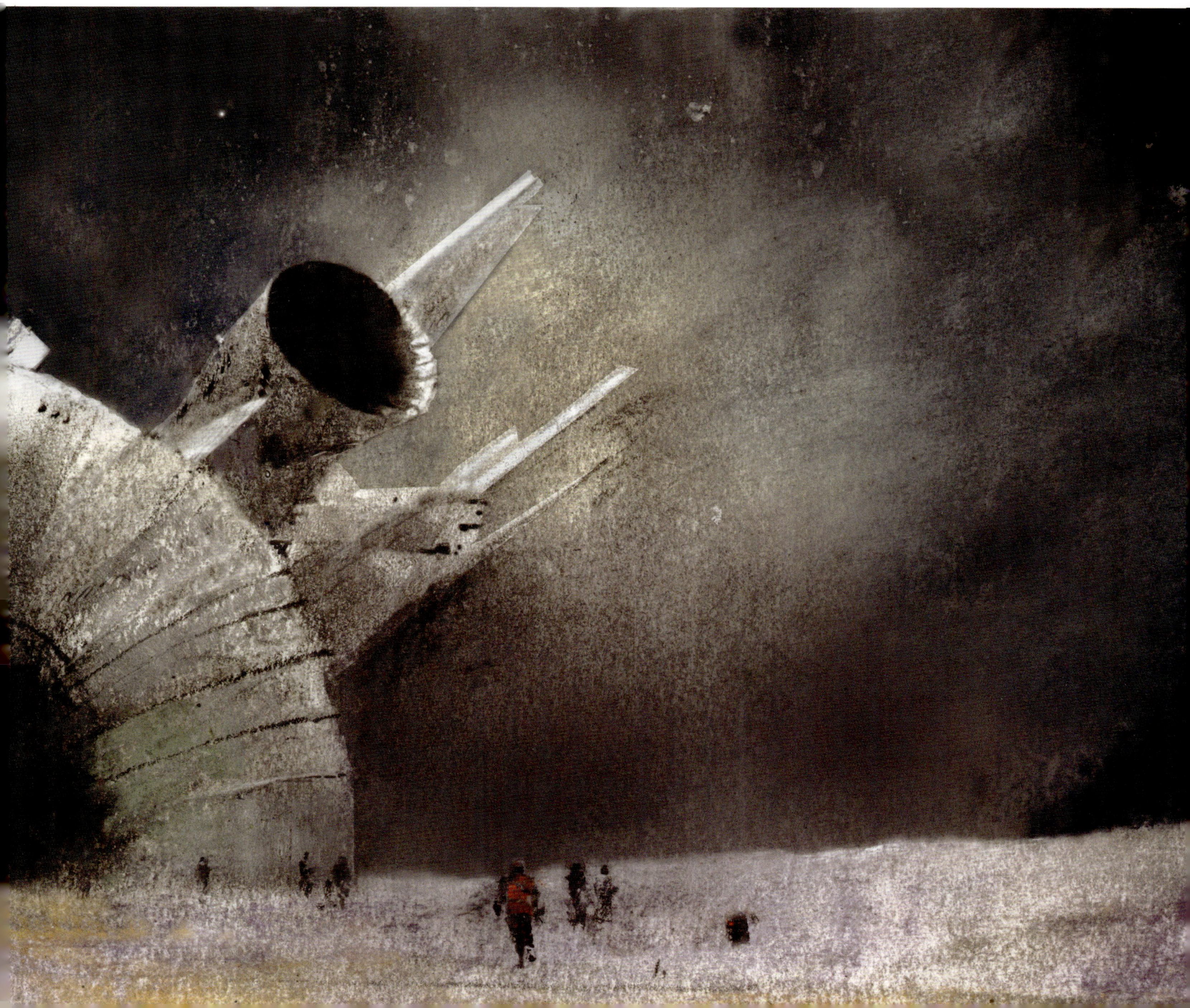

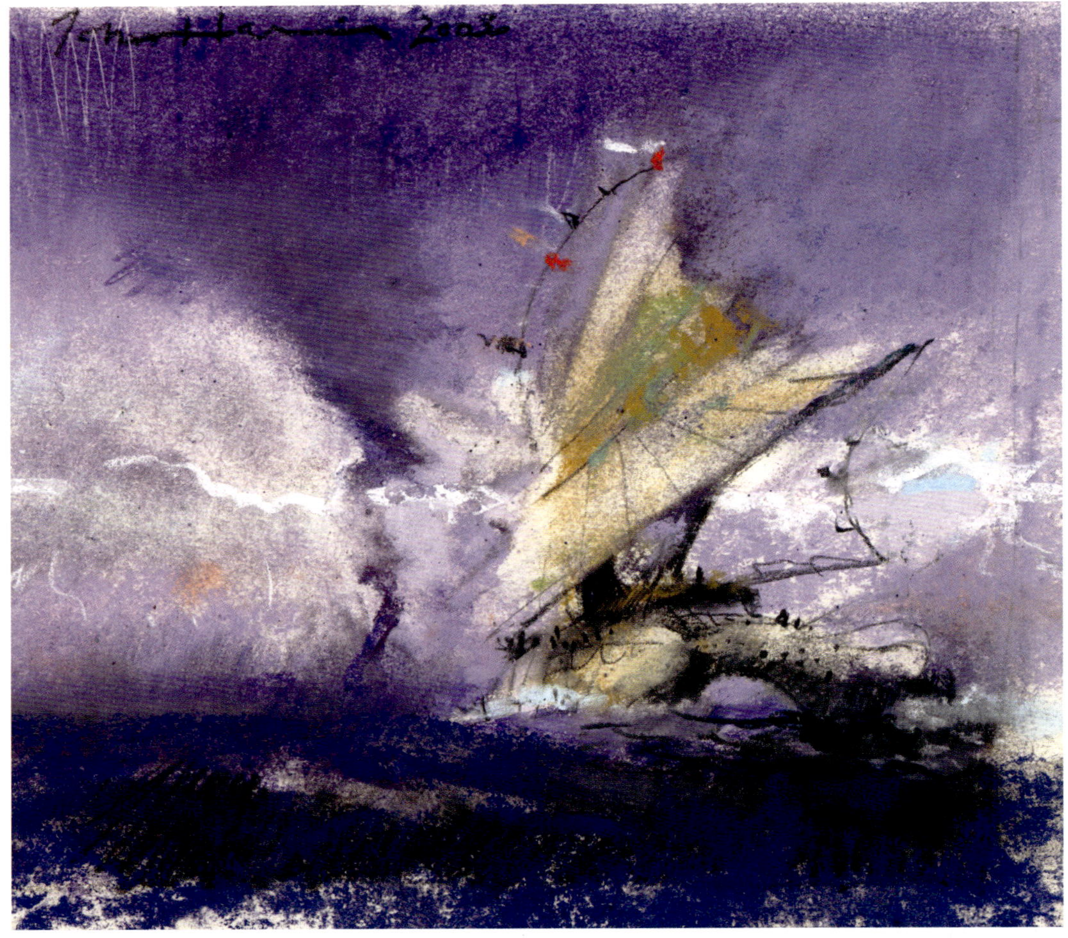

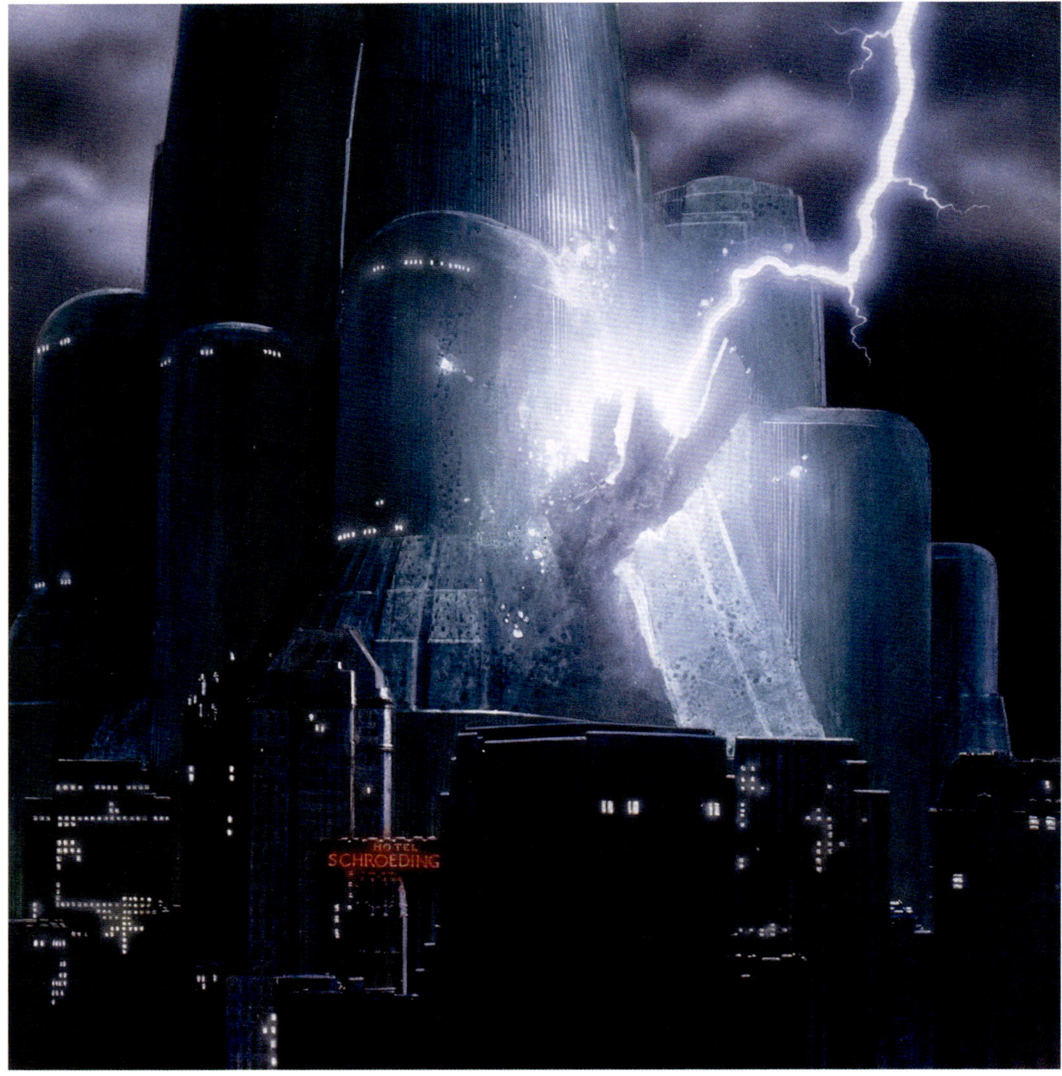

Top: *Noise*, preparatory sketch for the cover of the book by Hal Clement. 2002

Bottom: *Mass: Hotel Schroedinger*. 1997

Opposite: *Burning Watchtowers*, the cover of *The Best of Trek 16*. 1990

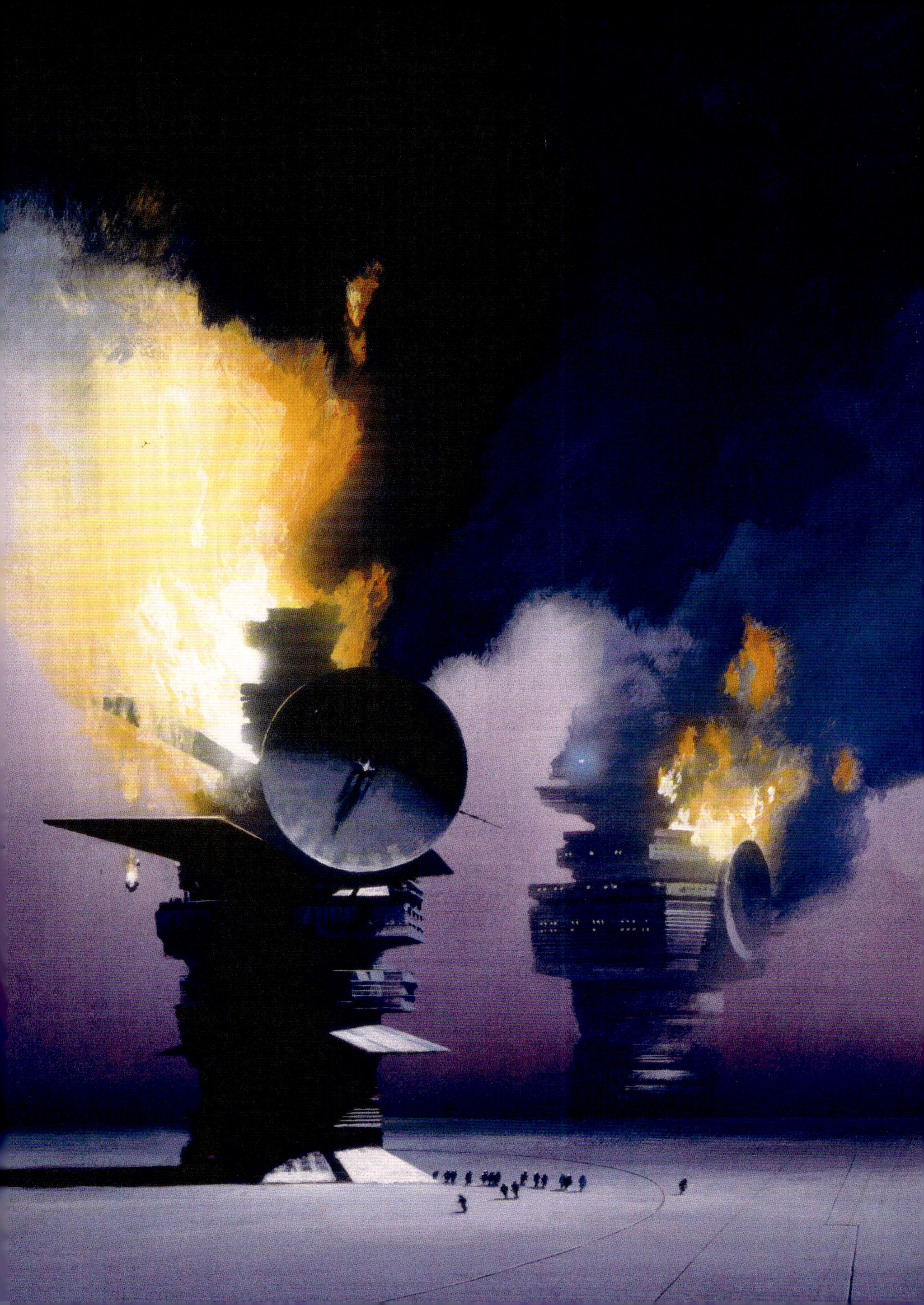

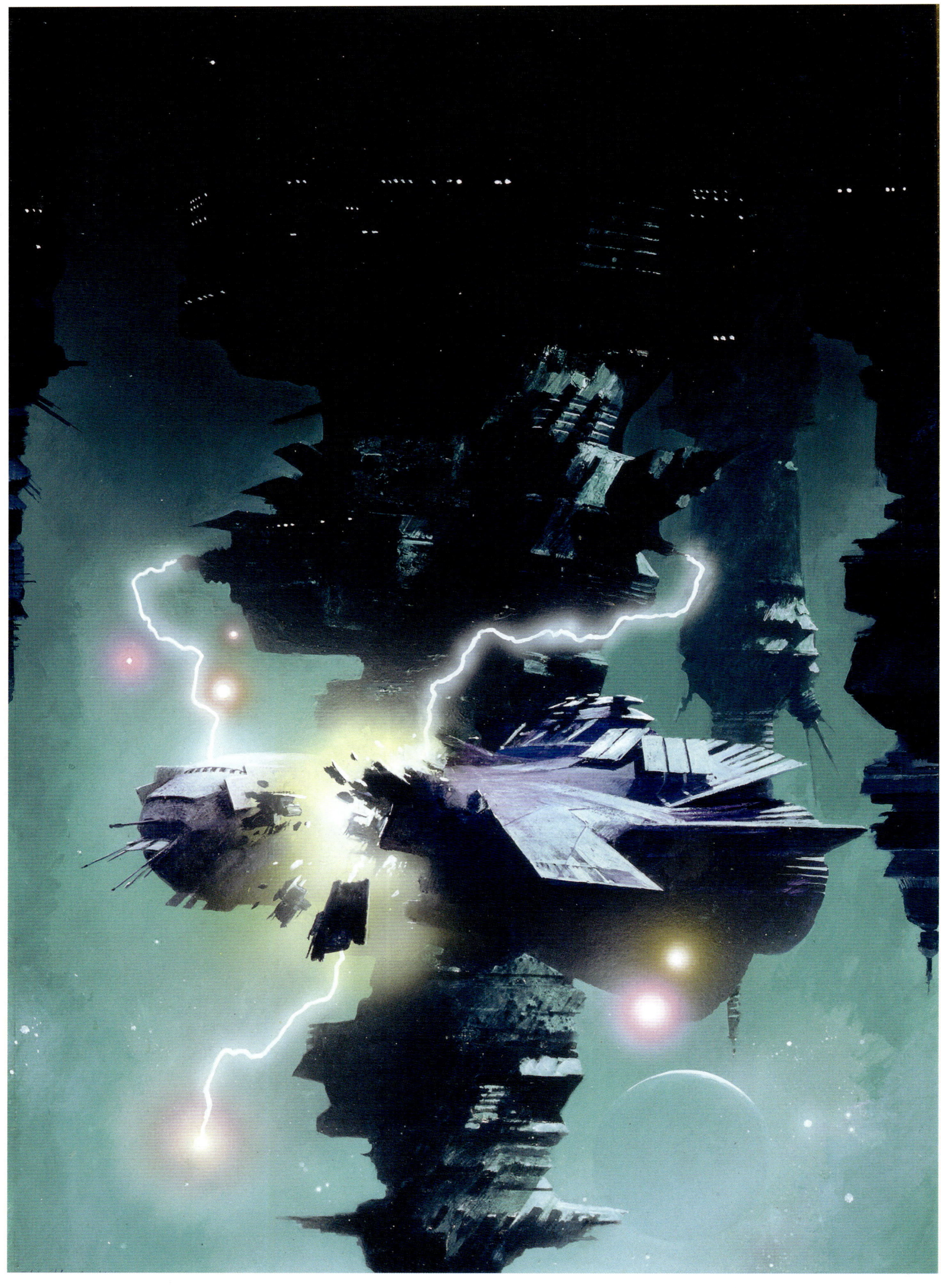

Above: *The Weapons of Chaos (Colors of Chaos)*, the cover of the book by Robert E Vardeman. 1998

Opposite: *Zoe's Tale*, the cover of the book by John Scalzi. 2007

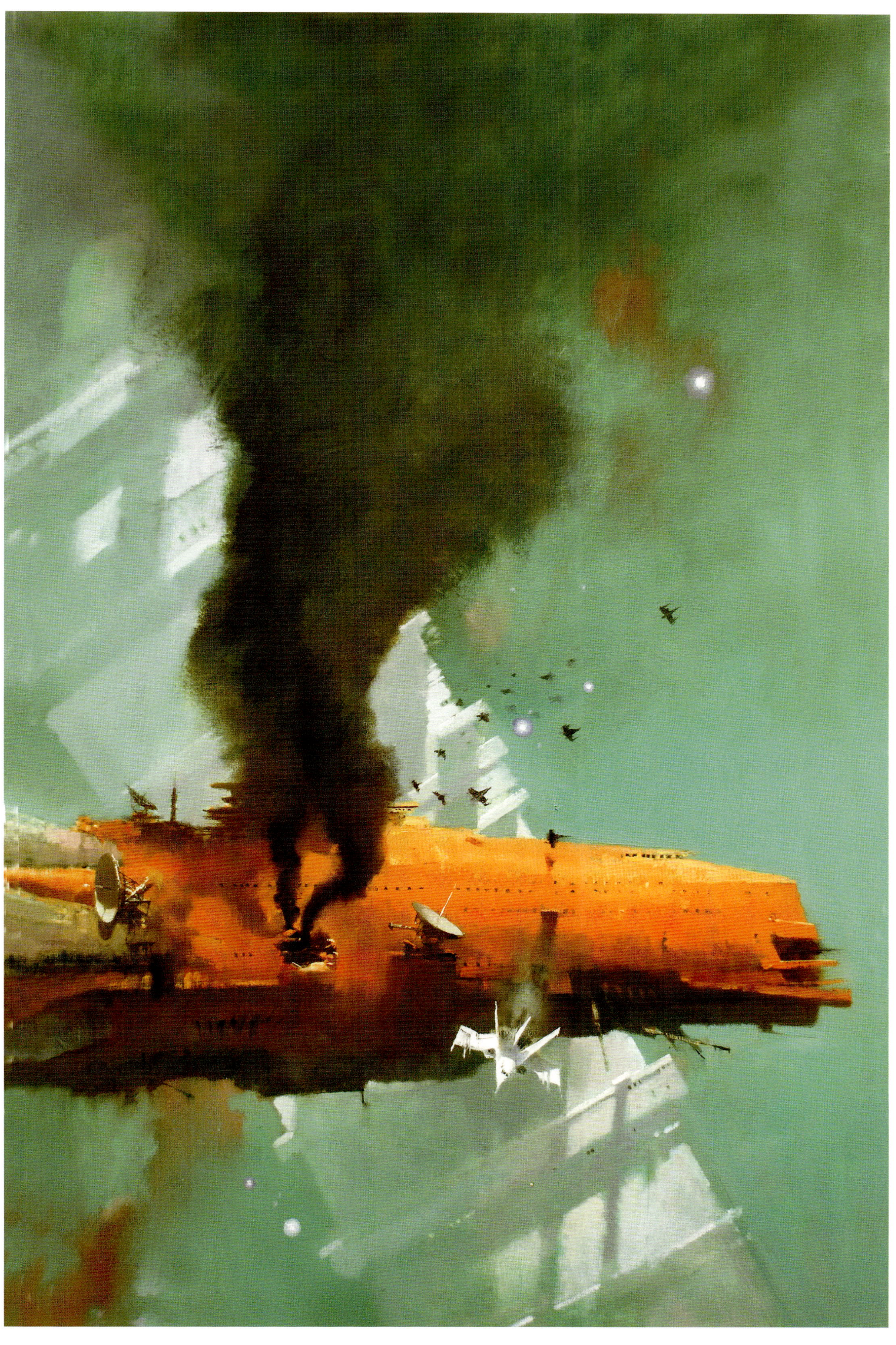

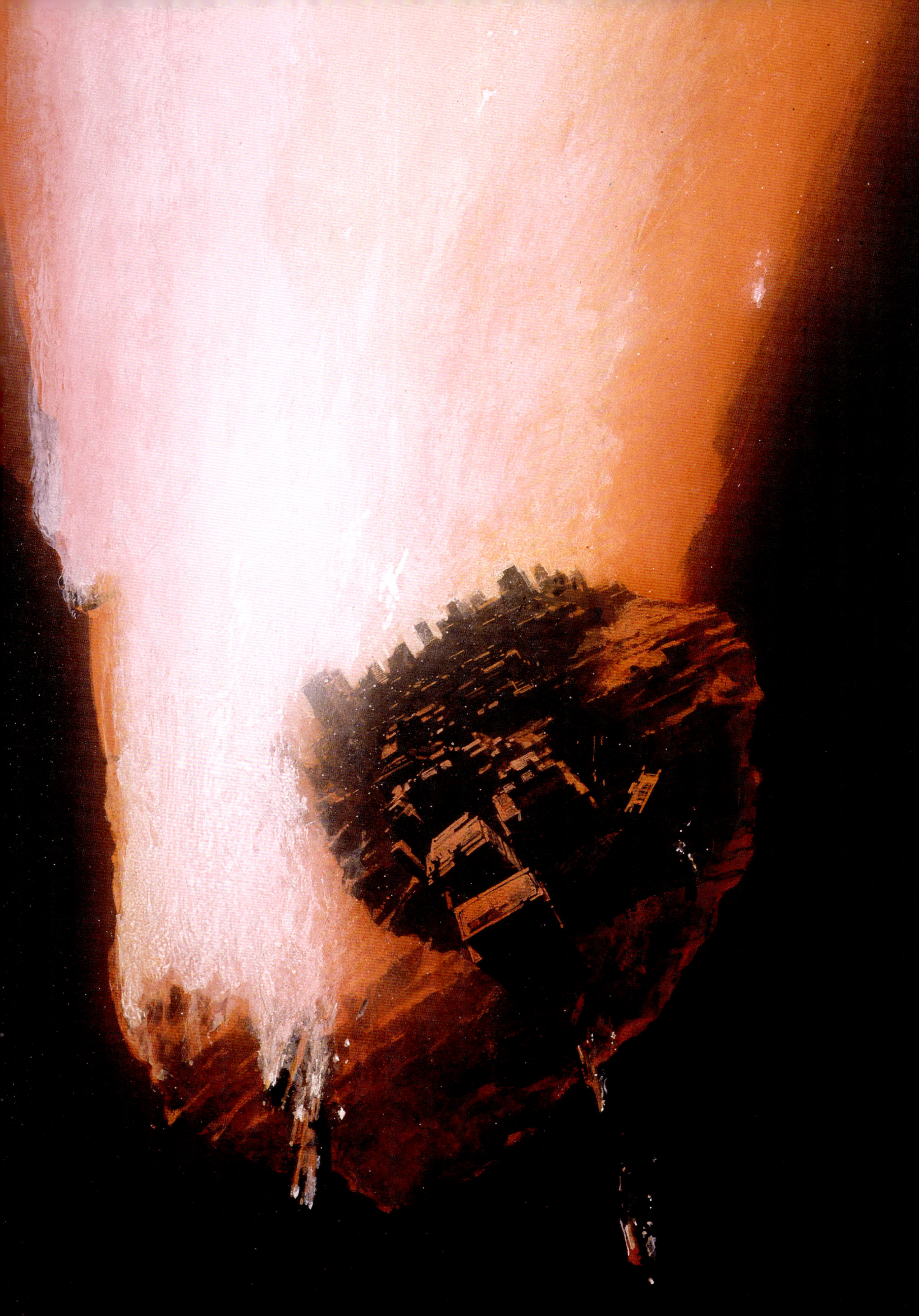

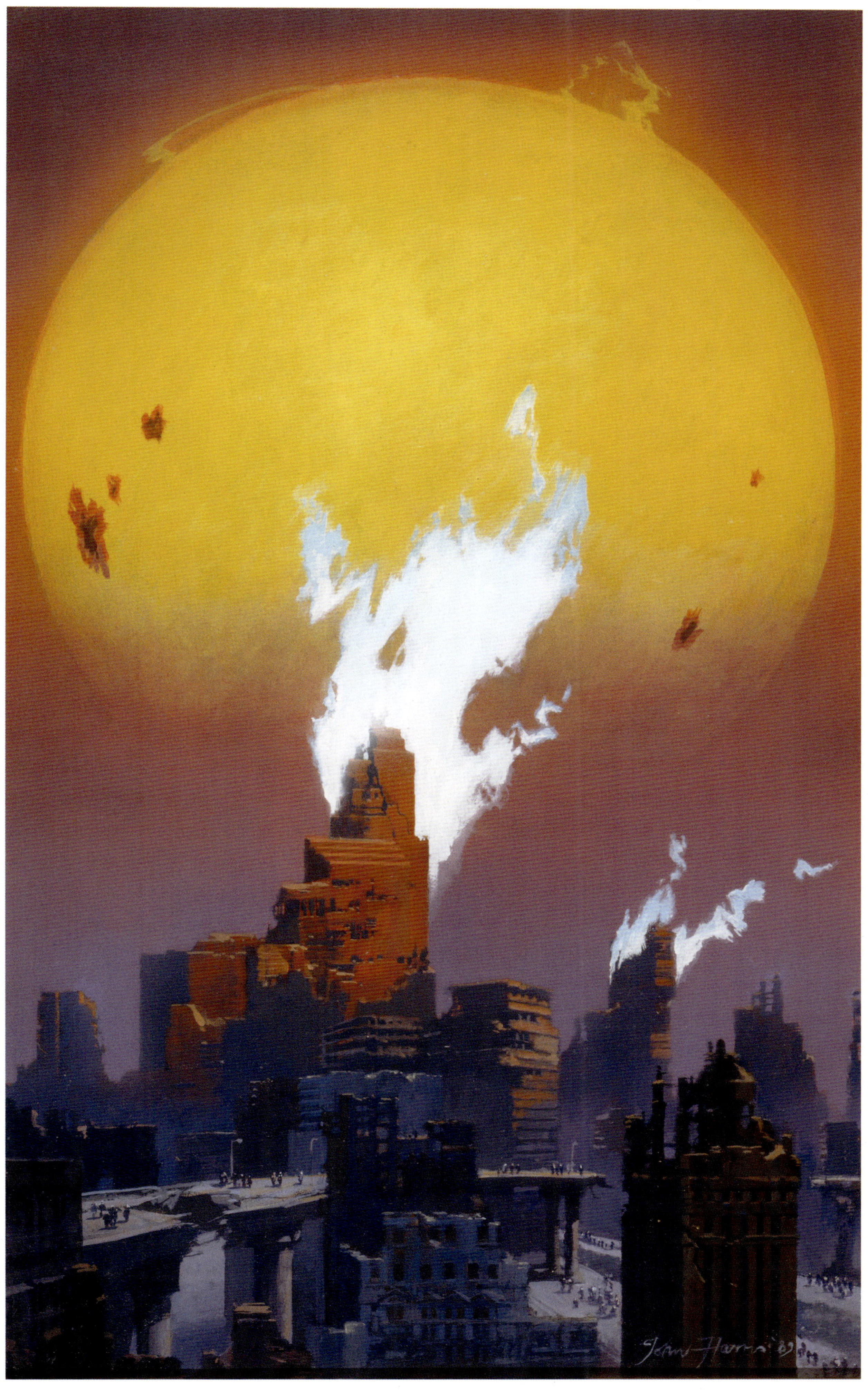

Above: *Dhalgren*, the cover of the book by Samuel R Delany. 1989

Opposite: *After the Fall*, the cover of the book by Isaac Asimov. 1977

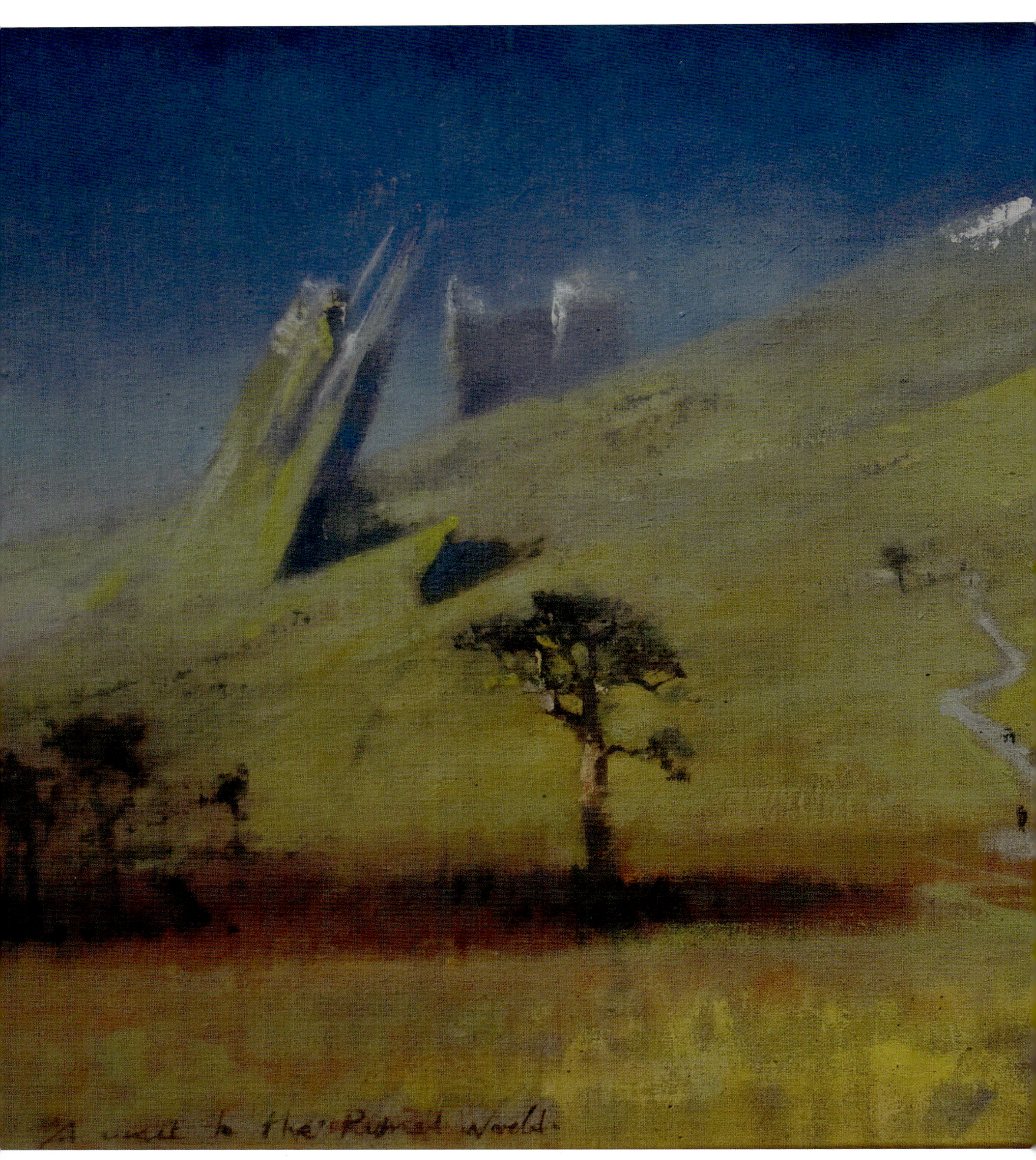

RETURN TO EARTH

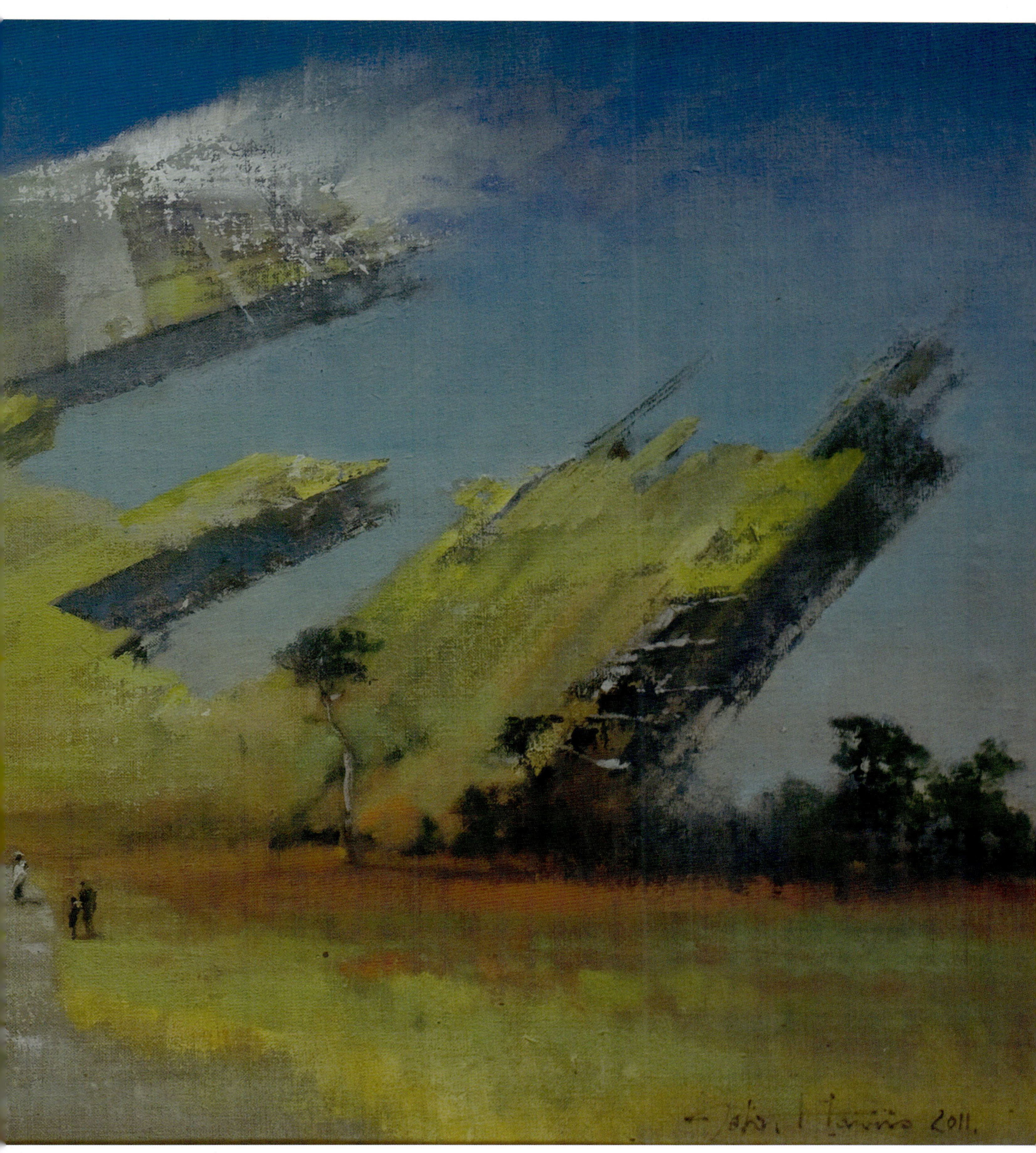

Previous Spread: *A Visit to the Ruined World*

Right: *The Gentle Giants of Ganymede*, a study for the cover of the book by James P Hogan. 1989

Opposite: *Mars Life*, the cover of the book by Ben Bova. 2007

Following Spread: *The Search*, 3 ft 6in. x 5 ft. 2012

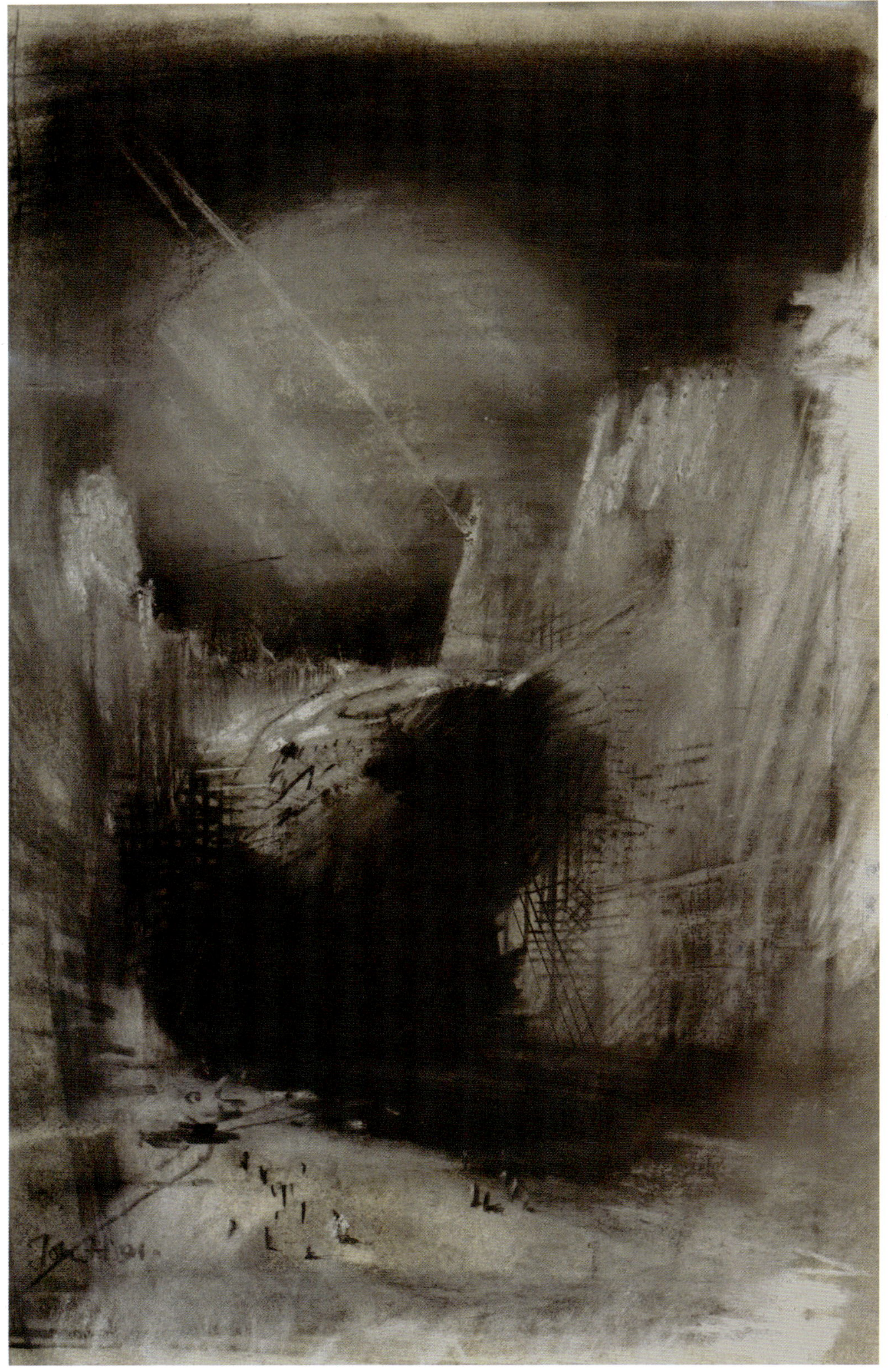

The passage of time works its alchemy on all things sooner or later, and even the most durable materials must eventually dissolve into the ground from which it came. But along that arc of melancholy, there can be moments of great beauty when created things – however hard – soften and mellow.

The moment when an artefact becomes overwhelmed by natural forces but is still visible seems especially poignant – but this is entropy, the fate of us all, and there is something fitting in that.

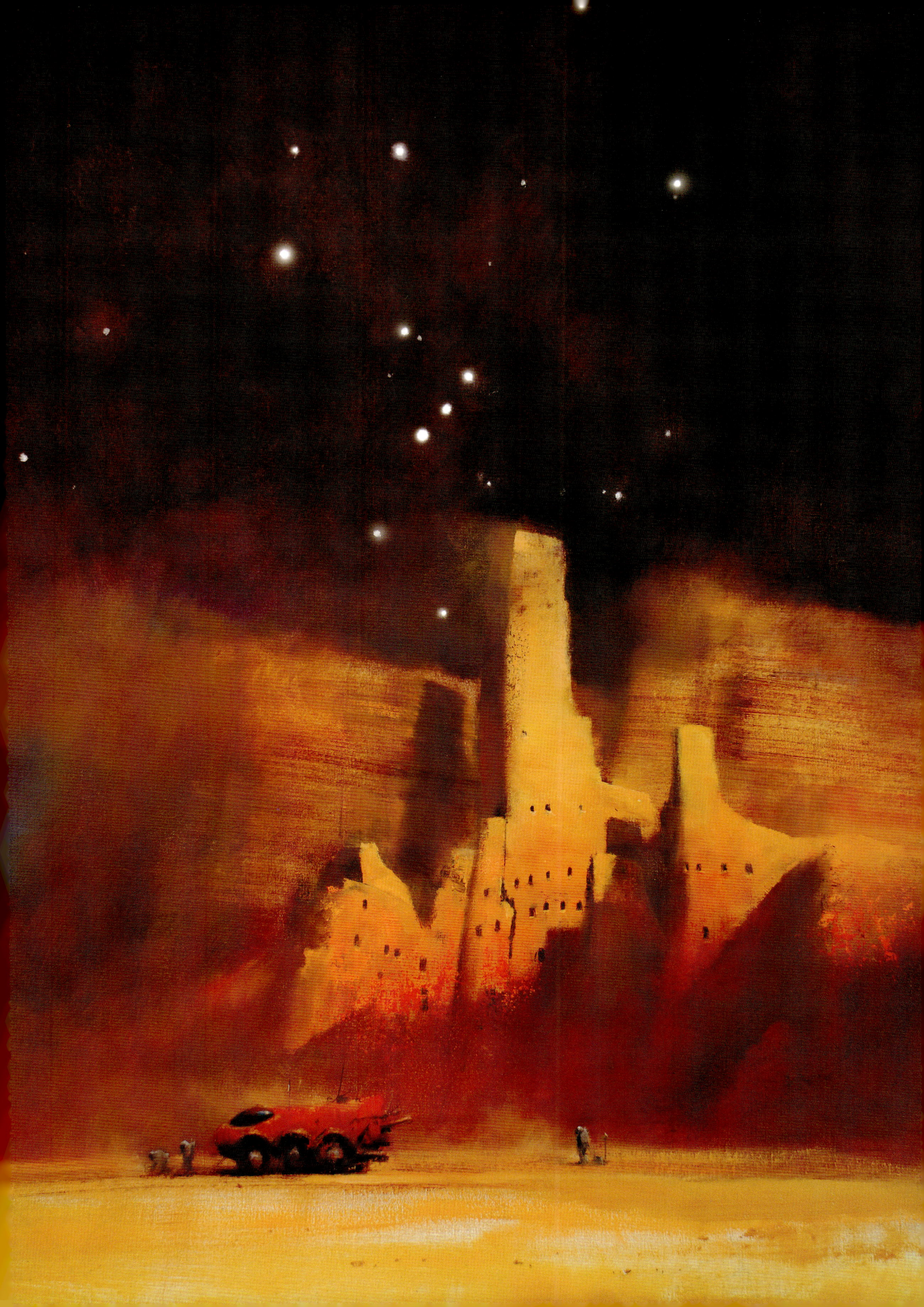

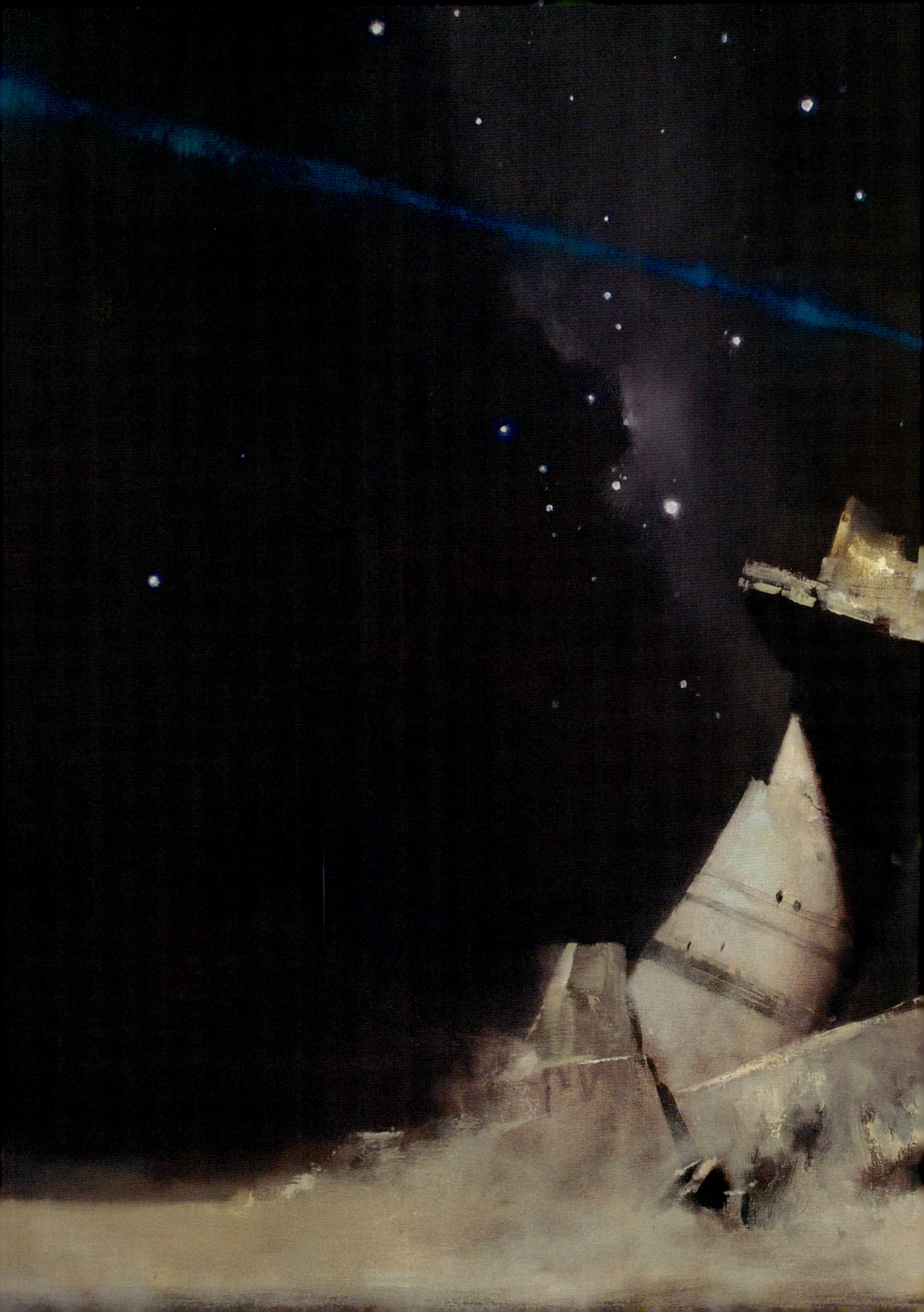

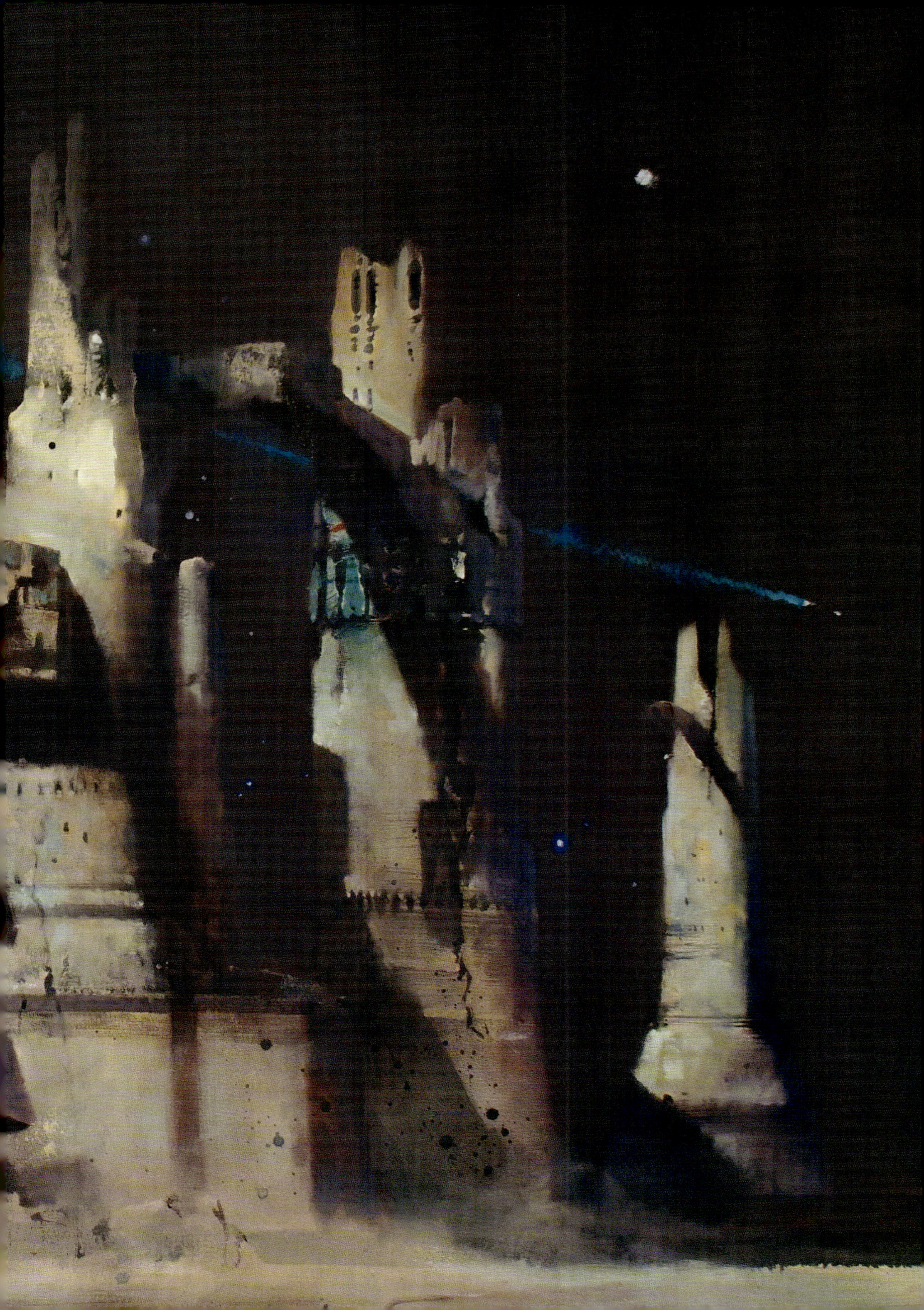

Right: *The End of Days*. 2010

Below: *Above the Wall*. 1995

Opposite Top: *The World at the End of Time*, a study for the cover of the book by Frederick Pohl. 1995

Opposite Below: *The Search*, a study. 2012

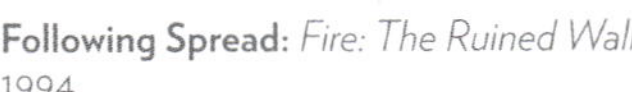

Following Spread: *Fire: The Ruined Wall*. 1994

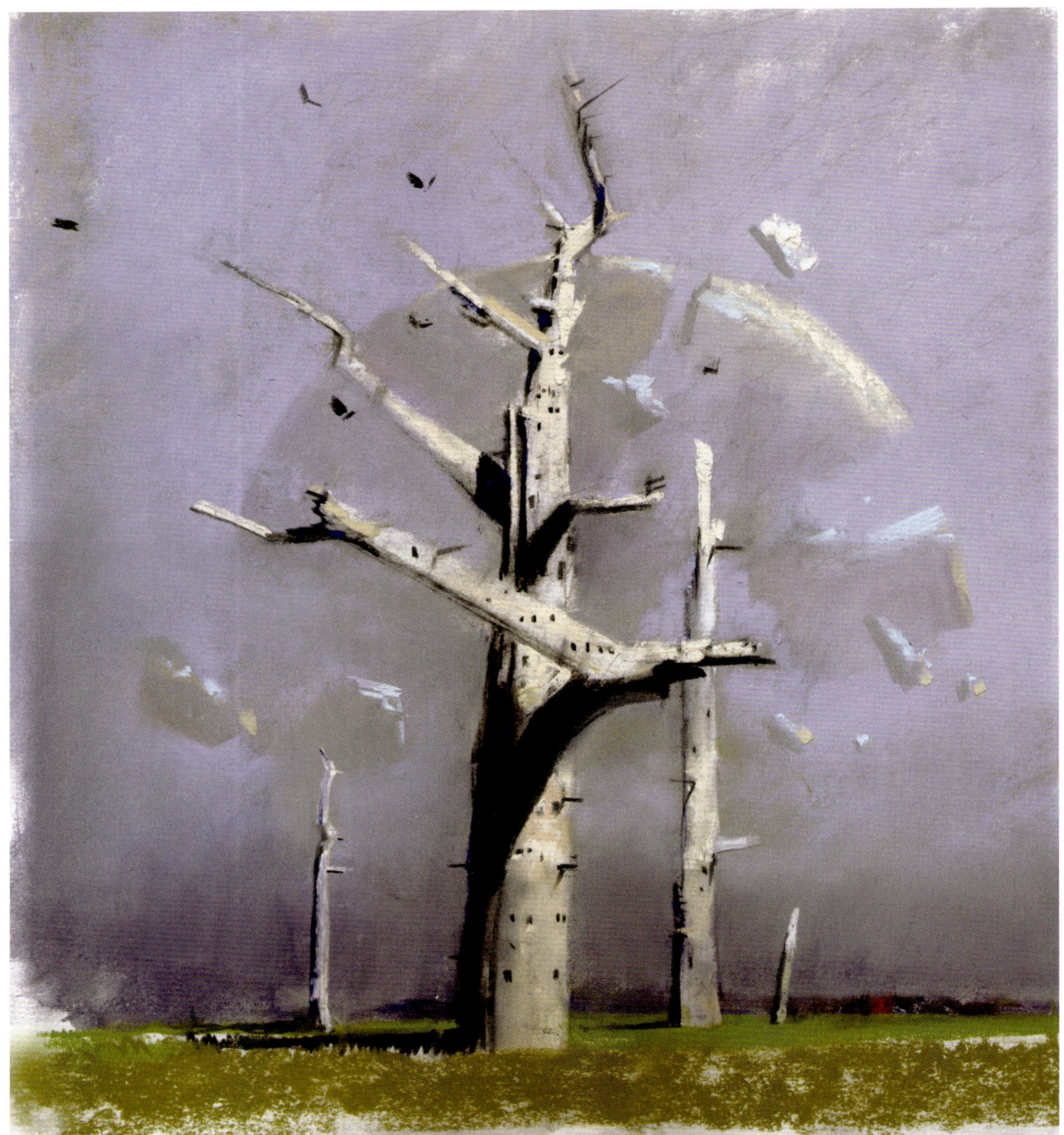

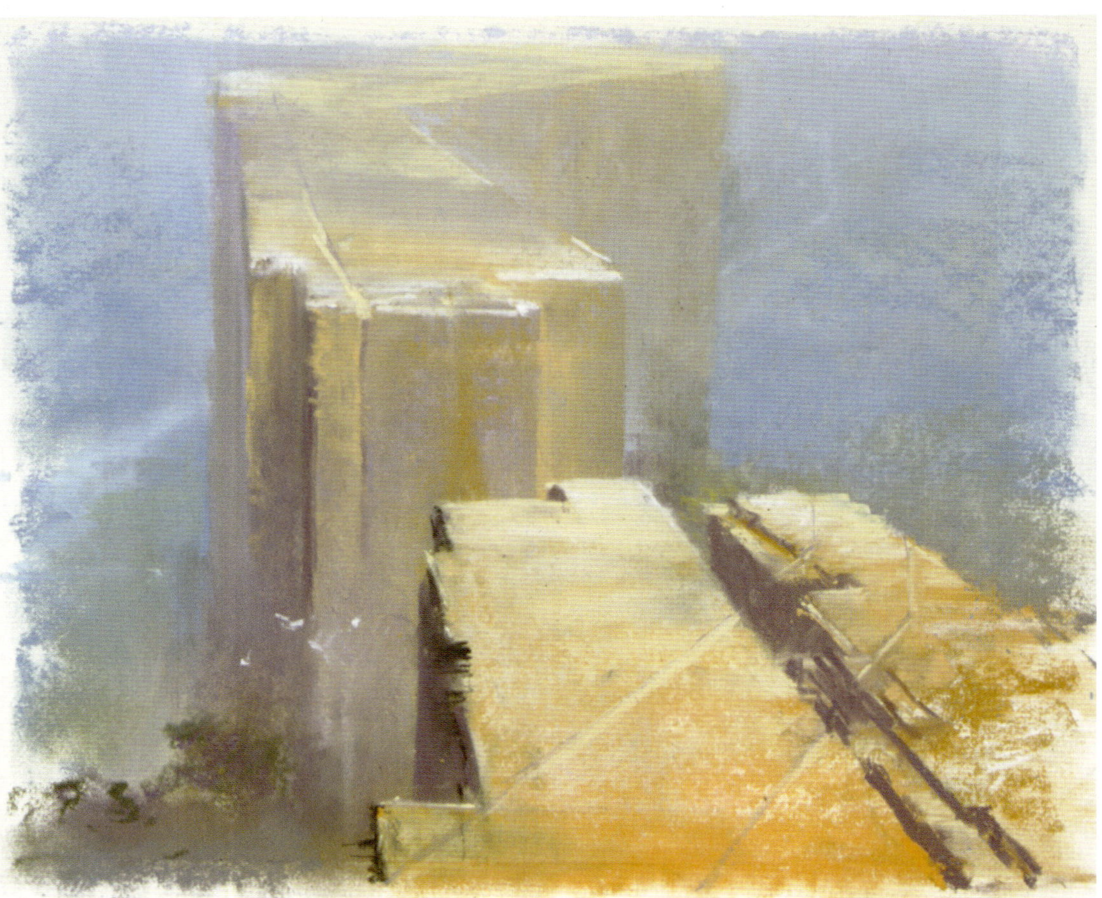

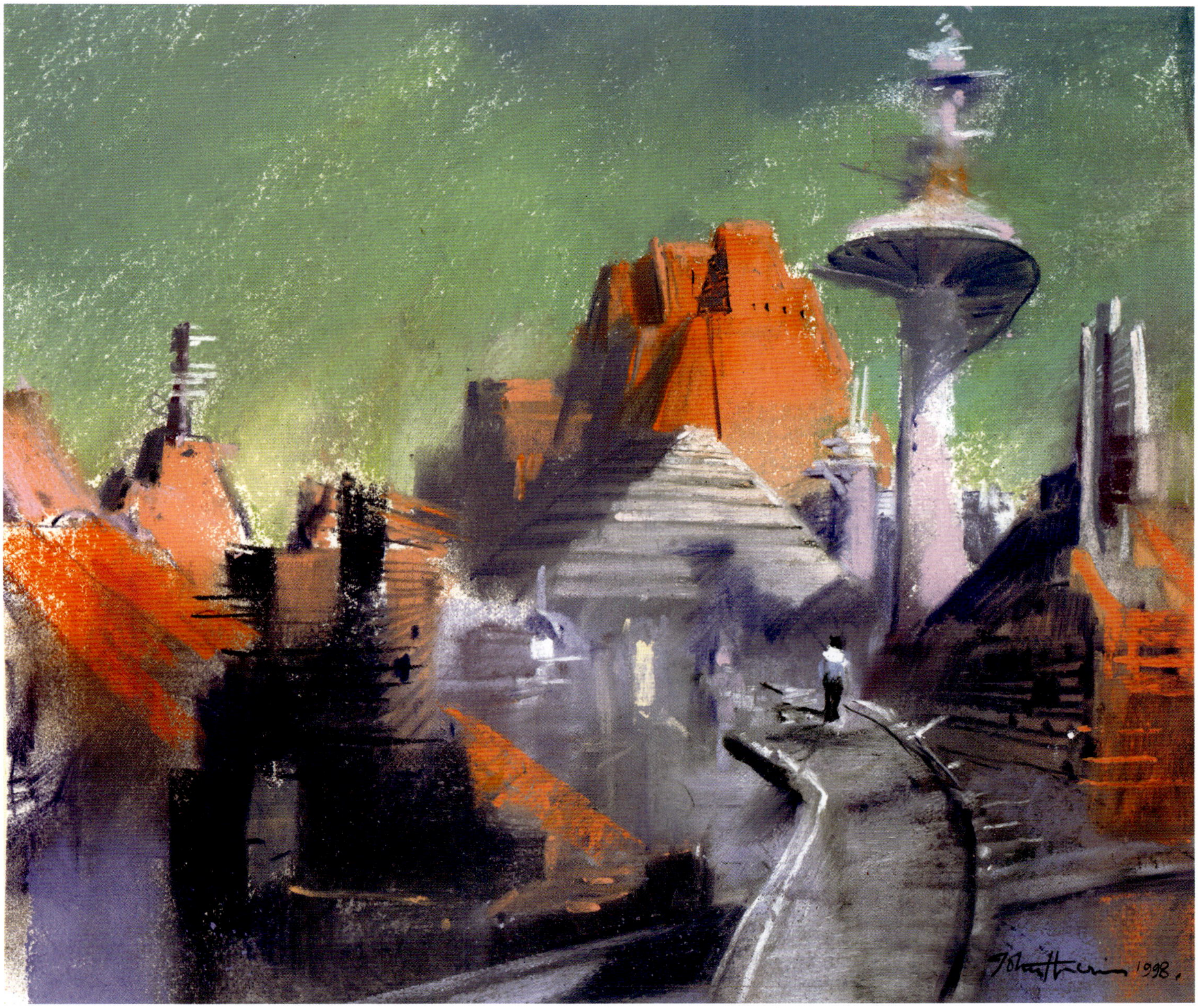

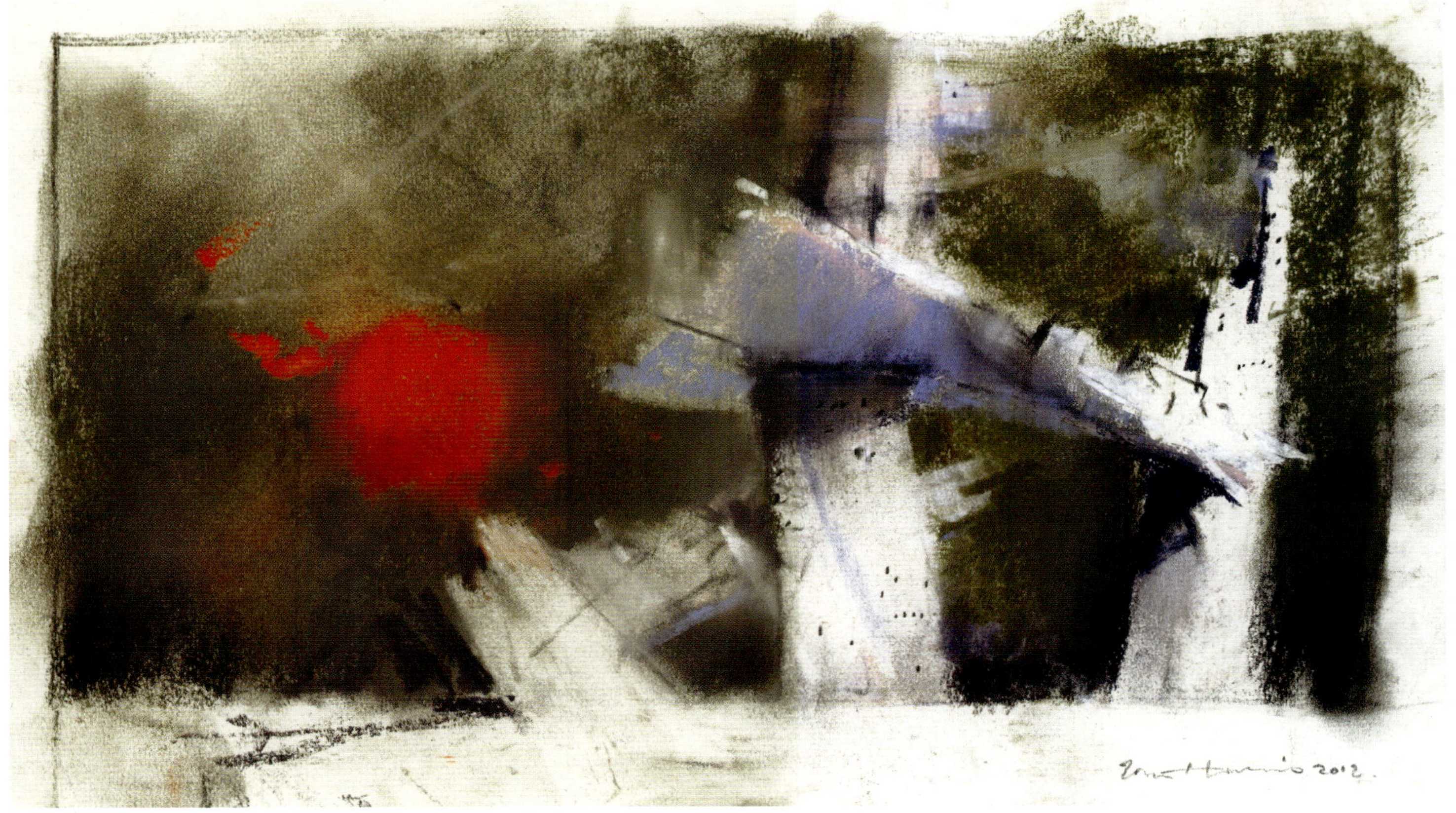

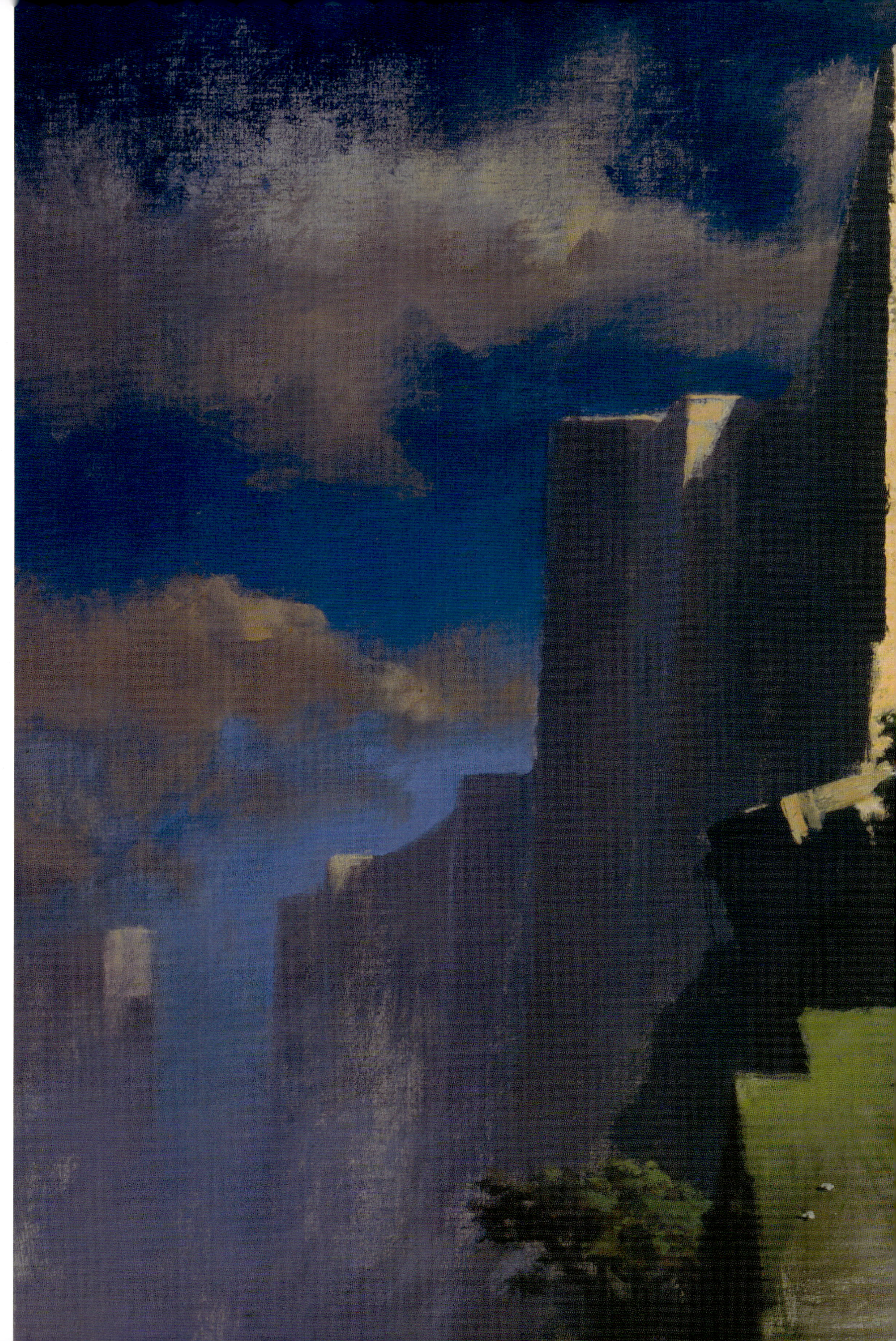

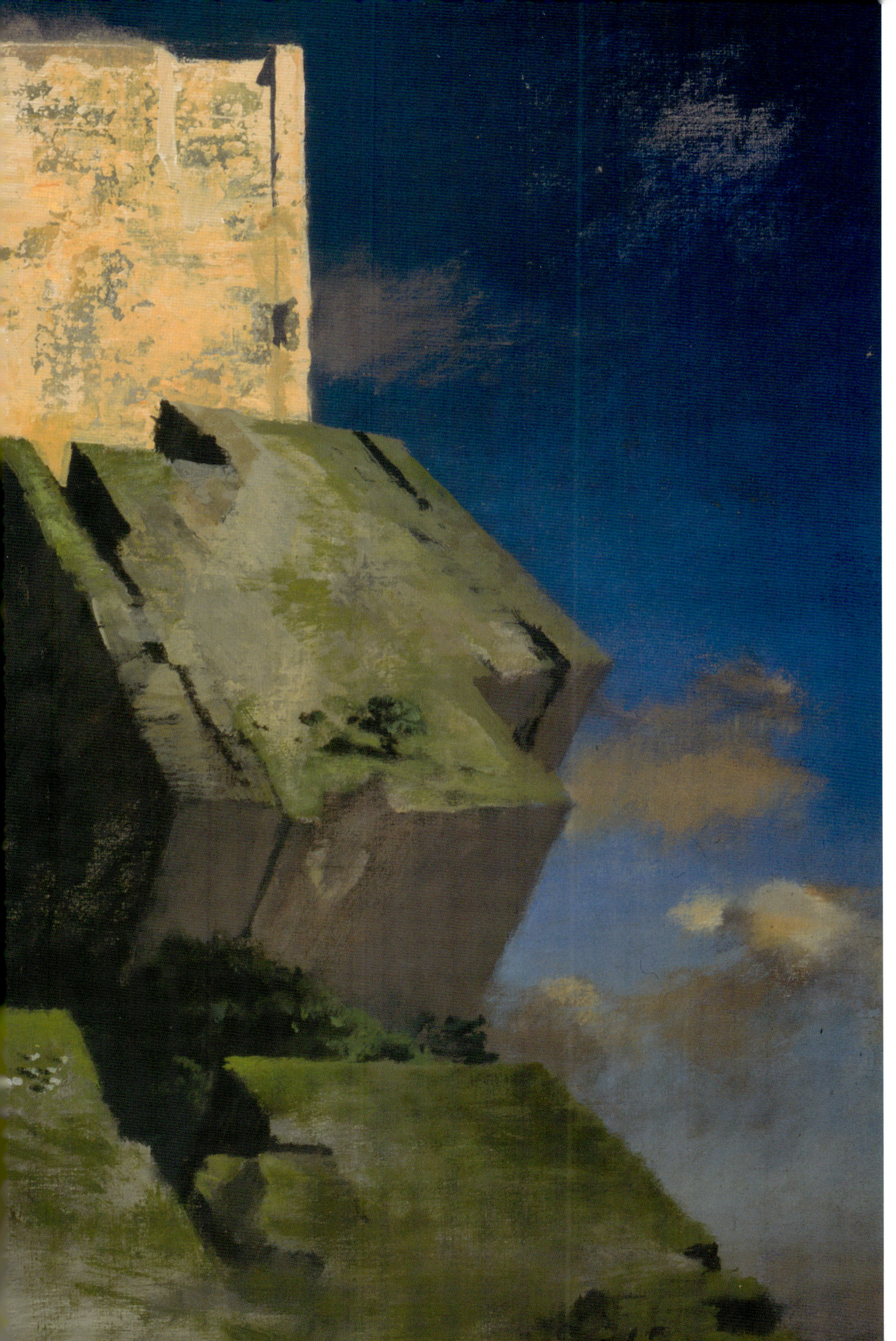

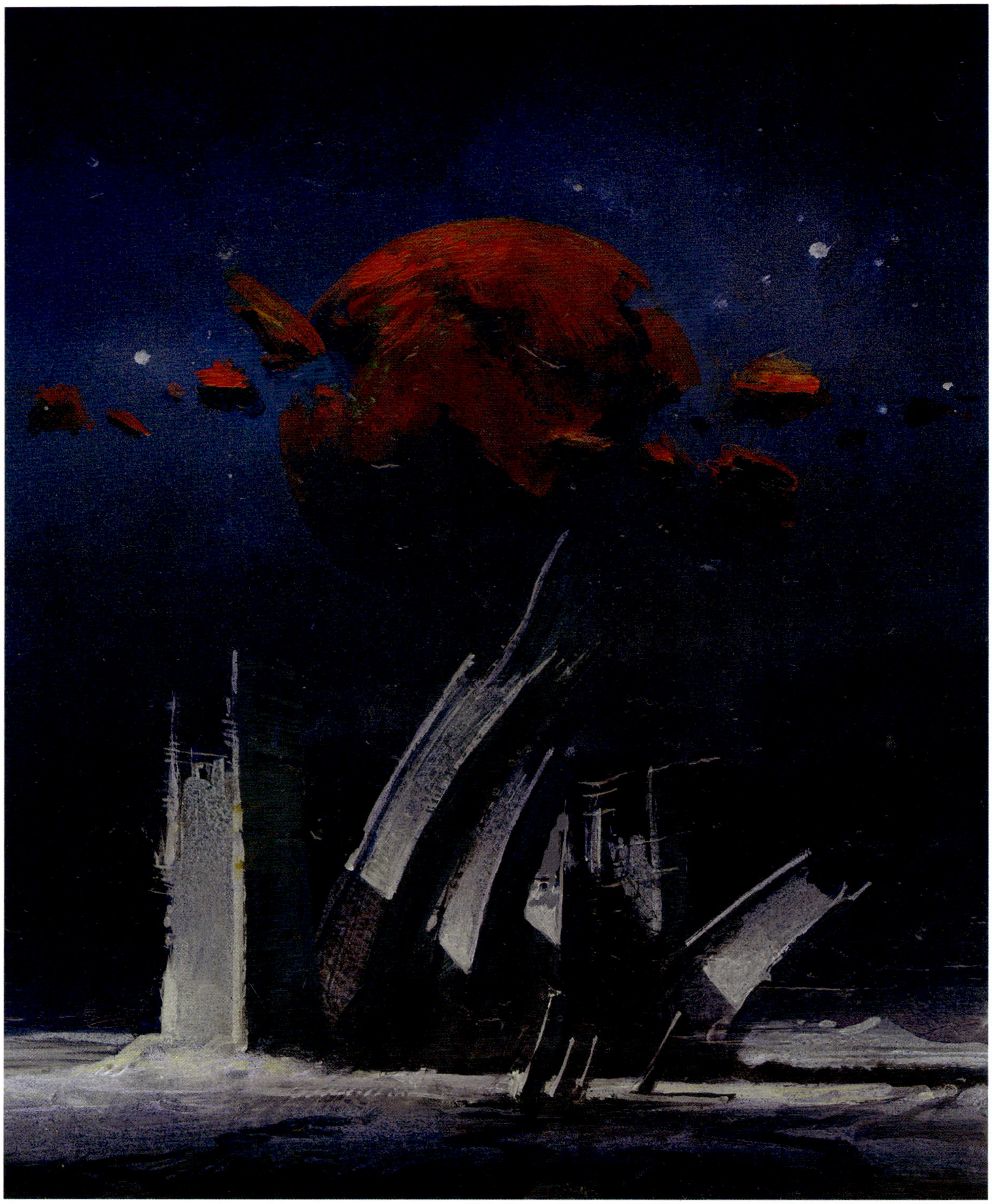

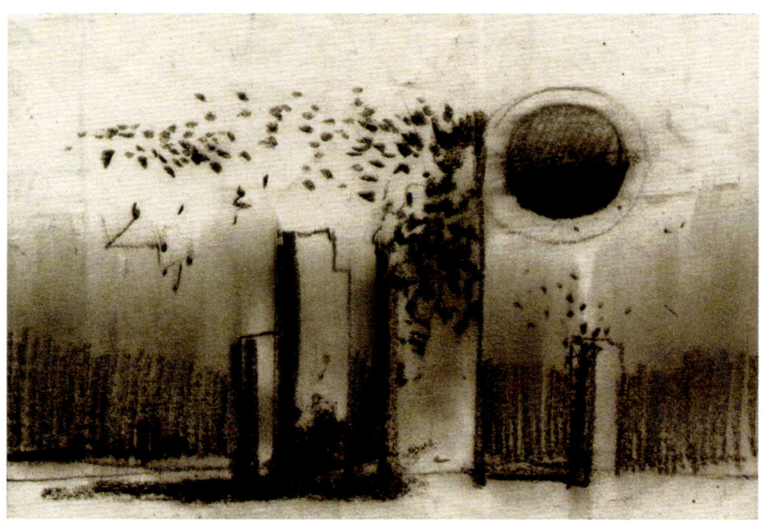

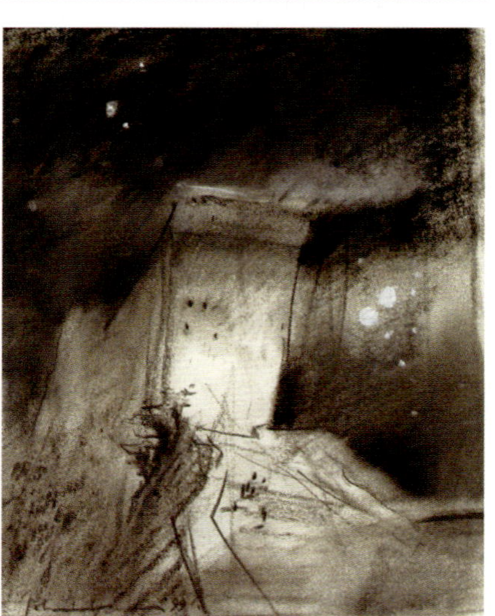

Top: *After Armageddon*. 1984

Above Left: *The Migratory Imperative*. 1989

Above Right: *Ruin*. 1991

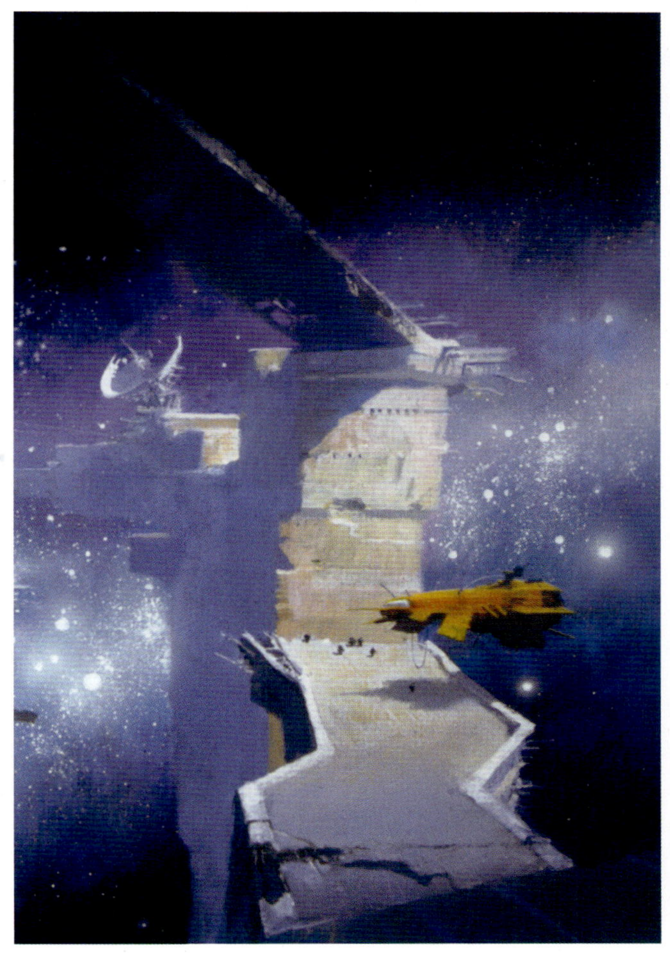

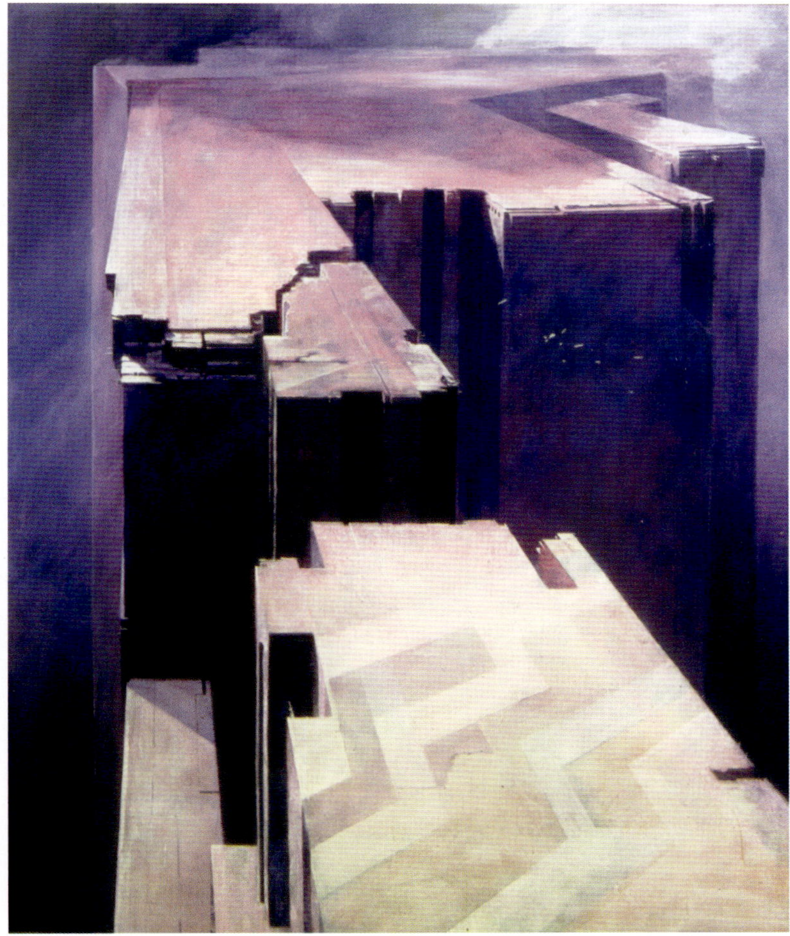

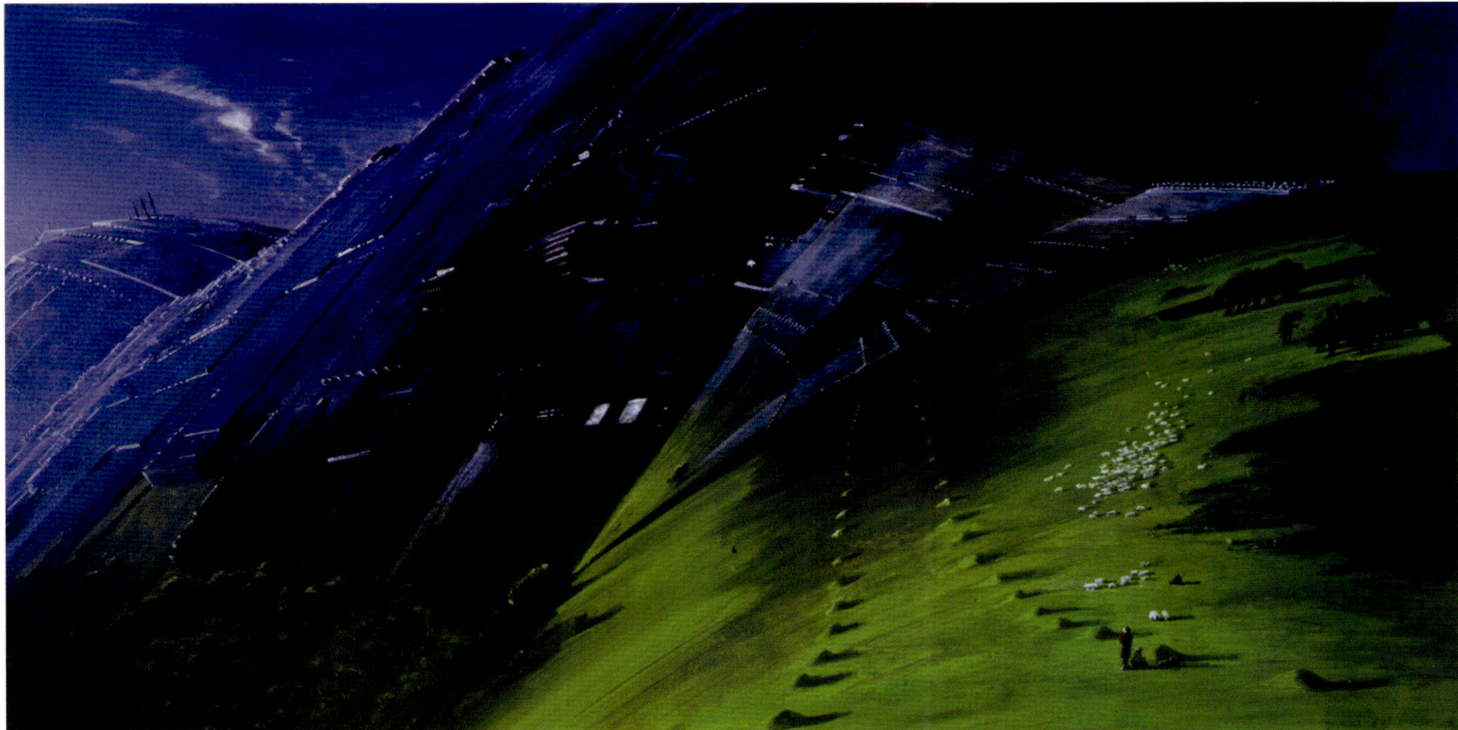

Top Left: *Stars Like Dust*, the cover of the book by Isaac Asimov. 1993

Top Right: *Mass: The Wall*. 1978

Bottom: *Mass: Shepherds on a Wreck*. 1979

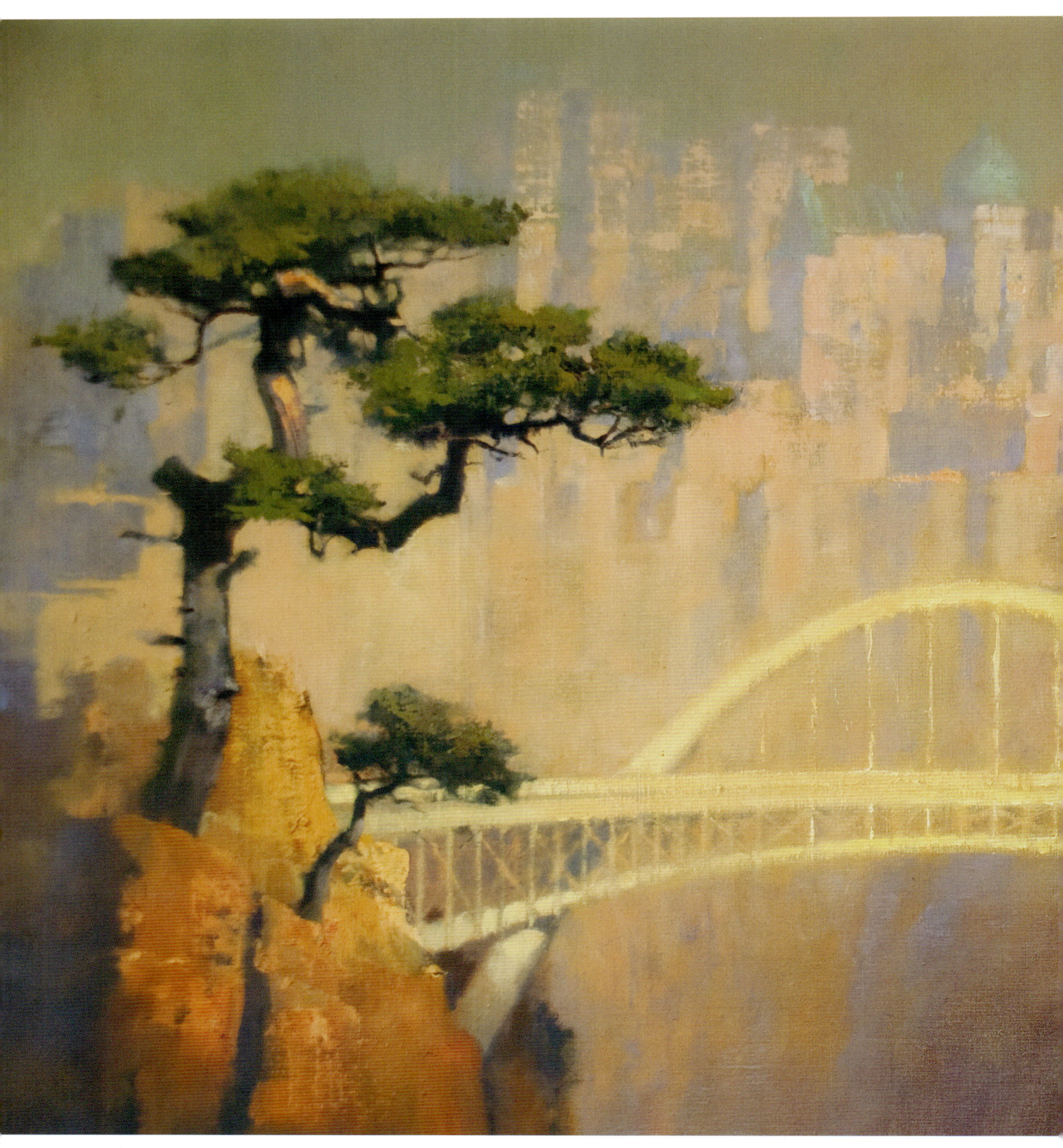

HIDDEN SUNS AND THE CITY OF FIRE

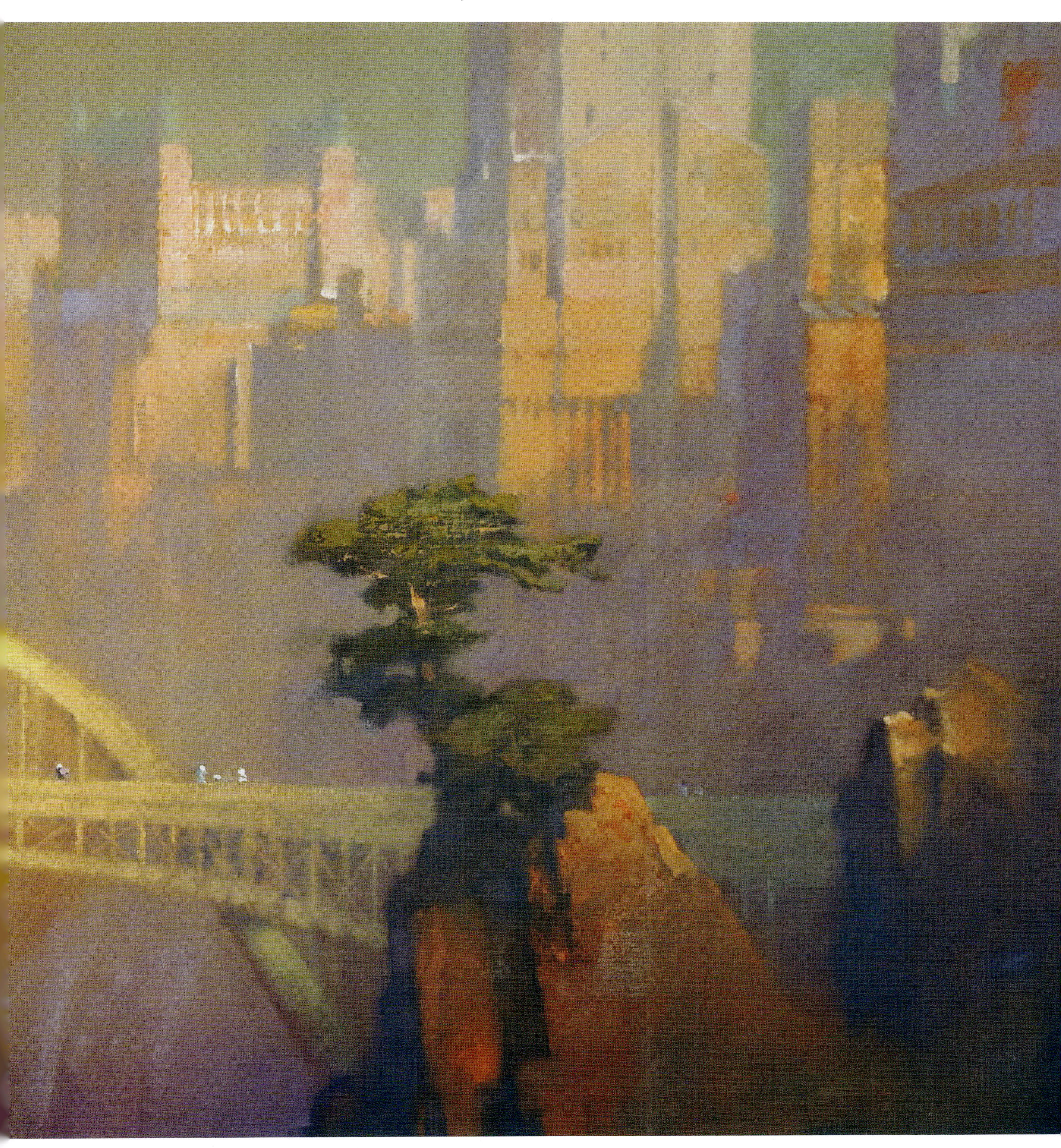

THE ROAD TO FIRE

All of the paintings in this section of the book were painted over a period of thirty years and more. Some have been worked on repeatedly during that time, and more are being added all the time. It is very much an ongoing project.

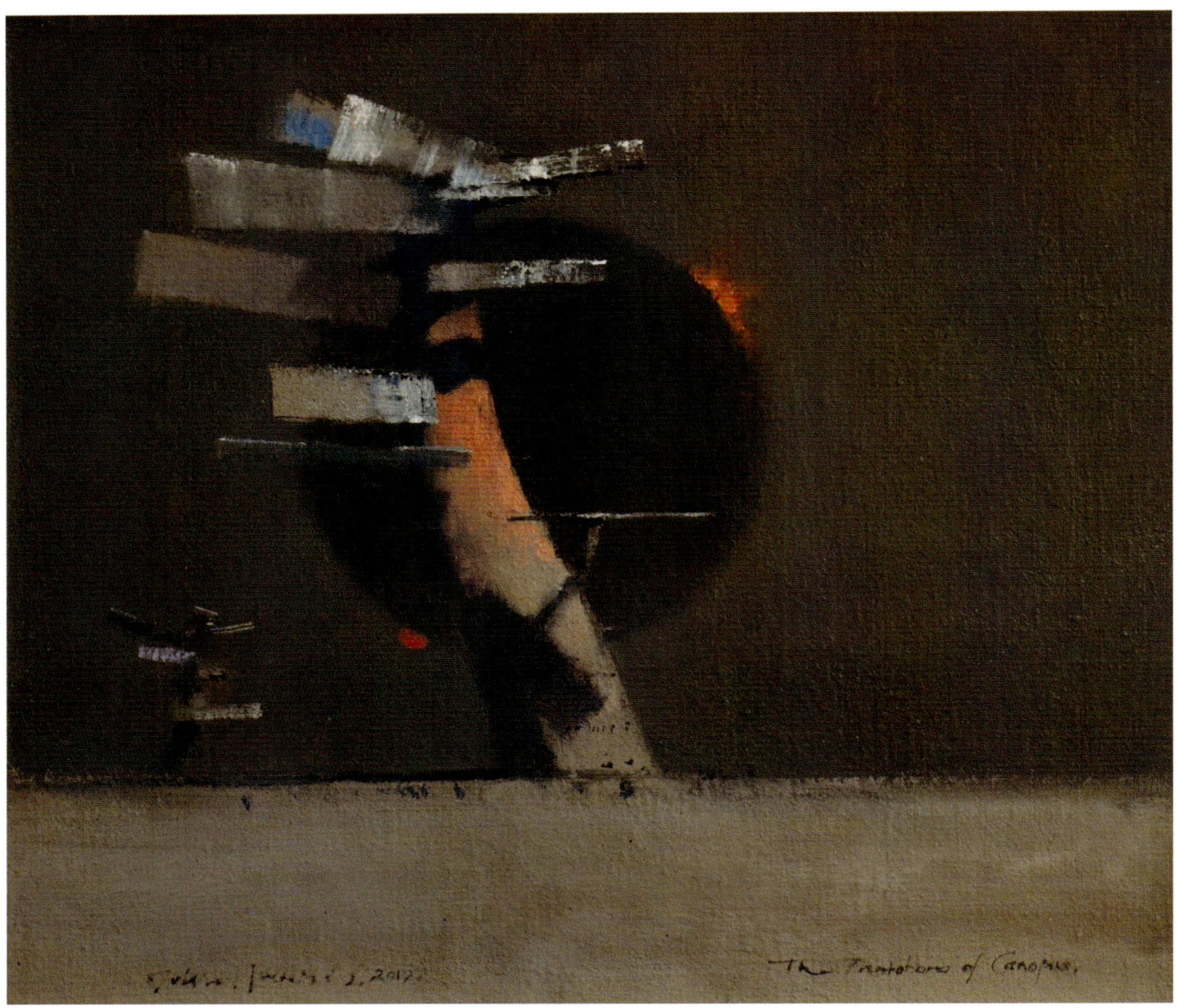

In the late 70s, I began a series of paintings which had been commissioned by Pierrot Publishing and which eventually became *MASS*. Amongst these pictures was one which I felt to be a bit of an anomaly. The piece was called *The Razor's Edge*, an allusion to the Katha Upanishad:

'The sharp edge of a razor is difficult to pass along,
Thus the wise say, the path to salvation is hard.'

When I had completed the picture, I had the feeling that it had come from another part of me, almost an alternate reality. The picture showed a girl walking along the top of a very tall wall, zig-zagging its way towards a temple in the light of a full moon. Around her lay a city which had the character of something that might have been found in Asia, certainly not of this age and probably very ancient .

For several years, the piece stuck there, not really belonging to the sequence of other images. Then, one day while I was going through my old work, I began to think about the kind of place it depicted, and what sort of culture would give rise to such an event. Almost immediately, I thought of it as a Rite of Passage. The feminine, lunar character of the image suggested a counterpoint of a male-oriented Rite involving the Sun, which developed into the idea of an event centring on a solar eclipse known as The Rite of the Hidden Sun.

From this, the whole culture assembled itself in my mind, complete with a city and history unlike anything I knew of. Over the intervening years, I have fleshed it out to incorporate well over seventy paintings and drawings, with several thousand words of text. The image of a hidden sun spilled over into a number of otherwise unrelated images, some of which are shown here. The main body of

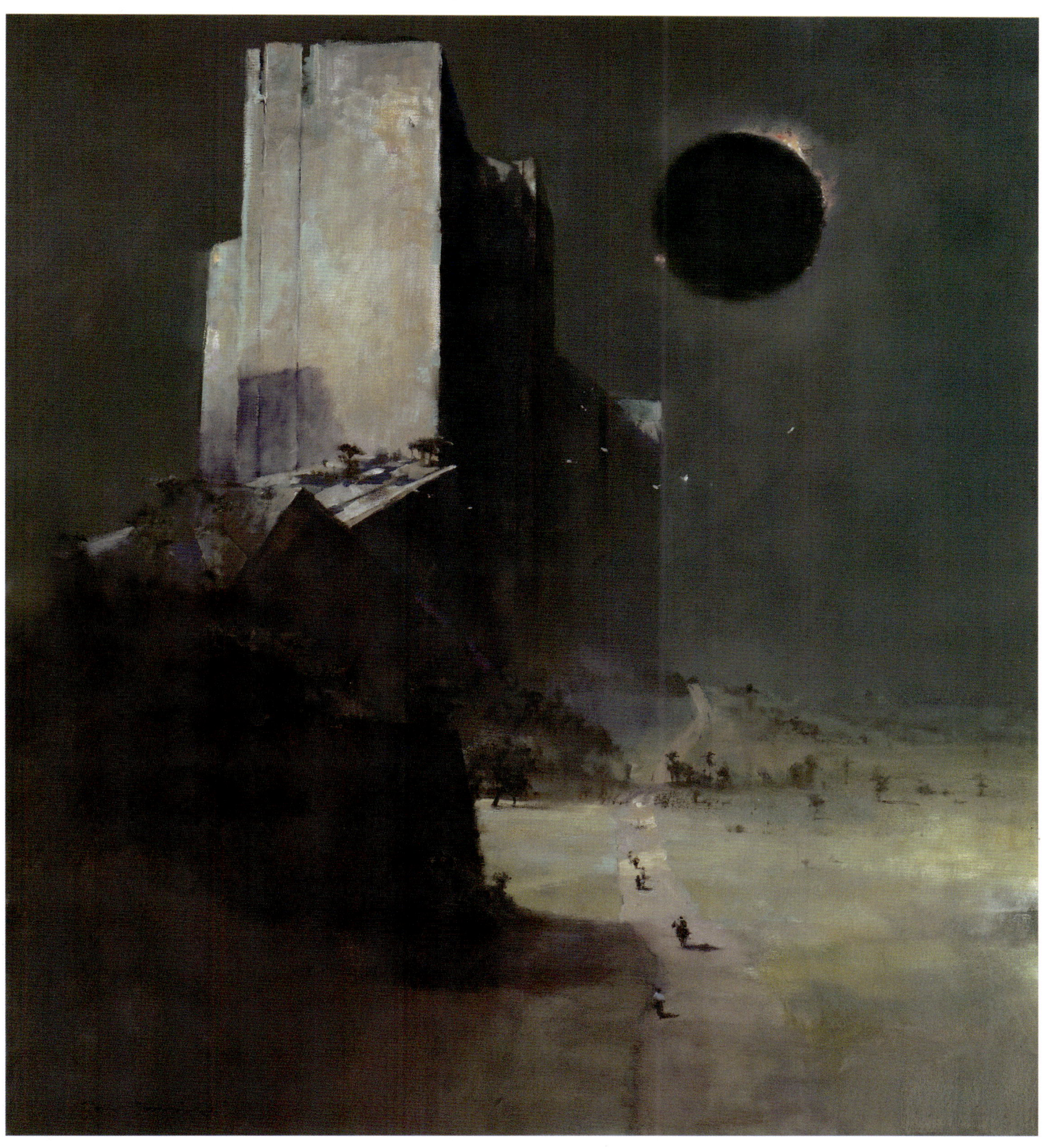

Above: *The Road to Fire.* 2013

Opposite: *The Photobors of Canopus.* 2011

Previous Spread: *Bridge of Cotl*

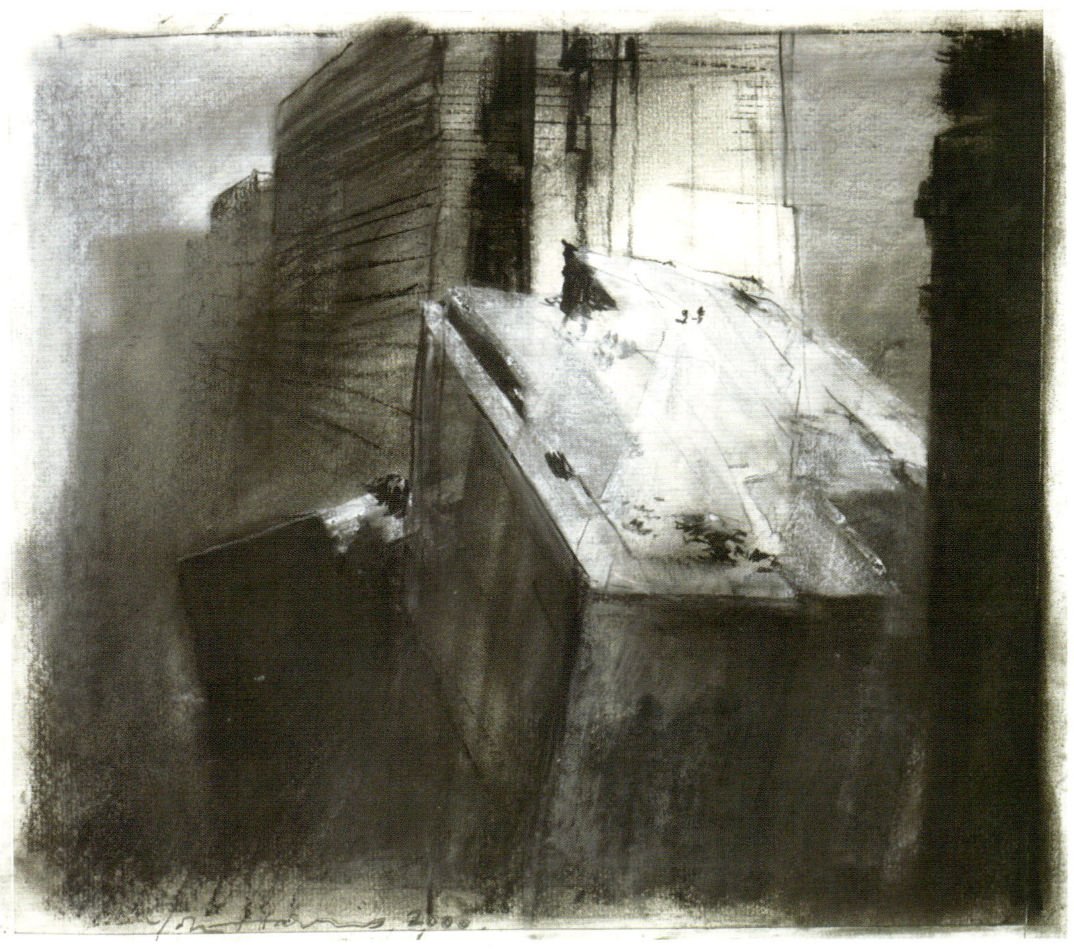

Above: *The Ruined Wall*, charcoal sketch
Opposite Top: *The Approach to The Wall*
Opposite Below: *The Wall in Summer*, a pastel study

this collection, however, relates to the city of Fire and the Rites associated with it.

As a whole, the images and the text that goes with them may be seen as having a separate identity to my other work. This is a conceptually driven project which has gone through several metamorphoses. From that first picture of the girl on the wall, now called *The Rite of the Silver Path*, it has become something similar to a graphic novel, an illustrated diary of an artist's travels through an unknown region. This element of discovering the unknown was one of the key motivations behind the series.

In the nineteenth century, artists from Europe travelled to all sorts of exotic places across the globe, bringing back paintings to a public who had never seen images of the pyramids or the walled cities of Asia. They must have created a real sense of wonder, and even longing, within many who saw them. Sadly, such a situation no longer exists. There is hardly any spot on the globe that has not been photographed or filmed.

I started this fantasy of an artist, travelling in an old-fashioned way, probably on a donkey, armed with sketchbooks and paints, towards the fabled city of Nandagni, recording along the way several improbable sights, such as an enormous ruined wall zig-zagging across a vast plain, or the ruins of giant 'sunflowers': solar generators capable, like their namesakes, of following the sun and still occasionally jerking fitfully, as if remembering their role. I imagined people suspended in cages over still water, waiting for the stars to appear; and eventually on reaching the city, discovering that it had been built on an active volcano, yet somehow seems to survive intact. And here the artist discovers that the secret of the city's survival lies, in some way which the artist does not understand, in the strange and threatening Rites of Passage which he observes.

So this odd, quixotic little task is really an unending journey into an imagined world, a place that no-one but this artist has seen, my own Shangri-la.

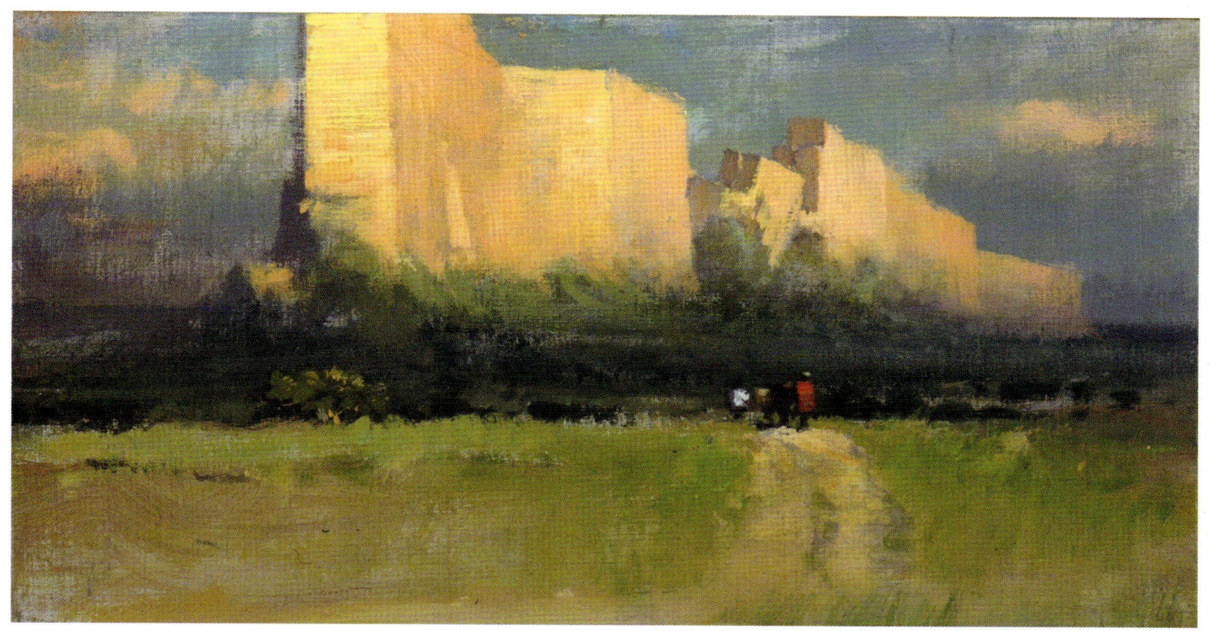

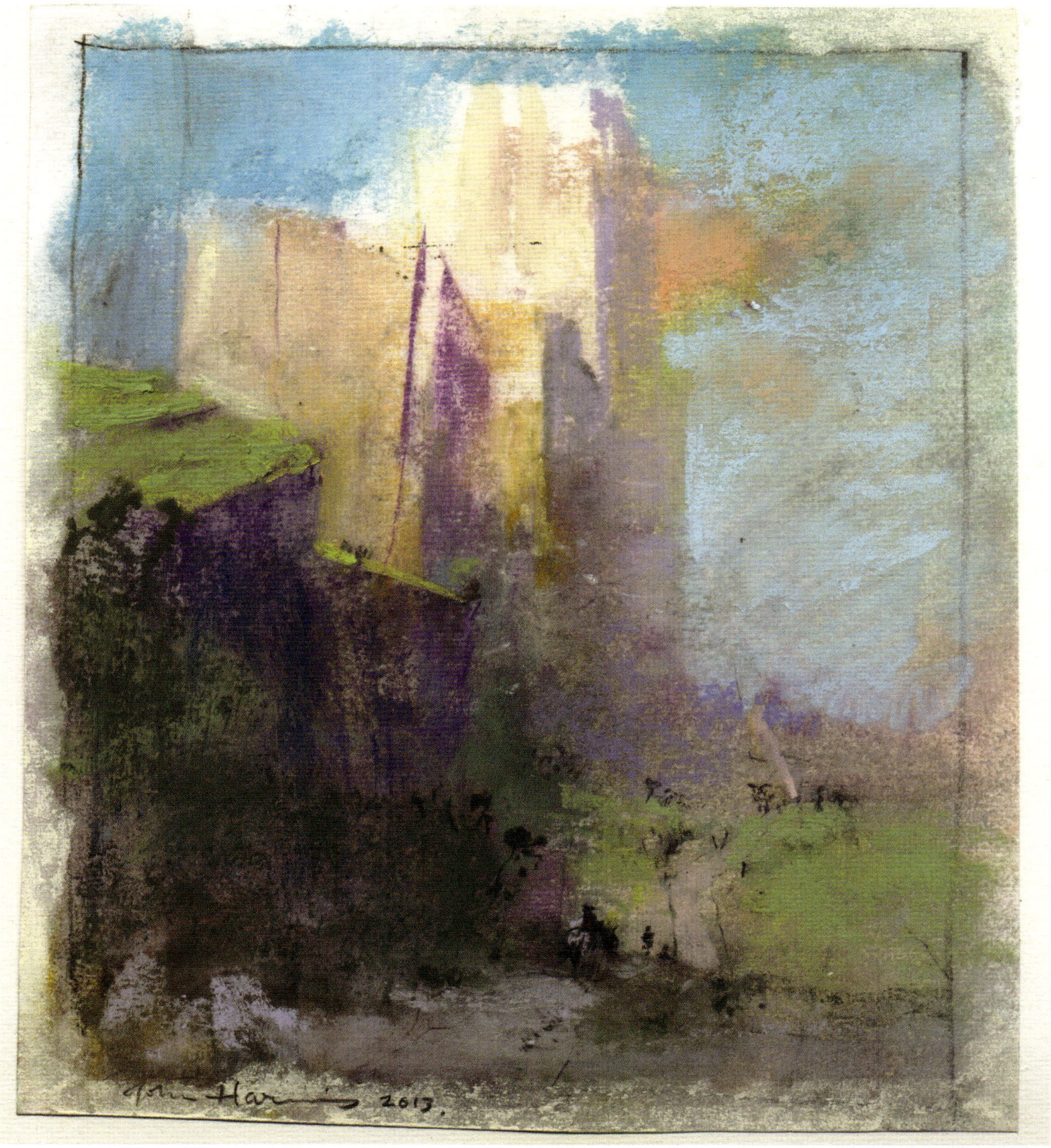

The artist's journey into the unknown regions begins with the Wall, a vast and crumbling structure whose makers and their purpose are lost in the mists of antiquity.

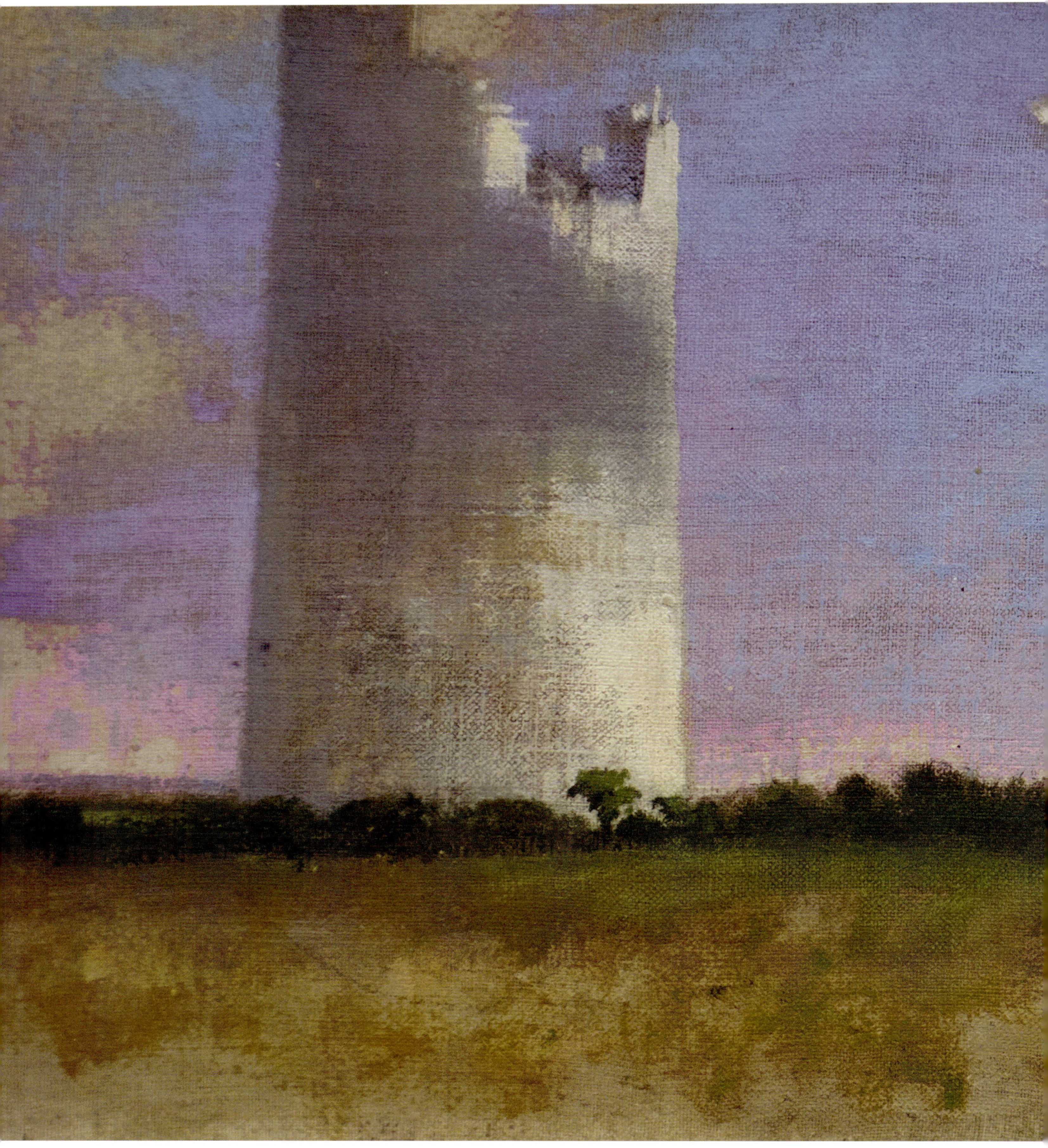

Above: *The Road to Drumm Dunn*

The 'sunflowers' on the road to Drumm Dunn, evidence of an ancient but sophisticated solar technology. They are now mostly in ruins but occasionally twitch in response to the sun.

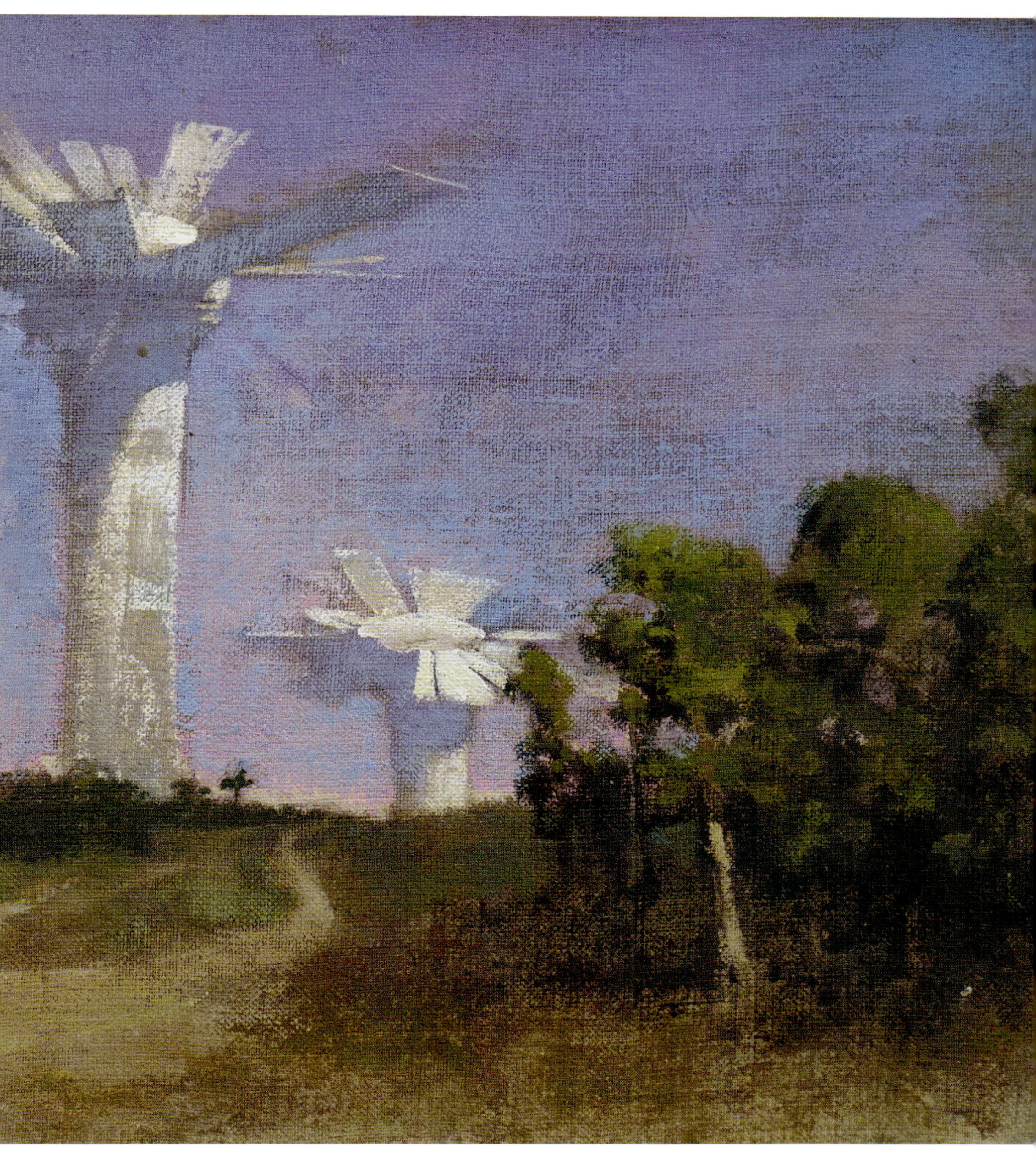

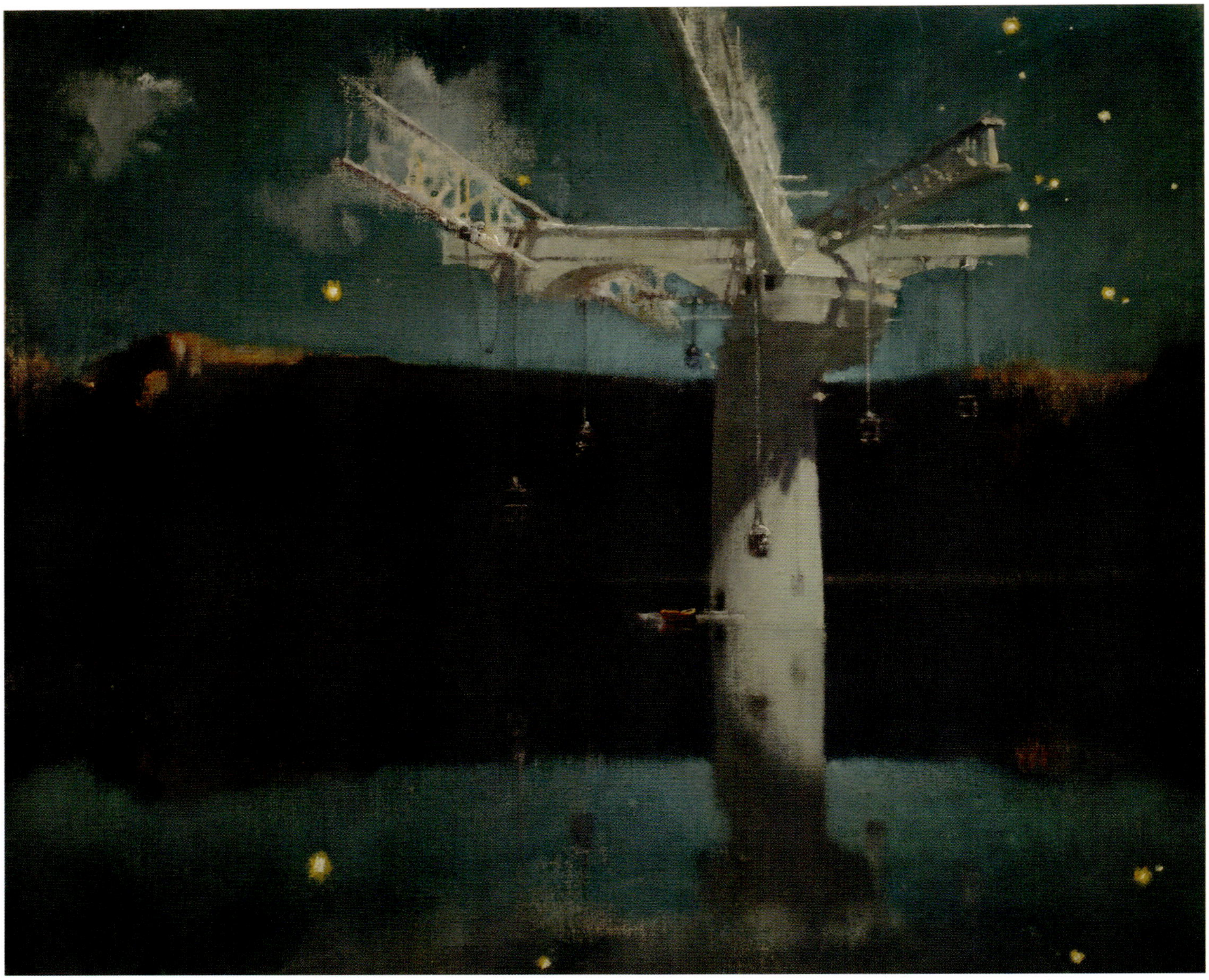

Drumm Dunn, set in the mountains, where people spend nights in contemplation in cages that hang over the still waters of a tarn.

Above: *Drumm Dunn*

Right: *The Watchers of Drumm Dunn*, a study

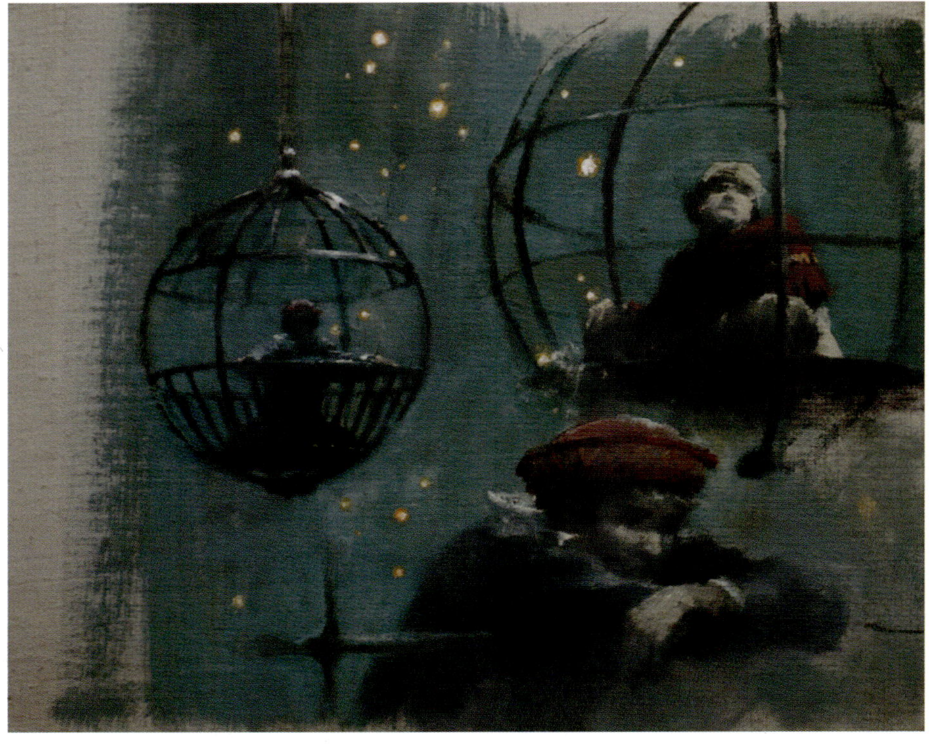

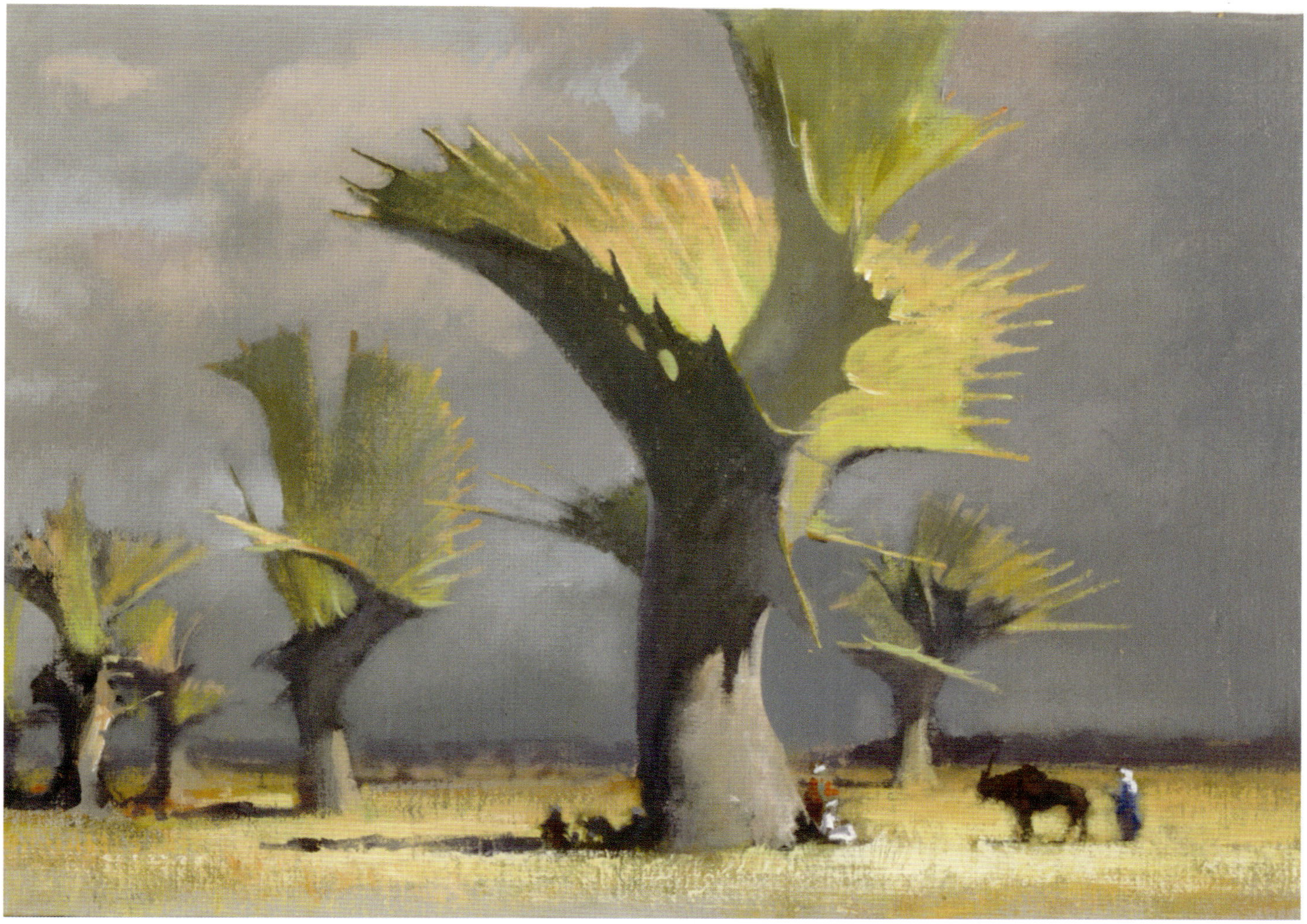

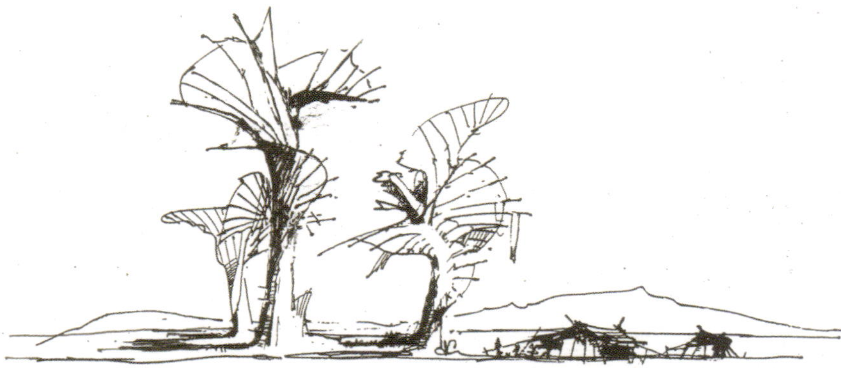

The desert region to the west of Drumm Dunn, peopled by nomads. The groves of Arantogas are a source of water for their cattle.

Above & Left: *Herdsmen in the Arantoga Grove,* painting and sketch

Below: *The Moon setting over Nandagni*

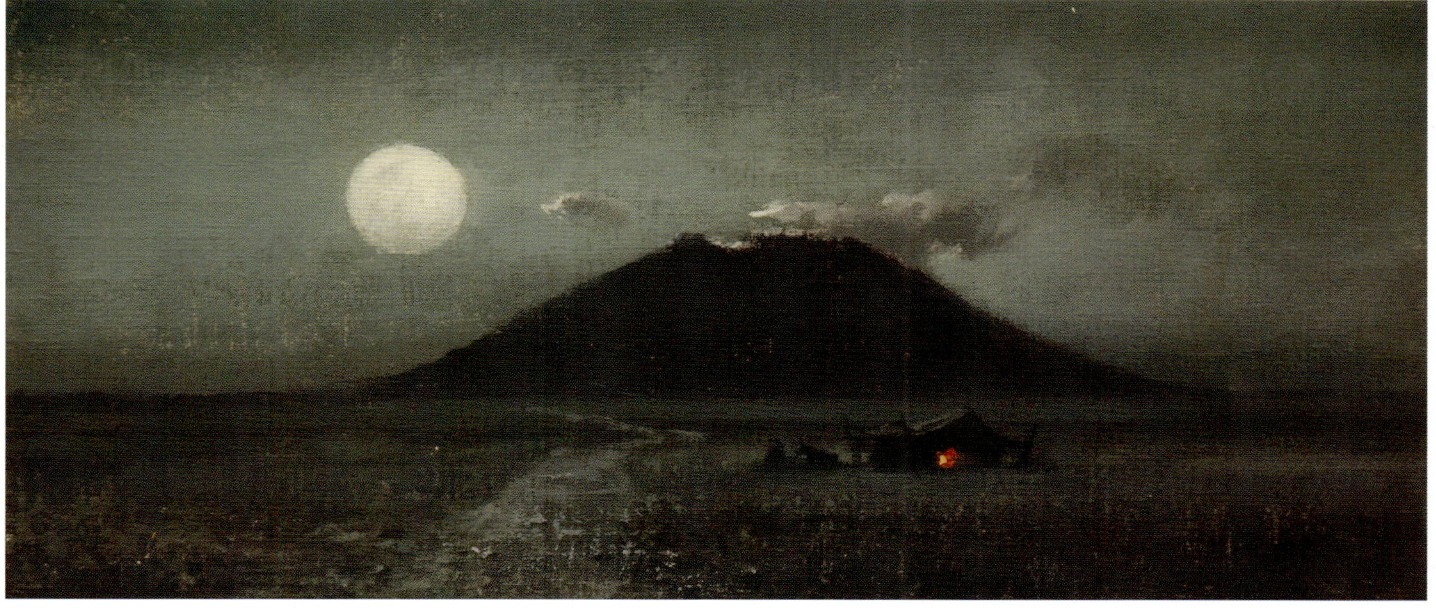

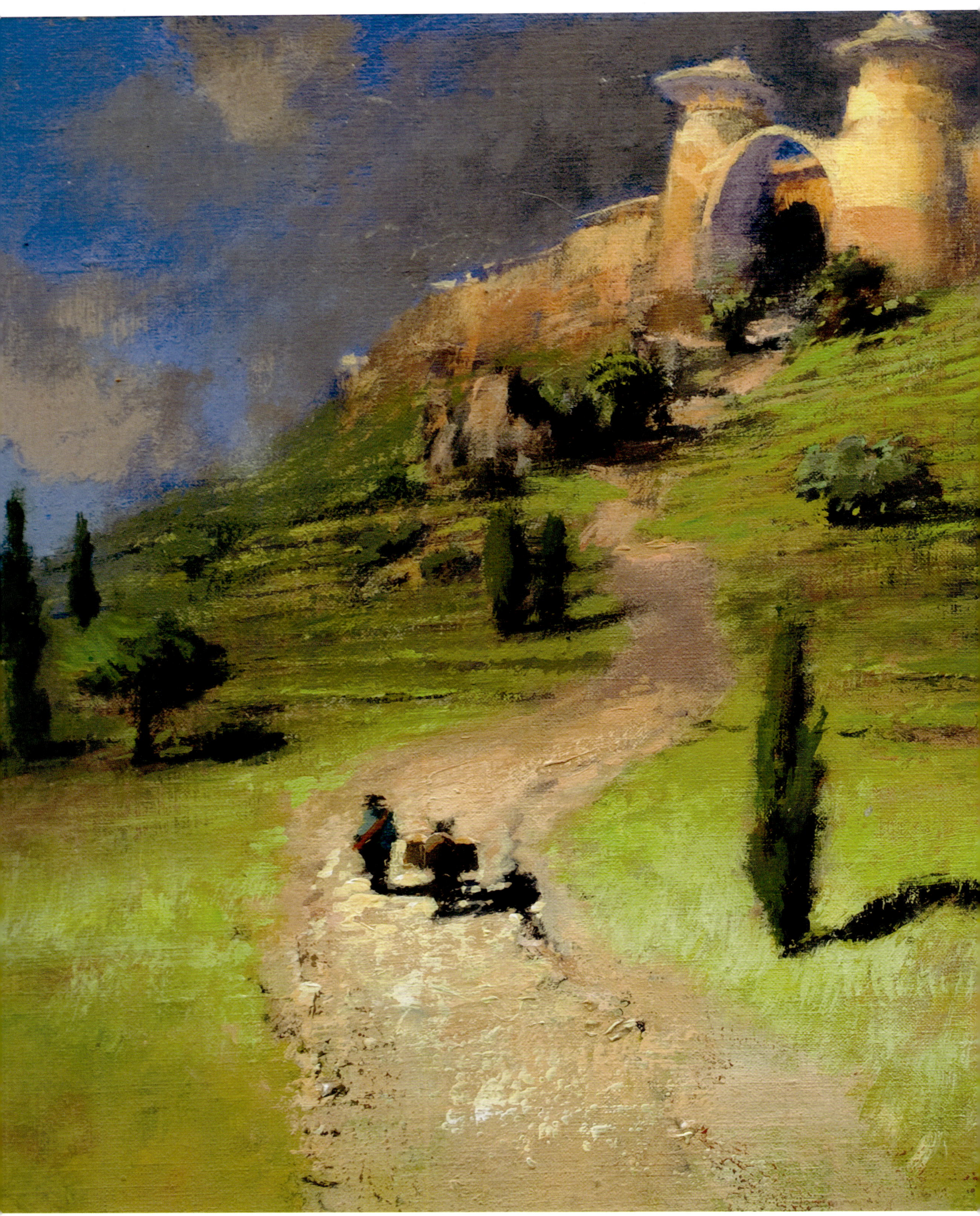

Above: *The Ascent to the Welcome Gate*

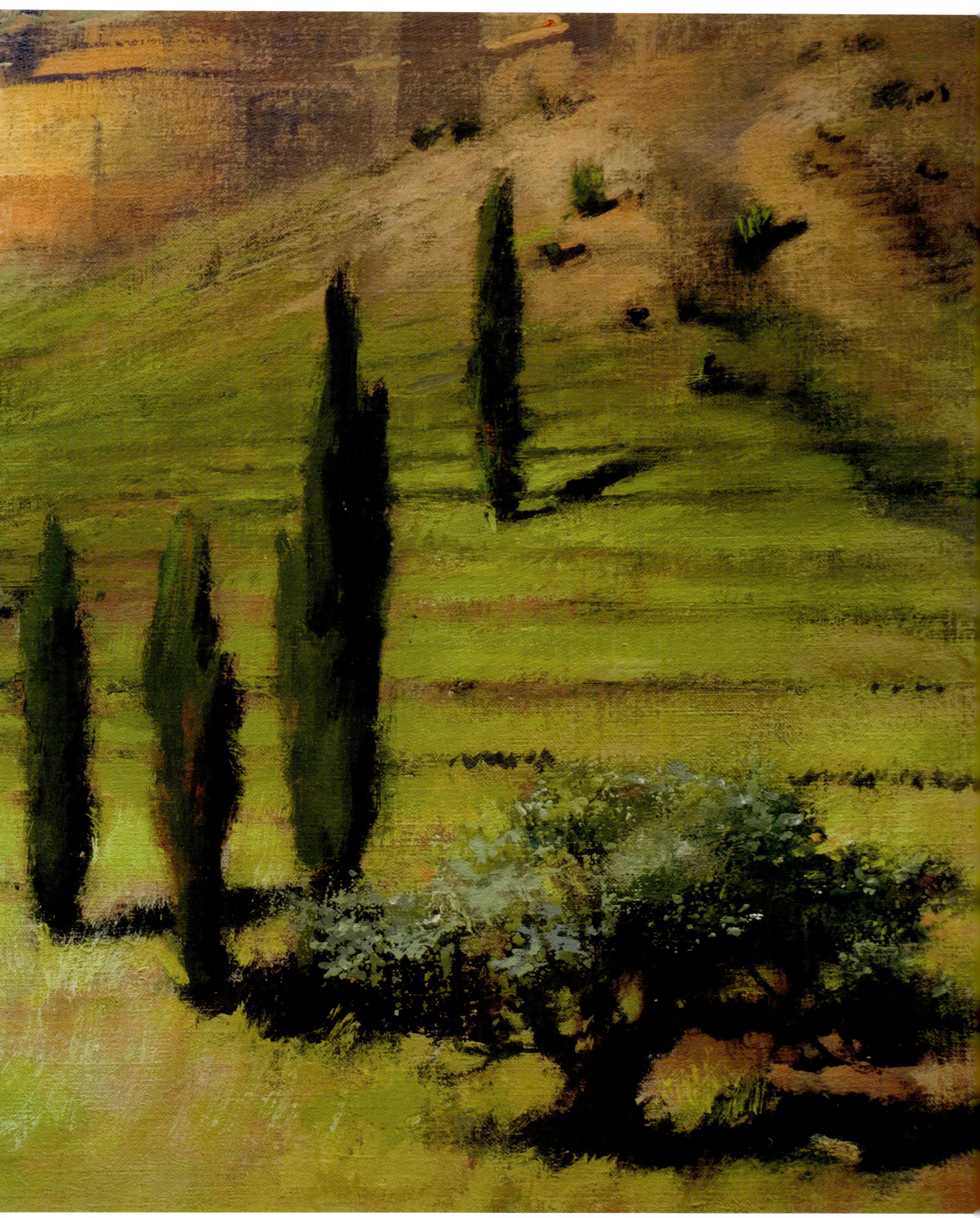

THE GATES AND THE RIM ROAD

Around the perimeter of the crater runs the Rim Road. At the cardinal points of the compass, the road is interrupted by four great gates, all very different from each other.

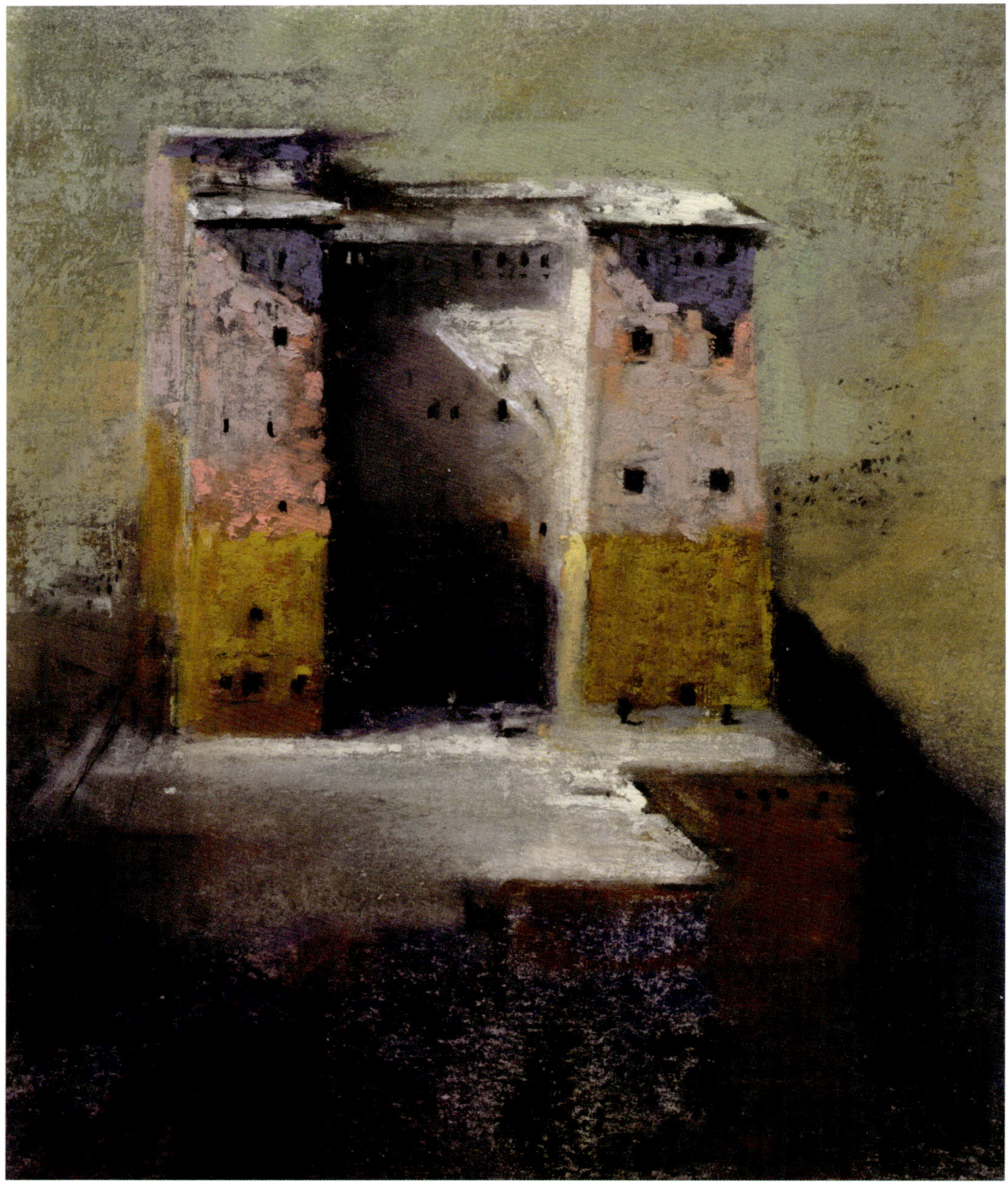

Above: *Four-Tower Gate*
Opposite: *The Street of Clouds*

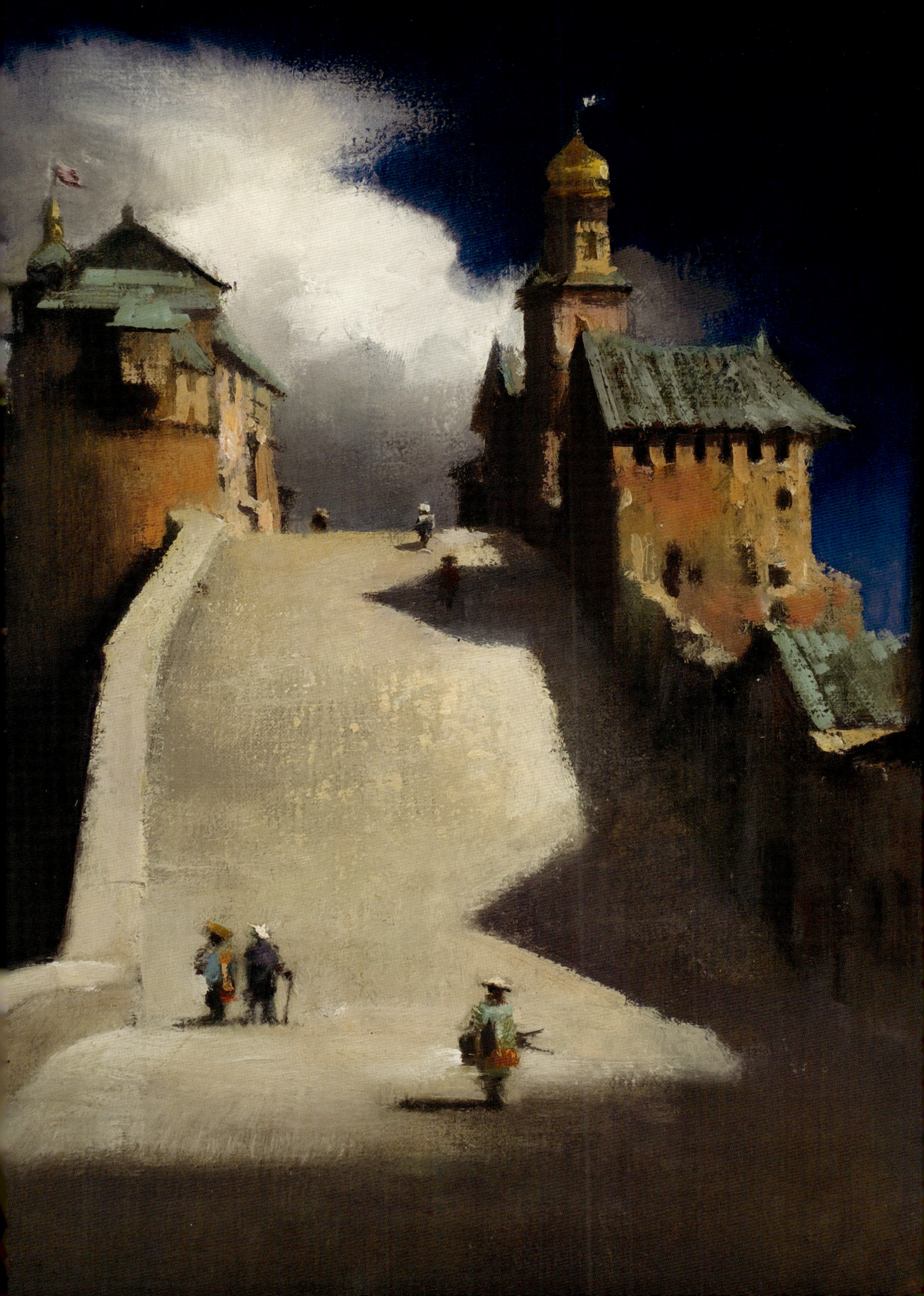

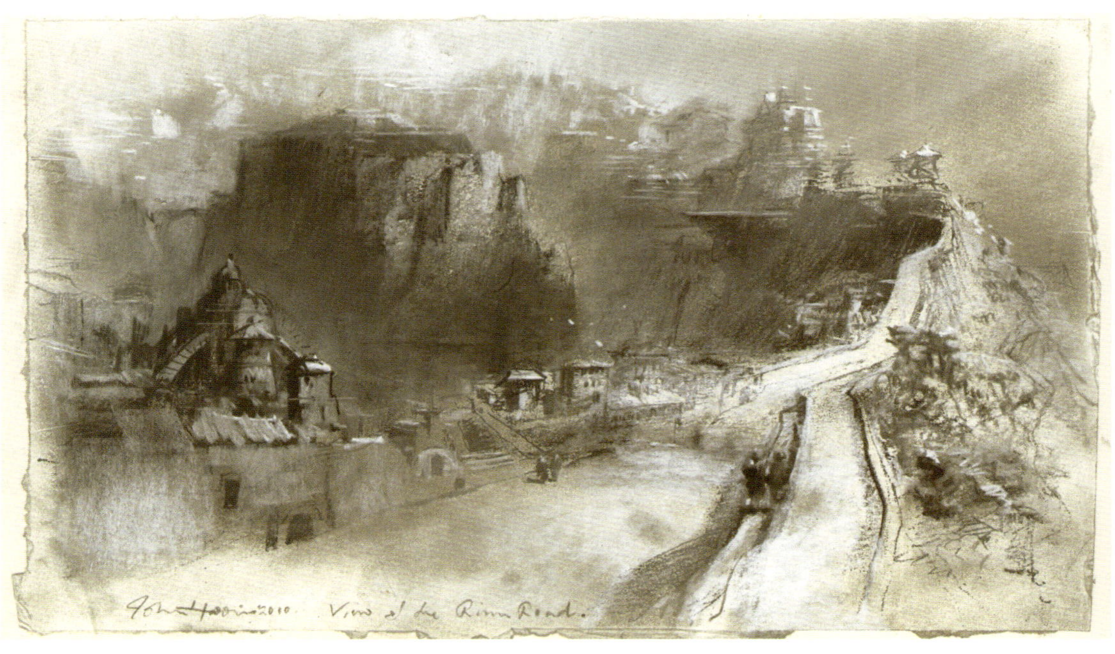

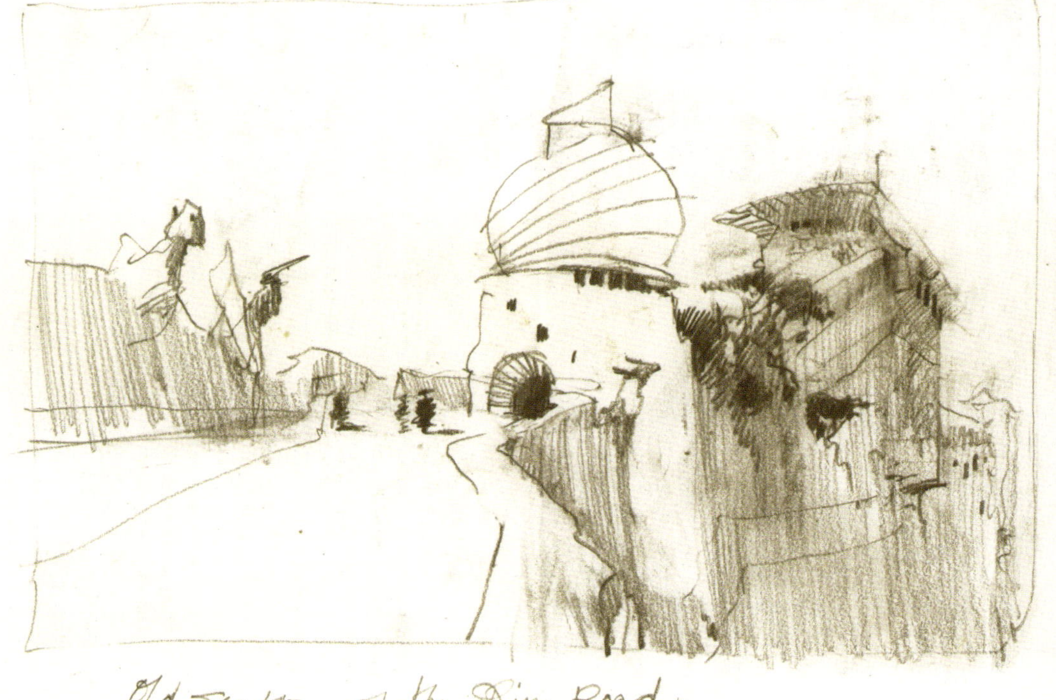

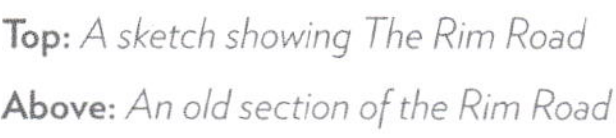

Top: *A sketch showing The Rim Road*

Above: *An old section of the Rim Road*

Right: *Flag Gate*

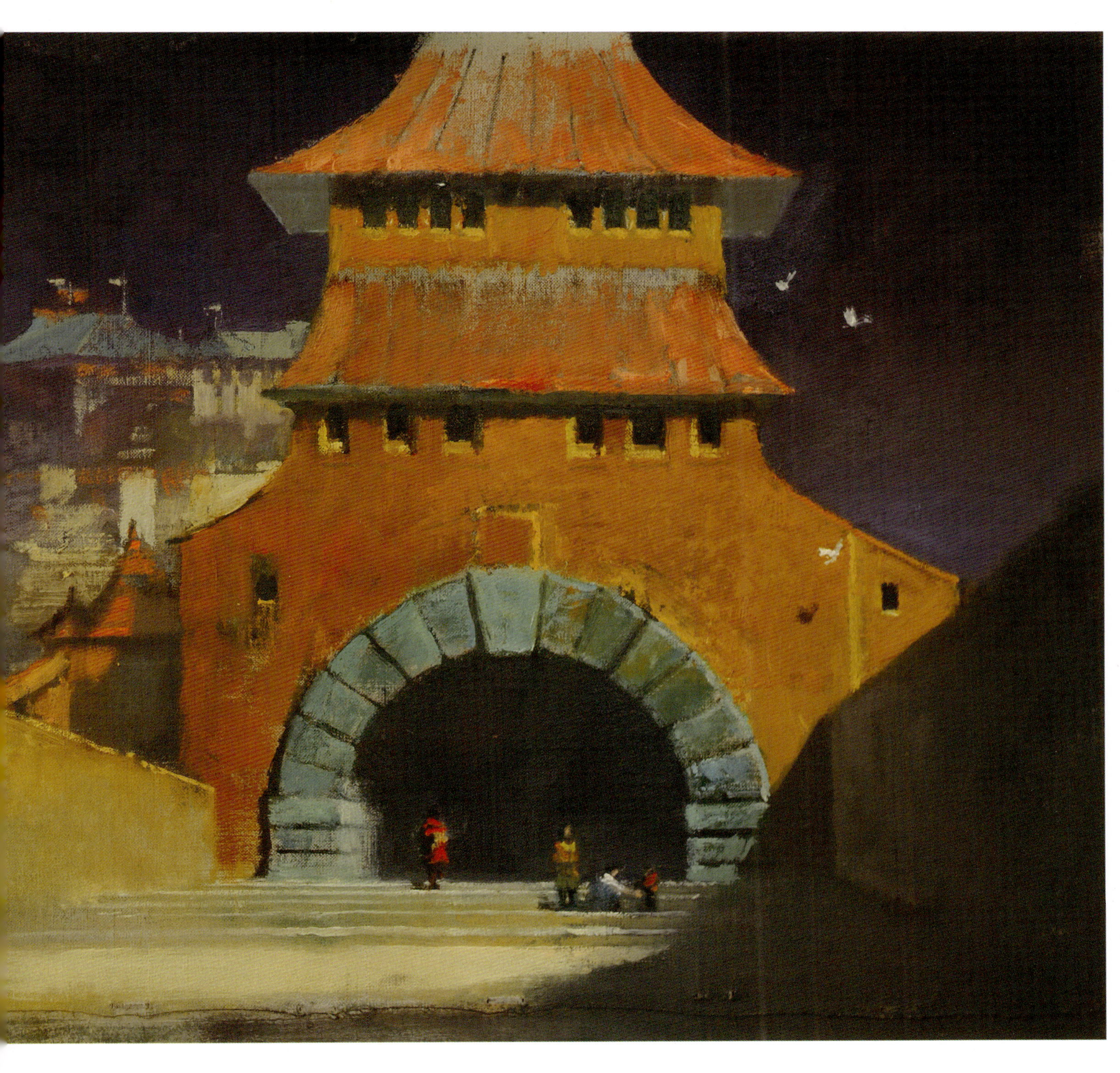

THE RITE OF THE SILVER PATH

This is the Rite associated with the full moon, and is undertaken only by women. It requires aspirants to walk the Zig Zag, with only the light of the moon to guide them, to the Shrine of the Flame. Only those who have mastered equanimity can attempt the feat. Once they arrive at the temple, they remain there for two years or more.

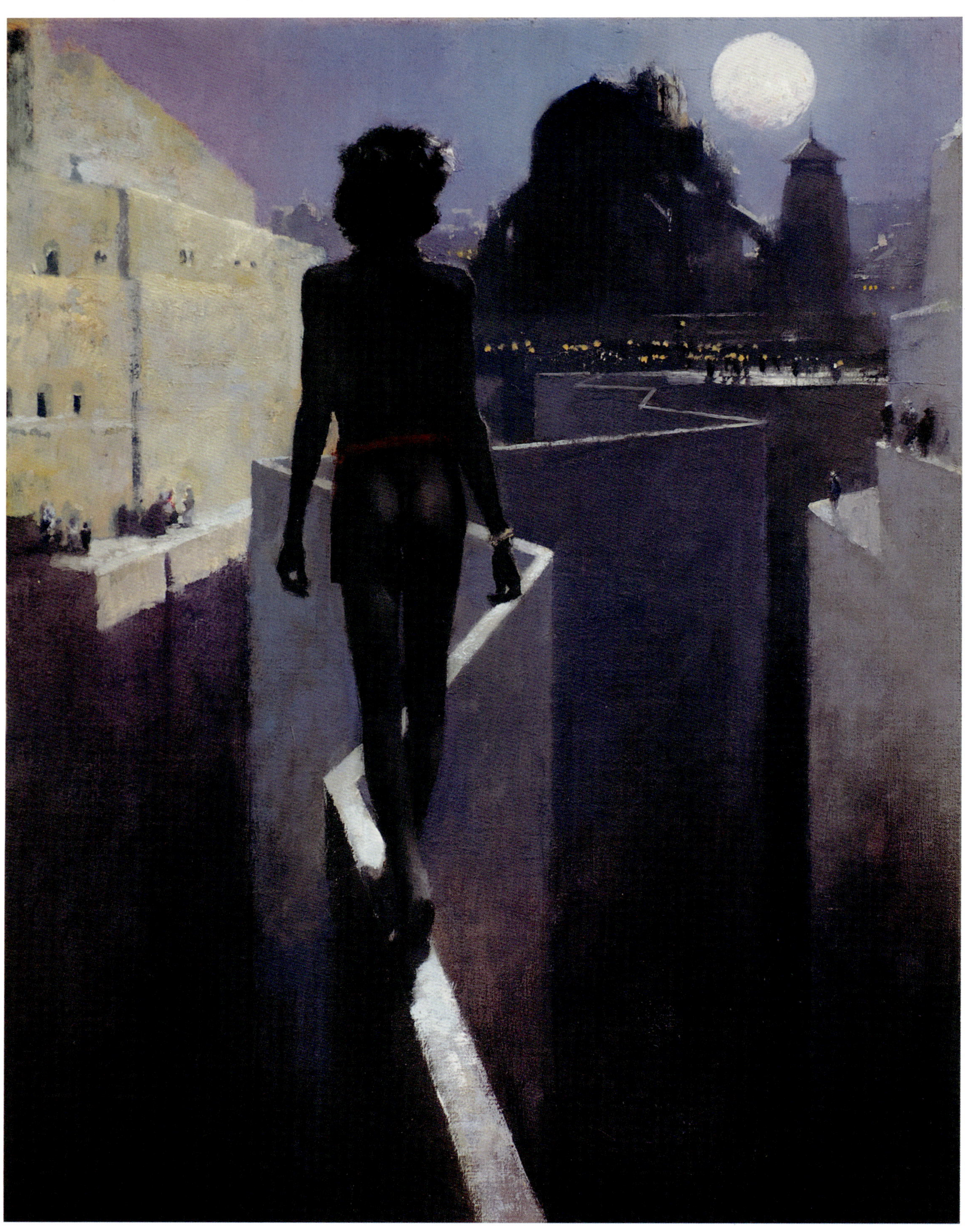

THE RITE OF THE HIDDEN SUN

The Threshold is the focal point, and it is where the Rite begins. It is from here that the young men, armed with bundles of silk, throw themselves out over the lava-filled crater, to ride the thermal storm. Their purpose is to reach the Core, a volcanic plug at the centre of the caldera.

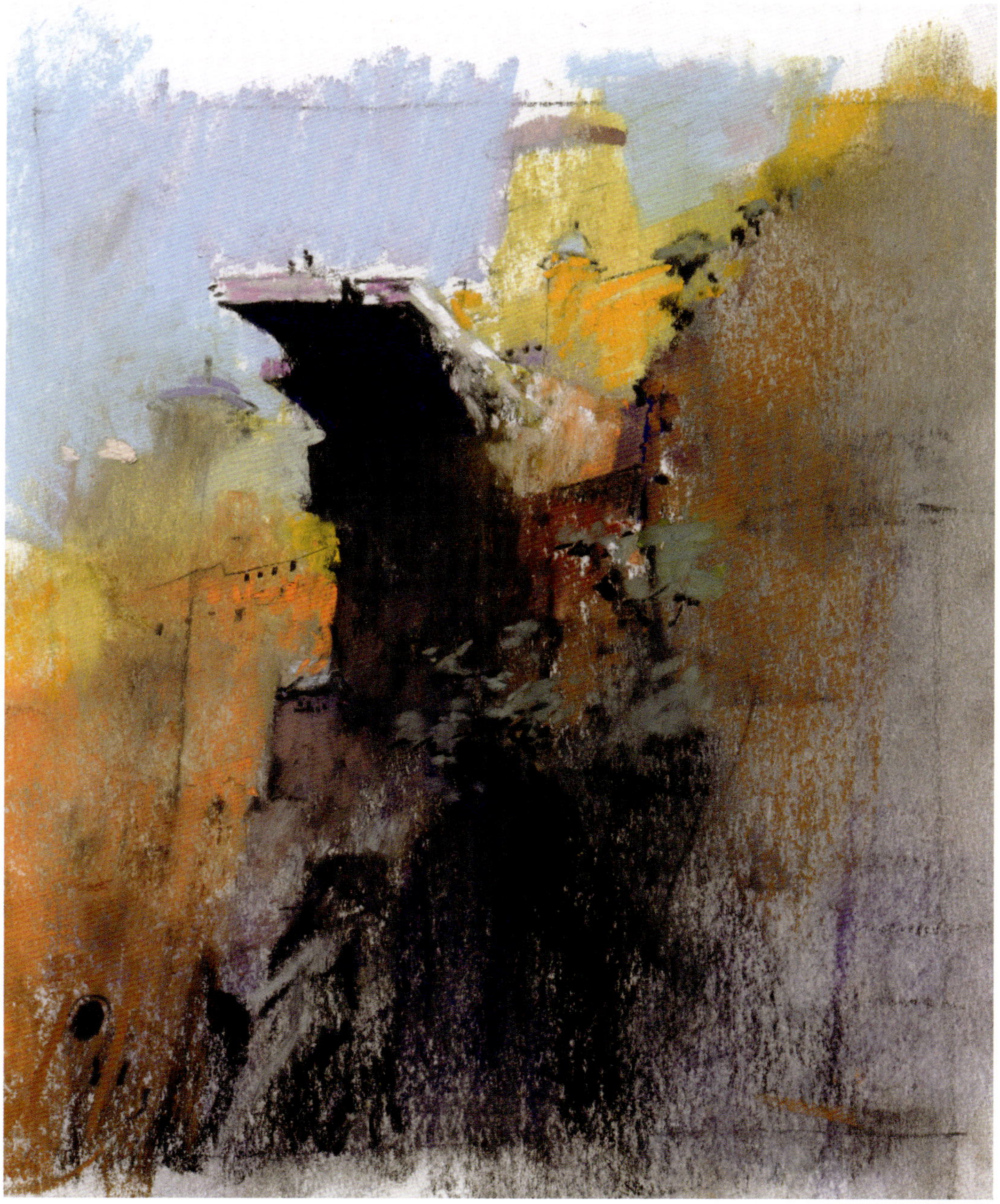

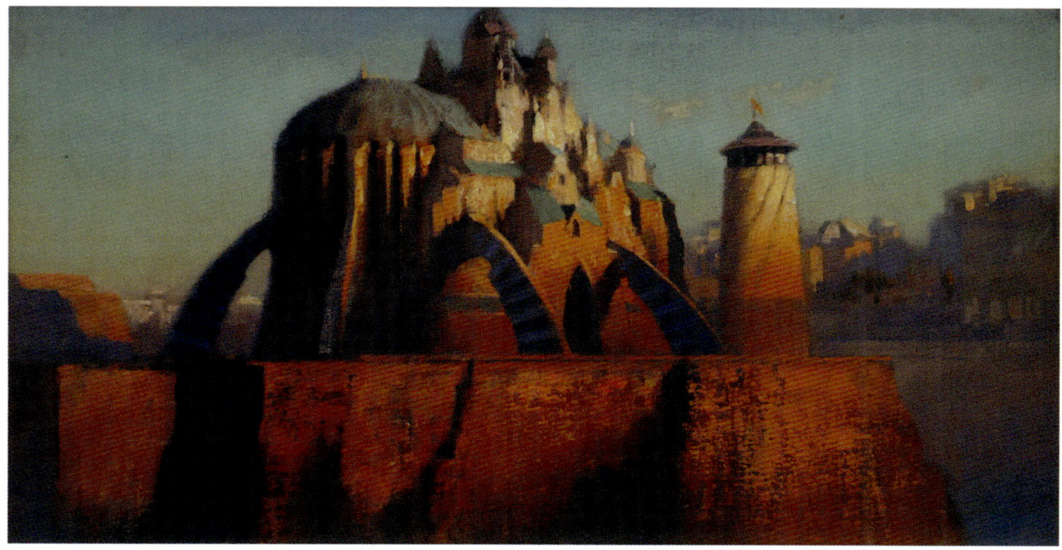

Top: *Below the Threshold*

Left: *The Shrine of the Flame*

Opposite: *The Rite of the Silver Path*

The Threshold is one of the few visible remains of the ancient structures that made up the geothermal station before the great quake, a thousand years before. It is all that was left when the bridge that originally connected the rim of the volcano to the Core collapsed. It is from this point, as the legend goes, that the young Humming Cotl launched himself out into the thermal storm with his canopy of silk in a desperate attempt to reach the Core and open the Valves. It was this act that led to the founding of the city and the Rite of the Hidden Sun.

Hundreds of years later, a second bridge was built, further round the rim of the crater, connecting to the Petty Core and on again to the Core. The people named it in honour of Cotl, and it is a tradition, that whenever a citizen steps onto the bridge, he or she makes a gesture towards the Sun, so that the founding father of the city, and his contribution, is never forgotten.

Right: *Threshold*

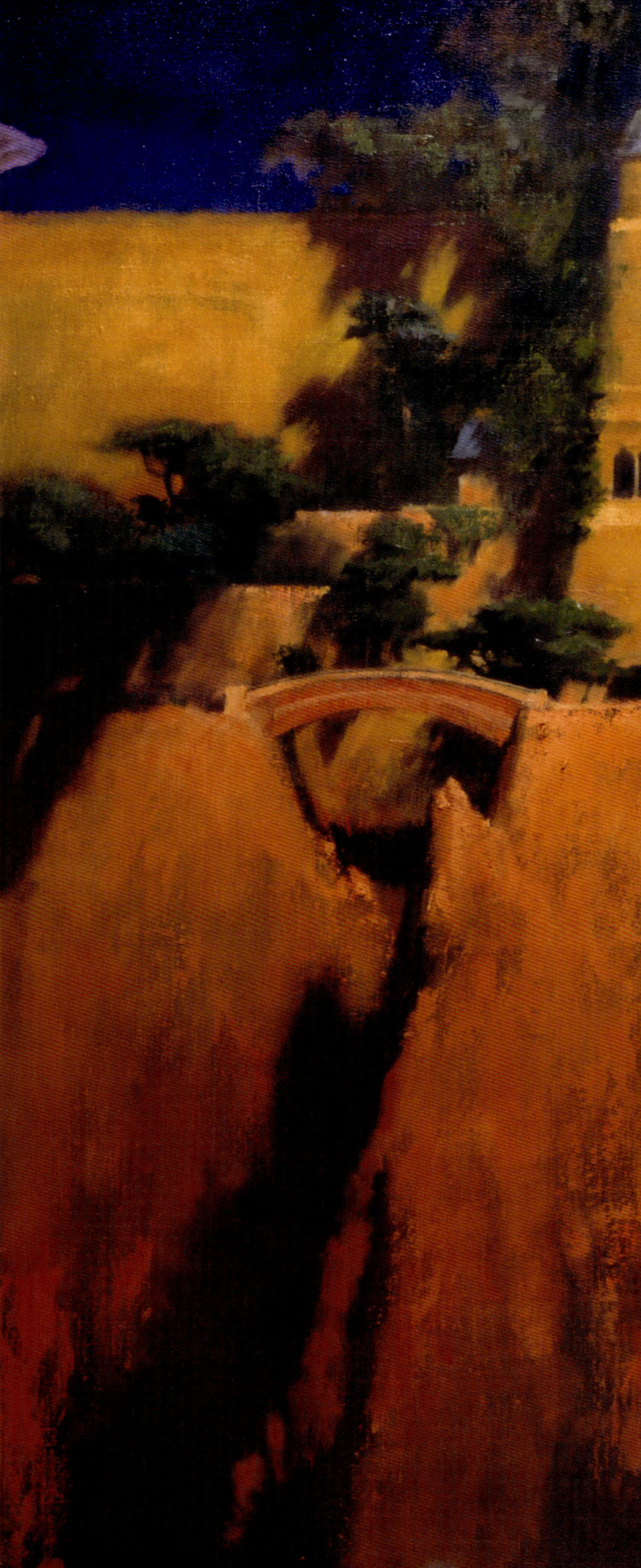

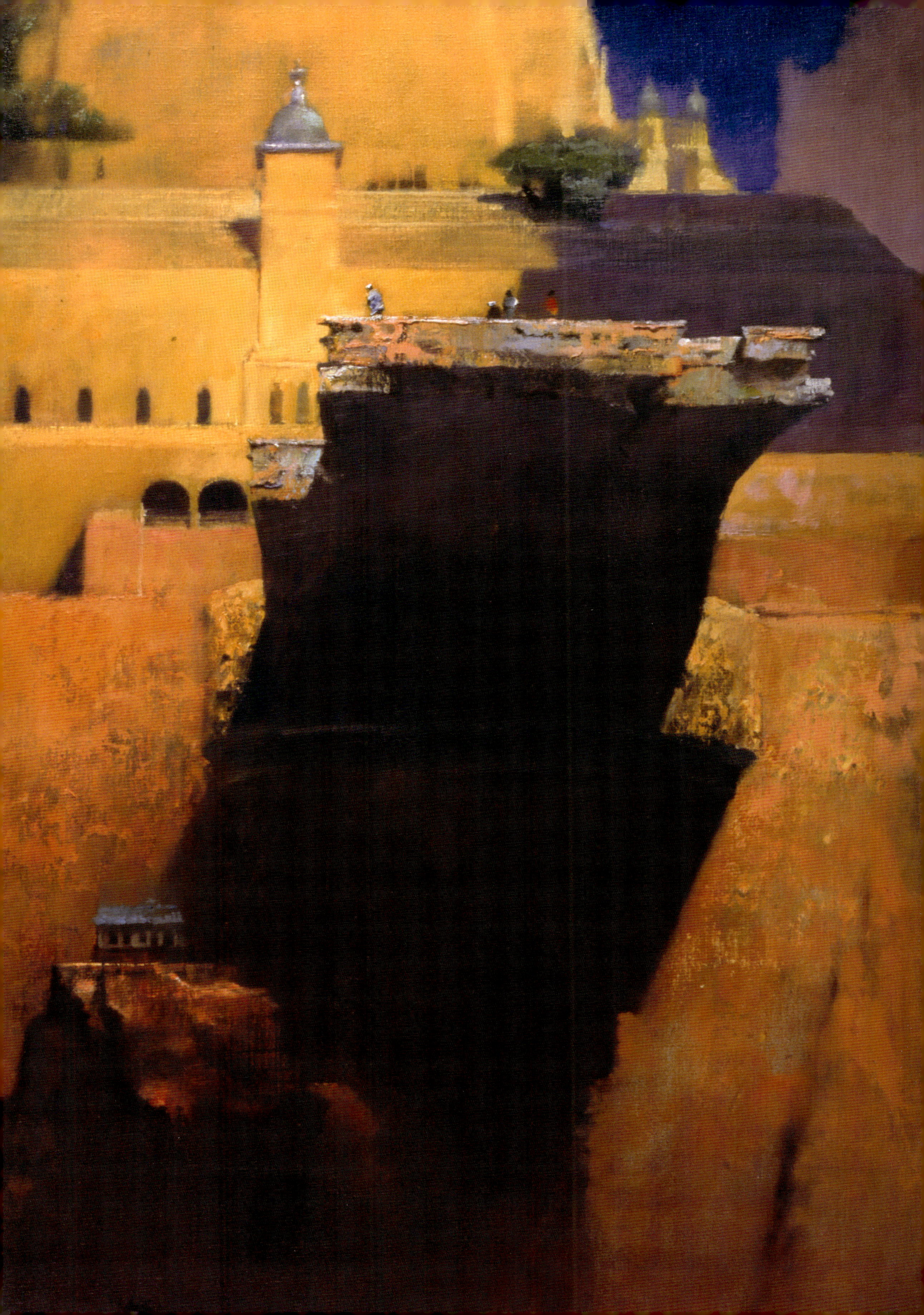

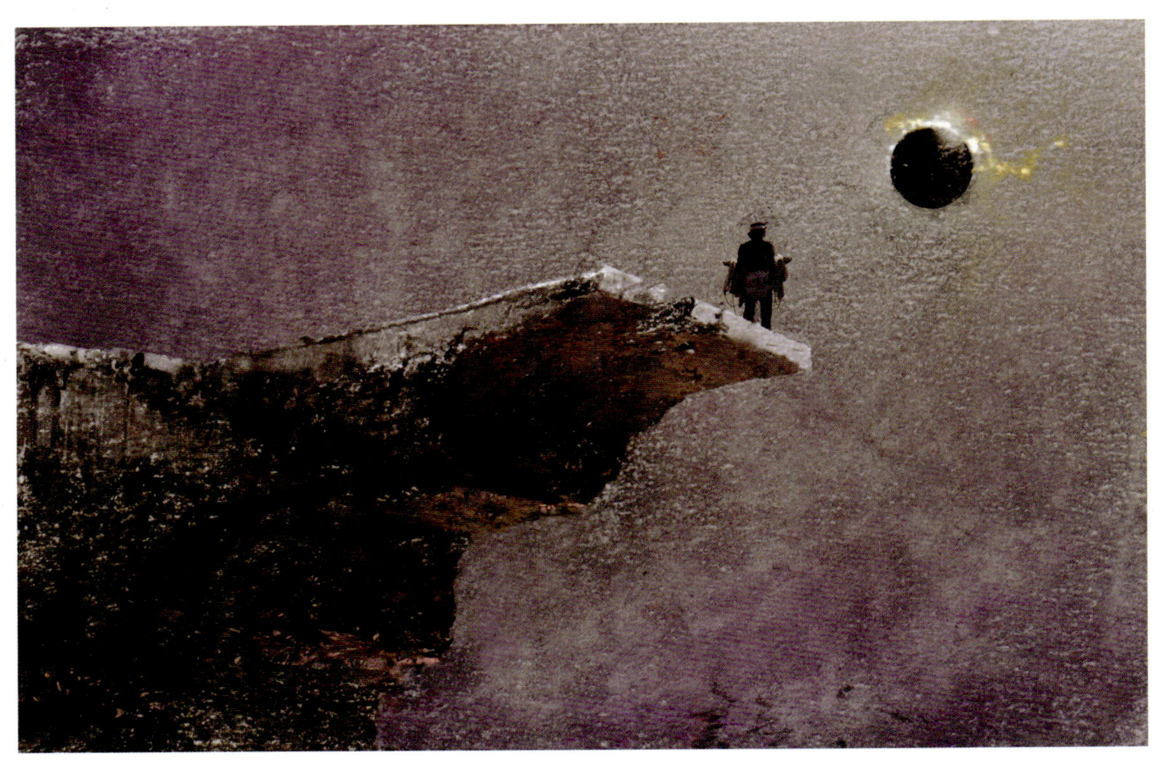

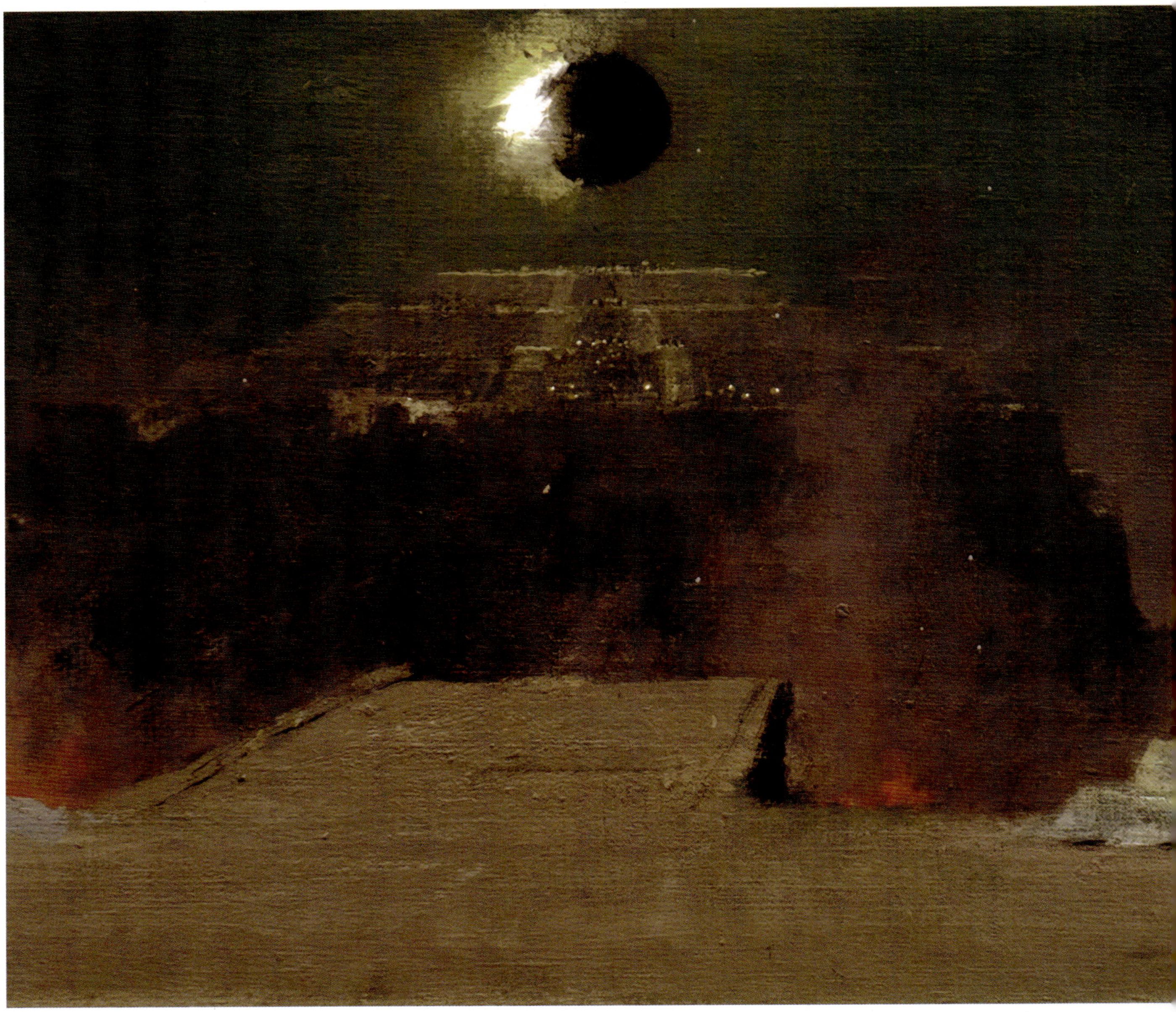

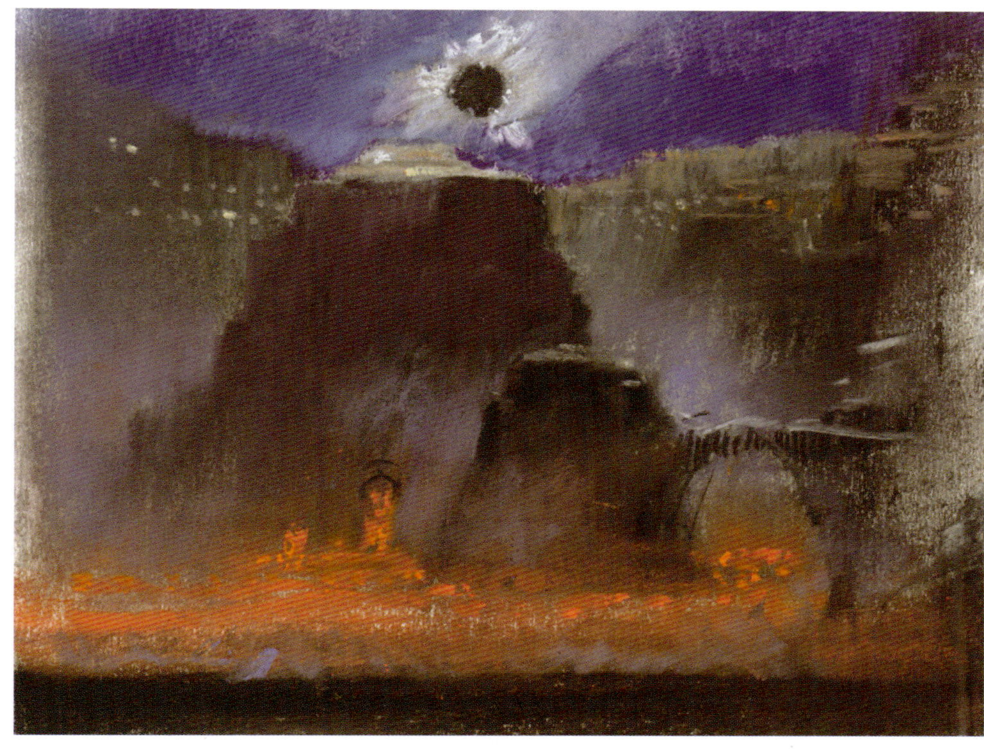

Left: *Eclipse over the Core*
Opposite: *Waiting for Totality*
Below: *Preparing for the Rite*

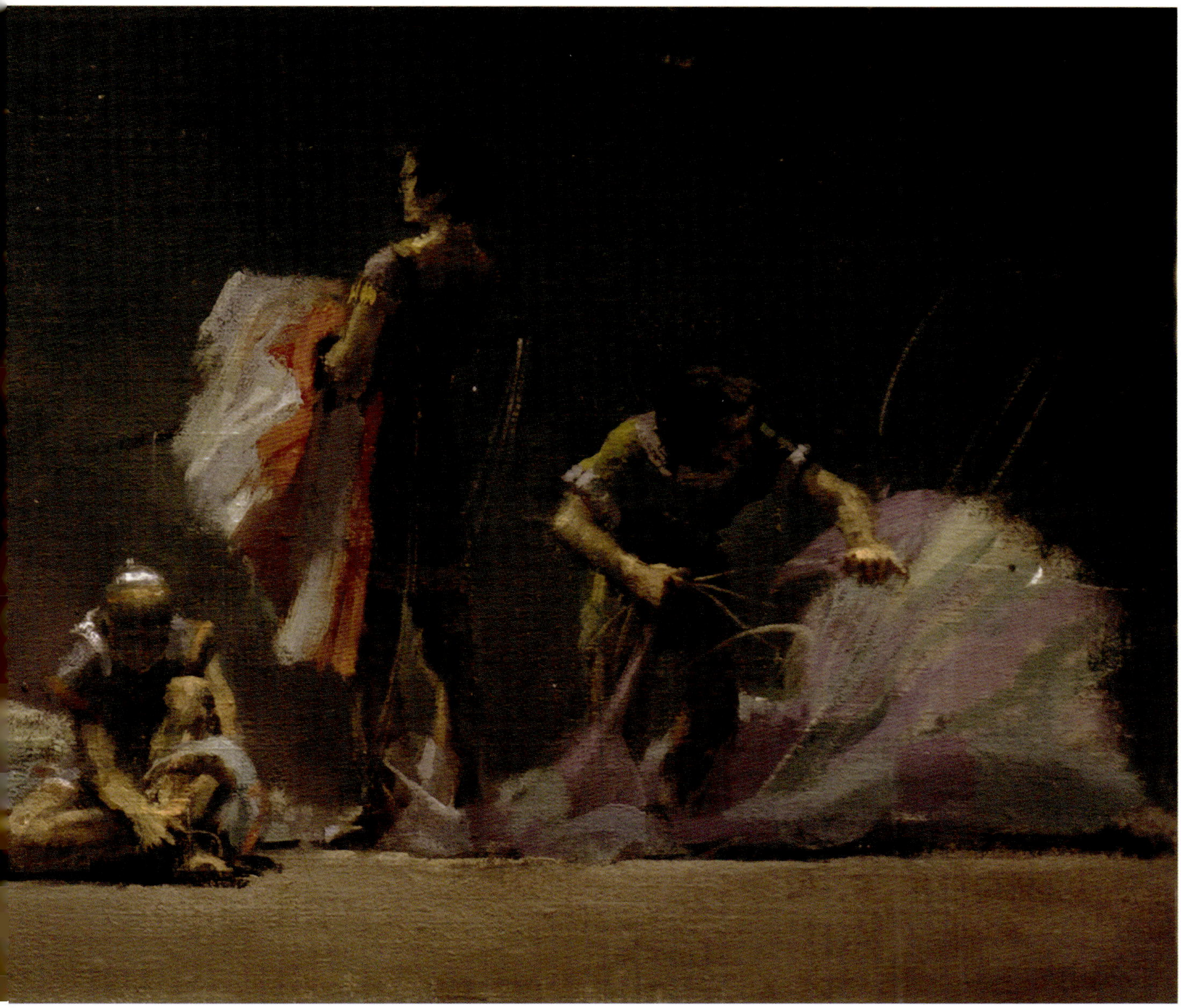

VIEWS OF THE CORE

These views of the volcano's central plug with its little outcrop (the Core and the Petty Core) show the Bridge of Cotl, built after the Great Quake.

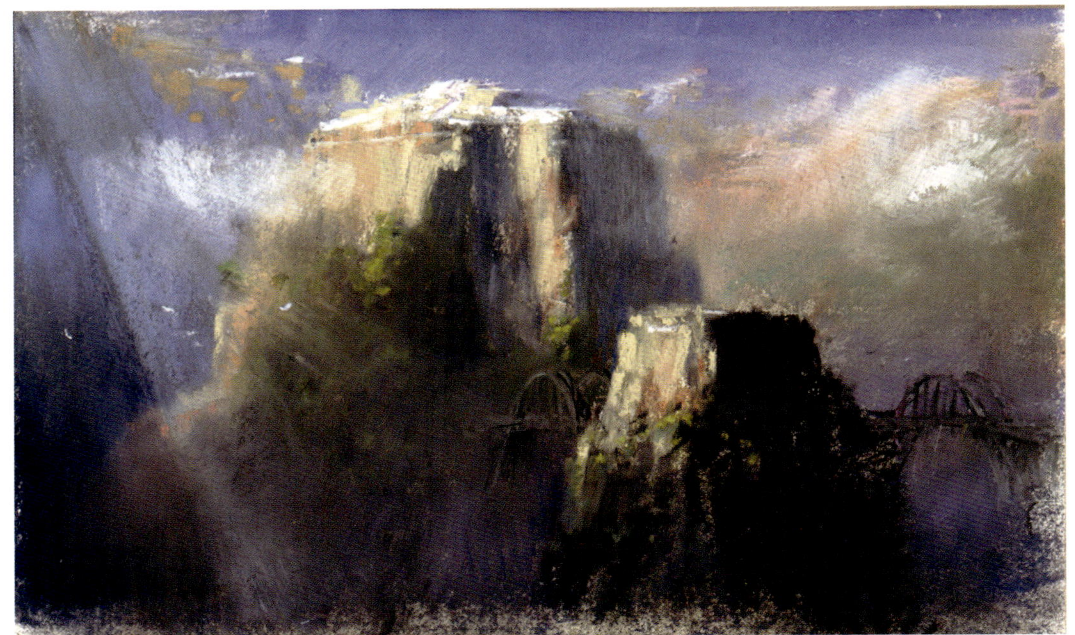

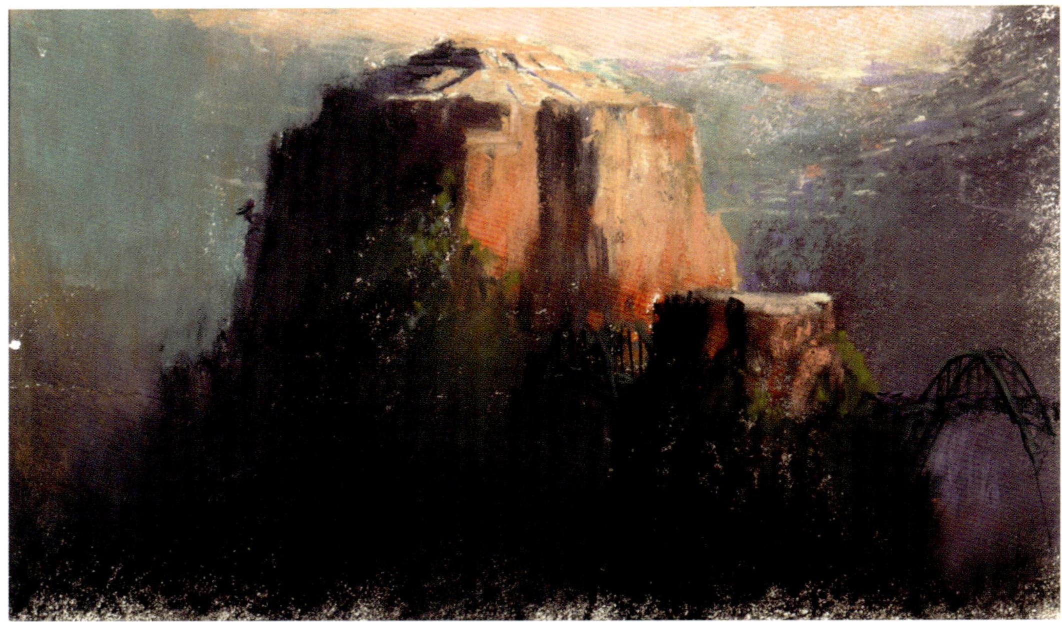

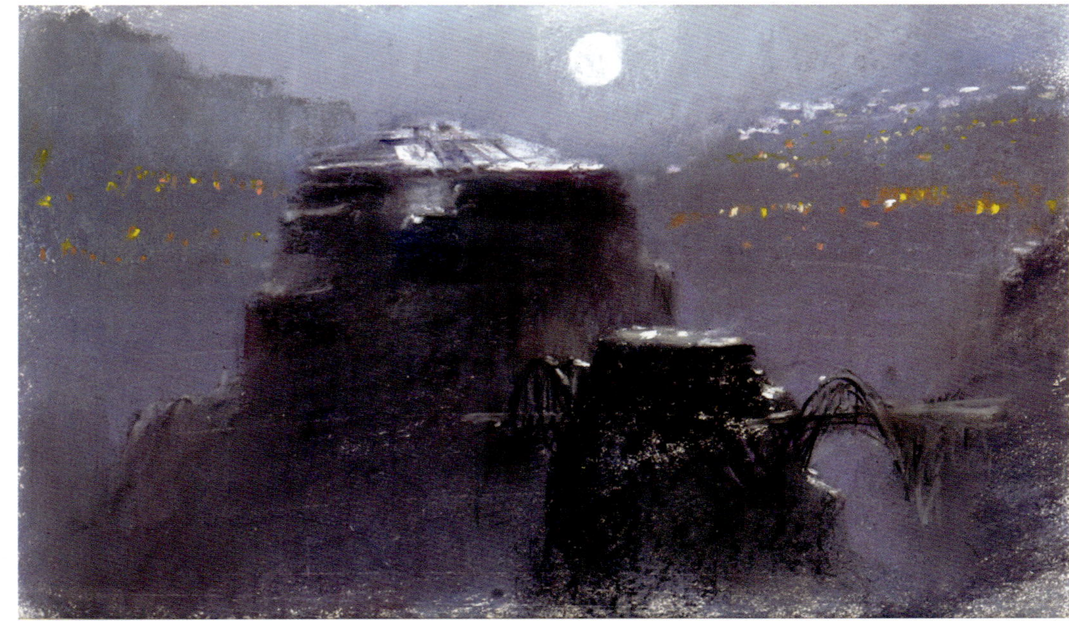

Top: *The Core midmorning*

Middle: *The Core, evening*

Bottom: *Moonlight over the Core*

Opposite: *Conduit*

Following Spread: *On The Terraces*

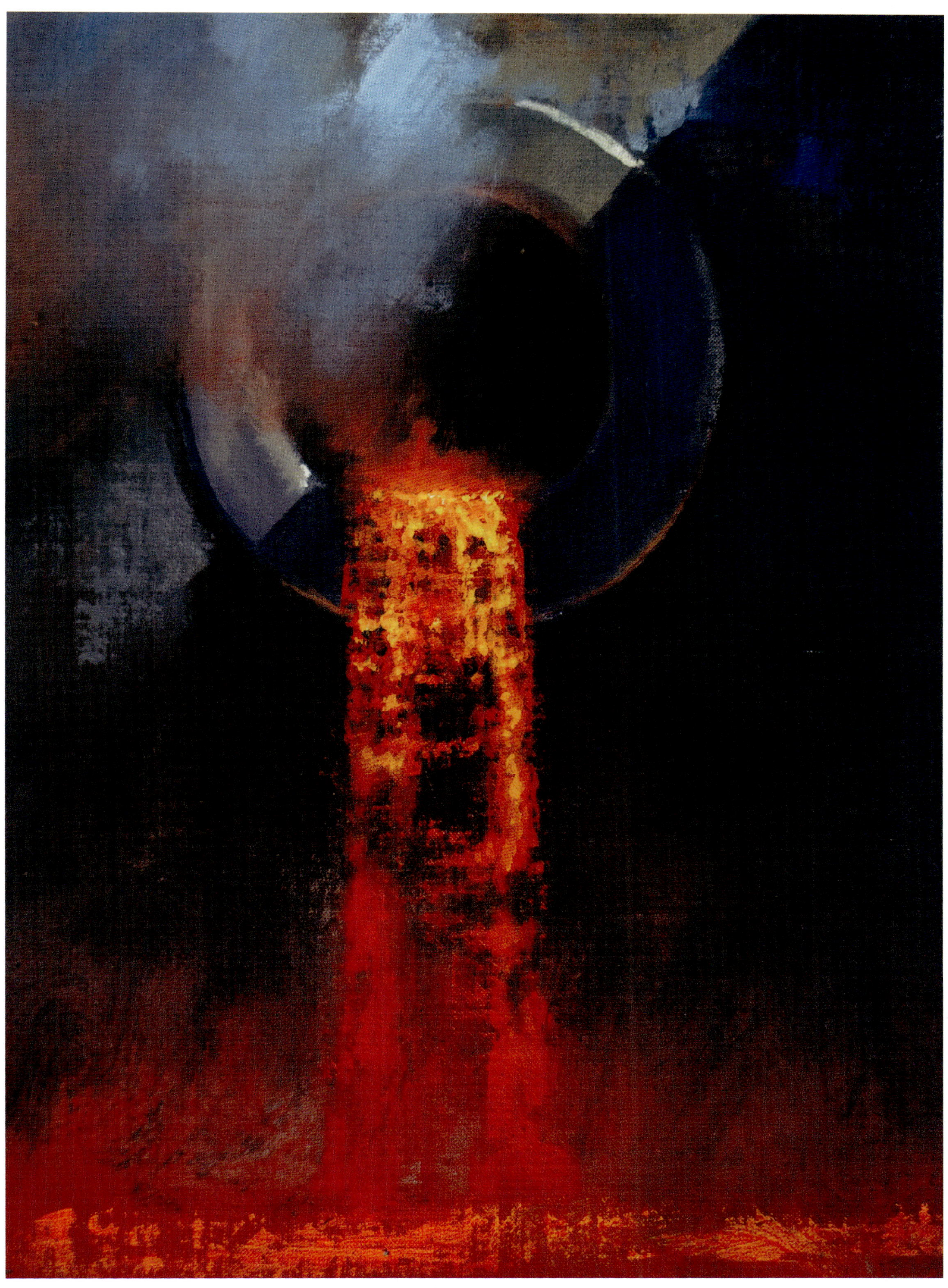

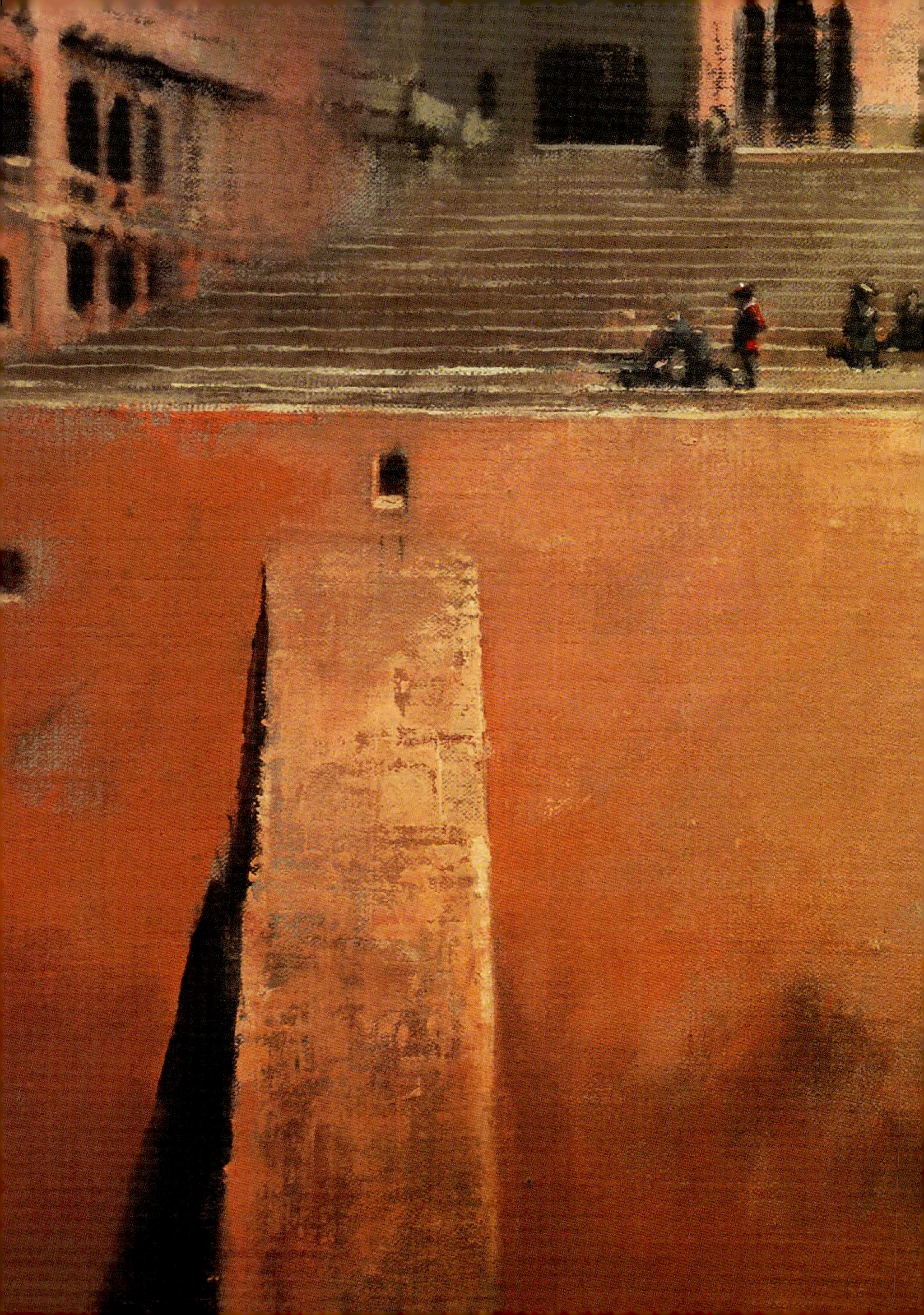

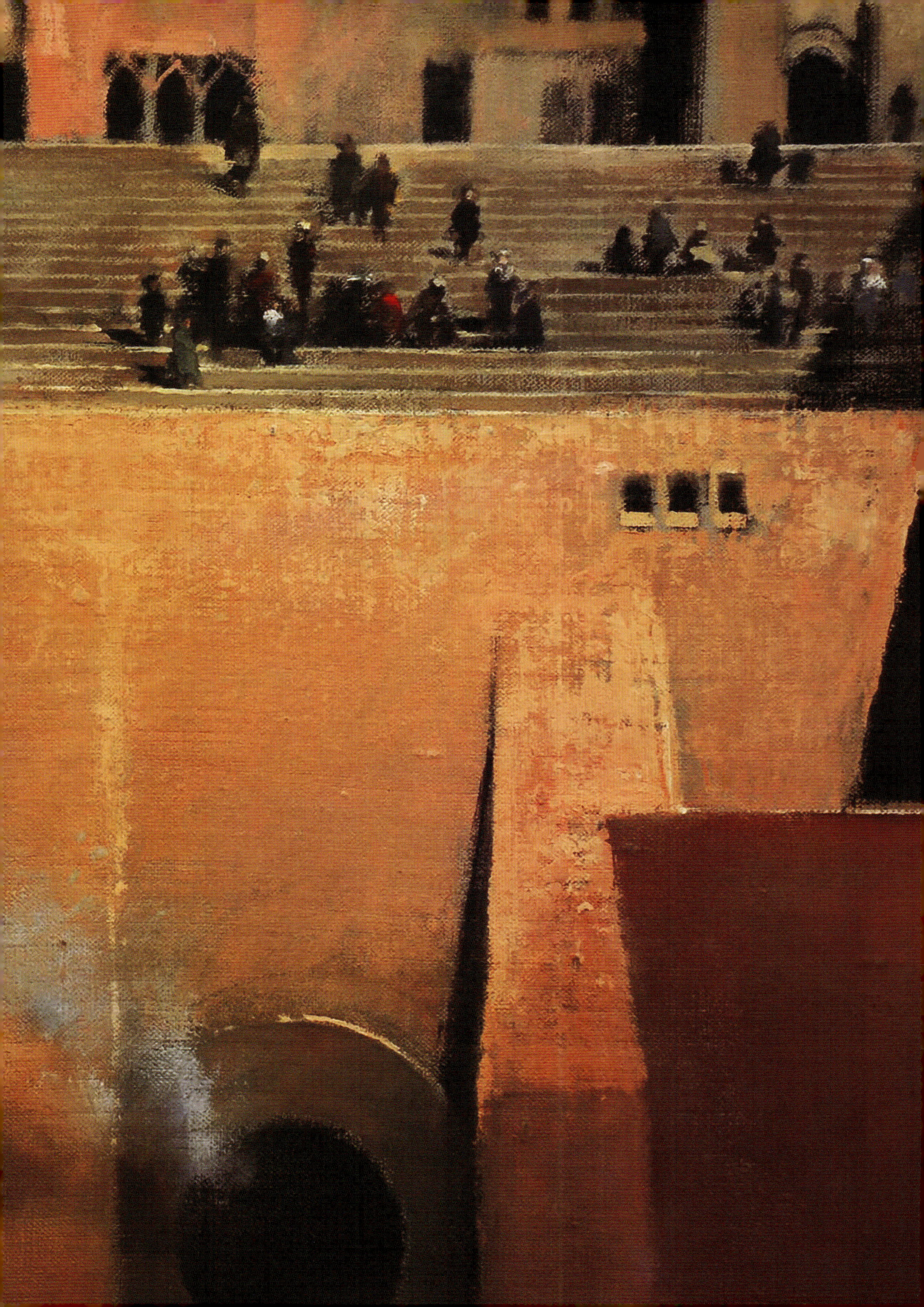

At the summit of the Core (which is the goal of the flyers) lies the Pyramid. This is the place where the elders of the City assemble to meet the flyers as they complete the Rite.

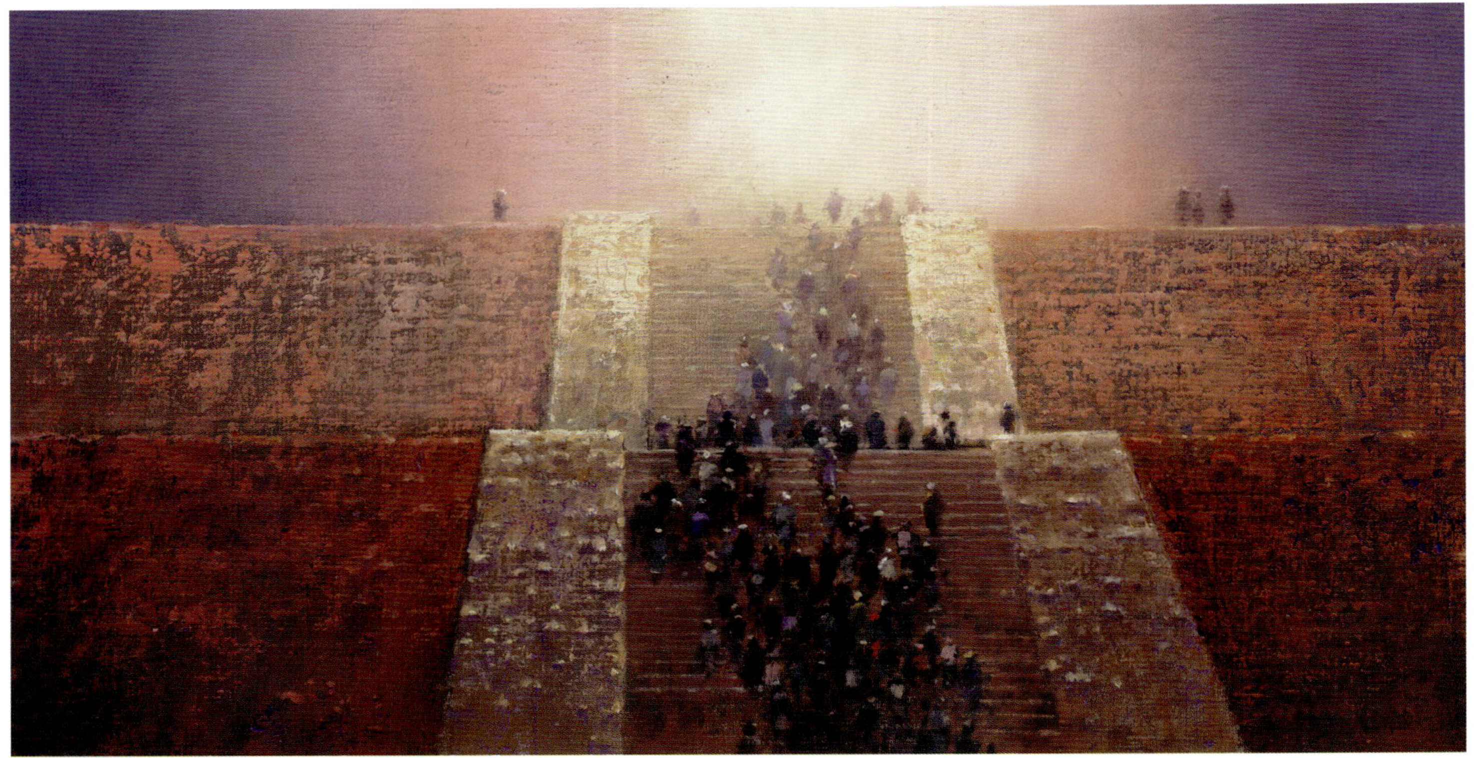

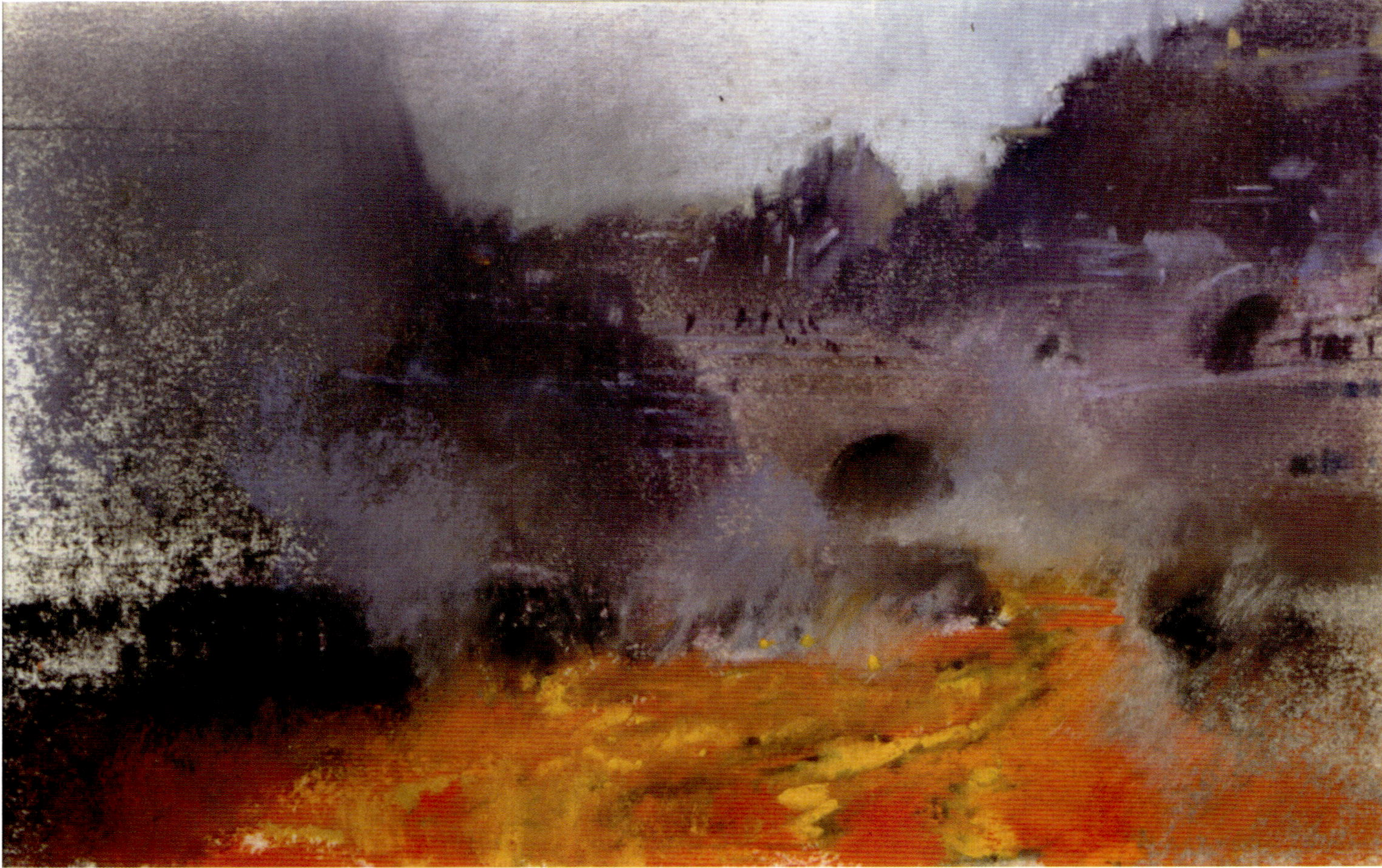

One of the many canals that fill with lava during the time of the eclipse.

Top: *The Tryst*

Below: *In the Caldera*

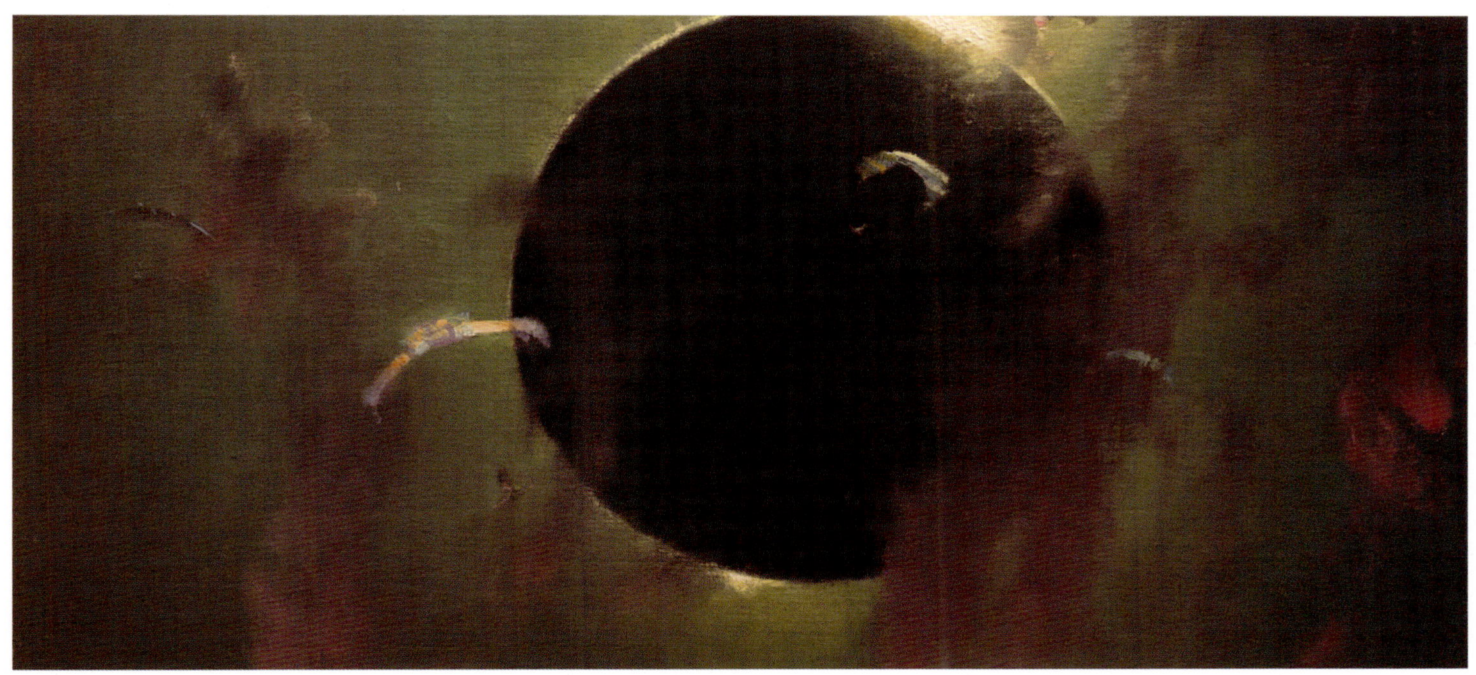

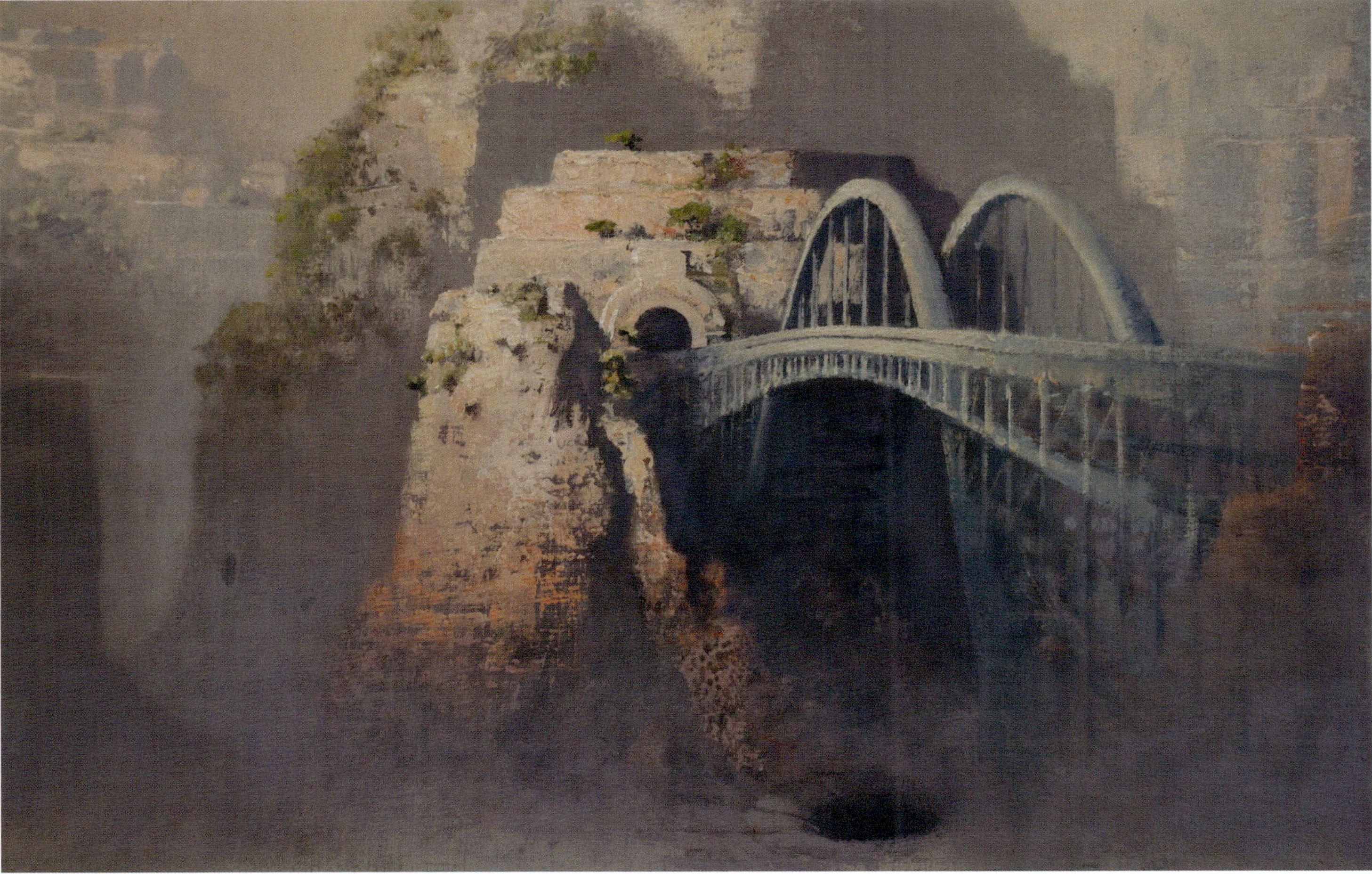

Top: *Thermal Storm*

Below: *The Petty Core*

The closing ceremony of the Rite of the Hidden Sun. The name given to this event is said to refer to a sound that is heard by the flyers as they transit over to the Core. Like a vast swarm of bees, this is apparently in some way connected to the knowledge that is revealed to the flyers, and lies at the very heart of the enigma of how the mountain remains a safe place to live.

Right: *The Celebration of the Hive*

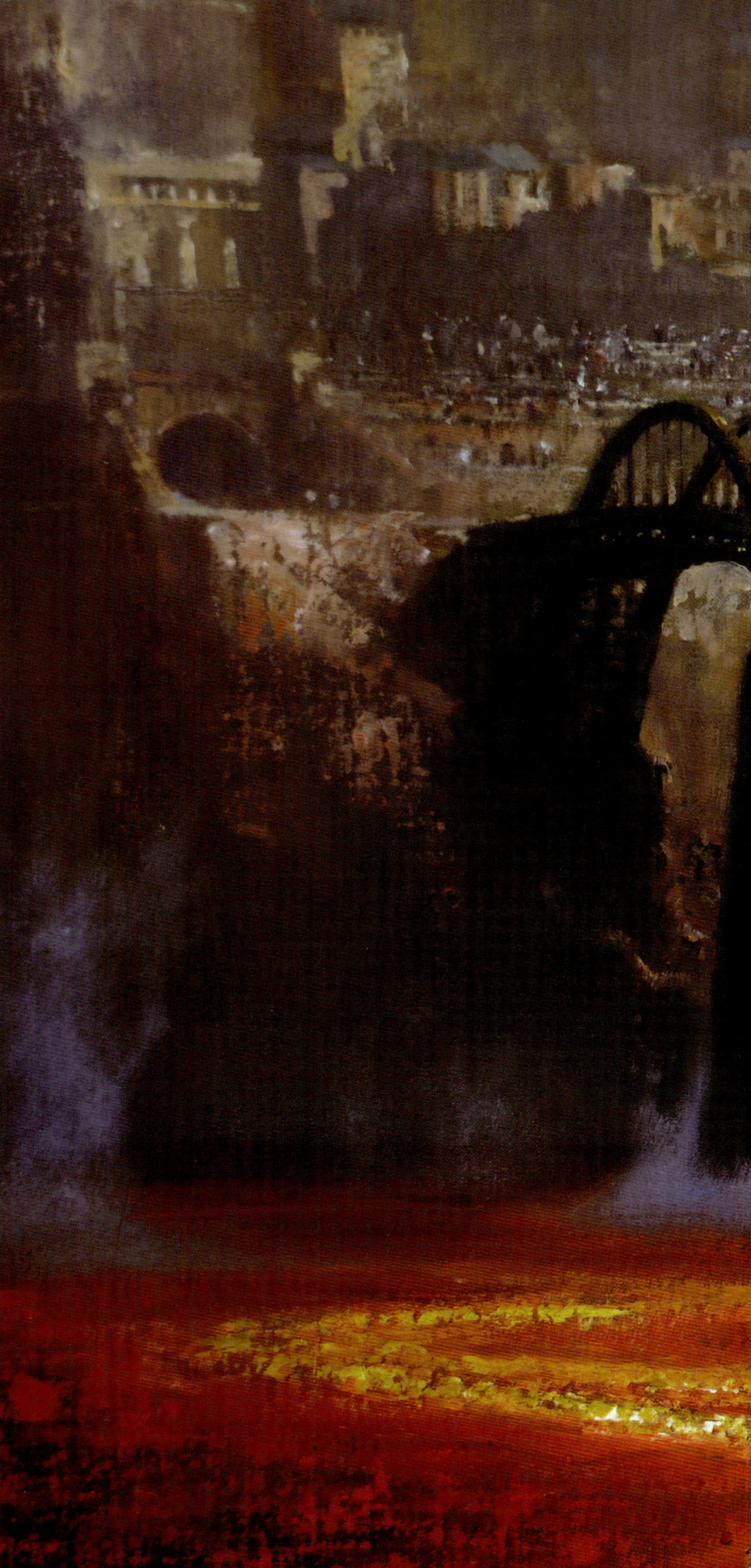

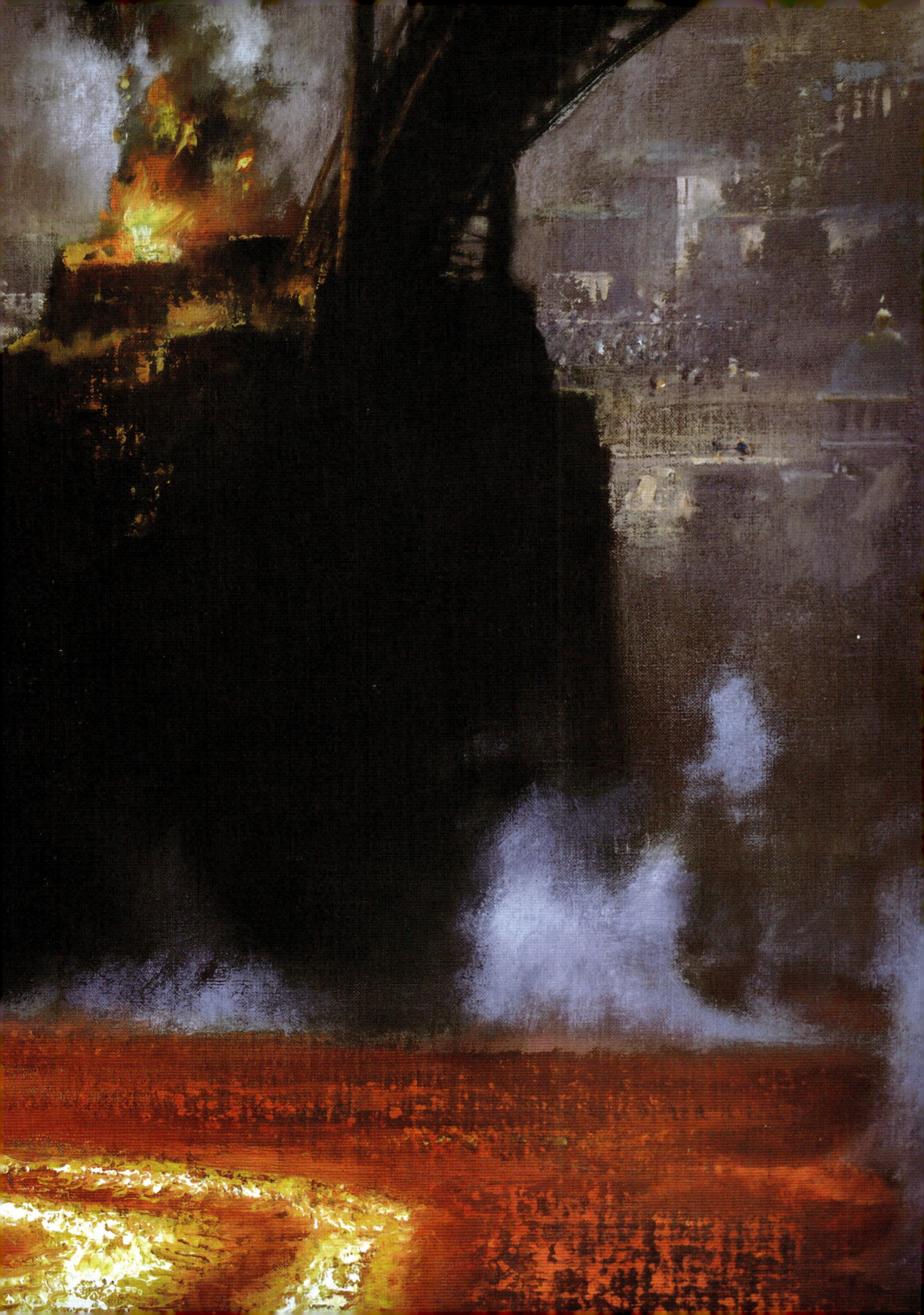

THE SINKS

Throughout the crater's ceramic-lined base can be seen large openings known as Sinks. These provide drainage for the lava to flow out onto the outer slopes of the mountain, via venturas. These ducts are scraped clean by massive machinery after each eruption, dating back to the time before the city as we know it was built.

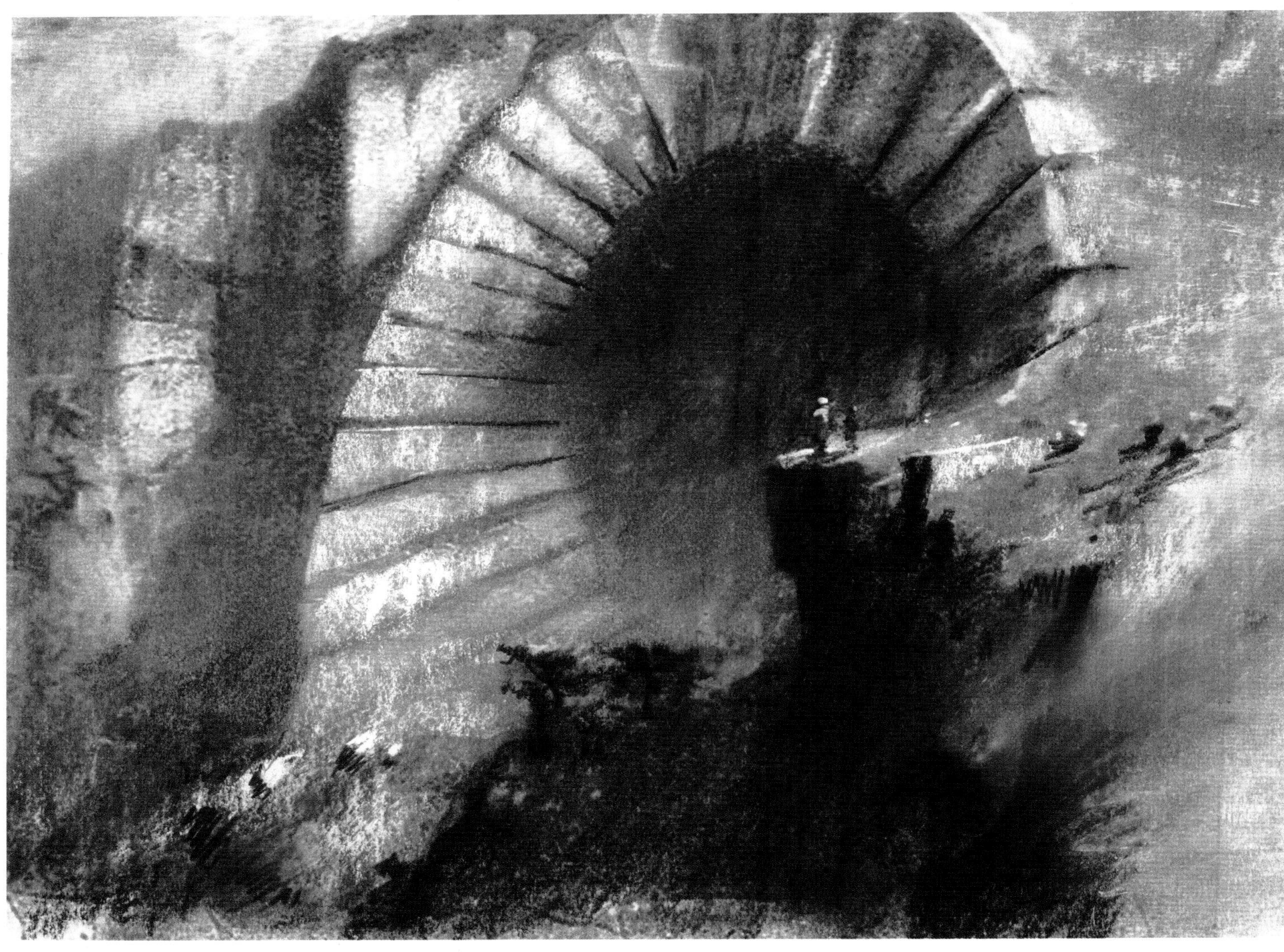

Above: *Ventura, the Outer Slopes*
Opposite Top: *Cleaning the Sinks*
Opposite Bottom: *The Big Sink*
Following Spread: *Cleaning The Ducts*

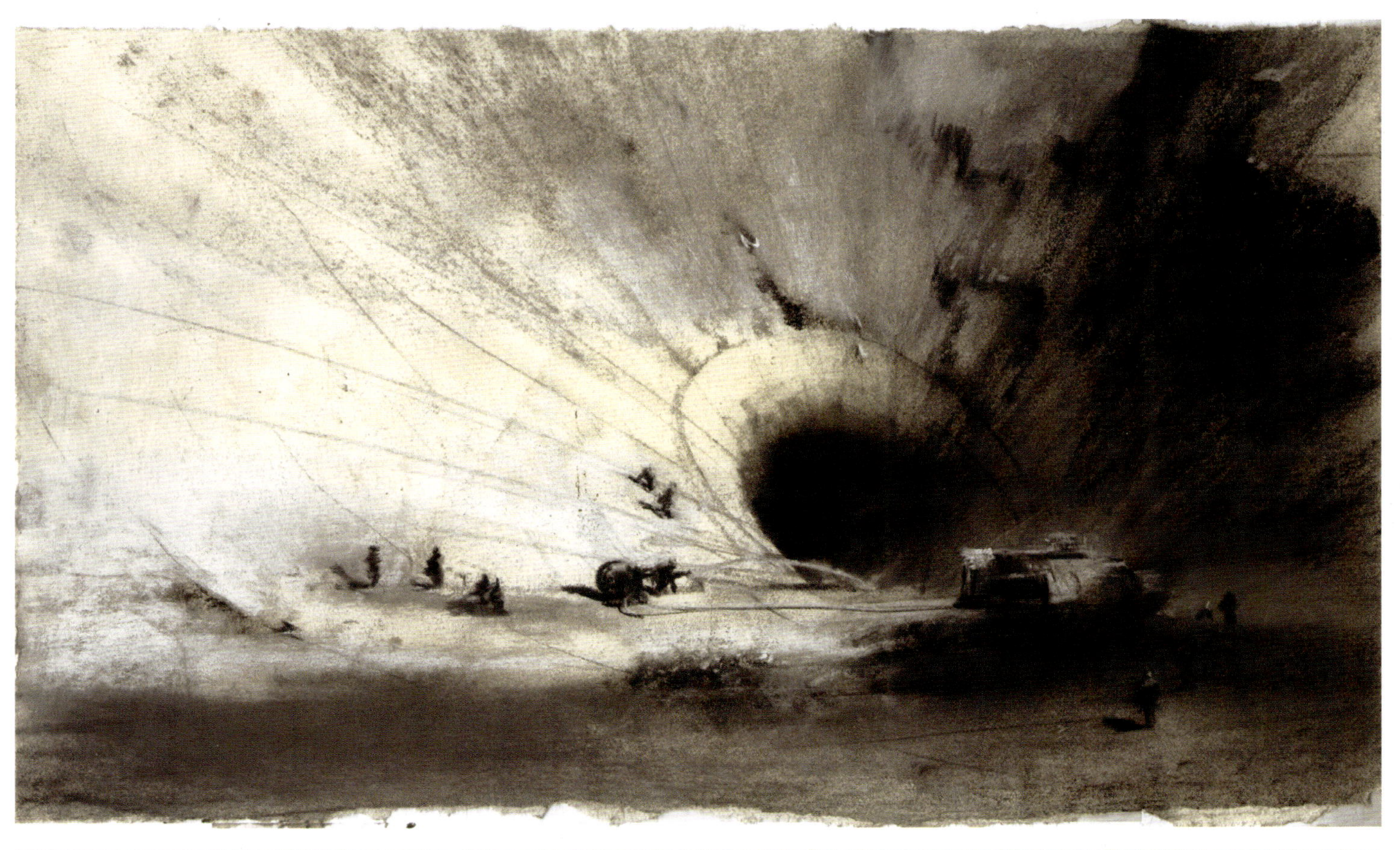

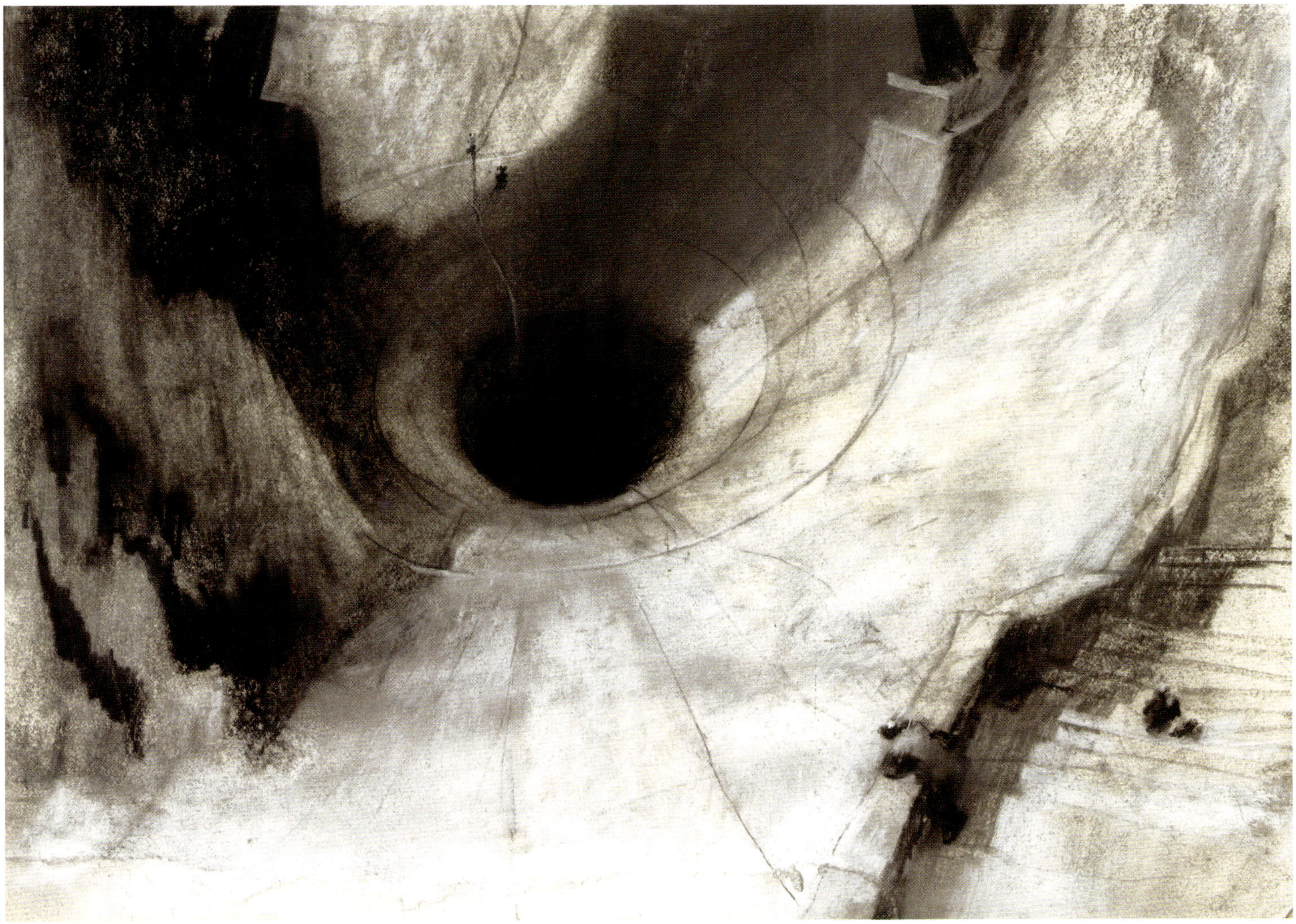

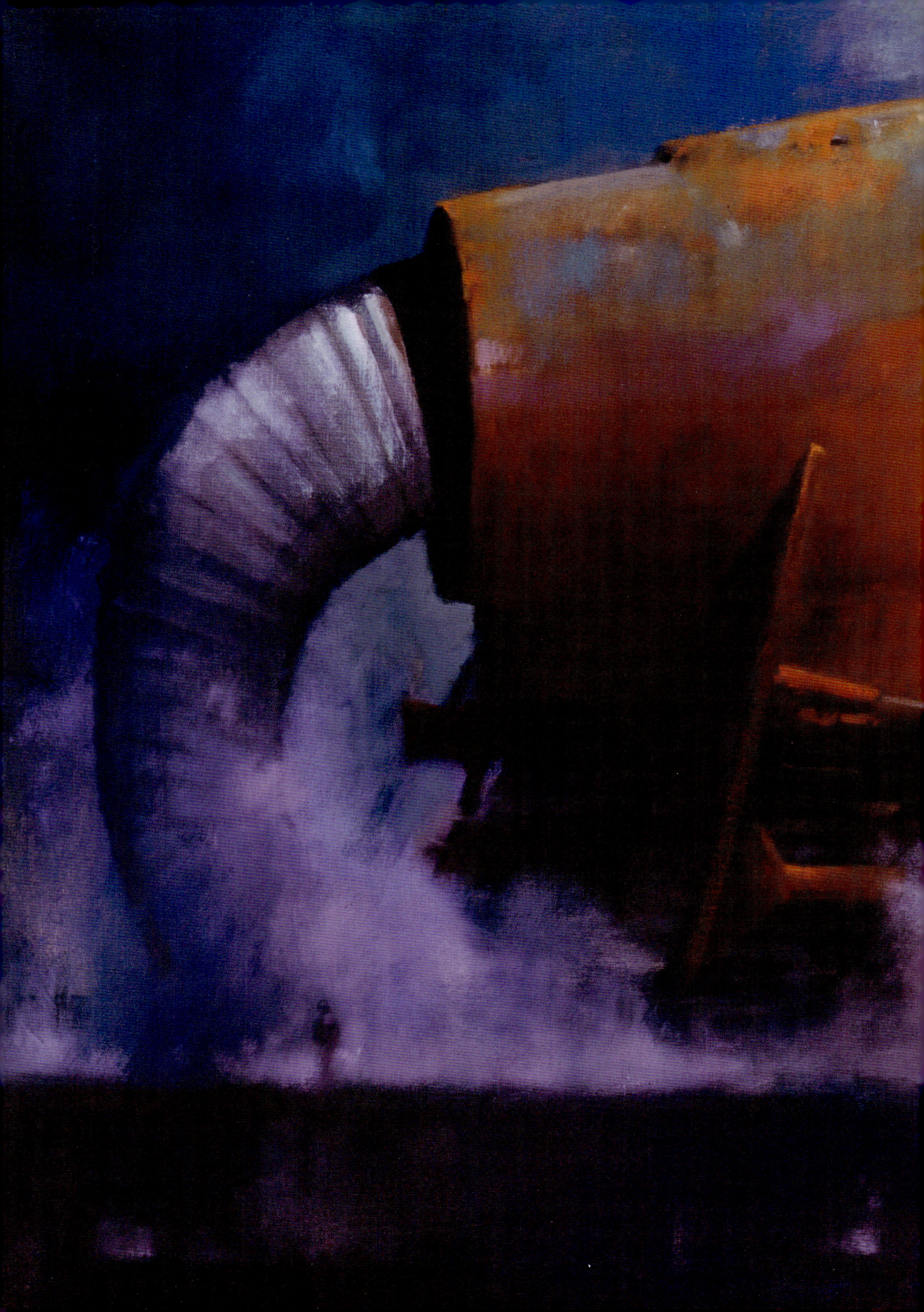

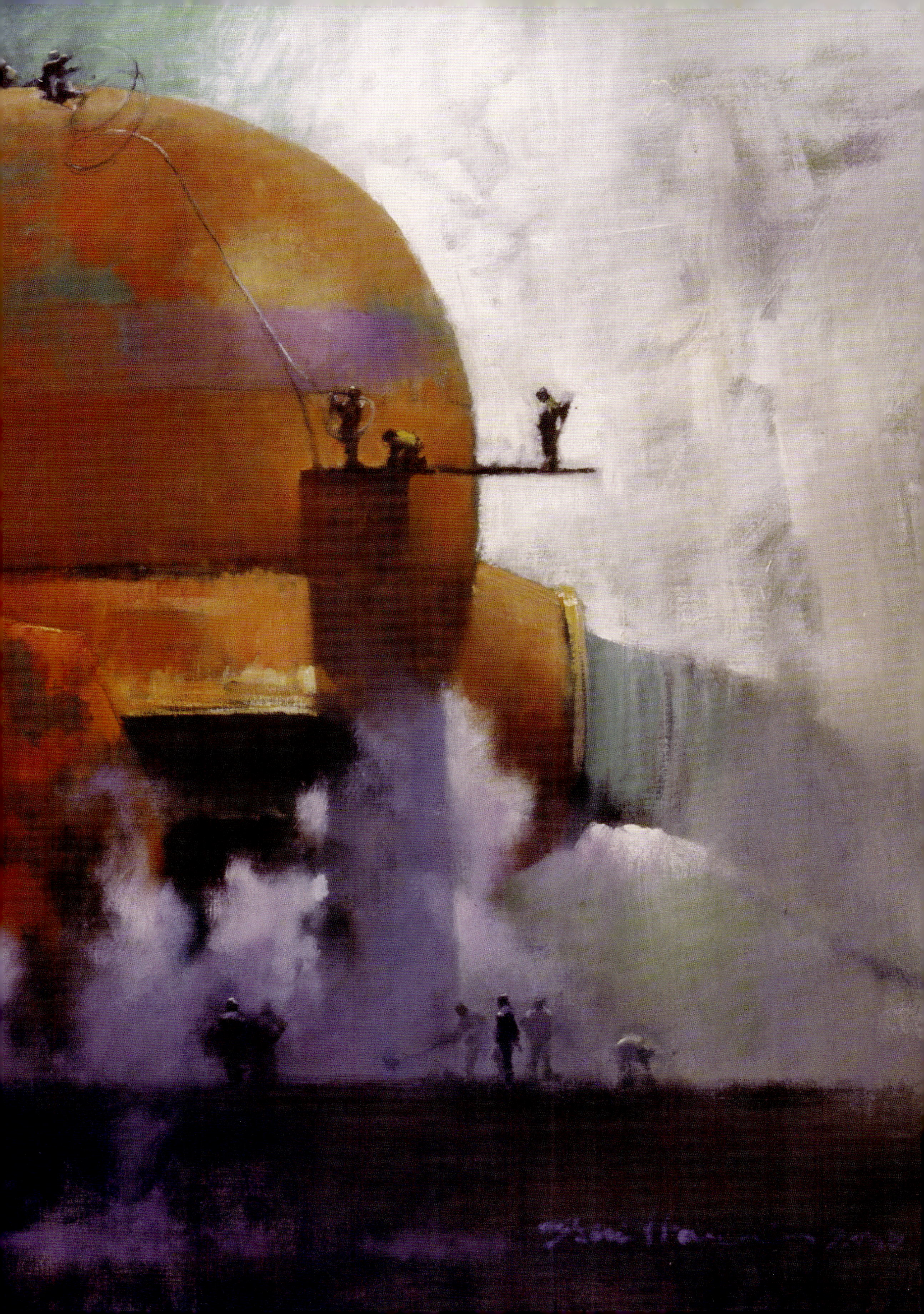

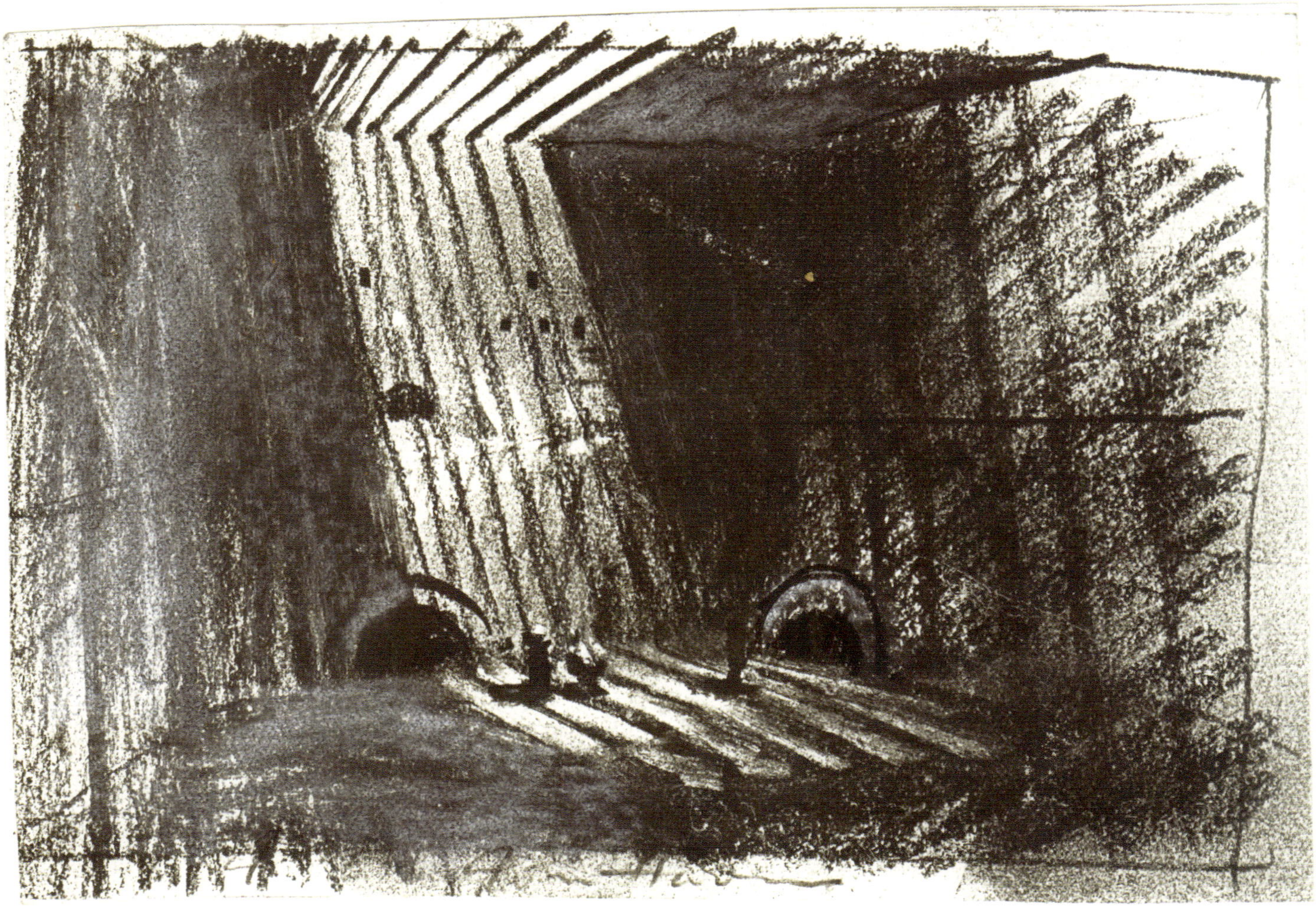

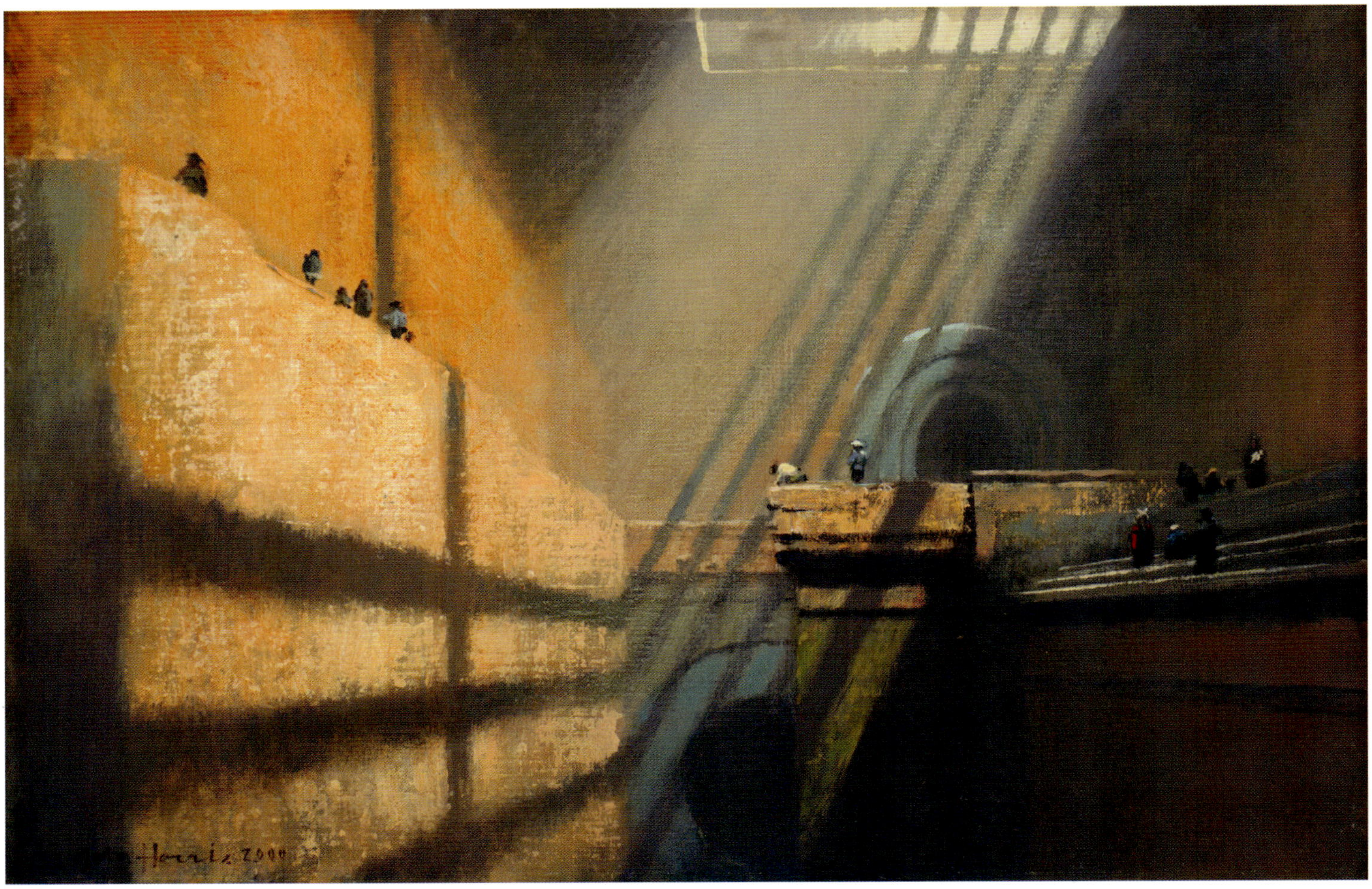

Top: *Inside the Chamber*
Bottom: *The Great Gallery*

In those days, the major part of excavations within the mountain related almost exclusively to its function as a geothermal station, such as the Turbine Room and the great Valve rooms.

Since then, many other chambers and passages have been added to accommodate the increasing urbanisation and change of the city's culture.

Right: *The Turbine Room*

Below: *The Key Valve*

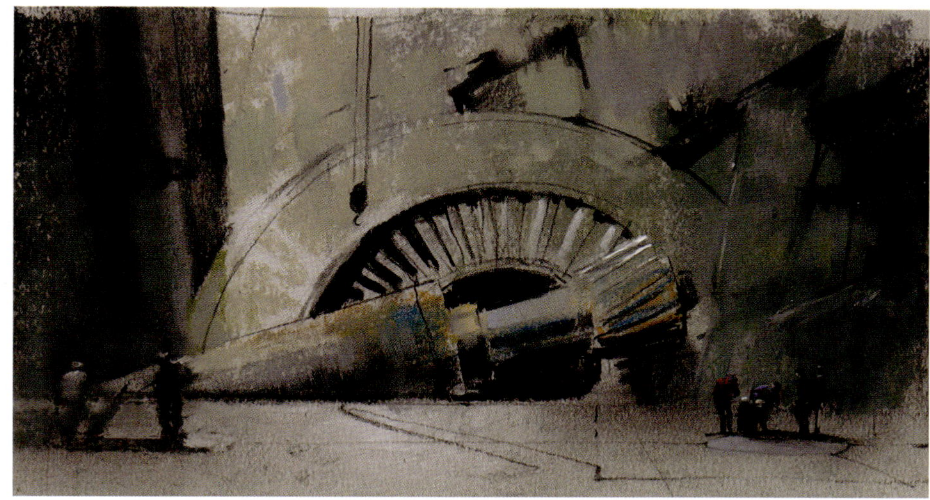

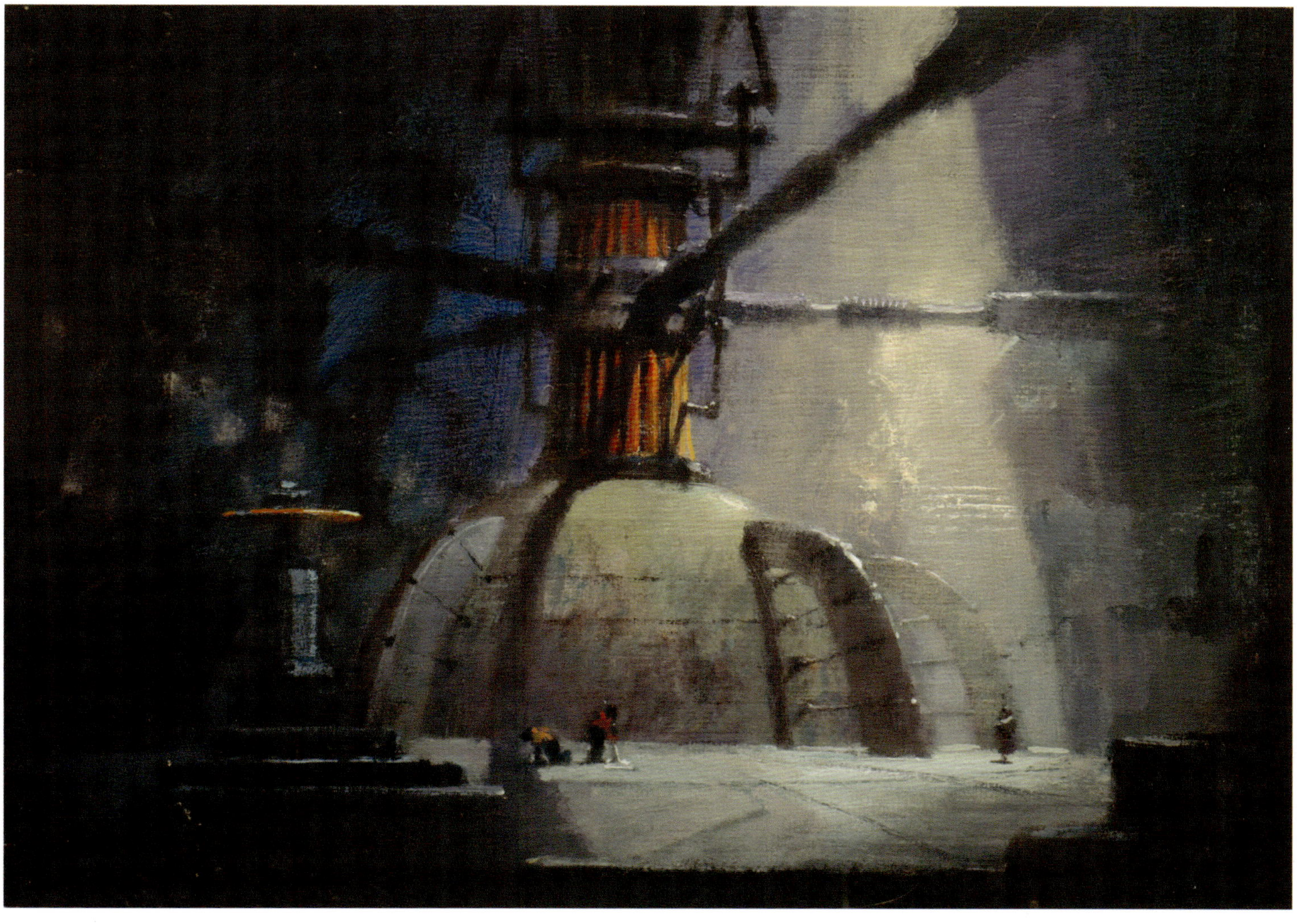

THE CAST

As the journals of the travelling artist unfolded, the story he had to tell became increasingly populated by an assortment of characters whose roles were inextricably tied up with the Rites. The Valve Keeper, a large imposing figure, who was, as his name implied, responsible for the hardware that kept the mountain functioning. The Attendant Sivian, an elusive shadowy figure to whom everybody in the city answered, but who was rarely seen (and then only with his dog). Arken, the prodigal one, who, unusually, travelled beyond the confines of the mountain and befriended Sol, the artist. And Mimu, the Valve Keeper's daughter, who became the reason for the artist's unthinkable decision to undergo the terrifying Rite himself.

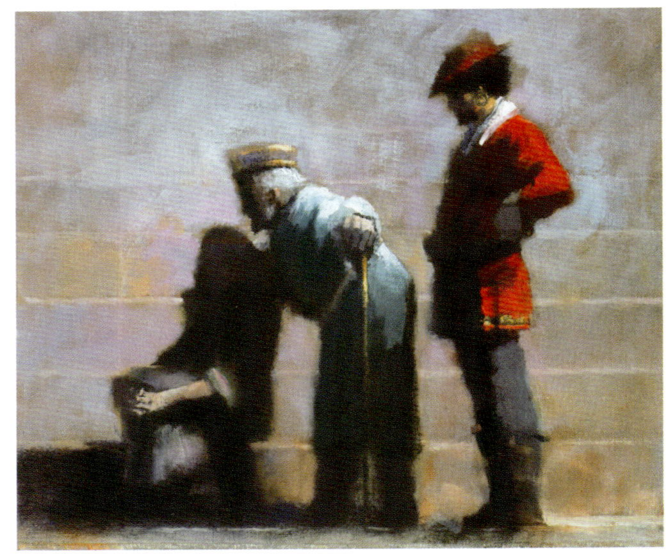

The Apprentice's Kin

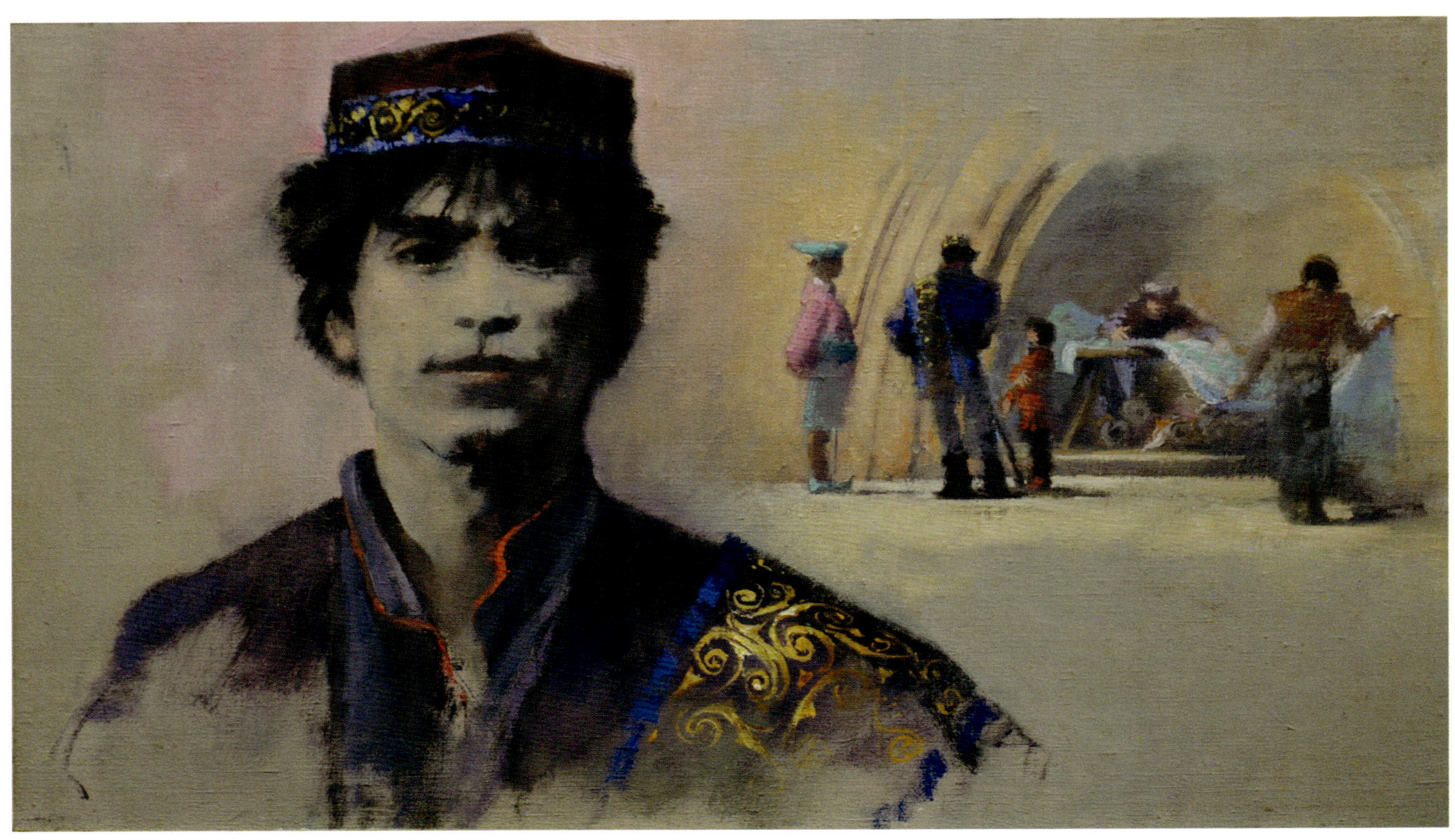

The Apprentice

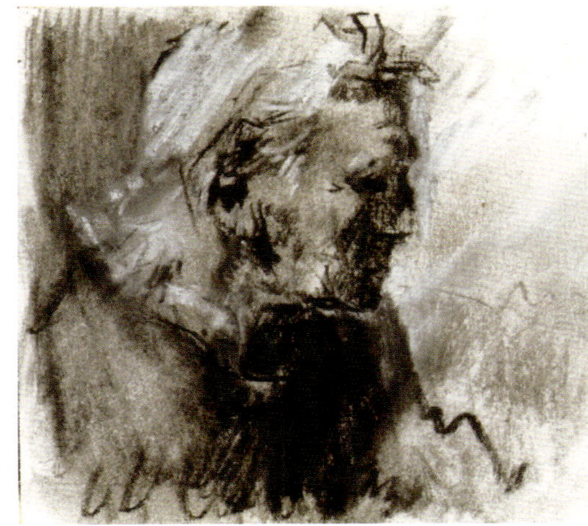

The Valve-Keeper

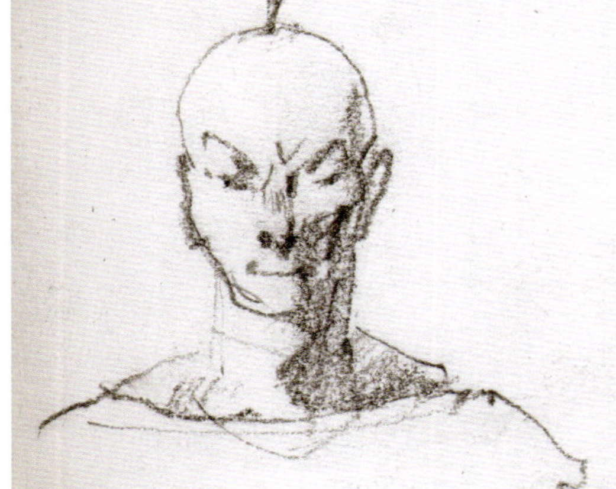

Sivian

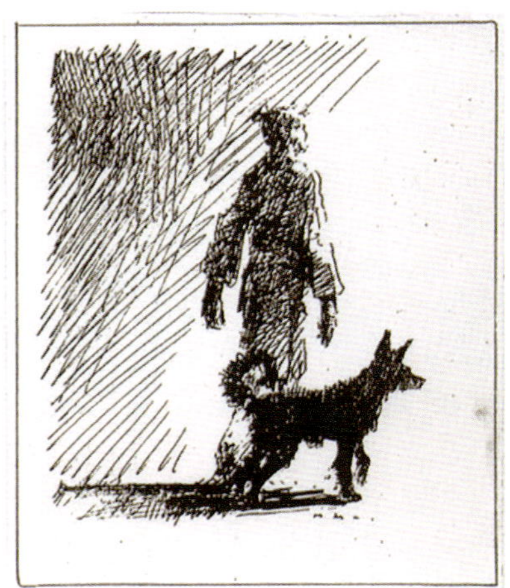

The Attendant

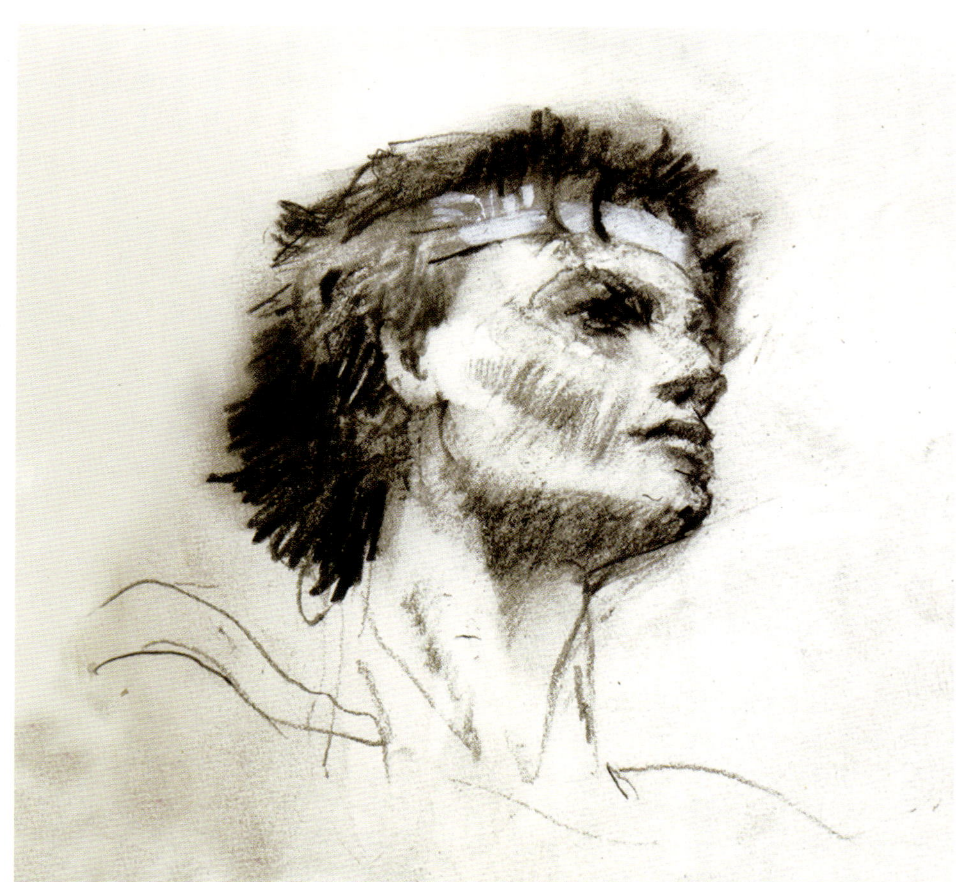

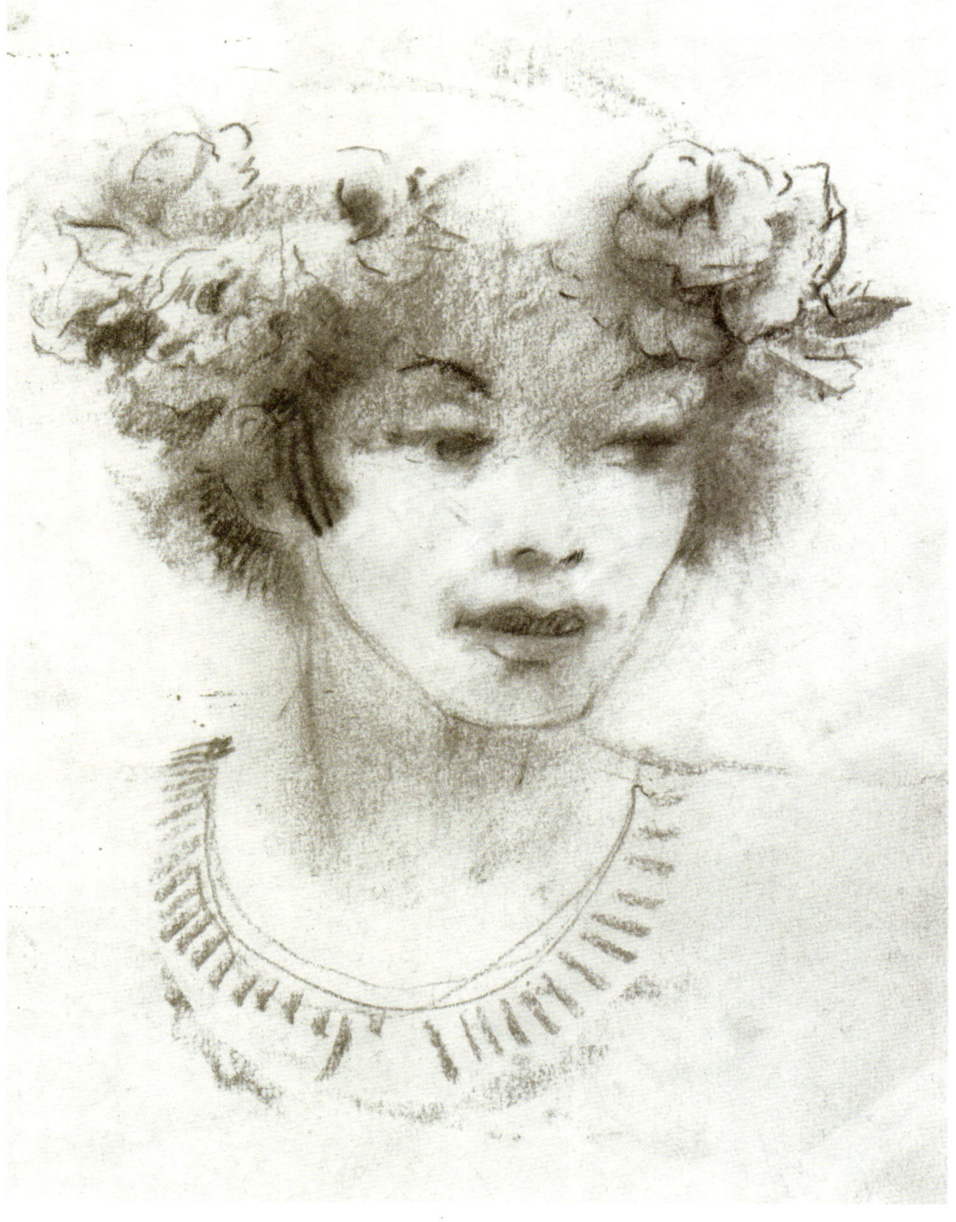

Left: *Sol*

Below: *Study of Mimu*

THE LEGEND OF HUMMING COTL

The city was already ancient before the era in which the artist arrived, but the people knew its history well. They claimed that it was as much as a thousand years old. Before that, it was simply a geothermal station, extracting energy from the magma and manned by no more than a hundred and fifty souls. It was run by an Attendant, or the Valve Keeper as he was called, who was directly responsible for the maintenance of the valve system that controlled the lava pressure within the caldera.

He had a son, Cotl, who, at the age of twelve, was learning his father's craft. Just two weeks before his thirteenth birthday, a total eclipse was due. In the hours before the eclipse, the lava pressure steadily rose, and, from the safety of the Rim, his father set the controls to open the valves within the Core. But then, unprecedented, the mechanism jammed. The Keeper moved to cross over the bridge to the Core and release the valves manually – but the stresses of the rumbling mountain broke the bridge and, helpless to prevent the inevitable explosion, he ordered an evacuation of the mountain.

Cotl was standing on the broken bridge, where he had been watching the lava pouring through cracks into the caldera below. Usually a silent child, he suddenly became animated and, bursting into unfamiliar speech, he said, "I can get there," pointing to the Core. Surprised to hear him speak at all, the Keeper gestured to the steaming void. "How?"

"I've been watching the birds," and ran off towards home.

Puzzled, but impelled by the crisis, the Keeper set about the evacuation. Cotl, out of breath, returned with a bundle of silk with lines and a harness attached to his body. He went to his father, caught him by the arm, and said, "Let me show you."

Without waiting for a reply, he ran to end of the broken bridge and launched himself into the void. The Keeper called out in horror, then stopped. He saw Cotl's body swept up under the ballooning canopy of silk, as the thermals from the lava far below, blew him away.

Across the void, he flew very fast, towards the Core, manipulating the canopy through the maelstrom of the thermal storm. From the rim his father watched, but in the dimming light of the eclipse, lost sight of his son. In despair, he returned to collect his staff and abandon the shaking mountain.

Cotl flew on, and glancing up, saw the moon's disk occluding the sun. As totality approached, he began to hear, through the roar of the mountain, another sound. At first just a quite hum, but growing louder, it seemed to come from the sun. He felt his body resonate as if a million bees swarmed within him. The corona flared into view and, with it, his own mind burst into understanding. The mountain spoke to him.

He landed on the Core and, knowing what to do, relieved the mountain of its pressure.

The eclipse passed, the lava bled away and the mountain was again quiet. The Keeper returned, not knowing how it happened that they and the mountain were still there. More amazing still, he found his son Cotl, waiting for him. After the rush of feelings from their reunion had passed, the Keeper was very pensive. Then, he spoke to Cotl. "How did you know which valves to open?"

Cotl knew that words would not do. We do not know how he answered, but from that day, Cotl showed others how to ride the thermals and answer that question for themselves. So was born the Rite of the Hidden Sun and Cotl, who had developed a habit of humming like a swarm of bees whenever he was alone, grew to be the leader of his people and the father of a culture that survives to this day.

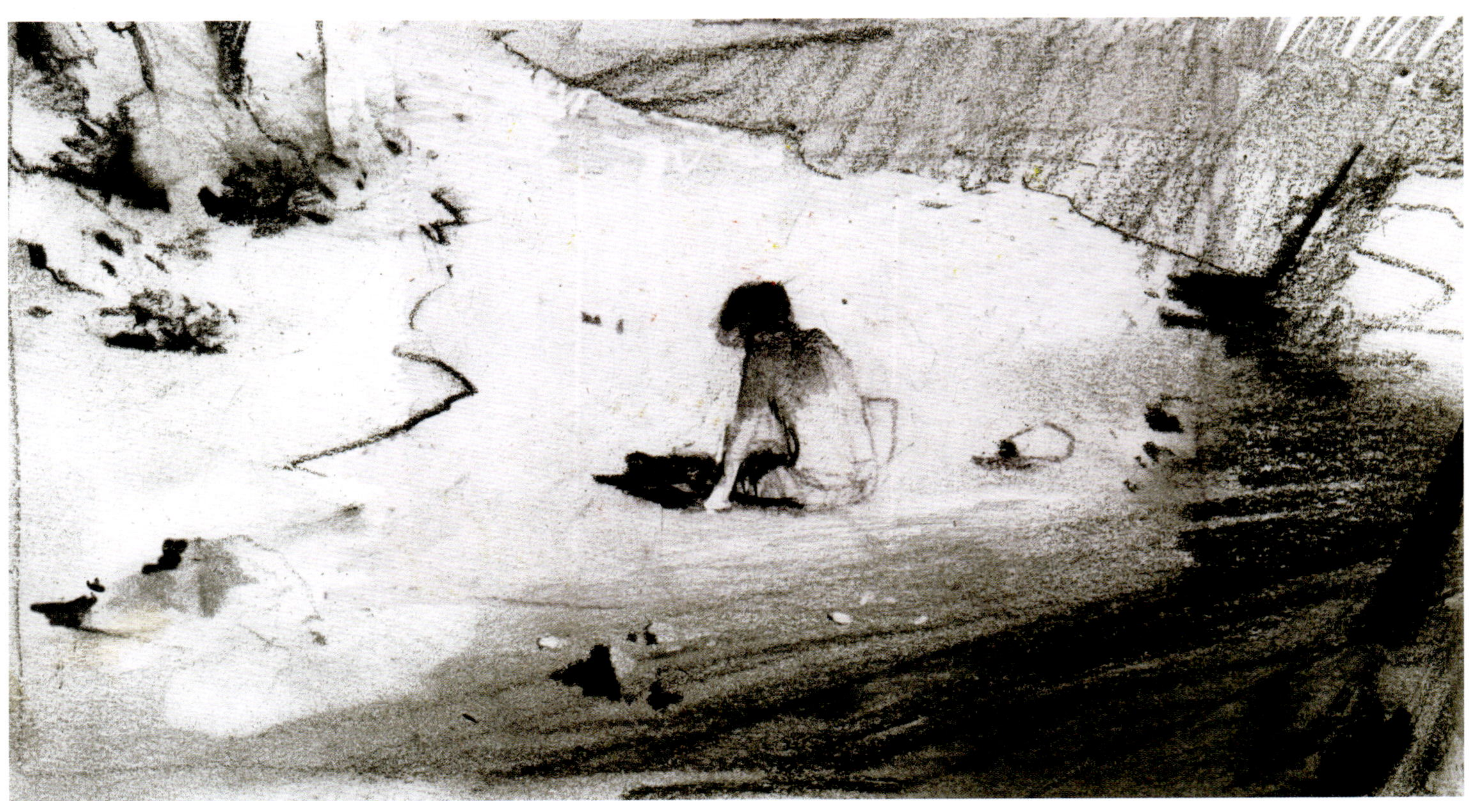

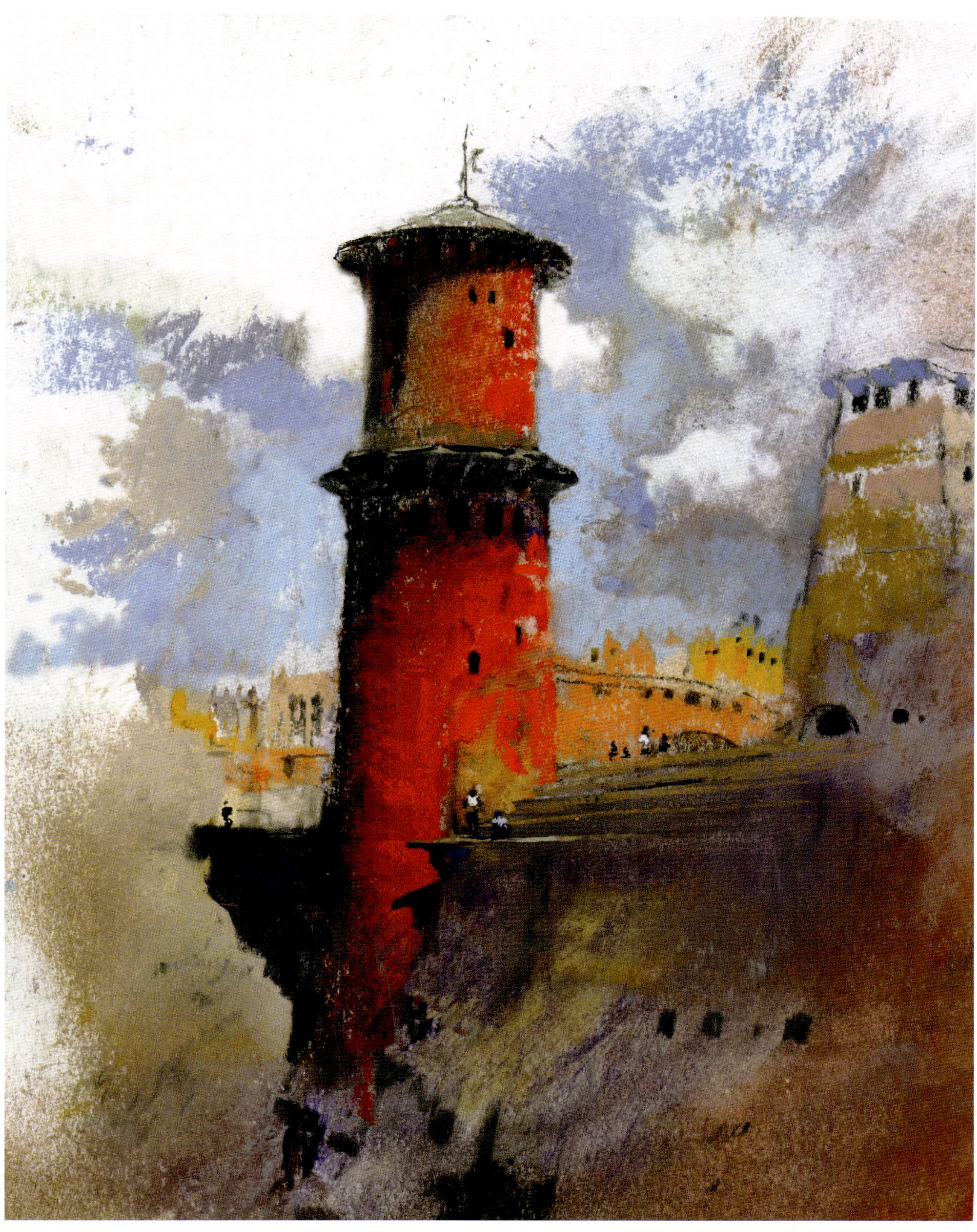

Above: *Valve Keeper's Tower*

Left: *Cotl Playing in the Sun*

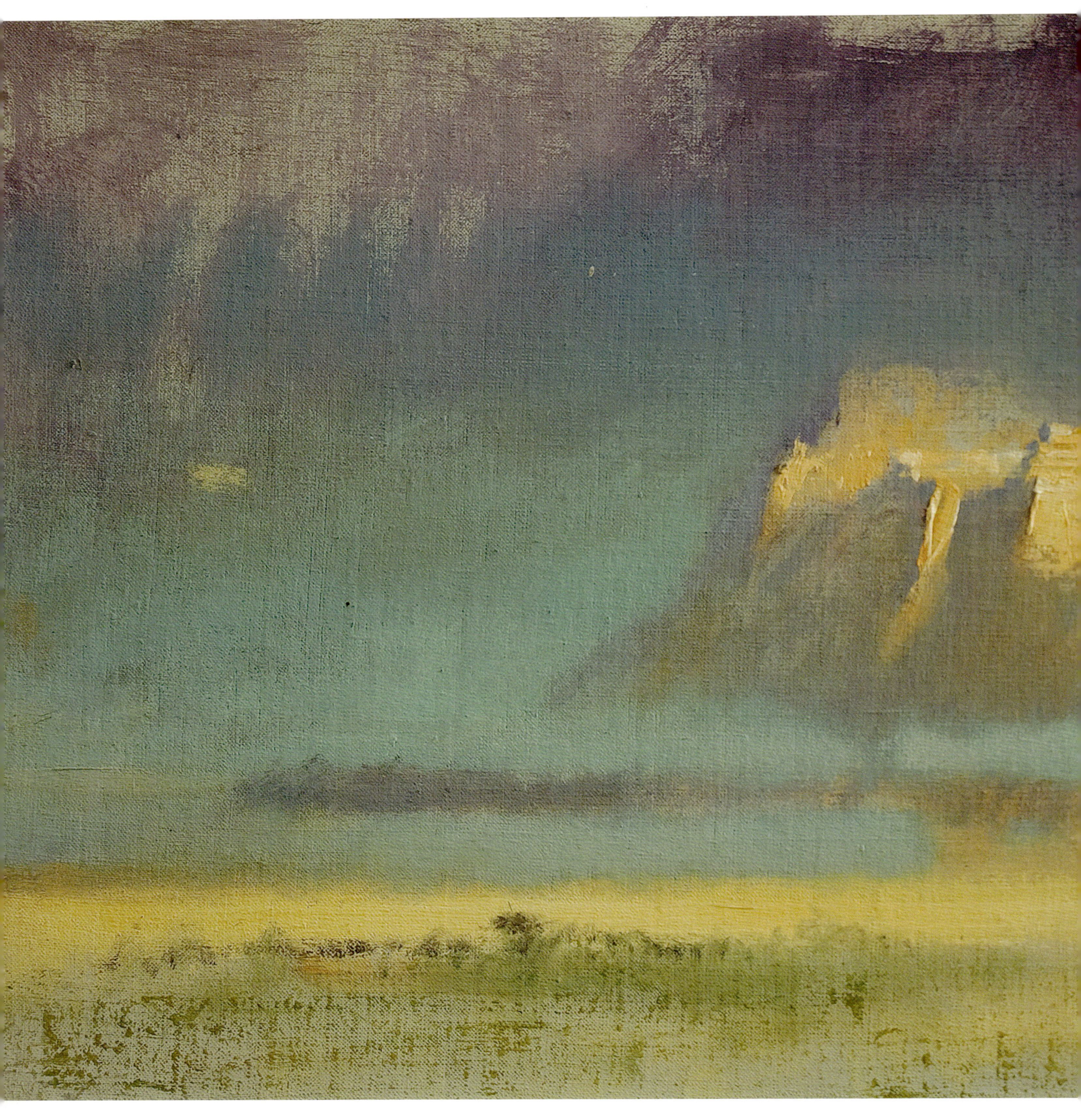

THE ABANDONED LANDS AND THE PLAIN OF CRYSTALS

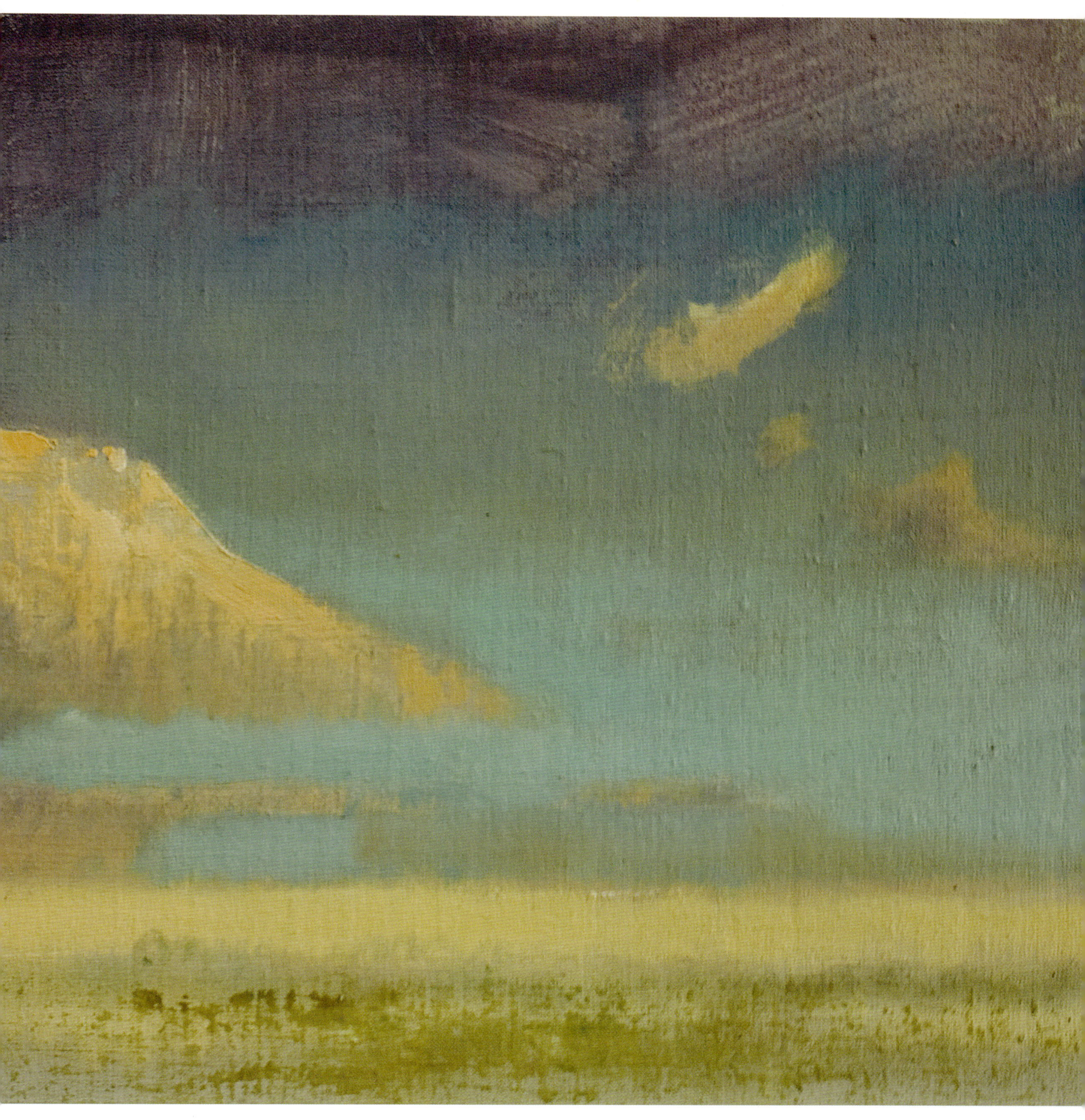

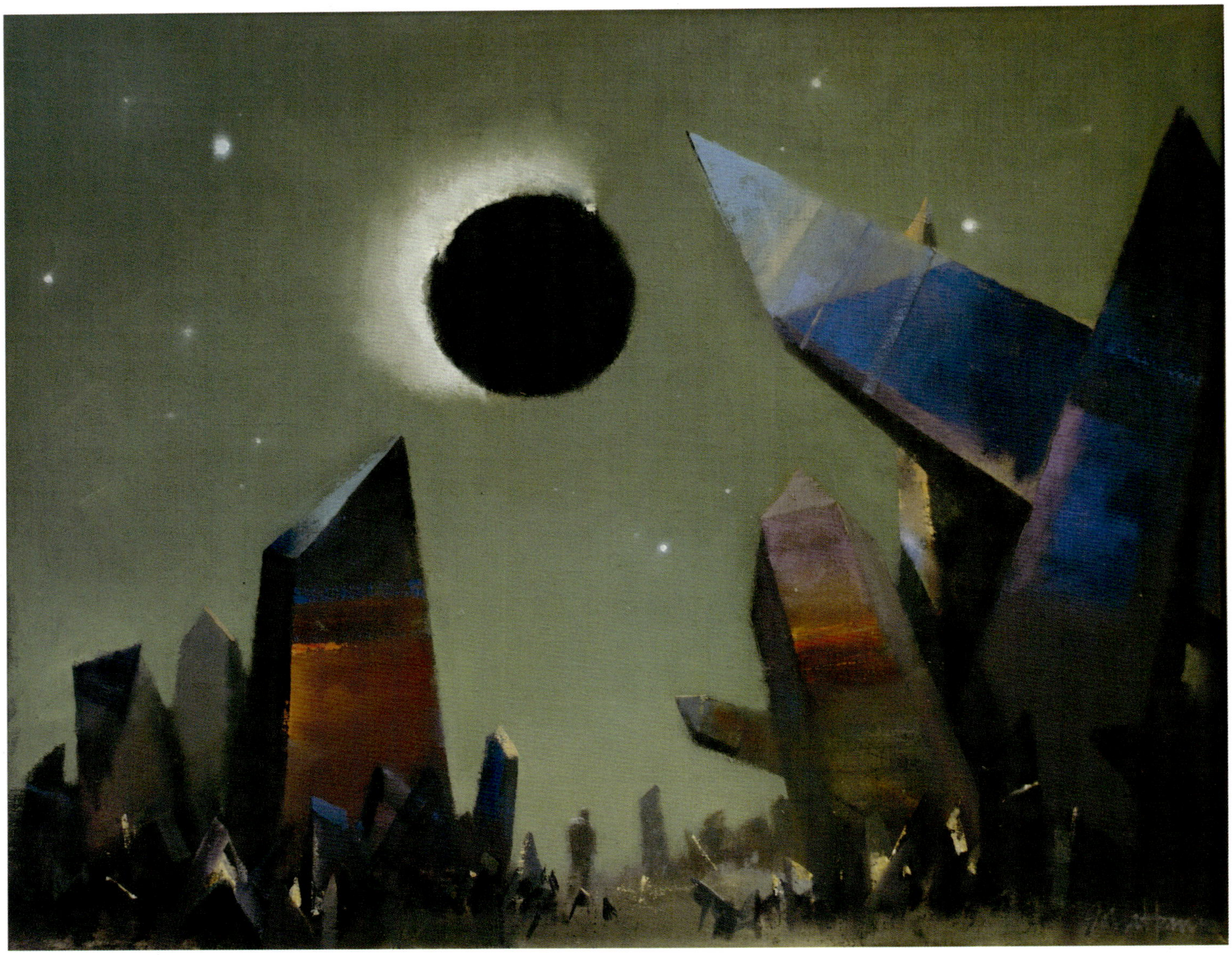

To the west of Haven lie the Abandoned Lands. There is a melancholy in this region which speaks of the retreat of life from a land that once had prospered, and is now only the haunt of crows. Beyond this are the bitter sands of the Plain of Crystals. It appears to be an inert and sterile world, but it is not quite as it seems...

Above: *The Exile*

Right: *The Lost Colonies of Drumm*

Opposite: *Travels In An Unknown Region*

Previous Spread: *Haven*

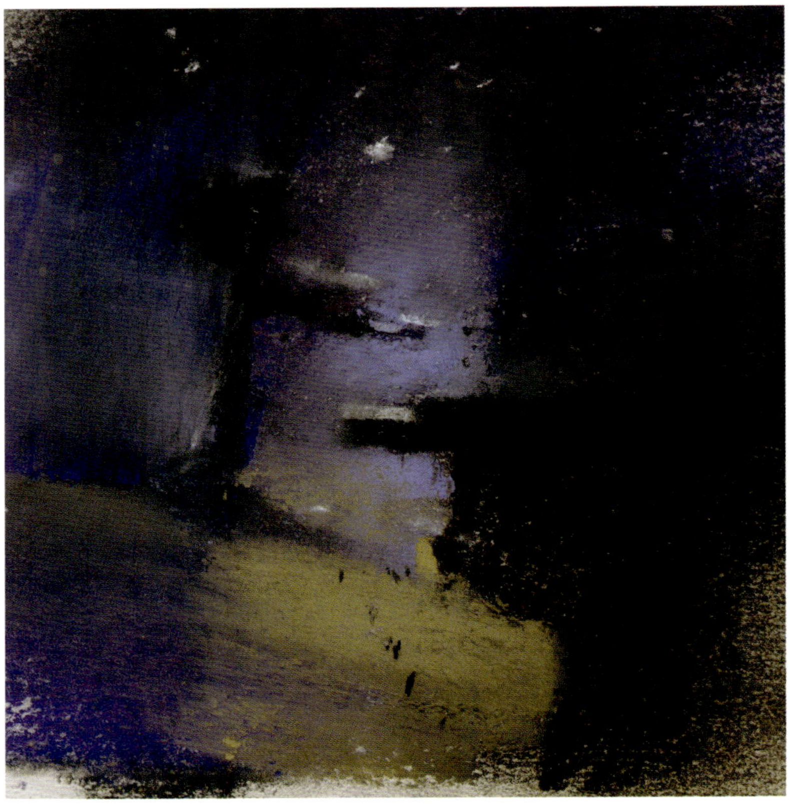

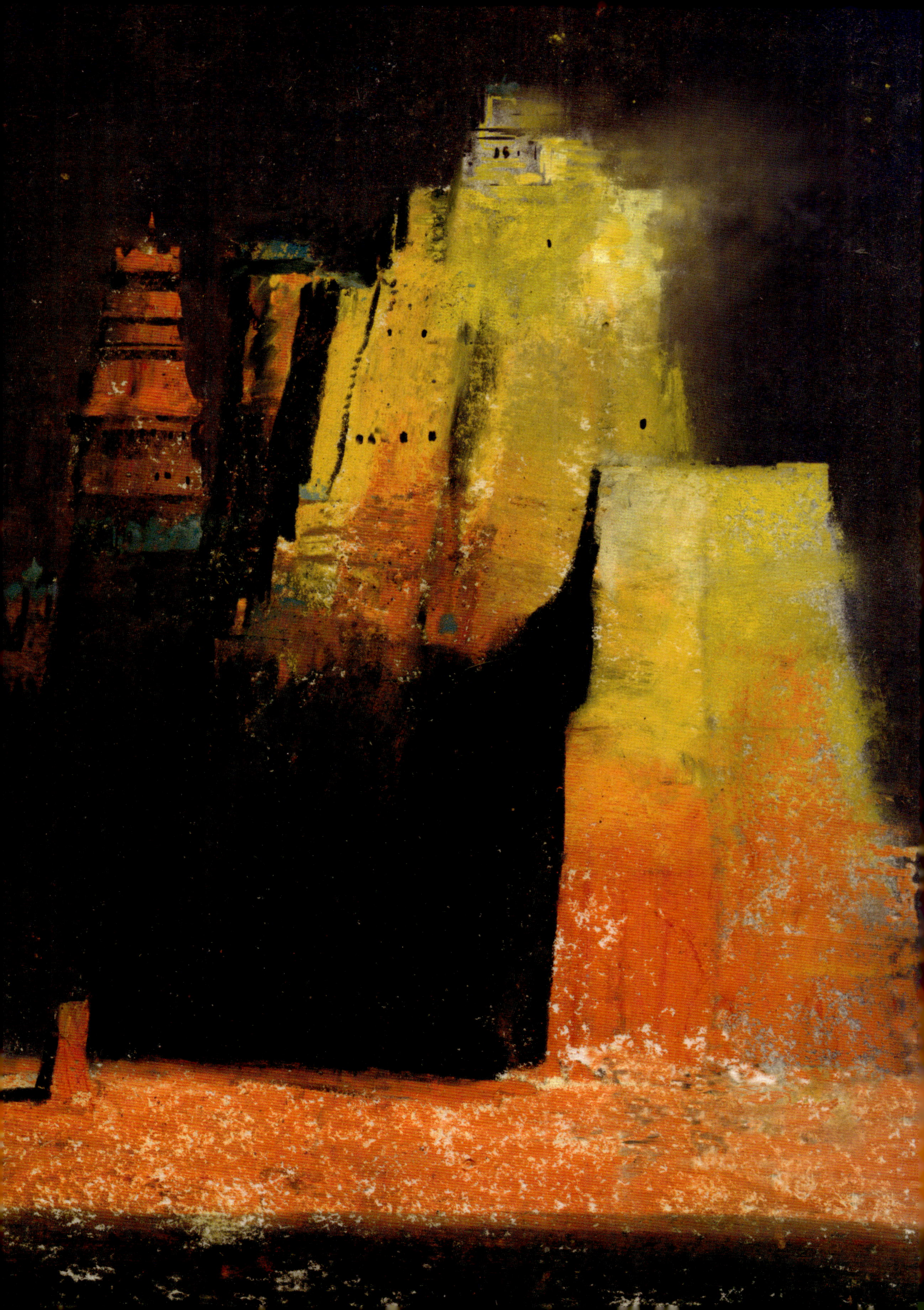

Whatever geological process caused these giant crystals to emerge from the otherwise featureless plain had also created reservoirs of vast electrical potential, which, under the right conditions, can release violent discharges. These fitful explosions dazzle the eye even in bright daylight and it is within this unpromising environment that the strangest form of 'life' has evolved. Silicon-based creatures that seem to exhibit some primitive form of social intelligence can frequently be seen scuttling around the crystalline structures, inserting metallic-like proboscises deep into the glassy ground, only to receive massive jolts of electricity, which then energise them into violent and erratic jerking fits. These are followed by squeals of pleasure or pain. It is hard to tell which.

Right: *Crystal City 1.* 2011

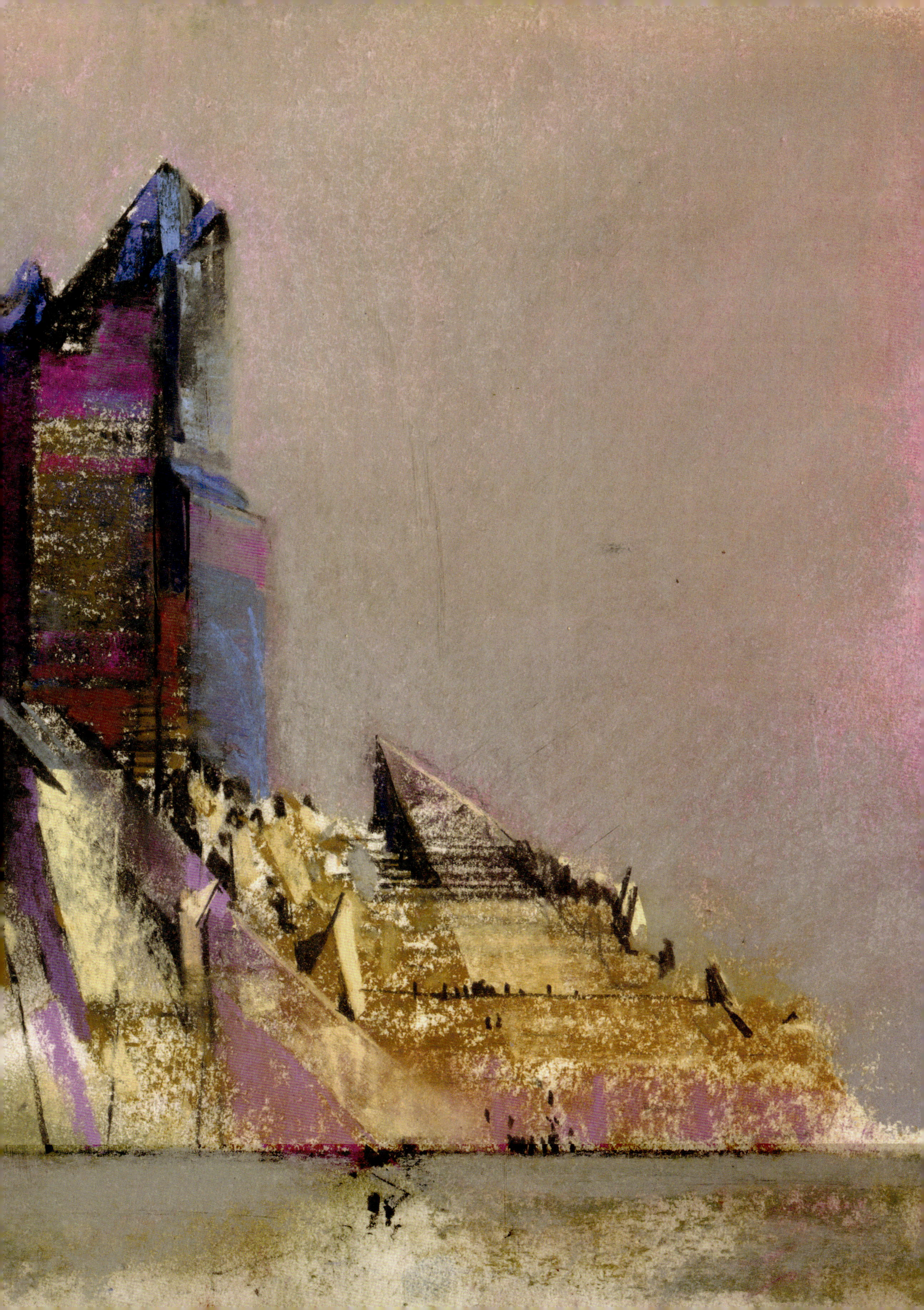

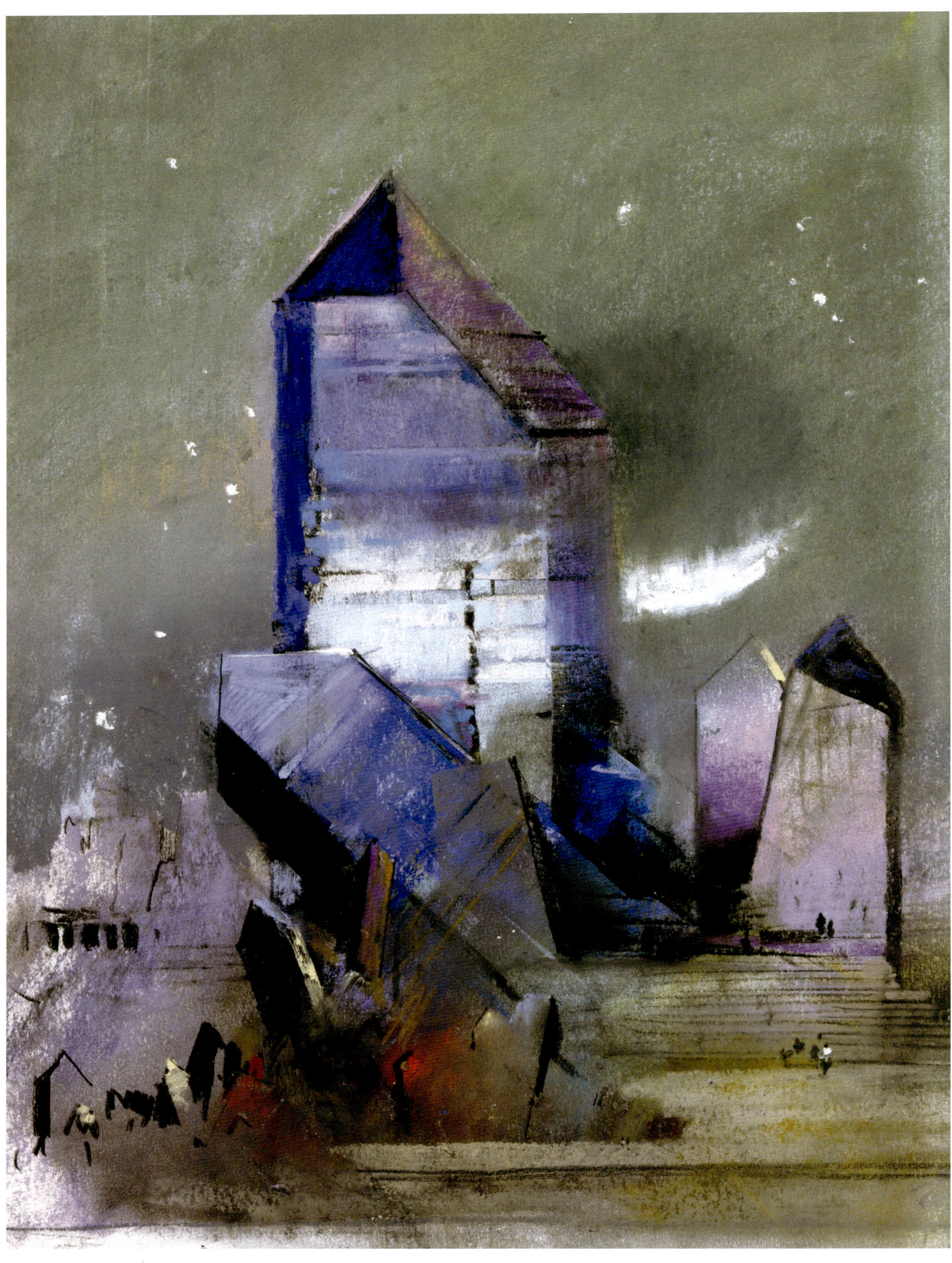

Above: *Crystal City 2*, 2011

Opposite Top: *The Pseudosapiens Duopods, electro-genetic beings*

Opposite Bottom: *Vespatron Feeding*, 2011

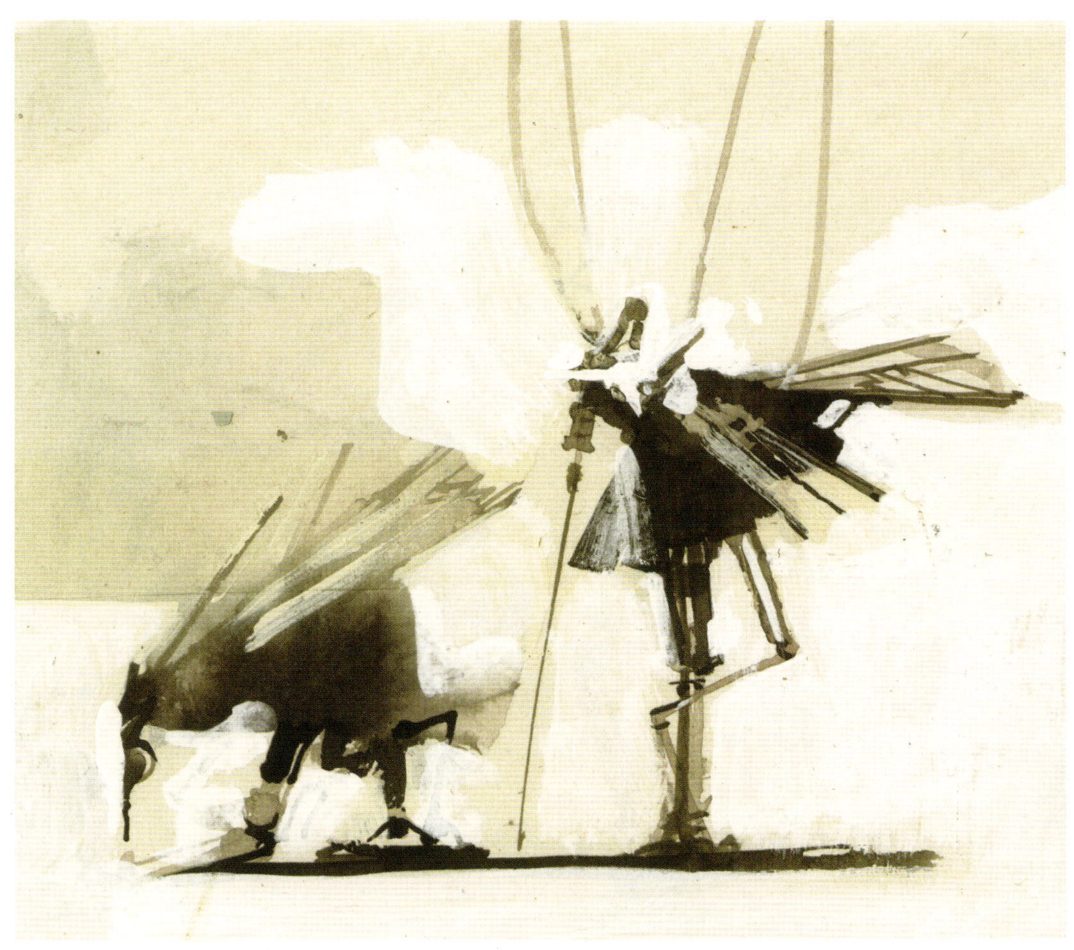

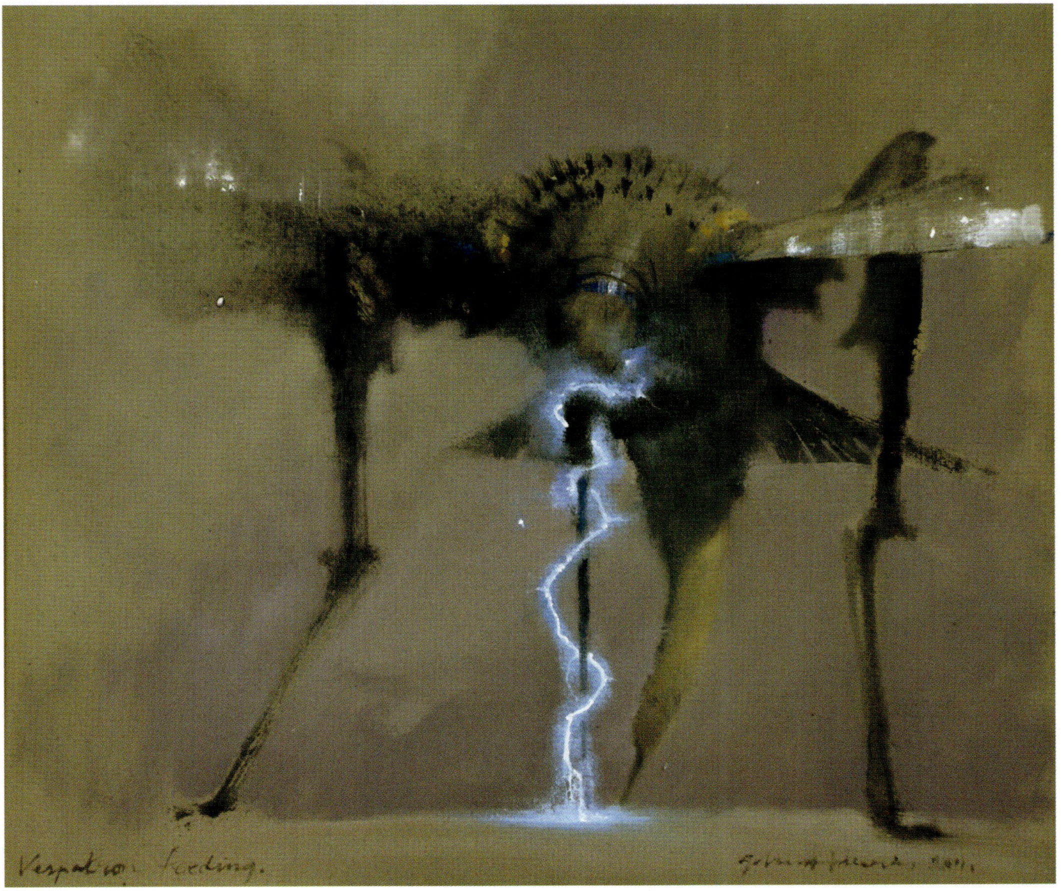

Life in the Plain of Crystals is very strange indeed. There is no organic life to speak of, but an entirely separate and apparently synthetic ecology may be found here. *Above,* silicon-based life forms, hunting for electrical sources around the crystalline structures which give this desolate place its name.

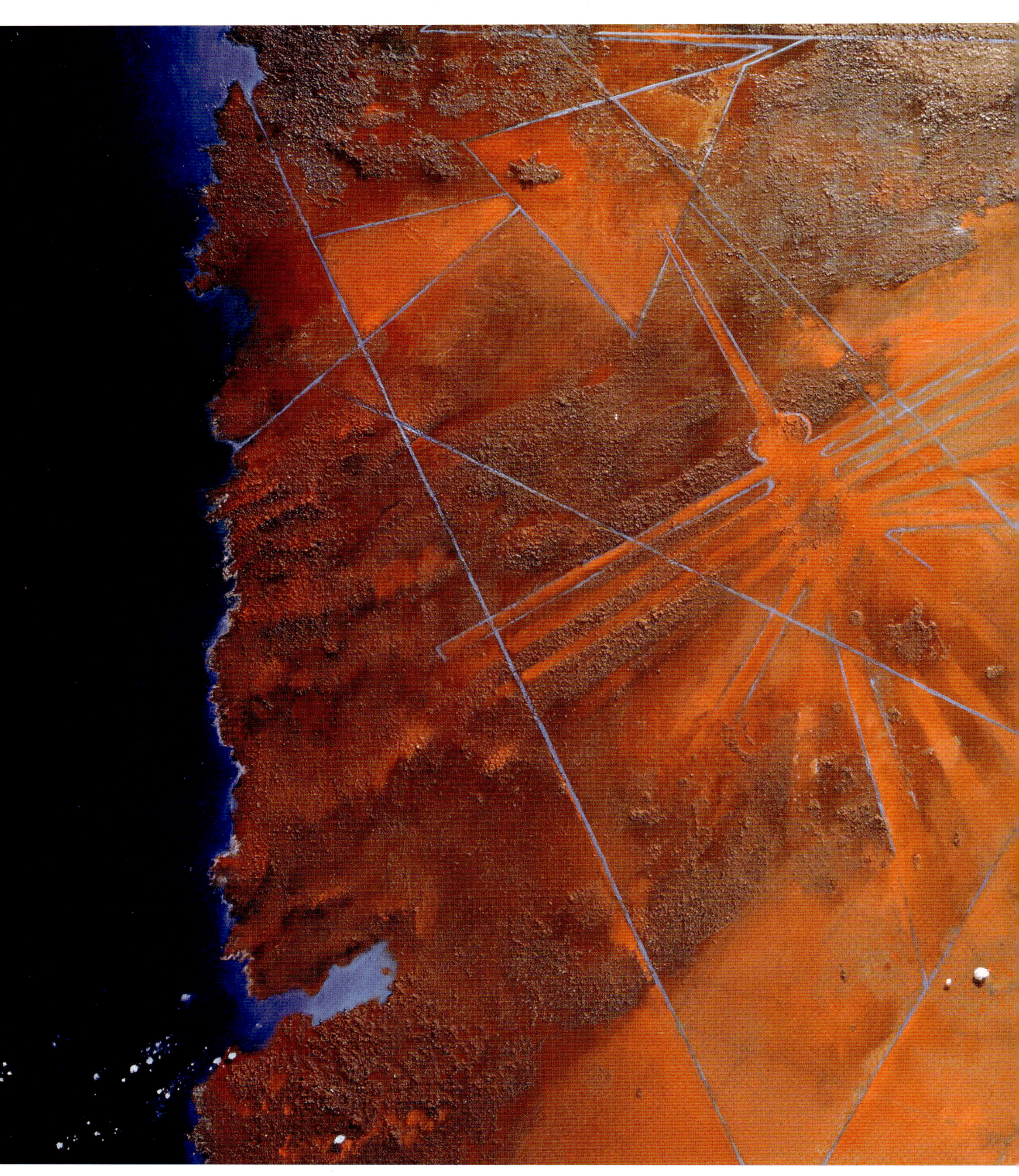

BEYOND THE HORIZON

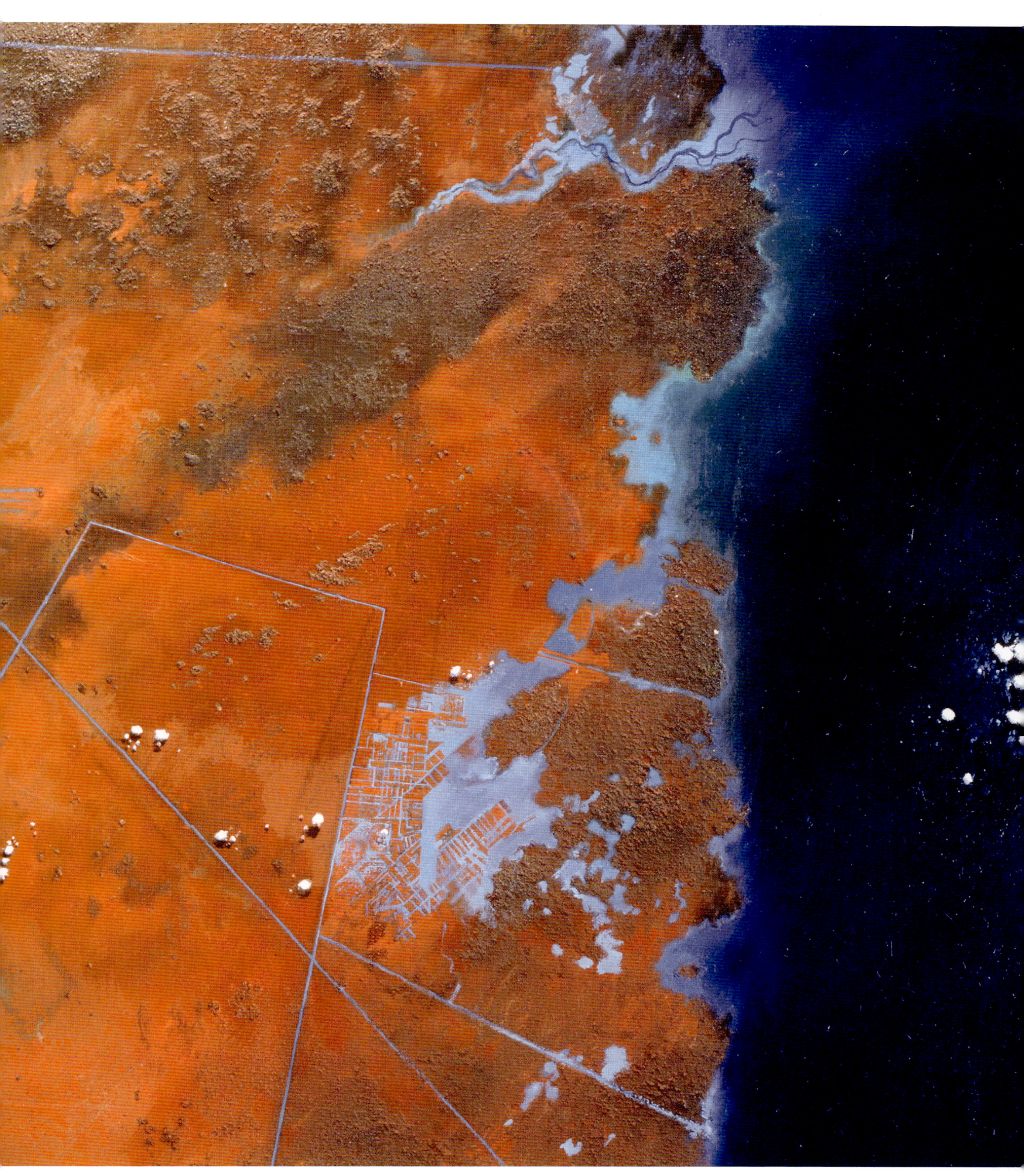

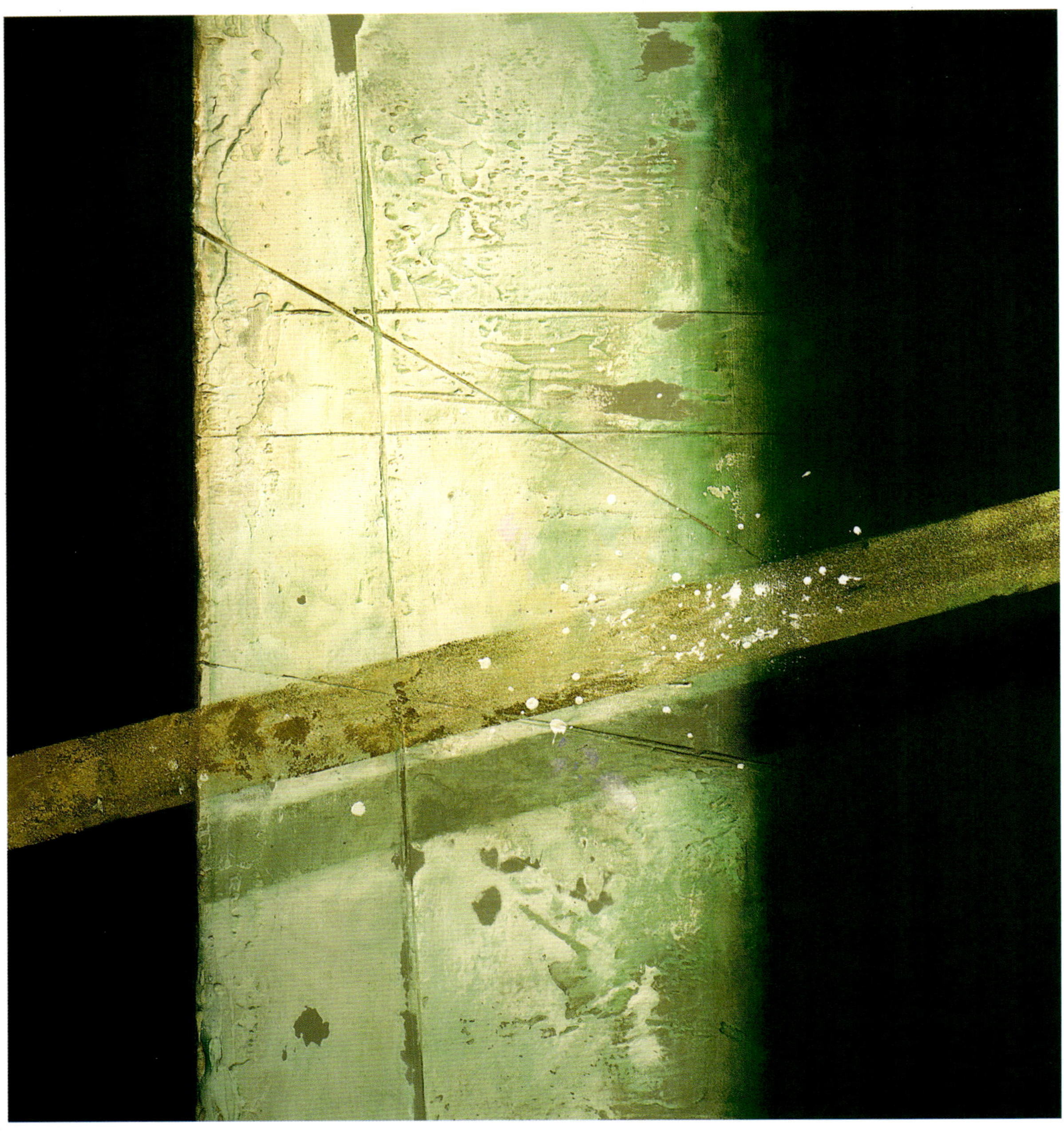

THE SECRET HISTORY OF THE EARTH

In 1985, I was commissioned by NASA to attend a launch and provide them with a painting to evoke the event, which opened up a train of thought which eventually led into an entirely different kind of work. The piece which I had completed in the winter of that year was a purely representational image of the launch (it now hangs in the Kennedy Space Centre), but in the process of creating the image, I had absorbed vast amounts of imagery from the NASA archives.

It wasn't until years later that the influence of this imagery surfaced. Thinking of the satellite photos of the Earth taken by NASA and others, I became aware of how much the traces of the past were visible on the surface of the Earth, not just of the activities of Man, but of the Earth itself, a slate constantly rewriting itself. Then, as I began to form images that echoed some of those characteristics, the physical materials that I was using (plaster, gold leaf, dry pigment etc.) began to dictate an entirely new visual language for me. The gradient of reflection, from the high shine of gold leaf to the almost absolute matt of raw pigment, the contrasts of texture, gritty earth to feathery dust: these are some of the elements of a language which developed and which became the focus of these pictures. Collectively, they have become something of a tone poem to the Earth.

I have always enjoyed the storytelling power of imagery and, paradoxically, the power of the materials that go into the making of a picture, their abstract nature of texture serving to enhance the 'illustrative' content of these images. The intent here, is to create a balance between the two, which I believe can generate an intensity which only the actual piece can fully express.

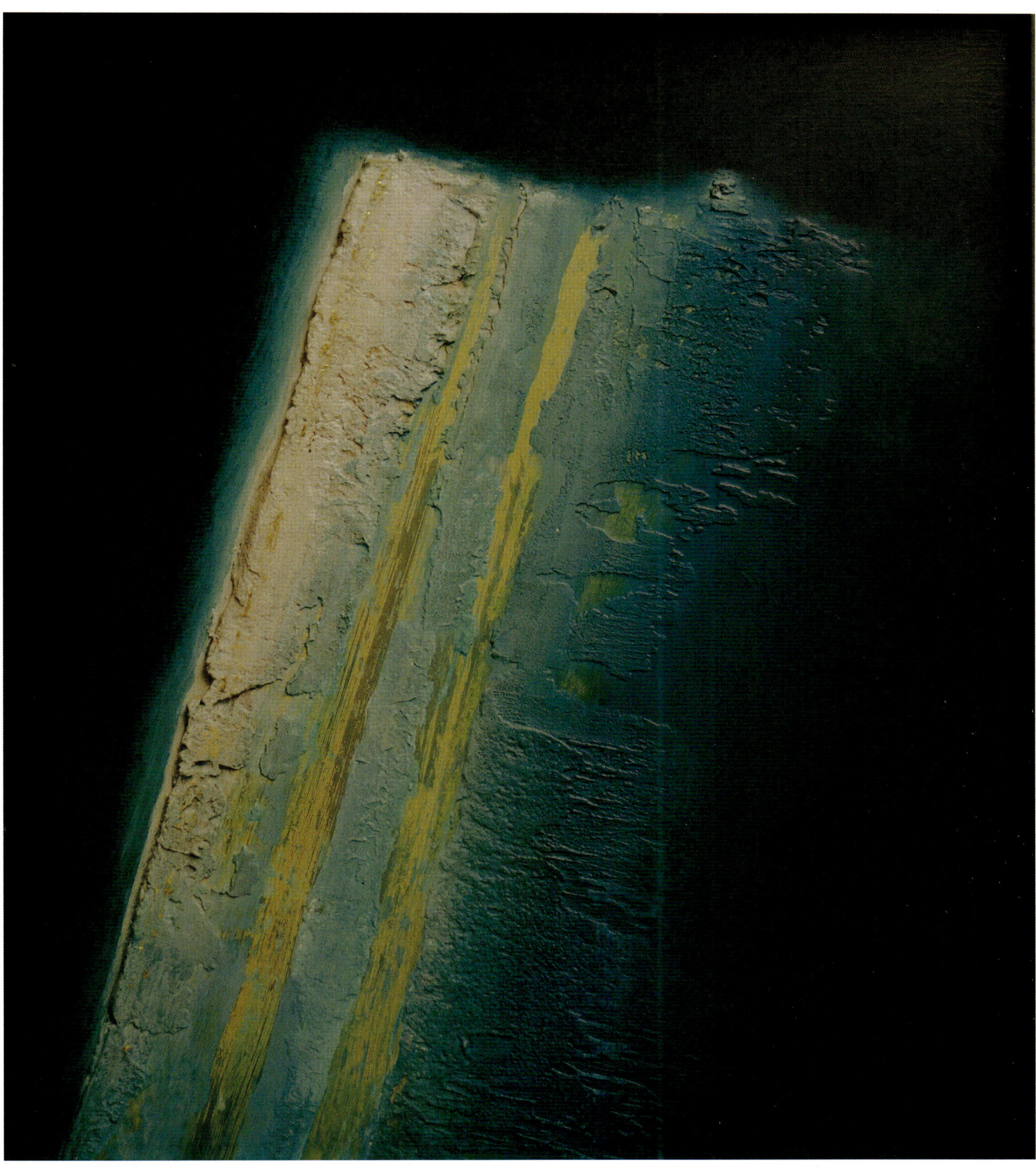

Above: *Above The Deep*

Opposite: *Transit*

Previous Spread: *A View from Above*

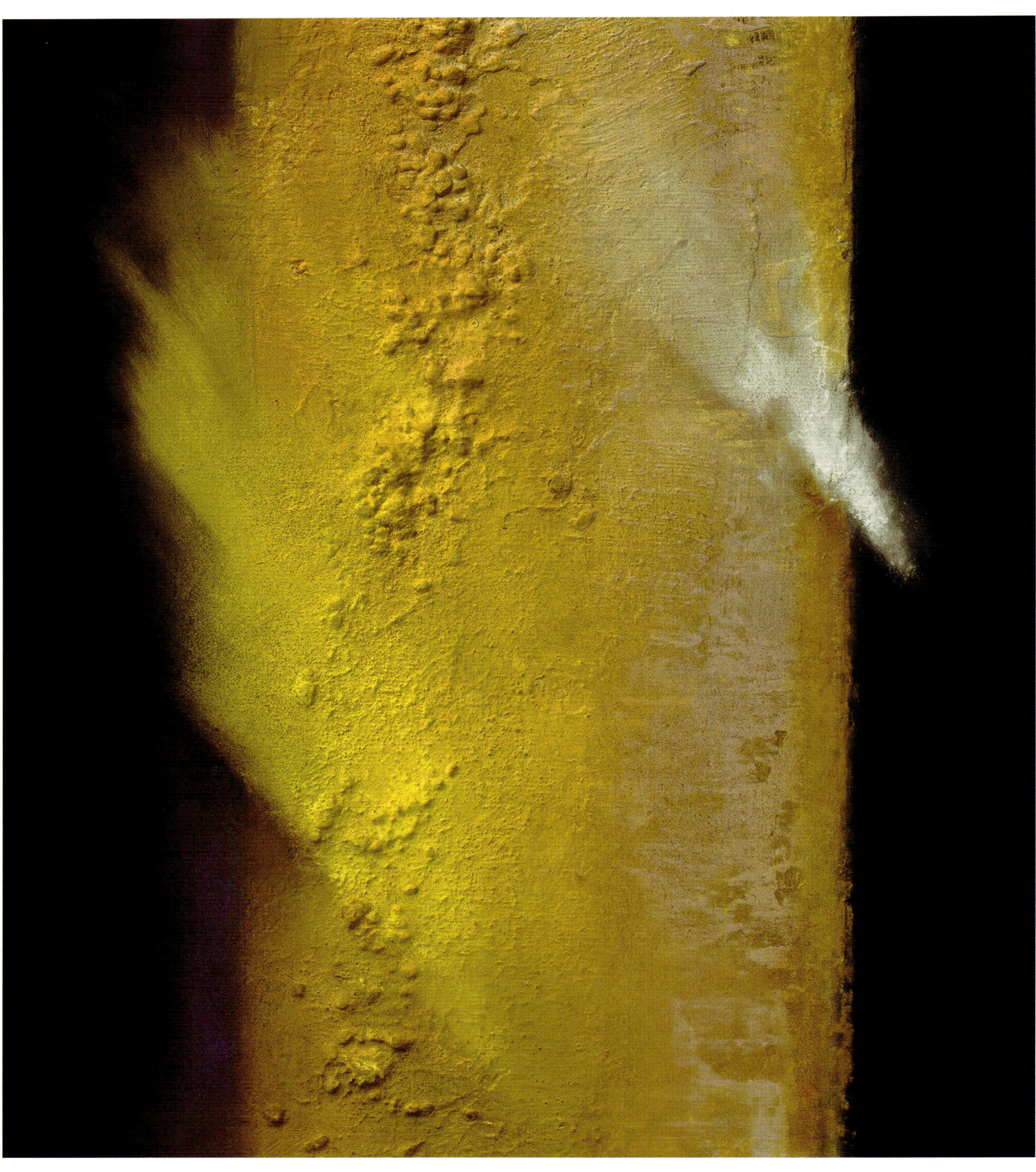

Above: *Sulphur Storm 1*

Opposite: *Sulphur Storm 2 (Human Traces)*

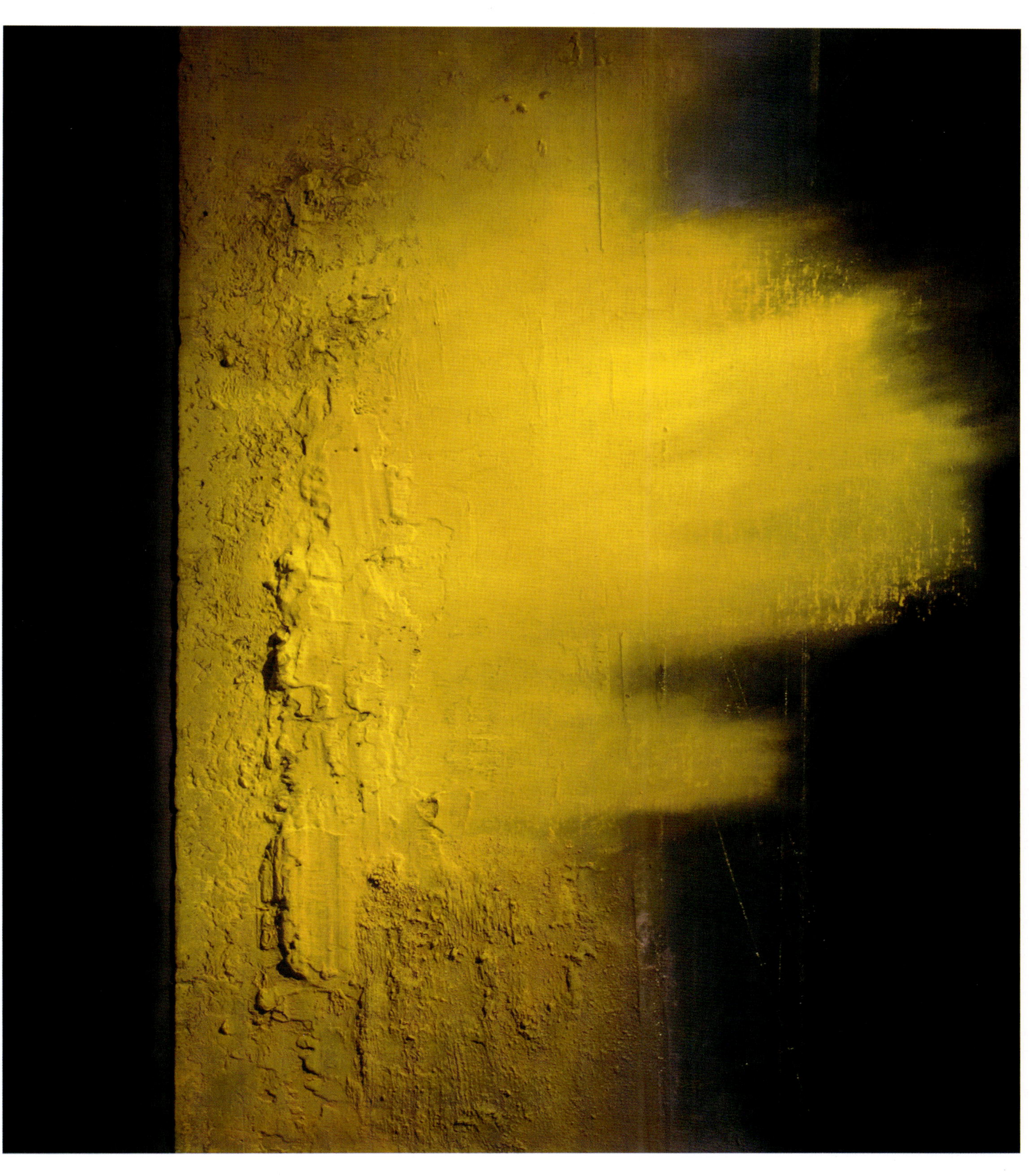

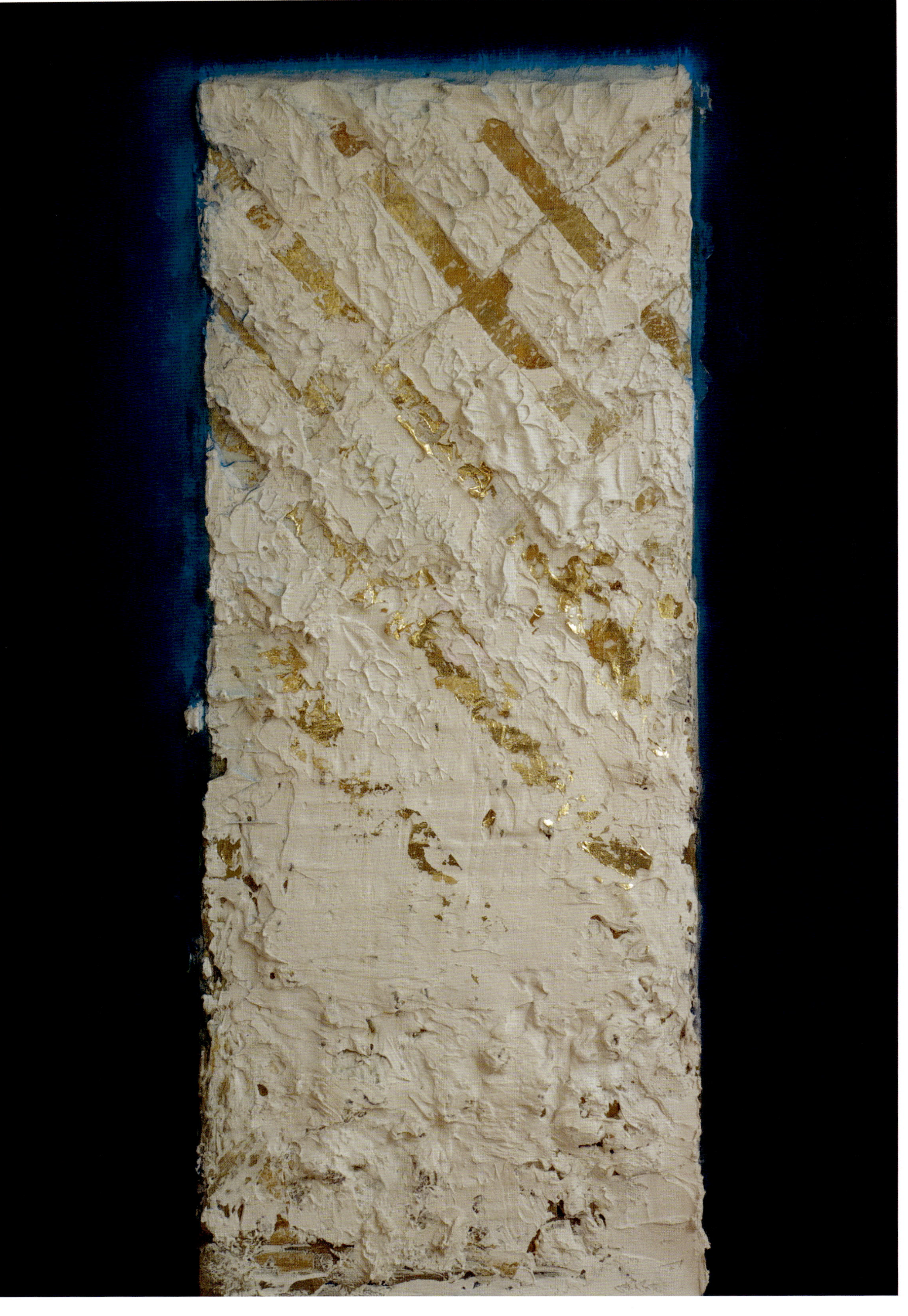

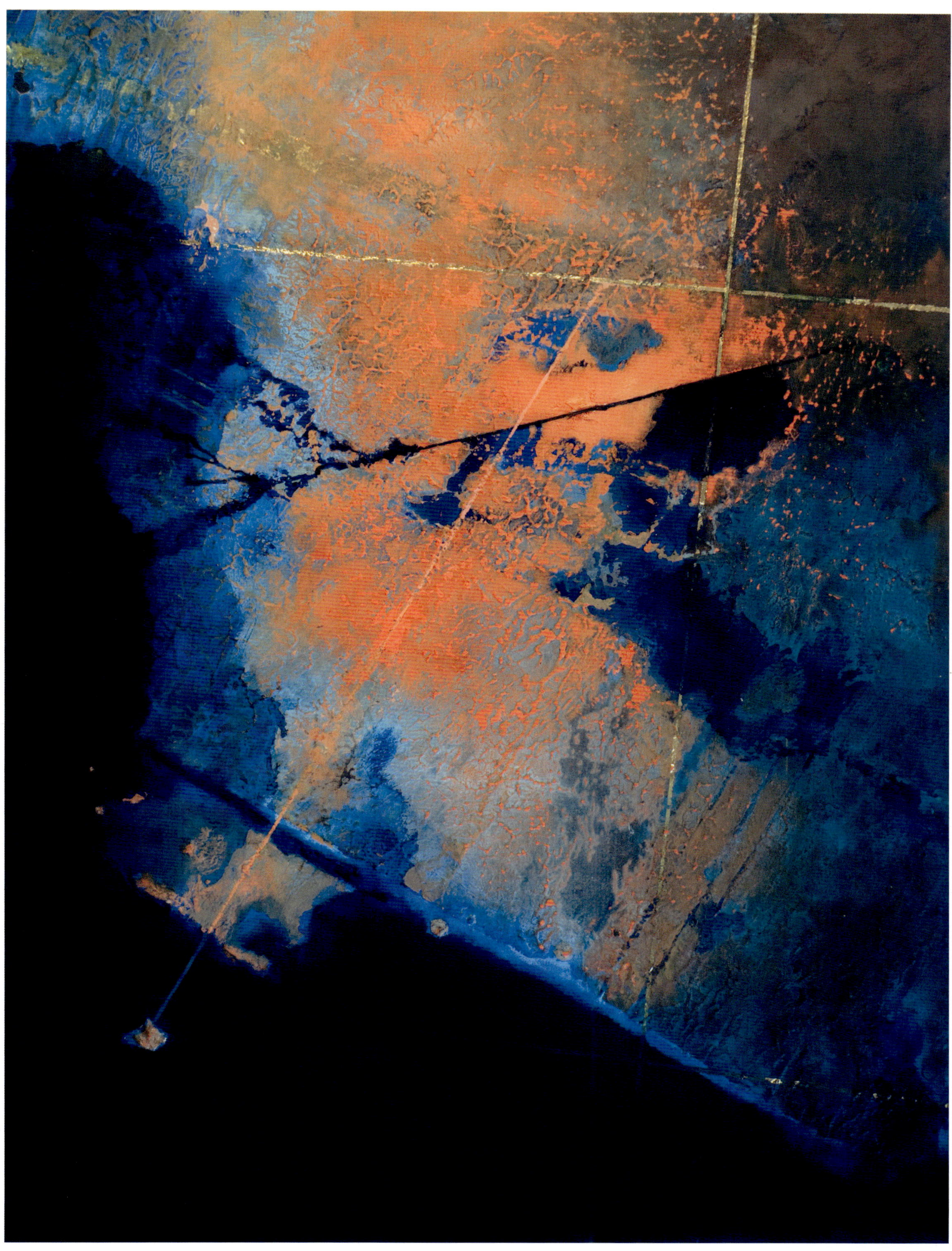

Above: *The Inundated Coast*

Opposite: *Iona*

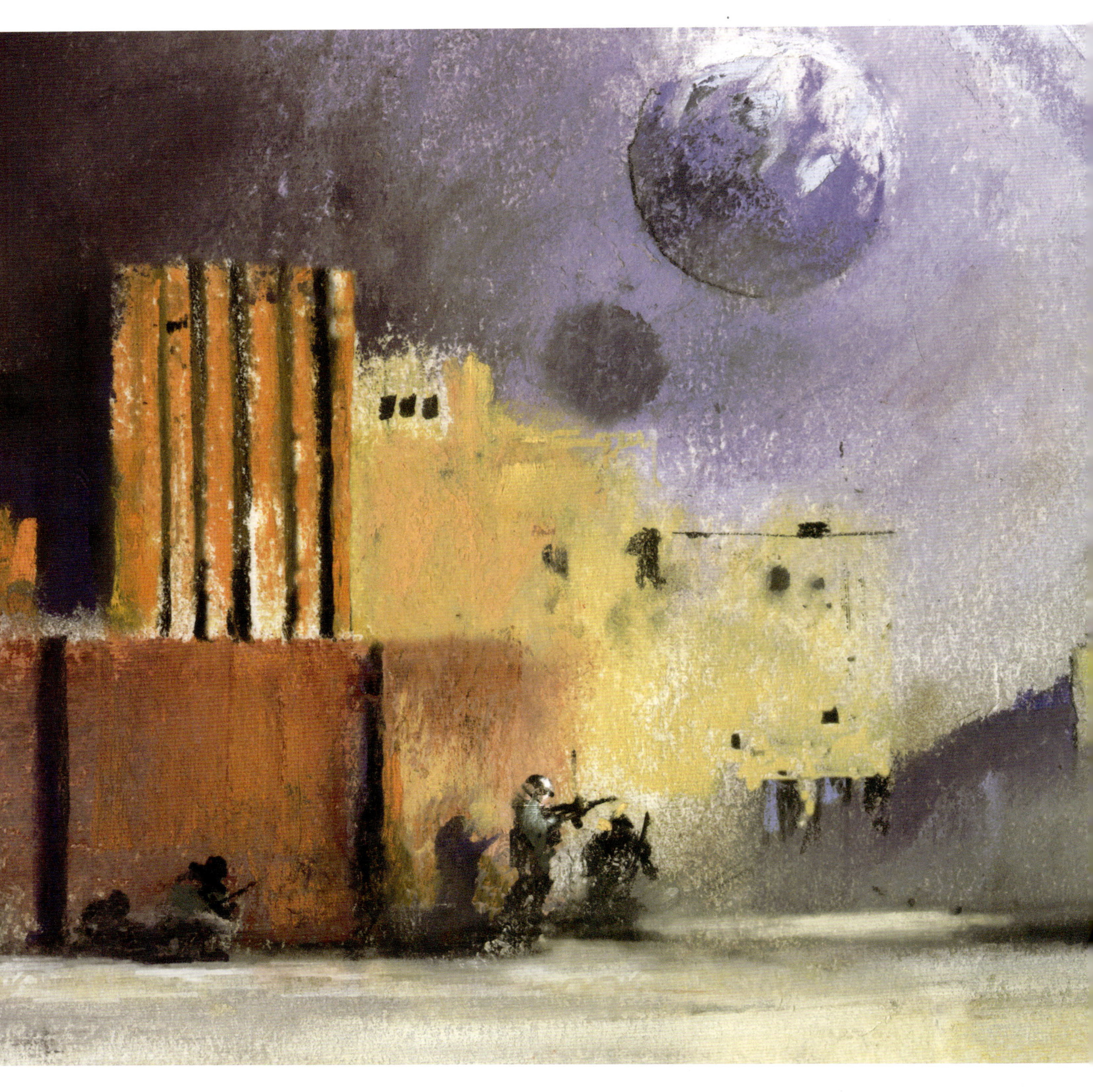

WORKS BY AUTHOR

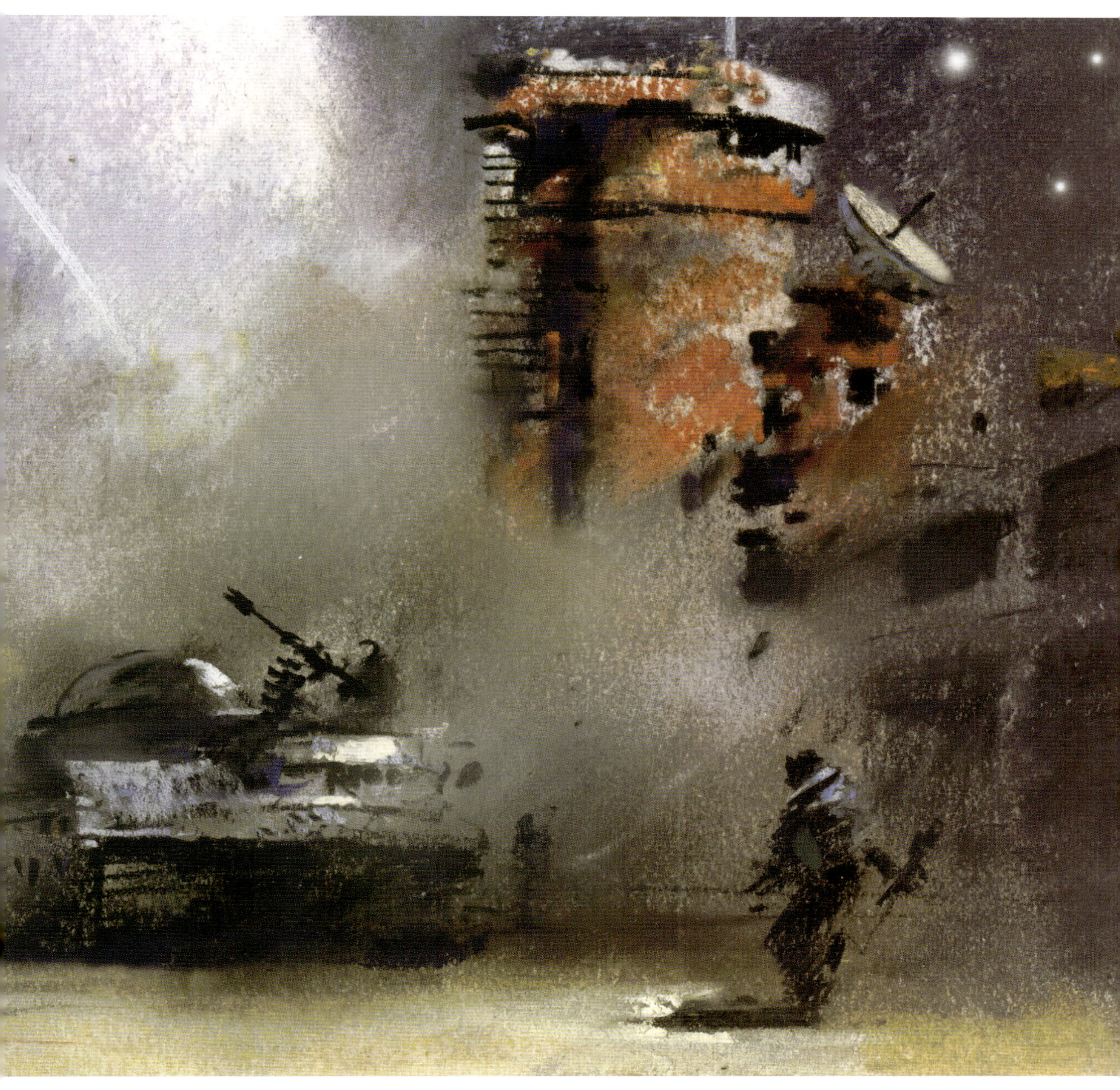

JOHN SCALZI

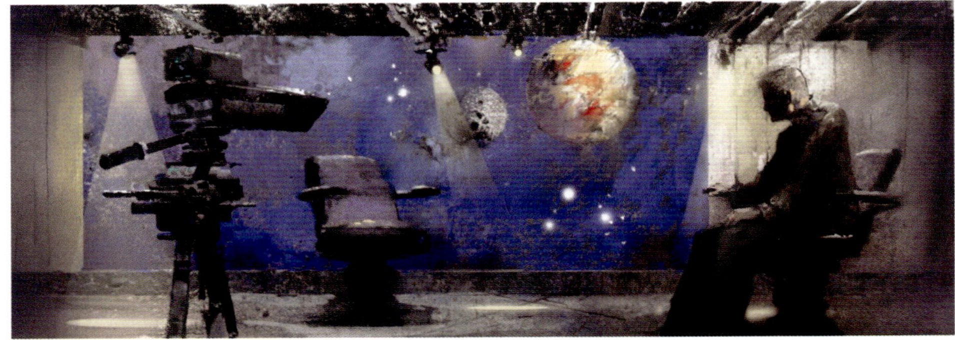

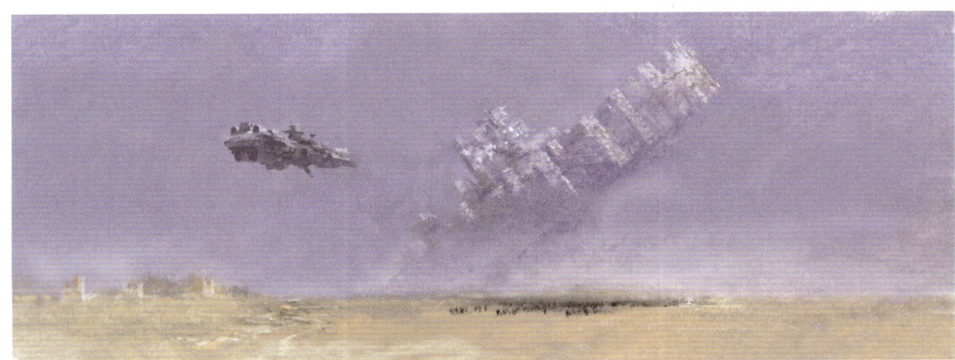

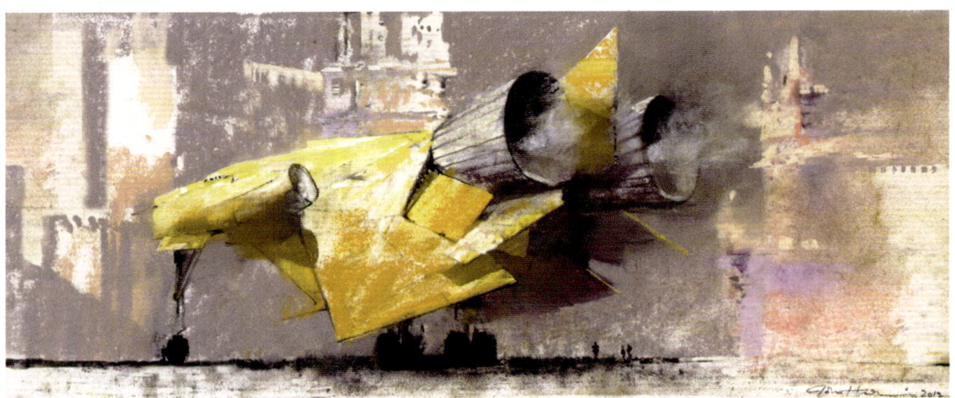

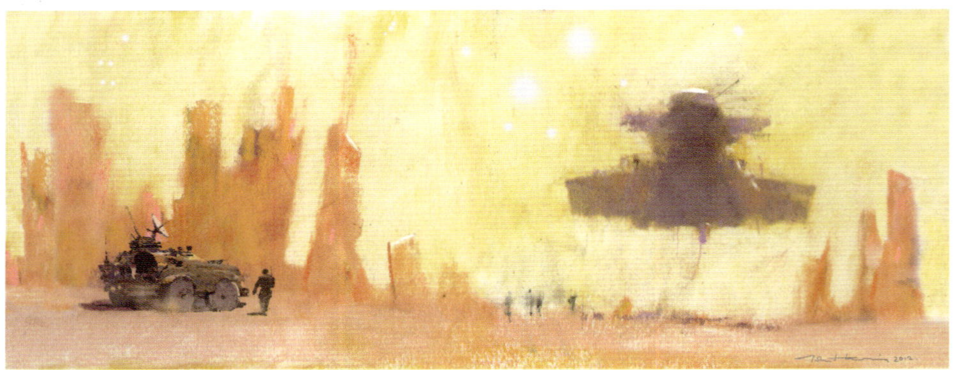

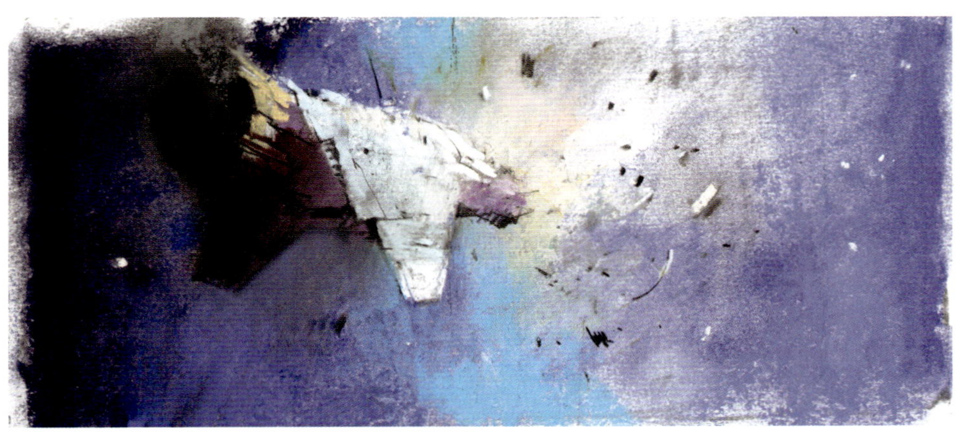

From Top to Bottom:

A Voice in the Wilderness

The Observers

This Must be the Place

Rendezvous

Walk the Plank

All commissioned to illustrate fragments of the book, *The Human Division*

Opposite: :
Old Man's War

Previous Spread: :
The Sound of Rebellion

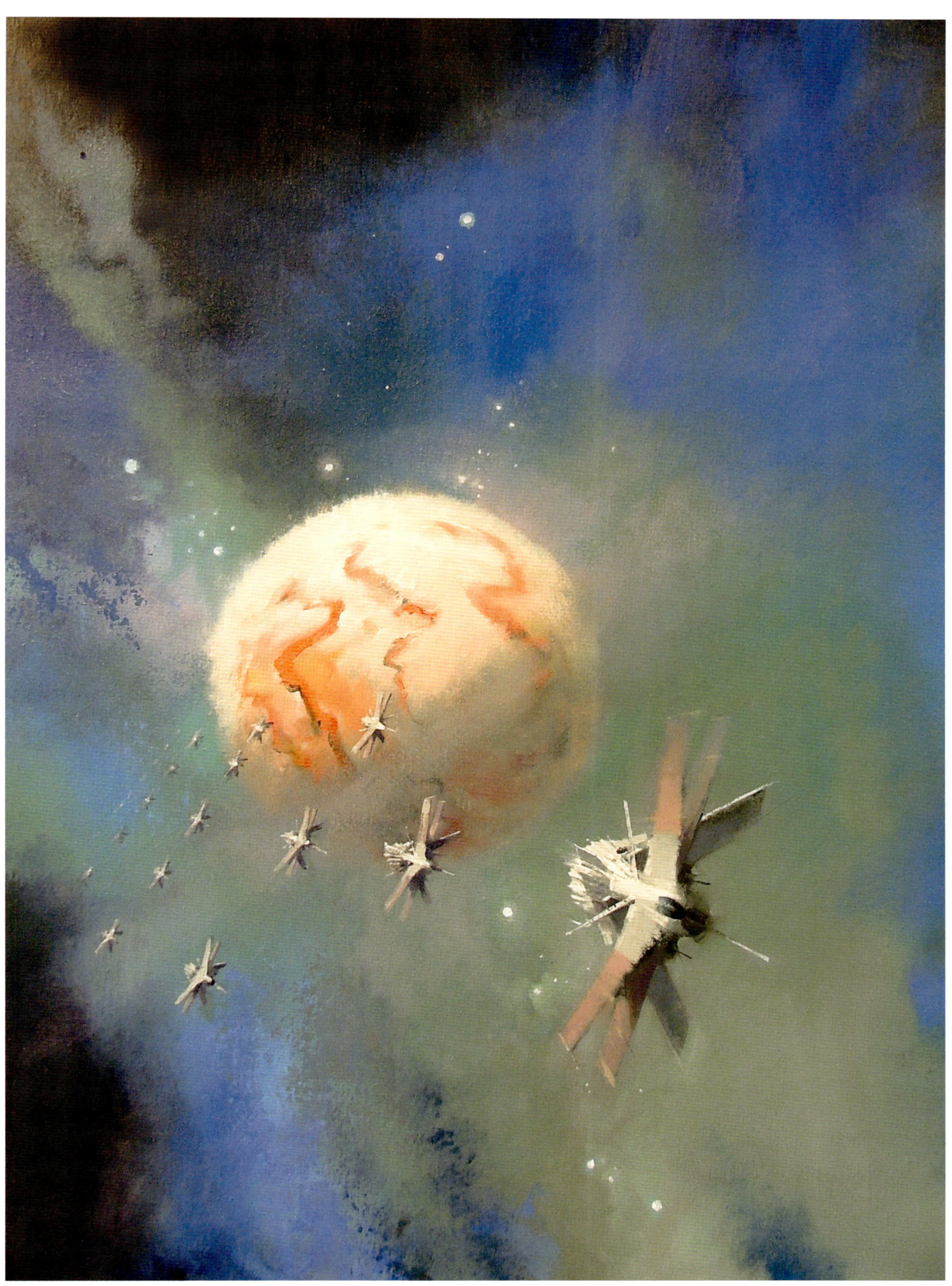

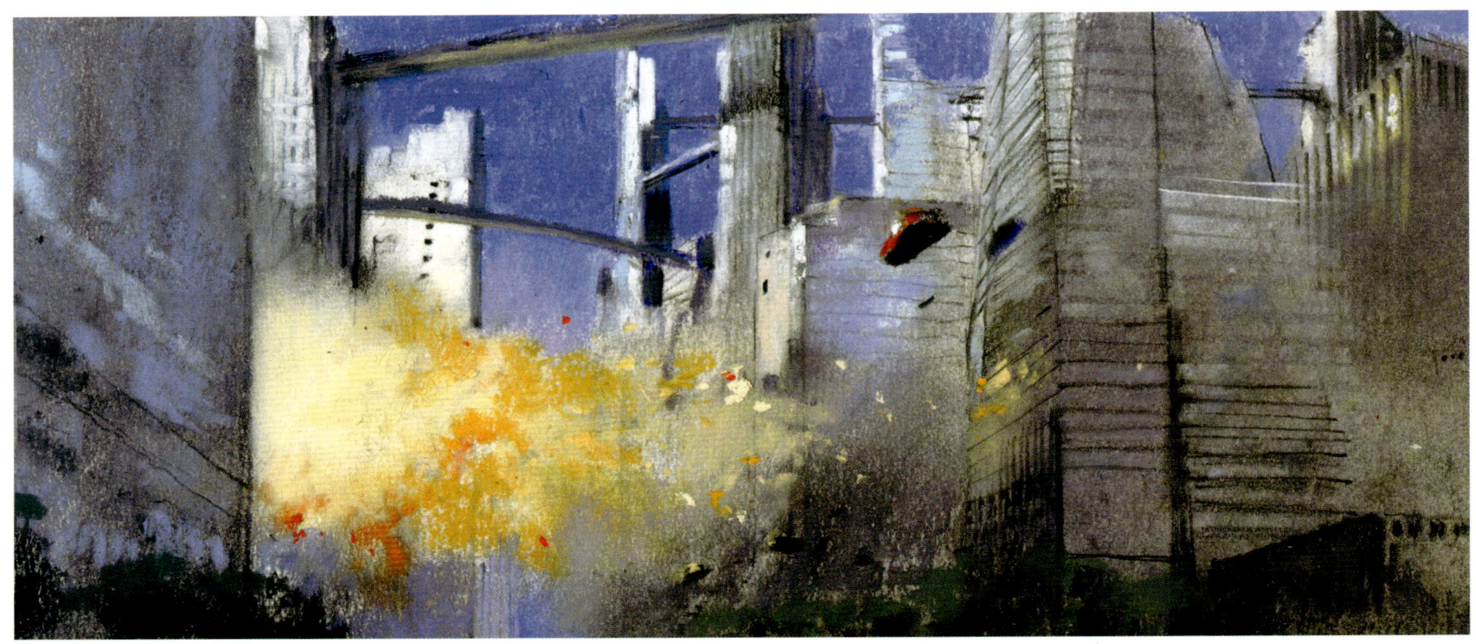

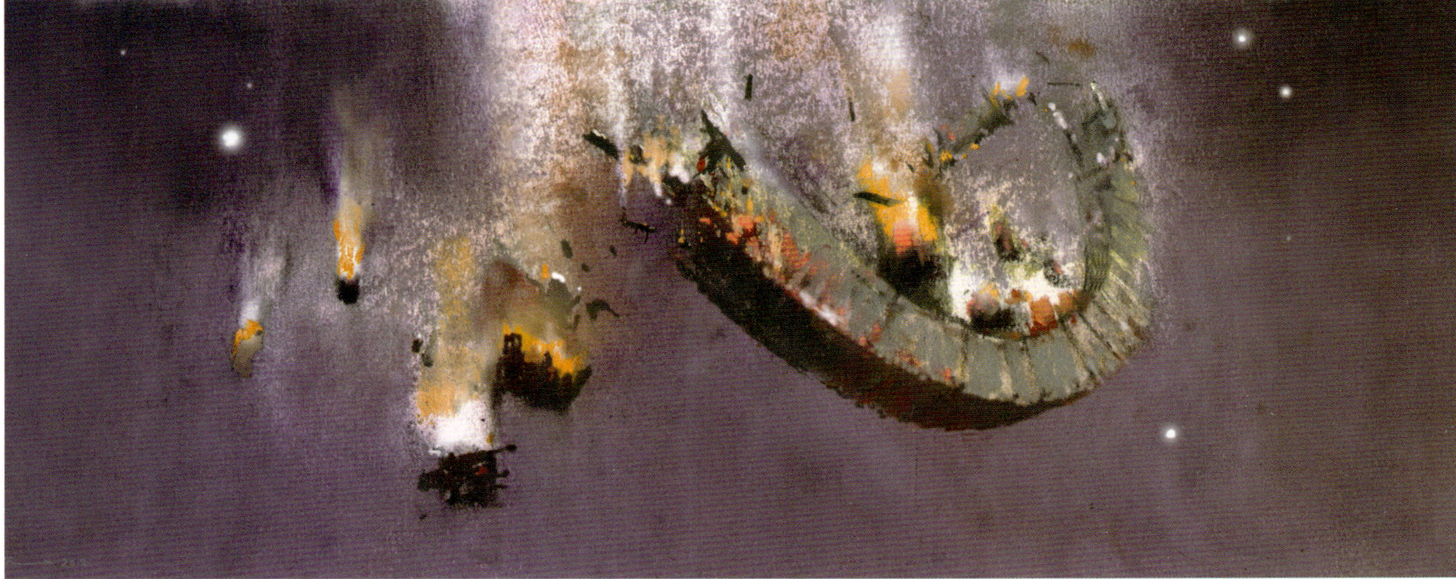

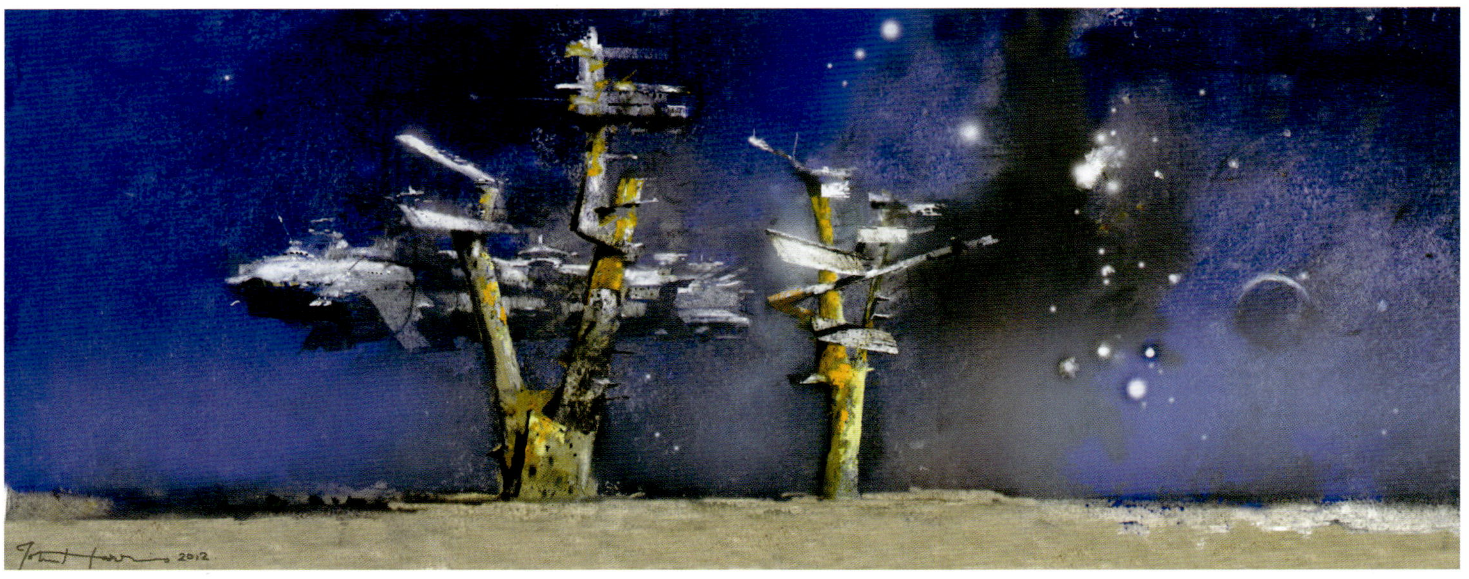

From Top to Bottom:
The Gentle Art of Cracking Heads
Earth Below, Sky Above
Tales from the Clarke

Opposite: *The Human Division (cover)*
All commissioned to illustrate fragments of the book, *The Human Division*

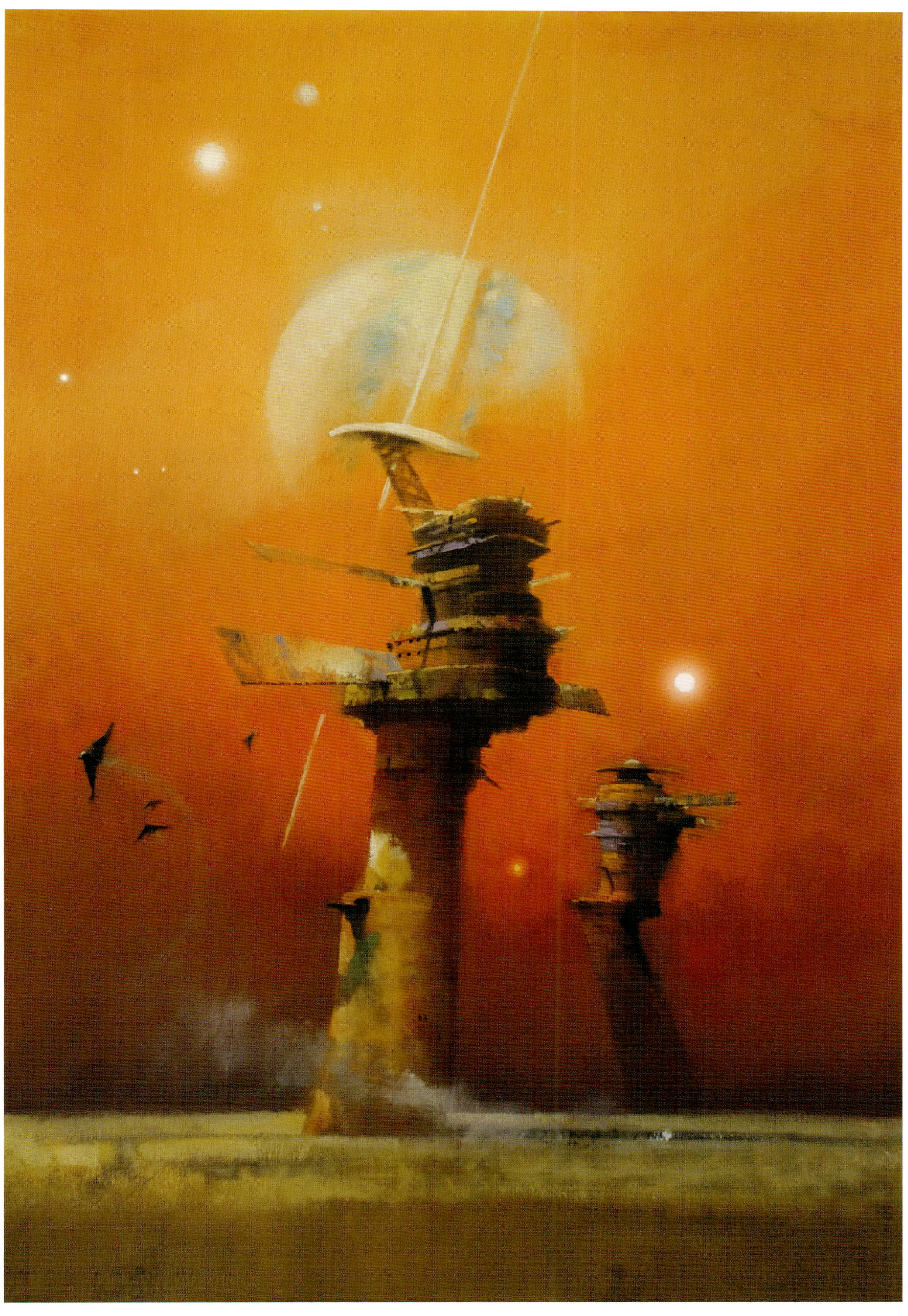

BEN BOVA

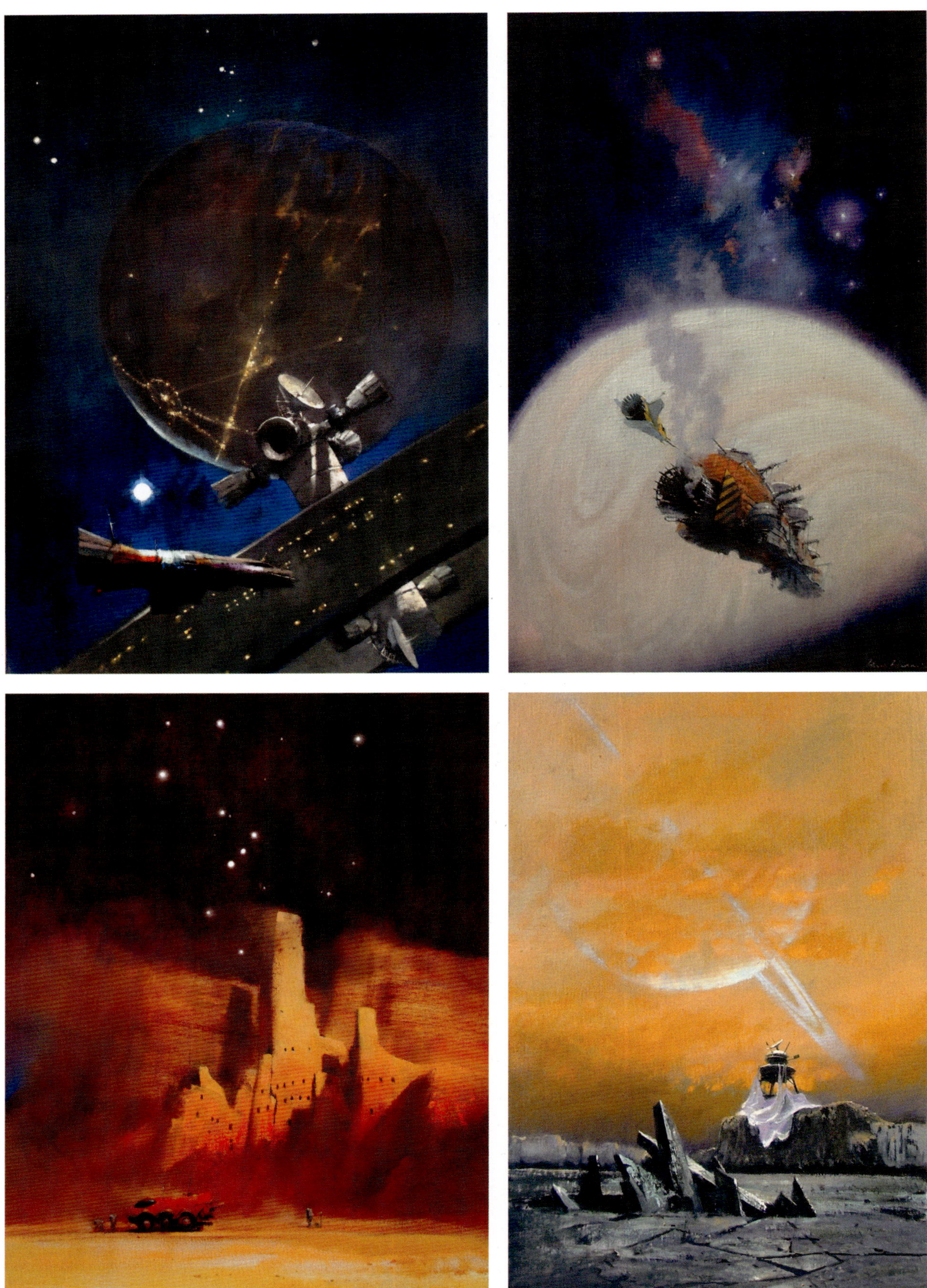

Top Left: *New Earth*
Top Right: *Venus*
Bottom Left: *Mars Life*
Bottom Right: *Titan*

JACK MCDEVITT

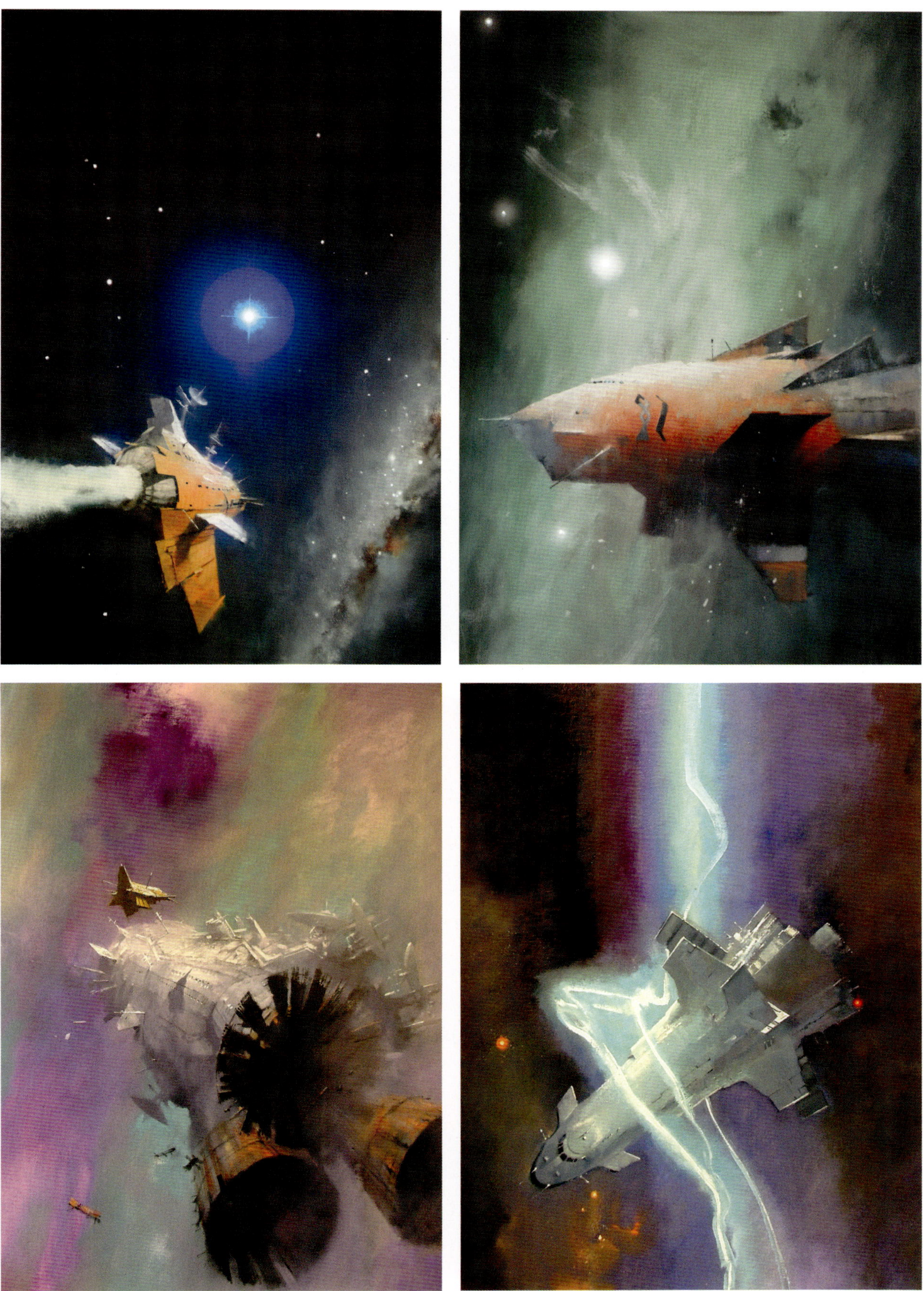

Top Left: *The Devil's Eye*
Top Right: *Firebird*
Bottom Left: *Seeker*
Bottom Right: *Polaris*

ORSON SCOTT CARD

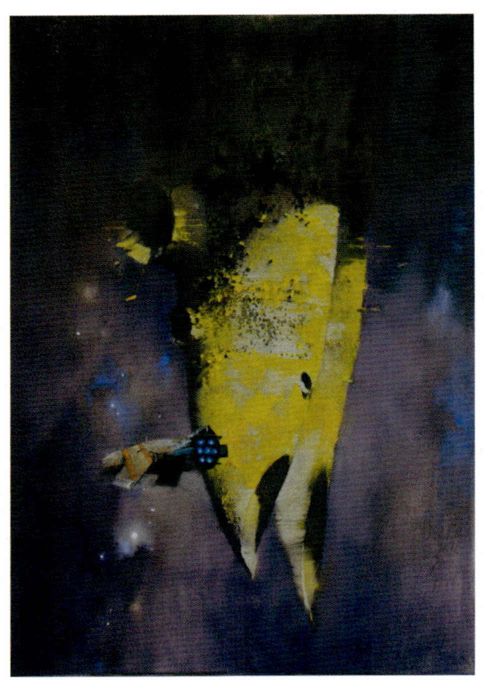

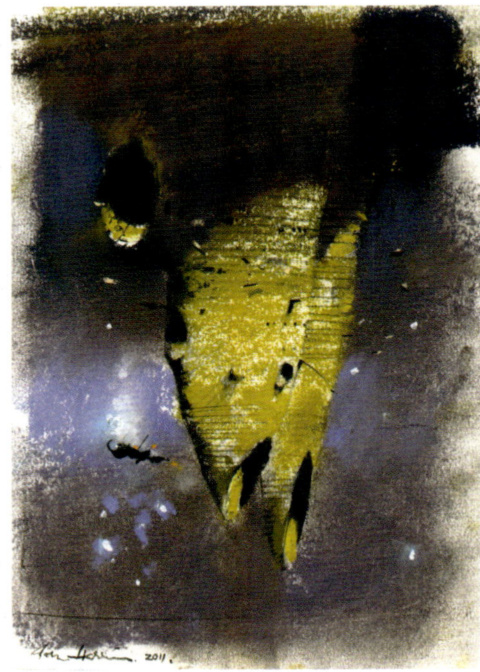

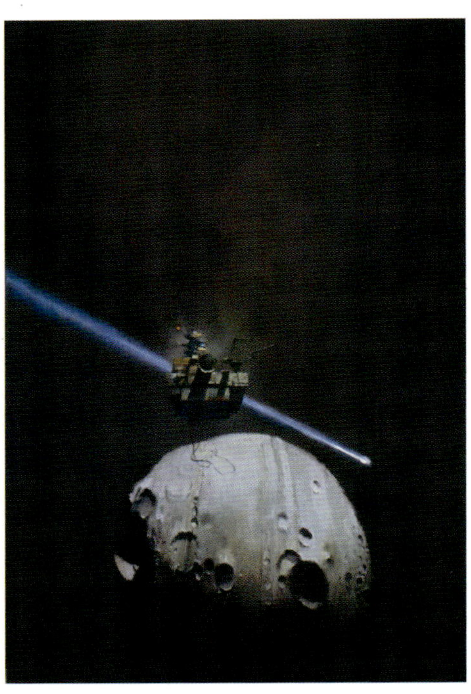

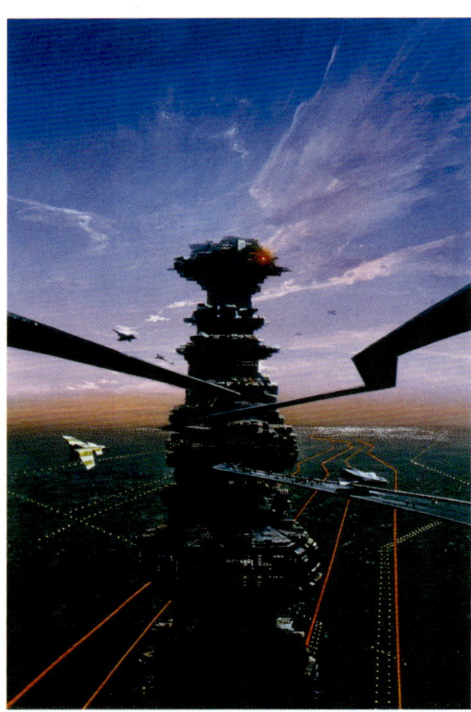

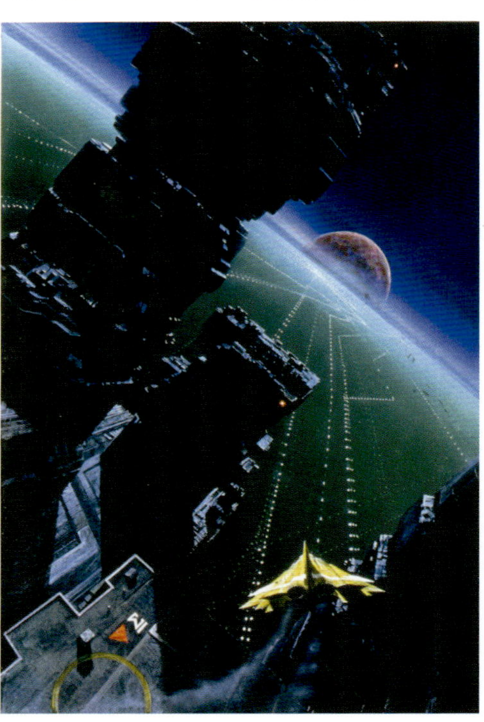

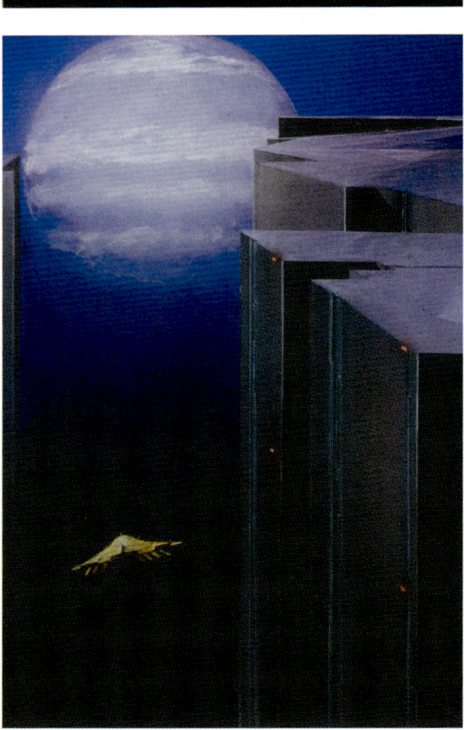

Top Row from Left to Right:
Shadows in Flight
Shadows in Flight (sketch)
Earth Unaware

Bottom Row from Left to Right:
Speaker for the Dead
Ender's Game
Xenocide

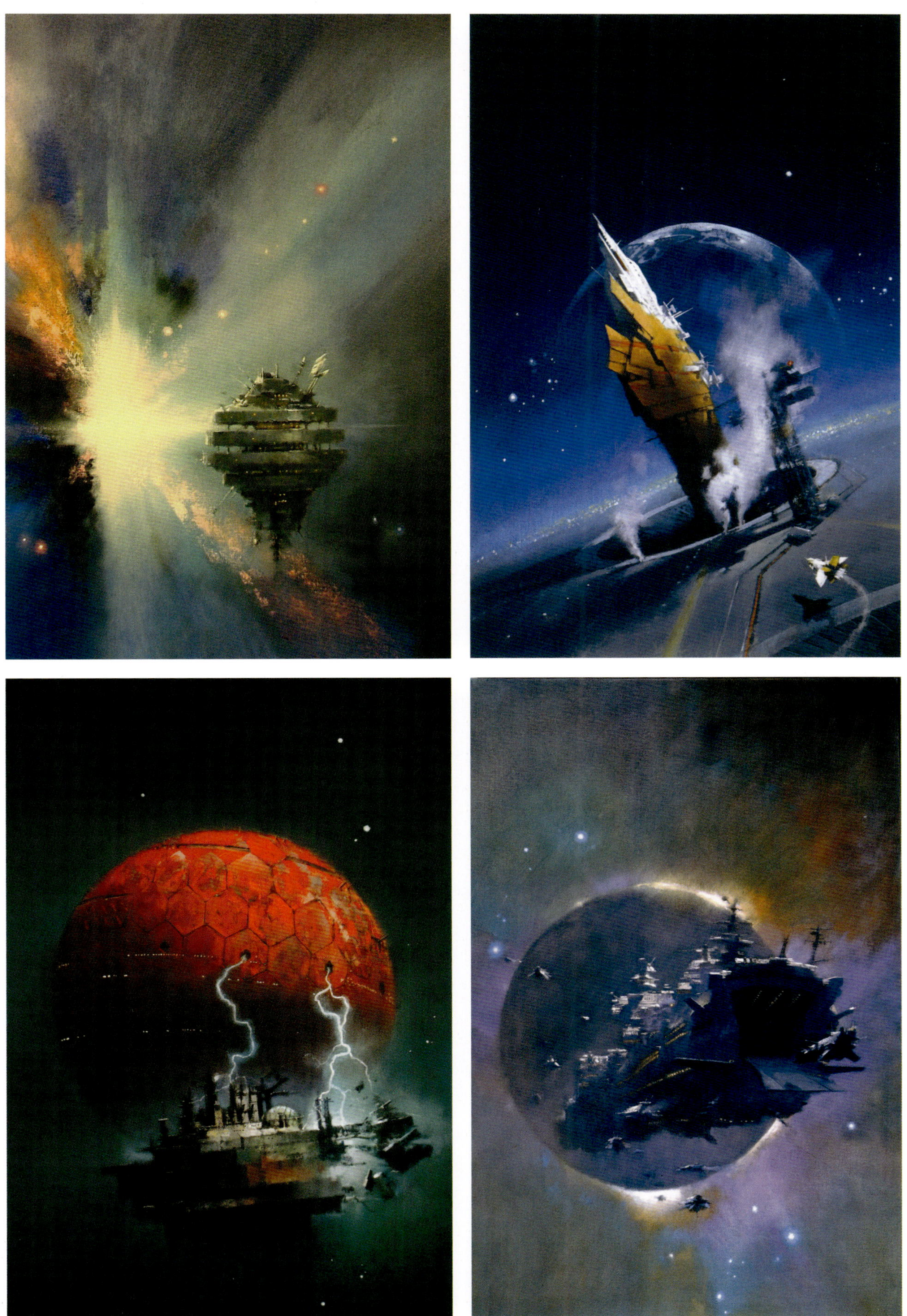

Top Left: *A War of Gifts*
Top Right: *Children of the Mind*
Bottom Left: *Earth Afire*
Bottom Right: *Treason*

INDEX OF IMAGES

ACKNOWLEDGEMENTS

A book like this, covering the production of nearly forty years of continuous work, involves a lot of people. It's an invidious task to list them all and I couldn't do it anyway. How do you measure who was instrumental and who incidental?

So if I've left anyone out who should be included, please accept my apologies – but here is a list of the most salient people I can think of at the moment, though it might be a different list tomorrow.

First and foremost is Alison Eldred who, along with Mick Jarvis and John Spencer (both now sadly gone), decided to represent me through Young Artists back in the seventies. As my friend and agent she has been an unflinching ally through rough and smooth, all my working life. All the boring stuff that is inevitably involved, she took on tirelessly and kept it all together. And Alan Lynch, who also comes from that beginning as Alison's arm in New York and then in his own right, who acquired the magical Irene Gallo of Tor, who has persisted in commissioning work from me with the absolute minimum of interference (how does she do that?). Philip Dunn and Sir Clive Sinclair, who first gave me the opportunity to really spread my wings. The late Bob Schulman of NASA who gave me the opportunity to paint a launch of the fabled shuttle *Enterprise,* and John Graham, my friend who acted as host and patron in the U.S. during those days. All those friends and patrons whom I have met through Pat and Jeannie Wilshire who each year pull out all the stops ('It's gonna blow, Captain!') to promote the Symposium of Imaginative Realism at Illuxcon, especially John Davis, Paul and LizAnn Lizotte, Beth and Mike Zipser. Alex Freidin Goss, for his work as film documenter of my efforts. Paul Lush for keeping my digital soul alive. John Melville, whose impeccable craft of photography recorded so many of my paintings. My fellow artists and friends, John Haysom, Jim Burns, Fred Gambino, Chris Moore and Ian Miller, all sailing along on the same ship, for their companionship and support. And now, most directly, all the team at Titan Books, particularly Omar Khan, editor, for his openness and generosity in allowing my voice full expression and fully taking it on board, along with Natalie Clay, the designer, for her flexibility in accommodating my little whims.

Ultimately, it's the background of one's family life that underpins anyone's work and helps give meaning to it all, so the final acknowledgement must go to my wife Sarah, and our two children, for being in my life at all. Thanks to you all.

To see the three films on John Harris's work: The Secret History of the Earth, Beyond the Horizon, and The Rite of the Hidden Sun, visit www.hiddensun.com